Studies in Latin American
Ethnohistory & Archaeology

Joyce Marcus
General Editor

Volume I
A Fuego y Sangre: Early Zapotec Imperialism in the Cuicatlán Cañada, Oaxaca, by Elsa Redmond, Memoirs of the Museum of Anthropology, University of Michigan, No. 16. 1983.

Volume II
Irrigation and the Cuicatec Ecosystem: A Study of Agriculture and Civilization in North Central Oaxaca, by Joseph W. Hopkins, Memoirs of the Museum of Anthropology, University of Michigan, No. 17. 1984.

Volume III
Aztec City-States, by Mary G. Hodge, Memoirs of the Museum of Anthropology, University of Michigan, No. 18. 1984.

Volume IV
Conflicts over Coca Fields in Sixteenth-Century Peru, by María Rostworowski de Diez Canseco, Memoirs of the Museum of Anthropology, University of Michigan, No. 21. 1988.

Volume V
Tribal and Chiefly Warfare in South America, by Elsa Redmond, Memoirs of the Museum of Anthropology, University of Michigan, No. 28. 1994.

Volume VI
Imperial Transformations in Sixteenth-Century Yucay, Peru, transcribed and edited by R. Alan Covey and Donato Amado González, Memoirs of the Museum of Anthropology, University of Michigan, No. 44. 2008.

Volume VII
Domestic Life in Prehispanic Capitals: A Study of Specialization, Hierarchy, and Ethnicity, edited by Linda R. Manzanilla and Claude Chapdelaine, Memoirs of the Museum of Anthropology, University of Michigan, No. 46. 2009.

Memoirs of the Museum of Anthropology
University of Michigan
Number 46

Studies in Latin American Ethnohistory & Archaeology
Joyce Marcus, General Editor

Volume VII

Domestic Life in Prehispanic Capitals

A Study of Specialization, Hierarchy, and Ethnicity

edited by
Linda R. Manzanilla and
Claude Chapdelaine

Ann Arbor, Michigan
2009

Printed in the United States of America
ISBN 978-0-915703-71-5

Cover design by Katherine Clahassey

The University of Michigan Museum of Anthropology currently publishes two monograph series, Anthropological Papers and Memoirs, as well as an electronic series in CD-ROM form. For a complete catalog, write to Museum of Anthropology Publications, 4013 Museums Building, 1109 Geddes Avenue, Ann Arbor, MI 48109-1079, or see www.lsa.umich.edu/umma/publications

Library of Congress Cataloging-in-Publication Data

Domestic life in prehispanic capitals : a study of specialization, hierarchy, and ethnicity / edited by Linda R. Manzanilla and Claude Chapdelaine.
    p. cm. -- (Memoirs of the Museum of Anthropology / University of Michigan ; no. 46) (Studies in Latin American ethnohistory & archaeology ; v. 7)
  Includes bibliographical references.
  ISBN 978-0-915703-71-5 (alk. paper)
  1. Indians of Mexico--Antiquities. 2. Indians of Central America--Antiquities. 3. Indians of South America--Antiquities. 4. Capitals (Cities)--Latin America--History. 5. Dwellings--Latin America--History. 6. Home--Latin America--History. 7. Neighborhood--Latin America--History. 8. City and town life--Latin America--History. 9. Ethnoarchaeology--Latin America. 10. Latin America--Social life and customs. I. Manzanilla, Linda. II. Chapdelaine, Claude.
  F1219.D67 2009
  307.3'36209809021--dc22

                         2009021406

Front Cover: A general view of Compound 5 in the southern portion of the Huacas of Moche site, with Huaca de la Luna and Cerro Blanco in the background (photo by Claude Chapdelaine, 1999).

Back Cover: A general view of the Oztoyahualco 15B:N6W3 apartment compound in the northwestern periphery of Teotihuacan, Central Mexico (photo by Linda R. Manzanilla, 1988).

Contents

PART I: MESOAMERICAN EXAMPLES

PART II: ANDEAN EXAMPLES

PART III: COMMENTARY

Contributors

Marshall Joseph Becker
University of Pennsylvania

Claude Chapdelaine
Université de Montréal

R. Alan Covey
Southern Methodist University

Ernesto González Licón
*Escuela Nacional de Antropología
e Historia, México*

Dan M. Healan
Tulane University

Julia A. Hendon
Gettysburg College

Kenneth G. Hirth
Penn State University

William H. Isbell
State University of New York, Binghamton

John W. Janusek
Vanderbilt University

Linda R. Manzanilla
Universidad Nacional Autónoma de México

Joyce Marcus
University of Michigan

Michael P. Smyth
Rollins College

John R. Topic
Trent University

Illustrations

Tables

Preface

Linda R. Manzanilla and Claude Chapdelaine

State capitals are geopolitical centers—usually urban sites—where people gather to interact, manufacture, exchange, and rule over a territory. In this book, excavated data from three spatial units are privileged: the single domestic structure, the compound, and the neighborhood. In these three spatial units, we have documented three topics: the indicators of craft specialization, ethnicity, and hierarchy.

Mesoamerica and the Andes have been chosen as two macro-areas where diverse state capitals existed. Different kinds of polities arose at different times and under different political conditions. For Mesoamerica, there are important contrasts between the central Mexican capitals and Maya capitals. In this volume, Teotihuacan, Xochicalco, Tula, and Monte Albán are taken into consideration, and contrasted to Tikal, Copán, Sayil, and Chac. For the Andean region, Tiwanaku, Huari, Huacas de Moche, Chan Chan, and Cuzco are tackled.

This book emerged from a 2006 symposium conducted at the 71st annual meeting of the Society for American Archaeology, held in Puerto Rico. The symposium, organized by the editors of this volume, was called "Domestic Life in State Political Economy at Prehistoric Capitals: Specialization, Hierarchy and Ethnicity." It emphasized a comparative approach between different kinds of polities and urban sites. By comparing different types of cities, we hope to clarify how important multiethnicity and craft production are in the shaping of the capital itself, and in shaping the political economy of the state.

From an archaeological perspective, the study of prehispanic states generally starts with the identification of capitals. These sites are the largest within a specific region, and they usually feature monumental buildings (administrative, civic, and ritual structures) with residential sectors surrounding them. The size and number of plazas, temples, elite residences, royal burials, storage facilities, workshops, streets, and fortifications vary from capital to capital but they indicate the power of a ruling elite.

The study of prehistoric capitals is still in its infancy. Long-term interdisciplinary projects are needed for a better understanding of these enormous archaeological sites. Some prehistoric capitals have been studied for more than forty years, although the consolidation of a site for tourism can handicap the pace of research. Thus it is the case that the capitals considered in this volume have not received the same amount of research. For example, the plan of the whole settlement cannot always be completed; in many cases, few residential compounds have been exposed in their entirety, and several tombs may have been looted well before the arrival of archaeologists. Considering these drawbacks, as well as the impossibility of grasping the complexity of the two most famous New World capitals of the Aztecs and Inkas (Tenochtitlan and Cuzco), which lie beneath huge modern cities or were destroyed during the conquest, archaeologists have been working continuously on the other major capitals in this volume. Furthermore, these capitals are well documented in comparison to so many small sites.

The group of scholars assembled here is trying to push our analysis of state capitals a step further. We do this by looking at the available excavation data, tackling all the elements and shared features of domestic life in houses, complex residences, neighborhoods, and specialized areas to address the nature of specialization, social hierarchy, and ethnicity.

New perspectives on residential units are offered for most sites, many of which reveal greater complexity than formerly thought. Nevertheless, the states followed different paths and their respective capitals include unique urban features. Some tendencies and patterns are evident but are not shared by all in kind or degree. Craft production was a major activity at most sites; the locus of production—near the center of the site or at the outskirts—may vary, but not the importance of craft manufacturing.

Centralization of power in the hands of a ruling class is often a basic element in the formation of social hierarchy. The social position of craftsmen is still open for debate, as is the mobility of an individual who may or may not be able to move from one class to another. Many examples addressed in this volume show a wide variety of socioeconomic groups crosscut by status and ethnic differences.

The identification of palaces or elite residences is another aspect of domestic life that can lead to a better understanding of social stratification and ethnicity. Determining population estimates of prehistoric state capitals is problematic, and great variation in these estimates is seen in the literature. Based on the assumption that a capital is the most important settlement in a given region and sits at the top of the settlement hierarchy, the total population in the capital should be high. Several cases presented in this volume show a smaller number of urban citizens than one might expect, but capitals controlled a hinterland inhabited by a much larger number of residents. It is thus important to distinguish the inner city from its periphery, an area that could include villages as far as 10 to 15 km distant, depending on the nature of the topography.

All the case studies in this volume are exciting, providing provocative ideas on what was going on in the core of these prehistoric state capitals. Sufficient data and ideas are now available to allow scholars to make their own comparisons and to refine their conception of domestic life in various regions of the New World. For students, this collection of new studies will serve to illustrate different aspects of states at their respective capitals, usually the most studied archaeological sites of these polities.

PART I
MESOAMERICAN EXAMPLES

Introduction

Mesoamerican Domestic Structures, Compounds, and Neighborhoods

Linda R. Manzanilla

Mesoamerica has been considered a mosaic of ethnic and linguistic groups, a macro-area where diversity and heterogeneity not only exist, but also shape interactions. Three different regions in Mesoamerica have been chosen for this book: the central highlands, the Valley of Oaxaca, and the Maya lowlands.

Particularly characteristic of the central highlands are huge capitals, large multiethnic settlements that were densely occupied and that provided goods and services to a vast hinterland. Nevertheless, the states they headed were different in type and extent. At the onset, Teotihuacan (particularly during AD 200–550) was a 20 km² head of an octopus-type state, where linear arrangements of sites were like tentacles extending out to enclaves located in regions where sumptuary raw materials and goods could be obtained (Manzanilla 2006). Teotihuacan was surrounded by a rural periphery within the Basin of Mexico, but it imposed a formal urban grid on the city, thereby revolutionizing the urban plan (see Millon 1973). It did so by channeling rivers, by placing the multiethnic population in formal foreign neighborhoods in the periphery, and by locating barrios of the Teotihuacanos near the city's core, each barrio probably headed by a noble "house" (Manzanilla 2006). It also inaugurated a new kind of domestic life situated in multifamily apartment compounds (see Manzanilla 1996), since the earlier Formative pattern had been a single-family 5 × 5 m hut set around a courtyard (a house group), as seen in Cuanalan (Manzanilla 1985).

Teotihuacan apartment compounds occur in three principal sizes (3600–3000 m², 2300–1200 m², and 700–250 m²); within the compound, each family has its apartment with rooms, porticoes, and patios in which to fulfill different domestic functions, including venerating the family patron god. This last characteristic separates Teotihuacan domestic life from contemporary Maya examples, where the extended family shared a common sanctuary (see, for example, the domestic compounds at Cobá, Quintana Roo [Manzanilla and Barba 1990]).

I have the impression that the neighborhood is the basic unit of social integration and work, as well as the unit of concentration and redistribution of goods. The compounds around the barrio center do not share the same production activities, but rather, display a diversity of crafts and offices needed for the functioning of the barrio. Most of the craftsmen do not specialize in one craft, but are masters of several arts. As Hirth notes for Xochicalco, there are no guilds in Teotihuacan. Nevertheless, there are hints that some specific industries are privileged in certain sectors of the periphery of the site: obsidian working to the north, lapidary work to the northeast and southwest, and pottery making to the south (see Manzanilla, Chapter 2). At Teotihuacan, dependent workshops are related either to the ruling elite (censers' plaques in the Ciudadela sector [Múnera 1985]; mica objects in the Xalla compound [Rosales de la Rosa 2004; Manzanilla and López Luján 2001]; dart points to the west of the Pyramid of the Moon [Carballo

2007]; perhaps greenstone and slate production) or to the noble houses that head the Teotihuacan barrios (costumes, headdresses, lapidary work). Independent production is located in the periphery, and may be in the hands of different foreign groups.

During the Epiclassic, at Xochicalco, Morelos (after the fall of Teotihuacan), a fortified capital of a small polity developed. Fourteen neighborhoods divided by boundary architecture and centered around civic architecture and/or elite residences are found. In those neighborhoods, Hirth (see Chapter 3) finds residential compounds that—under a single household head—share the organization of work, water facilities, and architectural space; thus, the basic economic unit at Xochicalco is not the neighborhood, but the joint family household (that is, families that reside together and collaborate in common or shared economic activities). Most craftsmen seem to be part-time and masters of several crafts. The terrace houses have a surface area of 210 to 348 m², a range smaller than the smallest of the Teotihuacan apartment compounds, and small Xochicalco compounds cluster between 300 and 800 m².

Following González Licón (see Chapter 1), Classic period Monte Albán (in Oaxaca), set on a modified mountaintop, was the capital of the Zapotec state; it housed the "middle" class in stone wall houses on terraces, and the ruling elite in large residences and palaces closer to the central plaza. These elite decorated their residential façades and displayed mural paintings on the walls; they lived in larger constructed spaces, and had more imported items. At Monte Albán, neighborhoods seemed to be administrative subunits of the state (Blanton 1978), a trait that is partially present at Teotihuacan, particularly in Xolalpan times (before this phase, we have detected independent movements of sumptuary goods by the intermediate elites of the wards, and thus a greater degree of autonomy of the barrio with respect to the central administration) (Manzanilla 2006).

At Tula during the early Postclassic, Healan (see Chapter 4) mentions the existence of apartment compounds (which may have been remnants of the Teotihuacan occupation of the valley) and house compounds (particularly in the Tollan phase). Neighborhoods such as El Canal (900 m², with a neighborhood temple), El Corral, or Dainí represent independent construction decisions, and not centralized policies, contrary to what happens at Teotihuacan. It seems that at Tula, as well as at Teotihuacan and Monte Albán, the neighborhood is the basic and most important social and economic unit.

In Mesoamerica, especially in Central Mexico, hierarchy is expressed by positioning the elite residences in a ring around the civic-ceremonial core. In some cases where the capitals have an acropolis or a mountaintop plaza, the ruling elite palaces are also placed on the highest ground. In the Maya area there are also examples of an acropolis (sometimes more than one), but it is also possible that elite houses are placed in "terminal groups" around the settlement.

In Central Mexico, much of the population of these capitals seems to have been involved in the production of goods or in construction activities, whereas in the Maya area, craft production is distributed in a wide variety of settlement types, and some particular manufacturing activities are placed in elite residences.

Three different sectors of the Maya area are considered in this book: Tikal in the Maya lowlands, Copán in Honduras, and two sites (Chac and Sayil) in the Puuc sector of the Yucatán Peninsula.

At Tikal (Guatemala), Becker (Chapter 5) points out 690 clusters of residential and civic buildings, and suggests that the differences in architectural patterning offer clues to ethnic diversity (which have long been postulated for the site). He proposes that the plaza plans represent a residential grammar that allows us to distinguish between foreigners of Mexican origin (Plaza Plan 4, evident only in urban sites, with a plaza and a central shrine) and the Maya (Plaza Plan 2, with a shrine to the east). He also detected possible enclaves of outsiders, including Group 6C-XVI that consisted of ninety structures arranged around five patios, some of which displayed *talud-tablero* architecture.

It is possible that the courtyards with sanctuaries to the east, and *without* a central altar, may be related to a Maya tradition (we also detected it at Cobá). Nevertheless, in Teotihuacan apartment compounds and barrio centers we found central altars *and* eastern temples in the same courtyard.

For Copán (Honduras), Hendon (see Chapter 6) refers to a biologically homogeneous population (the opposite of what happens at Teotihuacan) with social differences. Feasting seems an important activity for noble houses, a fact also hinted at in Teotihuacan neighborhood centers, where the intermediate elites foster the production of identity symbols. It is possible that the indicators of craft production at Copán (textiles, jewelry) were also related to the intermediate elites and their identities. Foreign neighborhoods are not evident at Copán as they are at Teotihuacan, although some hints of Lenca high-status occupation is suggested.

In contrast, in the Puuc capital of Chac (AD 500–750), Smyth (see Chapter 7) refers to important evidence for Teotihuacan-related individuals, soon after the collapse of the great Central Mexican metropolis. Smyth found apartment clusters using the same orientation as those at Teotihuacan; interior patios and rectangular altars; goggled figures in pottery; the use of specular hematite and cinnabar; caches with Thin Orange bowls; atlatl and pyrite incrusted disks; flakes of mica; and the cult of the Thunder God in nearby Chac Cave.

In summary, there are important differences between the Central Mexican and Maya examples, particularly in population density, in the importance of craft production and neighborhoods in the socioeconomic structure of capitals, and in the emphasis on multiethnic relations in Central Mexico. Precocious Teotihuacan represented one of the most complex and exceptional urban settlements of the preindustrial world, and set the standards for the Tollan-type of settlement in Central Mexico, of which Tenochtitlan was the last.

References

Blanton, Richard E.
1978   *Monte Albán: Settlement Patterns at the Ancient Zapotec Capital.* Academic Press, New York.

Carballo, David M.
2007   Implements of state power: Weaponry and martially themed obsidian production near the Moon Pyramid, Teotihuacan. *Ancient Mesoamerica* 18(1):173–90.

Cowgill, George L.
1987   Métodos para el estudio de relaciones espaciales en los datos de la superficie de Teotihuacan. In *Teotihuacan. Nuevos datos, nuevas síntesis, nuevos problemas*, edited by E. McClung de Tapia and E. Childs Rattray, pp. 161–89. Instituto de Investigaciones Antropológicas, UNAM, México.

Manzanilla, Linda
1985   El sitio de Cuanalan en el marco de las comunidades pre-urbanas del Valle de Teotihuacan. In *Mesoamérica y el centro de México*, edited by J. Monjarás Ruiz, R. Brambila, and E. Pérez Rocha, pp. 133–78. Colección Biblioteca del INAH. Instituto Nacional de Antropología e Historia, México, D.F.
1996   Corporate groups and domestic activities at Teotihuacan. *Latin American Antiquity* 7(3):228–46.

2006   Estados corporativos arcaicos. Organizaciones de excepción en escenarios excluyentes. *Cuicuilco* 13(36):13–45. ENAH.

Manzanilla, Linda, and Luis Barba
1990   The study of activities in Classic households, two case studies from Cobá and Teotihuacan. *Ancient Mesoamerica* 1(1):41–49.

Manzanilla, Linda, and Leonardo López Luján
2001   Exploraciones en un posible palacio de Teotihuacan: el Proyecto Xalla (2000–2001). *Mexicon* XIII(3):58–61.

Millon, René
1973   *Urbanization at Teotihuacan, Mexico. The Teotihuacan Map.* Pt. 1: Text. University of Texas Press, Austin.

Múnera, Carlos
1985   *Un taller de cerámica ritual en la Ciudadela.* Tesis de licenciatura en Arqueología, Escuela Nacional de Antropología e Historia, México.

Rosales de la Rosa, Edgar Ariel
2004   *Usos, manufactura y distribución de la mica en Teotihuacan.* Tesis de licenciatura en Arqueología, Escuela Nacional de Antropología e Historia, México.

—1—

Ritual and Social Stratification at Monte Albán, Oaxaca

Strategies from a Household Perspective

Ernesto González Licón

Introduction

Many things have been written about the Zapotec civilization and the strategies their leaders followed to consolidate and maintain power. Temples, administrative buildings, ceremonial structures, ballcourts, and hieroglyphic inscriptions are the impressive material representations of one of Mesoamerica's earliest stratified state societies that managed to survive for many centuries. Nevertheless, most of Monte Albán's structures were residential units built on artificially leveled terraces on the slopes of a hill where a population of 25,000 to 30,000 resided during the period of maximum development. An undetermined percentage of these people belonged to a sort of intermediate elite, or were people of middle status who may have been either wealthy commoners or minor elites. In this chapter, I discuss how these people, the wealthy commoners and the minor elite, lived from Early Classic (AD 200–500) to Late Classic (AD 500–700/750) times. The house, the material evidence of architectural history, is considered the physical enclosure where such people resided (Hendon 2002).

Considering that relationships are conducted by individuals or by families living in houses, we can best describe and analyze the impact the state had on Monte Albán's residents by using three archaeological indicators: residential patterns, domestic architecture, and funerary practices.

My goal is to document the economic, ideological, and social differences between elites and commoners in two chronological periods, the Early Classic and Late Classic, and determine the degree of heterogeneity within each social sector (González Licón 2003b, 2005). Specifically, I will describe and analyze data to gain information on two main topics:

1. The level of social inequality among domestic units using three scales: (a) within the domestic unit; (b) between domestic units from the same ward or barrio; and (c) among domestic units from different barrios.

2. The social differentiation in Monte Albán society through time with emphasis on the Early and Late Classic periods.

The Social Structure

The social structure of Monte Albán during the Classic period (AD 200–750) has at least three social segments:

(a) The ruling elite at the top, living in palaces and large residences close to the Main Plaza, and buried in well-made tombs with decorated façades, walls painted with polychrome murals, and abundant local and imported offerings.

(b) High-status commoners who are not part of the upper elite; they are wealthy commoners living in small- to medium-sized stone houses built on terraces on the hill, and are buried in tombs or graves with offerings. Here I am thinking of the families of specialized artisans, merchants, administrative assistants, and others involved in urban activities.

(c) The lower class of peasants, low-income artisans, or workers living in small wattle-and-daub houses on earthen platforms in the lower piedmont and valley floor. They were more involved in rural activities related to farming and supplying basic essentials to the city.

During the Early Classic (AD 200–500), social inequality within Zapotec society is evident; by the Late Classic (AD 500–700), these differences were more pronounced and were linked to stronger political power and institutionalized social stratification.

Social inequality is generally considered multidimensional and complex. In the archaeological context, the stratification levels or the presence of social classes are evidence of a permanent and unequal distribution of wealth. Thus, social hierarchies can be defined as a classificatory system based on status, roles, inequality, and heterogeneity. Differences among social strata are related to status and to vertical or hierarchical social positions. Here, status is defined as any social position that varies by strata, personal wealth, social prestige within the community, and political power or the ability to rule (Blau 1977; González Licón 2005; Ravesloot 1988). As a result, social stratification is considered the hierarchical arrangement of these levels or strata in a society. Nevertheless, even in highly stratified state societies, observed differences in the archaeological context are small and are therefore frequently mentioned as a "continuum" rather than as clear-cut social divisions. Identification and differentiation of each social stratum for comparative purposes are not easy tasks. To facilitate the analysis of the social structure, some researchers recognize the existence of only two social strata because sixteenth-century documents refer to two endogamous strata (e.g., Marcus 1992; Sanders 1992; Sanders and Price 1968; Sharer 1994): the rulers and the ruled, the elite and the commoners, or the nobility and the common people. Within each of these two strata, these archaeologists recognize many classes and statuses, such that a wealthy commoner could be buried with more goods than a minor noble (e.g., Marcus 1992). Others (Chase and Chase 1992) focus on three social classes, with an upper class corresponding to the nobility, a large minor elite, and an even larger low class of peasants, non-landowners, and slaves.

From the perspective of ethnohistoric sources, only two social strata were recognized. The ruling elite were on the top; they were a small group that tried to validate their position by claiming a divine origin or ancestor, and by requiring their members to marry other members of the upper stratum (Marcus 1992). The lower stratum was composed of commoners, which included peasants, non-specialized artisans, and slaves. Although it has been assumed that each social class had access to different types of goods and services, in the archaeological context the elite groups have been identified by their association with sumptuary objects, elaborate and larger residences, and more complex funerary ceremonies (Chase and Chase 1992).

These are some of the problems that I faced when working with the composition of the social structure in a given society. Identification of nobility or a high social class cannot rely solely on their association with some luxury objects. Therefore, I needed to develop a methodology incorporating multiple variables to evaluate qualitative and quantitative differences in the archaeological record. Unfortunately, this objective was not easy to accomplish. In this chapter I try to compare wealth differences between domestic units and individuals as a step in that direction. Size, architectural distribution, and the material assemblages of houses from five different parts of the city will be analyzed.

Strategies of Social Differentiation

Not many archaeological lines of evidence are available to infer the nature of social inequality at Monte Albán. It has been suggested (Blanton et al. 1996) that elites may follow two different strategies to remain in power. Each focuses on different aspects, and the changes associated with the emergence of sociopolitical complexity in early states may be related to two spheres of interaction, political and/or economic, and both are related to organization and production. As Blanton et al. (1996) mention, neither of these strategies is mutually exclusive; indeed, they are often used in tandem.

The Barrio

Based on Richard Blanton's (1978) settlement pattern research, Monte Albán was internally divided into fifteen barrios or wards. The barrio was considered an administrative subunit of the state and its internal organization usually incorporated elements that form the government structure.

The barrio represents a socioeconomic unit for communal activities performed with a certain degree of independence from other barrios. The presence of barrios has been documented in several major Mesoamerican cities for the Classic period. For Millon (1981), corporate groups based on kinship and economic activity occupied such barrios, and they functioned as a link between the different social sectors and the ruling elite. Archaeological excavations in the northern barrio of Mexicapam in the last couple of years have been an opportunity to search for indicators of economic specialization, ethnic affiliation, and social inequality of the inhabitants of Monte Albán (González Licón and Villalobos 2007).

The city had a form of organization in which the economic, political, and ideological strategies of the ruling elite were duplicated in microcosm in each of the barrios. In this way, I identify a barrio center by the concentration of administrative and ceremonial structures, along with elite residences. Even when the number, size, and urban layout of these architectural remains vary from one barrio to another, it is more or less recognizable. This conception of the barrio is my starting point for this research. Due to the impossibility of studying the whole city of Monte Albán, a sample of barrios must suffice, and does provide an opportunity to understand the city's internal organization.

The barrio represents a unit of organized specialized labor, ethnic affiliation, or a combination of both, where some ceremonial, administrative, and communal activities were performed with a certain level of independence from other barrios. Evidence of cities organized in barrios have been documented in Tula (Guevara 2003; Healan 1989), Teotihuacan (Gómez Chávez 2000; Manzanilla 1993, 2002, 2004, 2006; Storey 1992; Widmer and Storey 1993), and Tenochtitlan (Sahagún 1985), among others.

The Barrios of Monte Albán

Archaeological data for this chapter come from excavations in fifteen domestic units located in different areas of Monte Albán (Fig. 1.1). These areas include two relatively isolated barrios, El Pitayo and Mexicapam; a middle zone related to the Barrio del Plumaje ("Carretera" on the map); and the Central Area, close to the North Platform of the Main Plaza ("Estacionamiento" on the map). Productive activities varied according to the barrio location. More urbanized barrios, close to the Main Plaza, show a concentration of shell, jade, and turquoise, although it is not clear if these objects were worked there; it is also unclear whether their inhabitants were directly responsible for the production of food. The inhabitants of the Barrio del Plumaje combined their activities with ceramic vessel production.

It has been generally accepted that barrios were subdivisions of cities, where their inhabitants shared or had certain characteristics in common. Healan (1982) has suggested that each family occupied several domestic units and their members may have been related to each other; there was also a well-defined division of labor. Two other aspects of barrios are ethnic affiliation and economic specialization. It is not necessarily the case that every barrio has people from different cultures; each may or may not be occupied by migrants from some other village of the same ethnic group. The same can be said with respect to kinship as an integrative element. Kin ties or even religious orientation may be the principal reason for living together, without regard to the economic activities of their members. In many cases, members of these barrios were endogamous and larger barrios had more options for maintaining their unit (Pastor 1986). In this barrio form of organization, I sometimes found a correlation between territory and government, and in other cases between settlement pattern and kinship. In the Valley of Oaxaca, as in the case of Ocotlán and Etla, the barrios were also communities separated from the center, sometimes by a few kilometers (Paddock 1990).

During Colonial times in Oaxaca, the concept of a barrio had at least three meanings. The first one is territorial with ethnic characteristics and being part of a larger settlement; the other two have connections to kinship and religion (Millán 2003:50).

In the Mixteca Alta, the kinship relationships were organized around territorial units named *siqui*, with some similarities to the Nahua *altépetl* or town and the *chinámitl* or barrio. Each *siqui* had its own name, was considered a lineage initiated by a divine ancestor, and had several houses. Pastor (1986) describes the Mixtec *siqui* as an endogamous group of people sharing a territory in which a neighbor was seen as a relative. Spores (1967:92) agrees that Mixtec centers were organized in barrios, but he defines barrios as territorial and political units with no kinship component. In the *Mapa de Macuilxóchitl*, made in 1580 to explain the *Relación de Macuilxóchitl*, the communities surrounding this town are described as barrios (Acuña 1984). A final reference from the Colonial period (AD 1550) by Millán (2003:50) is the work of Zeitlin, who reports the existence of forty-nine barrios as the basic corporate units in the Zapotec village of Tehuantepec.

The word "barrio" had several meanings in the *vocabulario de fray Juan de Córdova*. For example, *naaqueche* is related to land ownership whereas *cozaana* is used to describe a collateral kinship element within barrio composition (Córdova 1987:32). These different conceptions of what a barrio was make it necessary to approach the subject with caution, but, at the same time, we hope to develop a methodology to enhance the possibilities of understanding the nature and function of the barrios, using the archaeological record.

The Archaeological Data

As mentioned above, the empirical data for this chapter are the results from fifteen excavated domestic units located at three different distances from the Main Plaza of Monte Albán. Although the inhabitants of Monte Albán adapted their settlement to the topographic conditions that a mountain demands (with each barrio having its own particular characteristics), proximity to the core of the city was more prestigious than being far from the plaza. The more distant barrios from the Main Plaza are El Pitayo and Mexicapam (Fig. 1.2). Barrio del Plumaje is an intermediate area located along the paved road to Carretera (see Fig. 1.1). The Central Area is located along the northeastern side of the North Platform, and is referred to as "Estacionamiento" in Figure 1.1 (González Licón 2003b; González Licón et al. 1994).

Social Inequality in the Early Classic

The Early Classic period (AD 200–500) represents abundance, development, and growth, but also large inequalities. Population at Monte Albán reached 16,500 inhabitants (Marcus and Flannery 1996). Evidence of contacts between Monte Albán and Teotihuacan in the central highlands is evident in the architecture, mural painting, ceramic styles, and hieroglyphic inscriptions that permeated the public, private, and funerary levels, but there is no evidence suggesting a Teotihuacan invasion or military occupation at that time or at any time. Some of the largest elite residences at Monte Albán were built during this period, such as those associated with Tombs 104 and 105 (Figs. 1.3, 1.4)

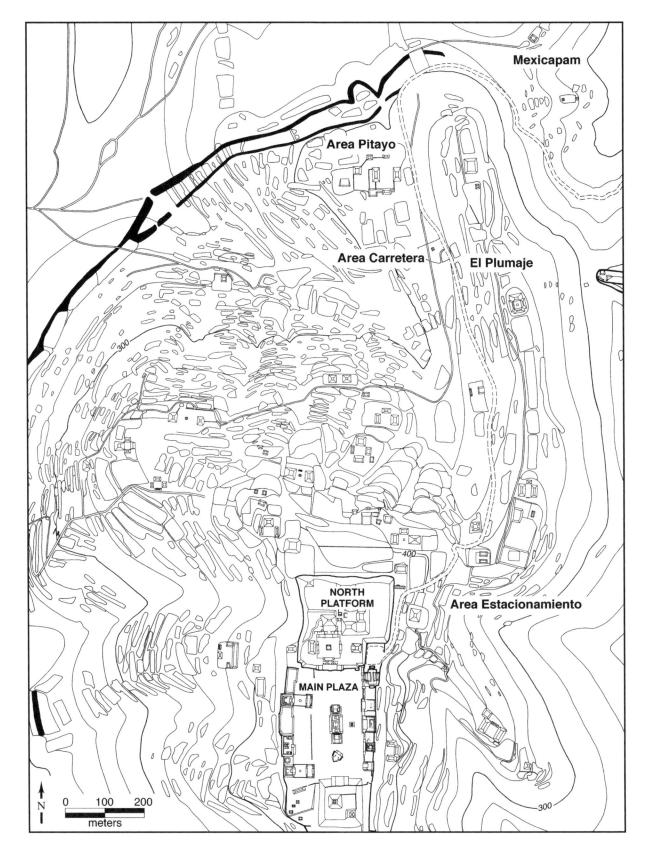

Figure 1.1. Topographic map of Monte Albán (redrawn from Blanton 1978).

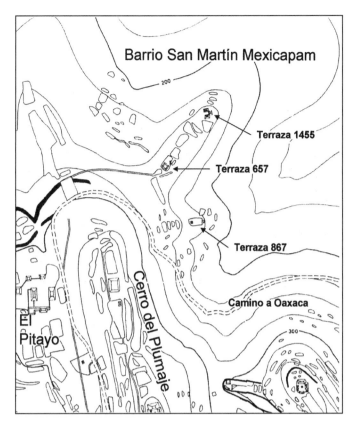

Figure 1.2. Topographic map of the Mexicapam barrio, Monte Albán (redrawn from Blanton 1978).

and the Palace of El Ocote on the northeast corner of the North Platform (Fig. 1.5).

A comparison of size, architectural layout, and magnificent effigy urns with other associated materials found in these elite tombs (Caso 1938, 1939, 1965; Caso and Bernal 1952, 1965; Caso et al. 1967; Marquina 1964) and in their funerary practices (González Licón 1997, 2004; González Licón and Márquez 1990) shows the social differences during this period.

The Early Classic (Period IIIa) was a time of prosperity and development for the ruling elite, but not for the common people, which is evident in their respective funerary treatment. Based on archaeological data presented in this chapter, social inequality was evident, but so also was a decrease in living conditions and health when compared to earlier Formative times for the people classified as middle status. From a gender perspective, for the minor elite, I concluded that males were buried with better and more numerous offerings. Decorated ceramics were more often associated with males, and domestic wares more often found with females, which can be interpreted as males performing

more ceremonies involving feasting and ritual, while females were engaged in a daily routine of domestic activities (González Licón 2003a, 2003b, 2007). With no relation to the social class that they belong to within each family group, there is also a strong hierarchy: adult males ate more meat and were buried with more offerings. Burial in the family tomb was mainly a male privilege.

In the last few years, there have been advances in understanding Monte Albán's population and its demographic tendencies, diet, diseases, and health, with attention focused on the minor elite and/or wealthy commoners (Brito 2000; Márquez et al. 1994; Márquez and González Licón 2001; Márquez et al. 2001; Márquez et al. 2002).

Taking into consideration the dietary data (González Licón 2003b), we can say that during the Early Classic more meat was being eaten than in previous periods, and individuals buried in tombs were consuming more meat than those buried elsewhere (Brito 2000; González Licón 2003b). Indicators of health and nutrition are given in Table 1.1 for Early and Late Classic times.

Comparing the dimensions of domestic units to the number of square meters of floor space gives us an idea about the considerable differences among them at Monte Albán; indeed, there is a positive correlation between size and social status. Therefore, floor space and dimensions of buildings are good indicators for the study of social differences among residents. Previous studies arrived at the same conclusion (Blanton 1978; Feinman and Nicholas 2007; Winter 1974). Blanton (1978) classified domestic units into six categories: (1) patio of 10 m², (2) patio of 16 m², (3) patio between 80 and 100 m², (4) patio between 80 and 520 m², (5) patio between 580 and 780 m², and (6) patio larger than 1,000 m² (Table 1.2).

In this chapter I analyze a group of domestic units (with no consideration of terrace size, where other features are frequently present). The residential units vary from 100 to 625 m² in constructed area, which I believe represent, more or less, the middle social classes of the Monte Albán population. Elite residences cover more than 1,000 m² (Table 1.3).

The differences in construction area presented here are a clear indicator of the social differences, not only of the middle sector but of Zapotec society during the Classic period as a whole. In other words, I find a strong hierarchical vertical differentiation, but also great heterogeneity, within each social class.

Larger houses offered better living conditions to their inhabitants, and more economic resources for their maintenance. The same differences that I recognized for each barrio can be seen when comparing one barrio to another. Inhabitants of the barrios closer to the Main Plaza generally had better houses and more wealth in their funerary assemblages. More distant barrios such as El Pitayo and Mexicapam had houses of smaller dimensions than barrios closer to the Main Plaza, such as the Estacionamiento. However, no matter where a barrio was located, the gender differences held constant. In all cases, adult males had more wealth than females, and adults had more than subadults.

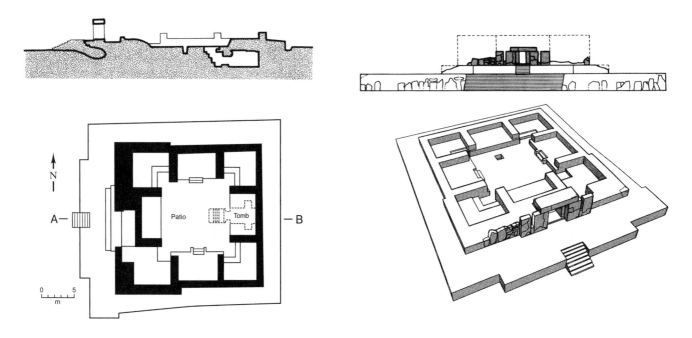

Figure 1.3. Elite residence of Tomb 105, Monte Albán (Flannery 1983: Fig. 5.5 and Marcus and Flannery 1996: Figs. 248–49; after Caso 1938).

Figure 1.4. Mural from the wall of Tomb 105, Monte Albán (after Marcus and Flannery 1996: Fig. 250).

Figure 1.5. Elite residence "El Ocote," northeast corner of the North Platform, Monte Albán.

Table 1.1. Indicators of health and nutrition of individuals at Monte Albán.

Health Indicators	Early Classic		Late Classic	
Hypoplasia on incisors	2/17	11.7%	no cases	
Hypoplasia on canine teeth	0/15	0%	0/14	0%
Criba orbitalia	1/30	3.3%	0/6	0%
Spongy hyperostosis	2/31	6.45%	0/6	0%
Tibia infection	9/30	30%	0/3	0%
Systemic infection	7/38	18.4%	0/3	0%
Periodontal infection	8/27	29.6%	3/6	50%
Abscess	3/39	7.6%	2/6	33.3%
Dental attrition	6/27	22.2%	2/5	40%

(Data from Márquez and González Licón 2001; Márquez et al. 2002)

Table 1.2. Type of domestic unit at Monte Albán.

Type	Patio Area (m²)	Total Area (m²)	% of Patio
1	10	150	6.6
2	16	250	6.5
3	80–100	350	25.7
4	280–520	500	56–104
5	580–780	600	n.e.
6	>1,000	>600	n.e.

(Blanton 1978)
n.e. = not estimated

Table 1.3. Domestic wards or sectors used in this research.

Unit	Patio Area (m²)	Total Area (m²)	% of Patio
Mexicapam	16	100	16
Pitayo	27–35	100–225	15–27
Plumaje	12–20	100–175	12
Central Area	25–80	215–625	11–12
North Platform	64	750	8.5

Figure 1.6. Main Plaza of Monte Albán.

Social Inequality in the Late Classic Period

During the period from AD 500 to 700/750, Monte Albán seems to have been an attractive place to live because it reached 25,000 people, ten times the size of the next largest town in the valley (Blanton and Kowalewski 1981) (Fig. 1.6). The settlement pattern had changed throughout the Oaxaca Valley. In the Zaachila-Zimatlán Valley, population decreased by approximately 95%, including the almost total abandonment of Jalieza, an important secondary center. The magnitude of population nucleation at Monte Albán during this period was similar to that experienced by Teotihuacan during the Early Classic.

The Northern Platform of Monte Albán was completed during this period. It is considered to be the residential quarters of the ruling elite. Several residential units have been explored within this great structure, in particular one located in the northeast corner of the North Platform, known locally as the Palacio del Ocote (González Licón 2003b, 2004).

For the Late Classic period, I found evidence of ceremonial activities in all three excavated areas. These ceremonies were performed in the patios of each household and included the deposition of figurines and skulls. No large effigy urns were present in the tombs, but incense burners were included as part of the funerary offerings. People in the three excavated areas were involved in ceremonies and rituals but they could not afford expensive items made of jade.

Within individual domestic units, changes can be seen from Early Classic to Late Classic times. The mortuary ceremonies, the forms of interment, and the amount and quality of offerings all indicate that each house continued to have a well-established hierarchical organization.

In Table 1.4, I present the changes by period of frequencies of ceremonial objects found in funerary contexts. In the column entitled "Other Objects," I include vases decorated with anthropomorphic or zoomorphic faces, Cociyo or other deity bridgespout jars, miniature vessels, stingray spines, turquoise chunks, and undrilled travertine disks.

Within this system, adult males had greater prestige, with some holding leadership positions; at their death, they received the privilege of being buried in the family tomb with abundant offerings. Obsidian, an imported artifact, continues to be well distributed in all houses but now, in funerary contexts, it is found only with females. This may be related to a change of roles in the residential units, with females involved in a wider range of productive activities, including those that required the use of obsidian artifacts, such as cutting, drilling, and scraping wood, bone, or leather.

During the Late Classic (Period IIIb), social inequality was strong. For the population studied by this project, living condi-

Table 1.4. Ceremonial objects related to funerary contexts.

Period	Object				
	Pipes	*Figurines*	*Effigy Urns*	*Incense Burners*	*Other Objects*
II (Late Formative)	2	2	5	1	5
IIIa (Early Classic)	6	7	6	3	27
IIIb (Late Classic)	0	7	0	32	39

Table 1.5. Distribution by gender and type of burial.

	Tombs	Graves
Males	59%	54%
Females	25%	20%
Subadults	16%	26%

tions declined, with an increase in health problems (see Table 1.1), evidently because their diet consisted mainly of maize, with almost no meat. Social stratification was more evident. Imported items were restricted to the ruling elite. Among the minor elite and wealthy commoner segment analyzed here, no shell, jade, or turquoise are present. In the family groups, prestige differences continued, but females were participating for the first time in other types of activities and were buried with obsidian blades or obsidian artifacts that were formerly associated only with males. Evidence for the performance of ritual ceremonies is extensive, with almost all of the households using ceramic figurines and incense burners.

Comparing houses within the same barrio reveals that there were differences, but not as large as in previous periods. For the barrios studied here, I found that there was one house that had more wealth than the others in the El Pitayo barrio. During the Late Classic, jade and turquoise were absent from the archaeological assemblages in these houses; the only imported good, besides obsidian, was shell, which turns out to be the only prestige marker for this period in non-elite houses. In remote barrios such as Mexicapam, shell objects were associated with children. Here, I found remains of obsidian cores, flakes, and prismatic blades, indicating their local manufacture/production. Prismatic blades were extensively used, with evidence that they were rejuvenated to create a new cutting edge.

In relation to ceremonial activities beyond the Main Plaza, I found evidence of ritual performances in the patios of the houses, including the offering of figurines and human skulls as seen in the El Pitayo barrio. Although it is difficult to determine their nature, in the houses of El Pitayo and Carretera I found several individuals with cranial trephination; one of them, an adult male with no evidence of disease or trauma, survived five trephinations before he died (Márquez and González Licón 1992)!

During the Late Classic, the use of effigy urns as representation of ancestors became more expensive for the common people. I found almost none of these objects as offerings, but I did find many more incense burners and *sahumadores*. This does not mean that people were participating less in ceremonies and rituals, but that they did not have the means to acquire the same objects that they did during the Early Classic period (Table 1.4).

For this period, elite residences reached their maximum splendor in construction, decoration, and richness. The layout of the elite houses was more extensive and complicated with secondary patios and more rooms, and an open space around each house. In the central part of the city, minor elite houses were closer to each other, with narrow corridors between them, covering most of the terrace area. Here, the cultivation of vegetables does not seem to have been possible except at a much reduced scale. In contrast to the scarcity of land for domestic gardens in minor elite houses, they did have occasional kilns for ceramic production, storage pits, and lithic workshops. Houses from the Estacionamiento area give a good idea of these features (Figs. 1.7, 1.8).

Demographic changes for the Late Classic were considerable; Blanton mapped 2,073 terraces, of which 2,006 were registered as residential. From this number, 37 were classified as elite residences with an average of 10 to 20 inhabitants in each. The other 1,969 terraces were occupied by commoner houses with an average of 5 to 10 persons in each, reaching a total population of 15,000 to 30,000 inhabitants (Blanton 1978).

Analysis of the funerary system has been an important element in explaining stratification and social inequality at Monte Albán. I have documented that a larger percentage of males (66%) than females (33%) were buried in tombs, and that more or less the same proportion occurs in graves (males 60%, females 40%) (González Licón and Márquez 1990; Márquez and González Licón 1992, 2001). The same proportion is maintained in the distribution of different age groups in tombs and burials, including subadults (Table 1.5).

I can conclude from this that differences with respect to sex and age of the individuals buried in tombs and burials can be explained in two ways—first, in relation to the hierarchical organization within the domestic group; and second, the social position of each household within the barrio and Zapotec society as a whole.

The level of prestige and recognition attained by a member of a household at the time of his or her death probably determined whether that person would be buried within the domestic unit. In almost every house belonging to the minor elite, a tomb was built to accommodate the corpses of their more prestigious family members; the patriarch or matriarch of the group received that honor at the time their death. They were buried with a funerary ceremony that included the deposition of several objects as offerings related to the material and spiritual realms. Each generation, perhaps every 20 to 30 years, another patriarch died and the same

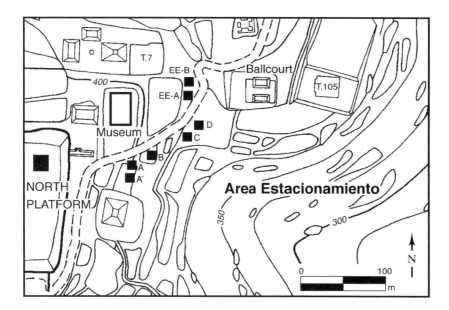

Figure 1.7. Houses (*A'*, *A–D*, *EE-A*, *EE-B*) in the Estacionamiento area (215–625 m² of total extension) of Monte Albán.

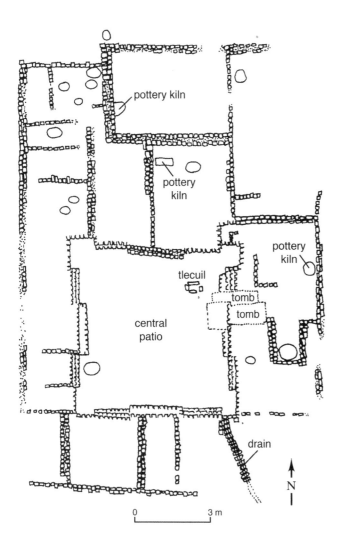

Figure 1.8. Estacionamiento-A residence, found east of the North Platform at Monte Albán; see Figure 1.7 (above) (redrawn from González Licón 2003b).

tomb was reopened to place the most recent dead, while the bones and objects associated with the previous burials were moved to the rear of the tomb. This practice explains our finding several individuals with no anatomical articulation, all located in the back part of the tomb with all the objects from the offerings piled up there; in the entrance and center of the tomb we see the last individual deposited, usually face up in fully extended position with the offerings still around it (Fig. 1.9).

The greater number of males in the tombs may be related to gender inequality, but also to a patrilineal form of organization. In this system, young people received less ceremony and just a few objects as offerings. Mortality rates in children were high and they were buried under the patio floor while adults were buried under the floor of the rooms.

Discussion

The patterns in sociopolitical organization and the degrees of social inequality presented here give us a good idea about the development of a sector of Zapotec society through time. The degree of social inequality between the inhabitants of Monte Albán differed from Early to Late Classic times. Proximity to the Main Plaza or to the barrio centers was related to prestige, and thus the larger and wealthiest houses and barrios were closest to the core of the city.

Evidence for the performance of ritual ceremonies has been documented in Monte Albán throughout its occupation. It is clear

Figure 1.9. Tomb 1991-11 at Monte Albán before excavation.

that the ideological realm was important not only to the ruling elite but also to the common people. For the elite, the development of the symbolic and ideological world was a way to increase their power. As a corporate society, they focused more on the internal production. The cohesion needed to achieve this internal wealth was provided by the ideology and was materialized in ritual and ceremony. The minor elite participated in public ceremonies and rituals, but also were involved in ceremonies within their own family group. By the Late Classic, Zapotec society was more socially differentiated. State organization imposed more tributary burdens; consequently, common people had less access to material things. In the ideological realm, it seems that the state monopolized and controlled public ceremonies, affecting or modifying those ceremonies conducted in the domestic spaces.

Taking note of the archaeological indicators mentioned earlier—settlement patterns, domestic architecture, and funerary practices—I can now define the existence of three social classes:

(a) The ruling elite on the top of the social scale, with more wealth, political power, prestige, and social recognition than the others. Members of this social class lived in larger and complex residences. These elite residences were located close to the center of the barrio or close to the Main Plaza. Their inhabitants had great funerary ceremonies and were buried with abundant and rich offerings. Their bodies were buried in large and spacious tombs with elaborate façades and painted walls, decorated with motifs depicting their religious beliefs. The ruler of Monte Albán and his extended family, many of whom lived in the North

Platform, belonged to this group (González Licón 2007). It has been suggested that at least one member of this ruling elite lived with his family in each barrio as a representative of the central authority, but there is no direct evidence for this statement.

(b) A sort of minor elite, integrated by those people who carried out economic activities related to the state and city government. Associated with this social class, I found a large variety of economic specializations including craftsmen, merchants, soldiers, bureaucrats, and many others who did not produce their own food. Members of this minor elite lived in all the barrios of the city, not too close but not too far away from the core. Their houses were built with stone walls and stucco floors with drainage systems to channel off the rainwater. In many of these houses, a family tomb, built under the main room, was where the most prestigious members of the domestic group were buried; other interments were placed below the stucco floors of the other rooms, while infants were placed below the patio floor. The objects that can be found as part of the offering were not as exotic, elaborated, or expensive as those from the elite group but included moderate-sized ceramic urns, assorted forms of vessels, figurines, shell, obsidian, and sometimes even jade objects.

(c) A lower class consisting of people living in small houses with earthen floors, limited use of adobe, and most with walls and roofs made of perishable materials. Due to their ephemeral nature, remains from these houses are not abundant in the archaeological record. Members of this social class were buried in earth pits, with almost no offerings (offerings consisted mainly of utilitarian objects).

In his study of the settlement pattern of Monte Albán, Blanton (1978) considered that only 2% of the domestic units of the city were occupied by the ruling elite. Flannery uses the estimate of 5 to 10 people living in a commoner house and 10 to 20 people living in an elite house, suggesting that the percentage of elite members in Zapotec society should be about 4% (Flannery 1983:136).

These considerations should be used with caution due to the inherent problems in the preservation and excavation of domestic units that cannot be representative of the whole social structure of the Zapotec society at that time (Kowalewski et al. 1992). In a recent study, Joyce Marcus (2004) estimates that commoners may compose at least 90% of the total population. Another problem worthy of mention is the difficulty in estimating the extent of the lower class population due to the perishable nature of the construction materials used in their houses, the smaller number and lower quality of their material possessions, and their dispersed distribution in relationship to the central part of the city or barrios. One of the main limitations in making these sorts of estimates is embedded in the definition itself of the social structure and each social class, but also in the extremely difficult task of deciding from the archaeological record which house or group of houses belongs to one social class and not to the other (González Licón 2005).

In our evaluation of social inequality in Monte Albán from Early to Late Classic, I can conclude that the differences are more quantitative than qualitative, but the social structure remains the same. Even considering that the information available is not completely comparable for each social sector, I try to look for patterns of social organization and ceremonial activities. It will be necessary to improve our methods to explain the archaeological record. Using as a working hypothesis the notion that the nobility always had everything and the lower class never had anything, some strategies adopted by the ruling elite may always be more recognizable among the minor elite. This proved to be true when comparing the possession of wealth or prestige goods such as jade and shell among the minor elite from the Early to Late Classic periods. During the Early Classic they have access to both, but for the Late Classic, jade is no longer available to members of this minor elite or middle class. With this approach I tried to describe economic and social changes in the Zapotec society, even though their causes remain to be fully explained.

Acknowledgments

The author wishes to thank Linda R. Manzanilla for her invitation to participate in the Symposium "Domestic Life in State Political Economy at Prehispanic Capitals: Specialization, Hierarchy and Ethnicity" (SAA 2006) and to be part of this volume. I also thank Linda, Claude Chapdelaine, and Joyce Marcus for their insightful comments and editorial assistance. Gratitude is extended to Roberto García Moll, President of Consejo de Arqueología del INAH; Enrique Fernández, Director of the Oaxaca INAH Center; and Nelly Robles, Director of the archaeological zone of Monte Albán. Part of the data discussed here is derived from the project "Desigualdad social y condiciones de vida en el barrio El Pitayo de Monte Albán, Oaxaca, a través del estudio de unidades habitacionales" (H43773), funded by CONACYT. In addition, I want to acknowledge the support provided by INAH.

References

Acuña, René (editor)
1984 *Relaciones geográficas del siglo XVI: Antequera*. 2 vols. UNAM, México.

Blanton, Richard E.
1978 *Monte Albán: Settlement Patterns at the Ancient Zapotec Capital*. Academic Press, New York.

Blanton, Richard E., Gary M. Feinman, Stephen A. Kowalewski, and Peter N. Peregrine
1996 A dual-processual theory for the evolution of Mesoamerican civilization. *Current Anthropology* 37:1–47.

Blanton, Richard E., and Stephen A. Kowalewski
1981 Monte Albán and after in the Valley of Oaxaca. In *Supplement to the Handbook of Middle American Indians*, Vol. 1, edited by Jeremy A. Sabloff, pp. 94–116. University of Texas Press, Austin.

Blau, Peter M.
1977 *Inequality and Heterogeneity: A Primitive Theory of Social Structure*. The Free Press, New York.

Brito, Leticia
2000 *Análisis de la población prehispánica de Monte Albán a través del estudio de la dieta*. Tesis de doctorado, UNAM, México.

Caso, Alfonso
1938 *Exploraciones en Oaxaca. Quinta y sexta temporadas 1936–1937*. Instituto Panamericano de Geografía e Historia, México.
1939 Resumen del informe de las exploraciones en Oaxaca durante la 7a y 8a temporadas, 1937–1938 y 1938–1939. Paper presented at the XVII Congreso Internacional de Americanistas, México.
1965 Lapidary work, goldwork, and copperwork from Oaxaca. In *Handbook of Middle American Indians*, Vol. 3, edited by Robert Wauchope and Gordon R. Willey, pp. 896–930. University of Texas Press, Austin.

Caso, Alfonso, and Ignacio Bernal
1952 *Urnas de Oaxaca*. Instituto Nacional de Antropología e Historia, México.
1965 Ceramics of Oaxaca. In *Handbook of Middle American Indians*, Vol. 3, edited by Robert Wauchope and Gordon R. Willey, pp. 871–95. University of Texas Press, Austin.

Caso, Alfonso, Ignacio Bernal, and Jorge R. Acosta
1967 *La cerámica de Monte Albán*. Instituto Nacional de Antropología e Historia, México.

Córdova, fray Juan de
1987   *Vocabulario en lengua zapoteca (1578).* INAH, México.

Chase, Arlen F., and Diane Z. Chase
1992a   Mesoamerican elites: Assumptions, definitions, and models. In *Mesoamerican Elites: An Archaeological Assessment*, edited by Diane Z. Chase and Arlen F. Chase, pp. 3–17. University of Oklahoma Press, Norman.
1992b   An archaeological assessment of Mesoamerican elites. In *Mesoamerican Elites: An Archaeological Assessment*, edited by Diane Z. Chase and Arlen F. Chase, pp. 303–17. University of Oklahoma Press, Norman.

Feinman, Gary M., and Linda M. Nicholas
2007   The socioeconomic organization of the Classic period Zapotec State. In *The Political Economy of Ancient Mesoamerica: Transformations during the Formative and Classic Periods*, edited by Vernon L. Scarborough and John E. Clark, pp. 135–47. University of New Mexico Press, Albuquerque.

Flannery, Kent V.
1983   The legacy of the Early Urban period: An ethnohistoric approach to Monte Albán's temples, residences, and royal tombs. In *The Cloud People: Divergent Evolution of the Zapotec and Mixtec Civilizations*, edited by Kent V. Flannery and Joyce Marcus, pp. 132–36. Academic Press, New York.

Gómez Chávez, Sergio
2000   *La Ventilla. Un barrio de la antigua ciudad de Teotihuacán.* Tesis de Licenciatura en Arqueología, Escuela Nacional de Antropología e Historia, México.

González Licón, Ernesto
1997   Funerary Practices and Social Organization at Monte Albán, Oaxaca, México: A Paleodemographic Approach from the Late Formative to the Early Classic. Paper presented at the 62nd Annual Meeting of the Society for American Archaeology, Nashville, Tennessee.
2003a   El papel de la mujer en Monte Albán a través del tiempo. Estudio de género. In *Primer Foro de Investigación Científica en la ENAH*, edited by Sergio Sánchez Díaz and Silvia A. Prado Camacho, pp. 31–44. ENAH, México.
2003b   *Social Inequality at Monte Albán Oaxaca: Household Analysis from Terminal Formative to Early Classic.* PhD dissertation, University of Pittsburgh, Pittsburgh.
2004   Royal palaces and painted tombs: State and society in the Valley of Oaxaca. In *Palaces of the Ancient New World*, edited by Susan Toby Evans and Joanne Pillsbury, pp. 83–111. Dumbarton Oaks Research Library and Collection, Washington, D.C.
2005   Evaluación de indicadores arqueológicos para estudiar el proceso de estratificación social en el Formativo mesoamericano. In *IV Coloquio Pedro Bosch Gimpera*, Vol. II, edited by Ernesto Vargas Pacheco, pp. 617–40. Instituto de Investigaciones Antropológicas, UNAM, México.
2007   Estado y sociedad: estudio de género en el Valle de Oaxaca. In *Las mujeres en Mesoamérica prehispánica*, edited by María J. Rodríguez-Shadow, pp. 171–86. Universidad Autónoma del Estado de México, Toluca.
2007   Arquitectura y complejidad: La Plataforma Norte de Monte Albán, ¿sede del Estado Zapoteca? In *Arqueología y complejidad social*, edited by Patricia Fournier, Walburga Wiesheu, and Thomas H. Charlton, pp. 153–70. INAH, ENAH, Promep, México.

González Licón, Ernesto, and Lourdes Márquez
1990   Costumbres funerarias en Monte Albán. In *Monte Albán*, pp. 53–138. Citibank, México.

González Licón, Ernesto, Lourdes Márquez, and Cira Martínez
1994   Salvamento arqueológico en Monte Albán, Oaxaca, Temporada 1991. In *Boletín del Consejo de Arqueología* 1991:128–34. INAH, México.

González Licón, Ernesto, and Alejandro Villalobos
2007   Excavaciones recientes en el Barrio "Mexicapam" de Monte Albán, Oaxaca: entorno urbano, emplazamiento y arquitectura. *Iberoamericana* XXIX(1):21–32.

Guevara Chumacero, Miguel Roberto
2003   *Buscando el origen del estado Tollan: La formación de organizaciones estatales secundarias.* Tesis de Maestría en Arqueología, ENAH, México.

Healan, Dan M.
1982   *Patrones residenciales en la antigua ciudad de Tula. Estudios sobre la antigua ciudad de Tula.* INAH, México.
1989   House, household and neighborhood in a Postclassic city. In *Households and Communities*, edited by S. MacEachern, D.J.W. Archer, and R.D. Garvin, pp. 416–29. University of Calgary Archaeological Association, Calgary.

Hendon, Julia A.
2002   Social relations and collective identities: Household and community in ancient Mesoamerica. In *The Dynamics of Power*, edited by Maria O'Donovan, pp. 273–99. Southern Illinois University, Illinois.

Kowalewski, Stephen A., Gary M. Feinman, and Laura Finsten
1992   "The Elite" and assessment of social stratification in Mesoamerican archaeology. In *Mesoamerican Elites: An Archaeological Assessment*, edited by Diane Z. Chase and Arlen F. Chase, pp. 259–77. University of Oklahoma Press, Norman.

Manzanilla, Linda
2002   Living with the ancestors and offering to the gods: Domestic ritual at Teotihuacan. In *Domestic Ritual in Ancient Mesoamerica*, edited by Patricia Plunket, pp. 43–52. Cotsen Institute of Archaeology, University of California, Los Angeles.
2004   Social identity and daily life at Classic Teotihuacan. In *Mesoamerican Archaeology*, edited by Julia A. Hendon and Rosemary A. Joyce, pp. 124–47. Blackwell Publishing, Oxford, UK.
2006   Estados corporativos arcaicos. Organizaciones de excepción en escenarios excluyentes. *Cuicuilco* 13(36):13–45.

Manzanilla, Linda (editor)
1993   *Anatomía de un conjunto residencial teotihuacano en Oztoyahualco.* 2 vols. Instituto de Investigaciones Antropológicas, UNAM, México.

Marcus, Joyce
1992   Royal families, royal texts: Examples from the Zapotec and Maya. In *Mesoamerican Elites: An Archaeological Assessment*, edited by Diane Z. Chase and Arlen F. Chase, pp. 221–41. University of Oklahoma Press, Norman.
2004   Maya commoners: The stereotype and the reality. In *Ancient Maya Commoners*, edited by Jon C. Lohse and Fred Valdez, Jr., pp. 255–83. University of Texas Press, Austin.

Marcus, Joyce, and Kent V. Flannery
1996   *Zapotec Civilization: How Urban Society Evolved in Mexico's Oaxaca Valley*. Thames and Hudson, London.

Márquez, Lourdes, Lourdes Camargo, Ernesto González Licón, and Minerva Prado
1994   La población prehispánica de Monte Albán: algunos parámetros demográficos. *Dimensión Antropológica* 1:7–36.

Márquez, Lourdes, and Ernesto González Licón
1992   La trepanación craneana entre los antiguos zapotecos de Monte Albán. *Cuadernos del Sur* 1:25–50.
2001   Estratificación social, salud y nutrición en un grupo de pobladores de Monte Albán. In *Primera Mesa Redonda de Monte Albán*, edited by Nelly Robles, pp. 73–95. INAH, México.

Márquez, Lourdes, Patricia Hernández, and Ernesto González Licón
2001   La salud en las grandes urbes prehispánicas. *Estudios de Antropología Biológica* X:291–313.

Márquez, Lourdes, Robert McCaa, Rebecca Storey, and Andrés del Angel
2002   Health and nutrition in pre-Hispanic Mesoamerica. In *The Backbone of History: Health and Nutrition in the Western Hemisphere*, edited by Richard H. Steckel and Jerome C. Rose, pp. 307–38. Cambridge University Press, Cambridge.

Marquina, Ignacio
1964   *Arquitectura prehispánica*. INAH, México.

Millán, Saúl
2003   *El cuerpo de la nube. Etnografía de las representaciones huaves sobre las jerarquías civiles y religiosas*. UAM-Iztapalapa, México, D.F.

Millon, René
1981   Teotihuacán: City, state and civilization. In *Supplement to the Handbook of Middle American Indians*, Vol. 1, edited by Jeremy A. Sabloff, pp. 198–243. University of Texas Press, Austin.

Paddock, John
1990   *De Oaxaca 1*. Casa de la Cultura Oaxaqueña, Oaxaqueños de antes A.C., Oaxaca.

Pastor, Rodolfo
1986   Ideología y parentesco en el señorío mixteco según las fuentes del siglo XVI. In *Origen y Formación del Estado en Mesoamérica*, edited by Andrés Medina, Alfredo López Austin, and Mari Carmen Serra, pp. 85–111. Universidad Nacional Autónoma de México, México.

Ravesloot, John C.
1988   *Mortuary Practices and Social Differentiation at Casas Grandes, Chihuahua, Mexico*. University of Arizona Press, Tucson.

Sahagún, fray Bernardino de
1985   *Historia general de las cosas de Nueva España*. Editorial Porrúa, México.

Sanders, William T.
1992   Ranking and stratification in prehispanic Mesoamerica. In *Mesoamerican Elites: An Archaeological Assessment*, edited by Diane Z. Chase and Arlen F. Chase, pp. 278–91. University of Oklahoma Press, Norman.

Sanders, William T., and Barbara J. Price
1968   *Mesoamerica. The Evolution of a Civilization*. Random House, New York.

Sharer, Robert J.
1994   *The Ancient Maya*. Stanford University Press, Stanford.

Spores, Ronald
1967   *The Mixtec Kings and Their People*. University of Oklahoma Press, Norman.

Storey, Rebecca
1992   *Life and Death in the Ancient City of Teotihuacan: A Modern Paleodemographic Synthesis*. University of Alabama Press, Tuscaloosa.

Widmer, Randolph J., and Rebecca Storey
1993   Social organization and household structure of a Teotihuacan apartment compound: S3W1:33 of the Tlajinga Barrio. In *Prehispanic Domestic Units in Western Mesoamerica*, edited by Robert S. Santley and Kenneth G. Hirth, pp. 87–104. CRC Press, Boca Raton, Florida.

Winter, Marcus
1974   Residential patterns at Monte Albán, Oaxaca. *Science* 186:981–87.

Zeitlin, Robert N.
1993   Pacific Coastal Laguna Zope: A regional center in the Terminal Formative hinterlands of Monte Albán. *Ancient Mesoamerica* 4(1):85–101.

2

Corporate Life in Apartment and Barrio Compounds at Teotihuacan, Central Mexico

Craft Specialization, Hierarchy, and Ethnicity

Linda R. Manzanilla

Introduction: Teotihuacan's Corporate Structure

Few cities in the preindustrial world are as complex, multiethnic, planned, and exceptional as Teotihuacan. The confluence of diverse groups—some fleeing volcanic eruptions at the beginning of the Christian Era (see Plunket and Uruñuela 1998), others attracted by the work and trading opportunities in the city or the availability of goods—brought occupants together in a place they regarded as the center of the known world. Exceptional in size (20 km² [Millon 1973]) (Fig. 2.1), urban planning (Fig. 2.2), settlement pattern (a huge city surrounded mostly by rural sites), corporate strategy (Paulinyi 1981; Pasztory 1992; Manzanilla 1988, 1993, 1997a, 1998, 2001, 2006a; Blanton et al. 1996), and multiethnic character embedded deep in its structure (Price et al. 2000; Rattray 1988, 1989, 1993; Spence 1990, 1996), Teotihuacan did not resemble any other contemporary site in Mesoamerica.

To organize groups of different origin that had different interests and strategies, Teotihuacan invested much of its energy in building a planned city that had: an urban grid evoking the four quarters of the universe, with an underworld (the original quarry tunnels under the city); majestic monumental architecture echoing the natural orography; the most important mural paintings emphasizing fertility and abundance; and an inclusive society where all the different types of ball games could be played and all the languages spoken. Teotihuacan was the center of its world, the archetypal *Tollan* (Manzanilla 1997b).

Without written texts that can let us glimpse how this complex culture integrated all the different ethnic groups and social strata, archaeology must rely on very careful observations of how identities are expressed in material traces related to various behaviors and practices—culinary, attire, funerary, ritual, and social (Manzanilla 2007a).

In this chapter, I will put forth some ideas on how ethnicity, specialization, and hierarchy intertwine in corporate domestic compounds and in neighborhoods at Teotihuacan. The study of these two different scales of spatial analysis has implications for understanding how the city of Teotihuacan functioned and collapsed.

The Apartment Compounds

One of the main characteristics of Teotihuacan, in contrast to contemporary societies in Mesoamerica, is that various families, linked by kinship and shared activities as well as friends and possibly servants, dwelled in the same building, called a multifamily apartment compound. Even though most of the Teotihuacan apartment compounds may have housed Teotihuacan families, at Oztoyahualco 15B:N6W3 we detected some affiliated mem-

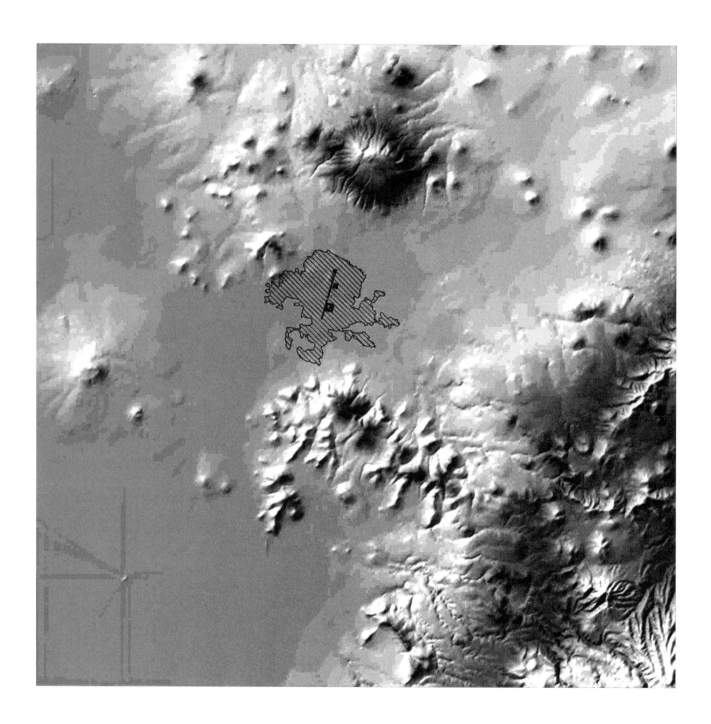

Figure 2.1. Location and size of the city of Teotihuacan in the Teotihuacan Valley (Manzanilla, in press; photo by Gerardo Jiménez).

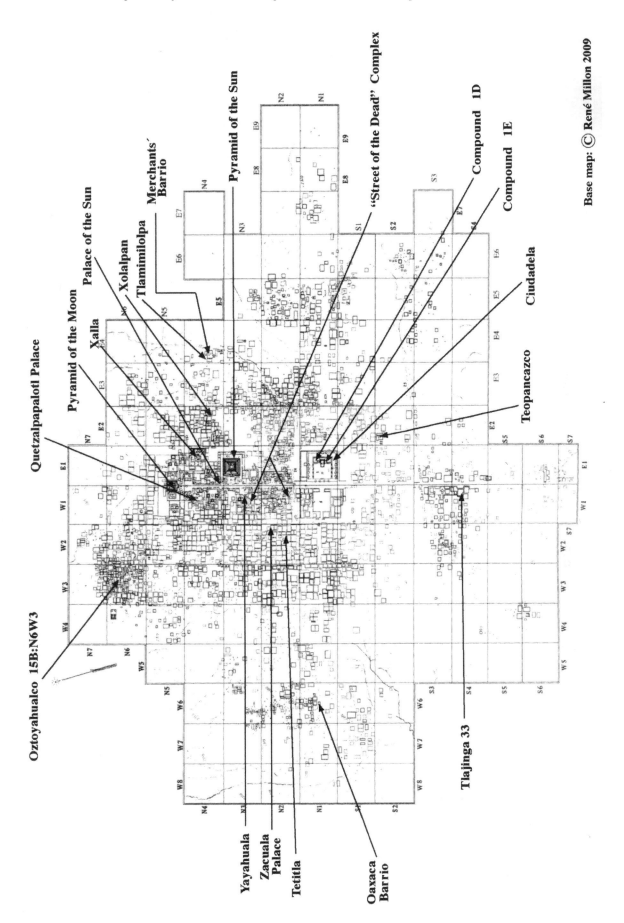

Figure 2.2. Map of the city of Teotihuacan by René Millon's project (1973), with some of the main sites (© René Millon 2009).

bers that came from other regions, as indicated by the data from strontium isotopes (Price et al. 2000).

Each household has a series of rooms, porticoes, and courtyards in which the people of the household live and reproduce. This domestic structure differs from Maya compounds (Manzanilla and Barba 1990), where each household has its own kitchen and sleeping areas but shares a domestic shrine ("the religious family," following Kulp 1925, in Blanton 1994:6). In the Teotihuacan apartment compounds, each household had its own kitchen, storeroom, sleeping area, and service courtyard, but also its own ritual courtyard, where its members venerated the familial patron god. One possible explanation for this unusual arrangement in Mesoamerica is the strong multiethnic component of Teotihuacan society, addressed below.

Even though they were dwelling together, not all the families and supporters who shared domestic spaces were at the same socioeconomic level: there seems to be a hierarchical organization within each compound (Manzanilla 1996), as was evident in multifamily T-shaped compounds (similar to "augmented corporate households" called *é* in Sumerian) in Samarra, Ubaid, and Uruk times in Mesopotamia (Maisels 1990:112, 166). At Oztoyahualco 15B:N6W3—a typical Teotihuacan compound (Manzanilla 1993)—only one family revered the God of Thunder as a patron deity and had access to foreign raw materials and goods (jadeite, slate, allochthonous fauna, and so on); in its domestic sector, it had the largest ritual courtyard (Manzanilla 1996). Other families had Fire God sculptures, probably as patron gods. The poorest of all had a rabbit (Manzanilla 1993; Manzanilla 1996; Barba et al. 2007). In other compounds, monkeys, birds, canids, or bats may have been representations of patron gods. These are represented as small sculptures on top of temple models or on top of altars set in ritual courtyards, as well as in the preponderance of these animals in the set of zoomorphic figurines in each compound (Riego Ruiz 2005).

Corporate life within each apartment compound may be detected in certain kinds of activities that the "augmented corporate household" offered to the neighborhood or urban setting. With respect to Oztoyahualco 15B:N6W3, located in the northwestern periphery of the city, we detected the extensive application of stucco not only for the plastering of the compound, but also to areas surrounding it (Manzanilla 1993).

The Barrio Compounds

The hierarchical organization of apartment compounds is even greater in the barrio compounds, where buildings housing groups of different statuses are contiguous and arranged around the barrio ritual sector (Manzanilla 2003b). Much remains to be learned about the relationships among the people in these compounds: kin, servants, clients, cadet lineages, and so on.

There are many indicators of foreign neighborhoods at Teotihuacan, located in the periphery of the city (Millon 1973, 1992; Rattray 1987, 1988, 1989, 1993; Spence 1990, 1996; Gómez-

Chávez 1998, 2000), which I address below (Fig. 2.3). In contrast to ethnic barrios, neighborhoods where Teotihuacanos lived may have taken three different forms:

(a) Neighborhood centers (that is, barrio centers) with open three-temple plazas (Manzanilla 1997b:120), surrounded by apartment compounds where a particular craft activity predominates in each. This form is perhaps the earliest manifestation of the different groups of people that settled in the Teotihuacan Valley after the volcanic eruptions of the first century AD, and thus these barrio centers are evident in the oldest sector of the city, the northwest sector. In many sectors along the main axis of the city, these three-temple plazas were incorporated into larger compounds, such as the Western Plaza of the Street of the Dead Compound.

(b) Elite neighborhoods (such as La Ventilla) with formal architectural compounds for each barrio function—that is, cult, administration, craft activity, residence, and an open space (Gómez-Chávez et al. 2004). Excavations in the La Ventilla 92-94 sector by Cabrera and Gómez have given us additional data with respect to the spatial organization of this particular neighborhood, which includes a barrio temple, an administrative building (the Glyph Courtyard), the apartment compounds of common people, and a huge open space that for Gómez-Chávez et al. (2004:175–76) was a place for exchange, festivities, and the playing of ball games. They also propose that Group Five Prima, near the Moon Pyramid, may have had a large open space associated with a barrio temple. I would add two more sectors with these characteristics—Tepantitla to the northeast, and Teopancazco to the southeast—that may have functioned as barrio centers, with large open spaces for ball games and popular gatherings (Manzanilla 2006a), as we propose below.

(c) Multiethnic neighborhoods headed by noble "houses," particularly evident in the southern periphery, such as Teopancazco (Manzanilla 2000, 2003c, 2006a, 2006b). This example will be discussed below.

At Teotihuacan, neighborhood centers are the seat of intermediate elites, as Elson and Covey (2006) describe them. They are dynamic social units in urban sites. Intermediate elites can shed light on the social organization of these units as well as on the transformational processes and the tensions in multiethnic settlements.

These intermediate elites may have been organized as noble "houses." A "house" or *maison* is a large corporate group organized by shared residence, subsistence, production, origin, and ritual (Gillespie 2000a:1). Following Lévi-Strauss (1982:174), they may have cultivation, hunting, fishing, and gathering areas, perpetuated through the transmission of their name, titles, and goods. The social group called *maison* is represented by the house itself; by the relics, emblems, masks, dress, and so on; and by the hunting, gathering, and food-producing lands (Gillespie 2000a:3, 2000b:25–26).

They may have displayed *oikos* economies, in the sense that Pollock (2002:117ff.) proposed for Early Dynastic Mesopotamia, following Max Weber. In third millennium BC Mesopotamia, the economy was reorganized as a result of having so many people

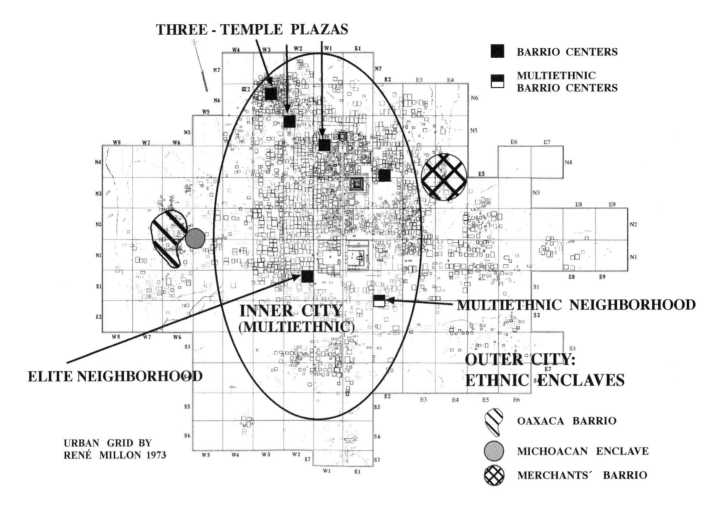

Figure 2.3. Foreign barrios in the periphery and Teotihuacano barrio centers in the inner city (drawing by Linda R. Manzanilla and Rubén Gómez-Jaimes; base map by René Millon 1973).

concentrated into cities. With less of their population residing in rural sites, tribute exaction diminished. The result was that the largest and wealthiest domestic units employed a substantial labor force of kin and non-kin domestic units (that is, a complex network of economically related units) to produce most of what was used or consumed. Pollock (2002:117–18) mentions extended families in coresidence, wealthy estates of public officials, temples, and royal palaces. These "great households" formed large socioeconomic units with workshops, storehouses, fields, orchards, flocks, managerial personnel, and dependent workforce. The personnel lived part of the time in the city and received food rations.

I propose that the noble "houses" of Teotihuacan settled in barrio centers, had *oikos* economies as described by Pollock (2002) for Mesopotamia, and integrated people and personnel who performed different functions. Expanding on what Gómez-Chávez et al. (2004:175ff.) proposed for La Ventilla, and adding a sector for the military personnel as well as an alignment of kitchens and storerooms, Teotihuacan neighborhood centers,

such as Teopancazco (square S2E2 in Millon's [1973] map), have seven components (Fig. 2.4):

1. The first component is the **ritual** sector, with (a) a larger plaza than any apartment compound known (275 m²), with an altar near the center, and (b) a large temple located to the east of the patio, with a sanctuary on top (ca. 57 m²) and façade to the west (Manzanilla 2006a). Chemical traces suggest processions of priests walking to and from the altar to the four cardinal points and up the temple (Pecci et al., in press), spilling organic liquids containing *Salvia* seeds (Martínez-Yrízar and Adriano-Morán 2006), as depicted in the famous mural painting found at the site (drawn by Adela Breton; Marquina 1922: ch. III, t. I, láms. 34 and 35; Cabrera Castro 1995:160) (Fig. 2.5).

Another ritual element in barrio centers that differs considerably from other contexts in the city are large displays of decapitated males associated with cinnabar, surrounding primary burials with theater-type censers (Manzanilla 2006a). We also recovered feasting debris, perhaps the remains of communal banquets on

KITCHENS - STOREROOMS

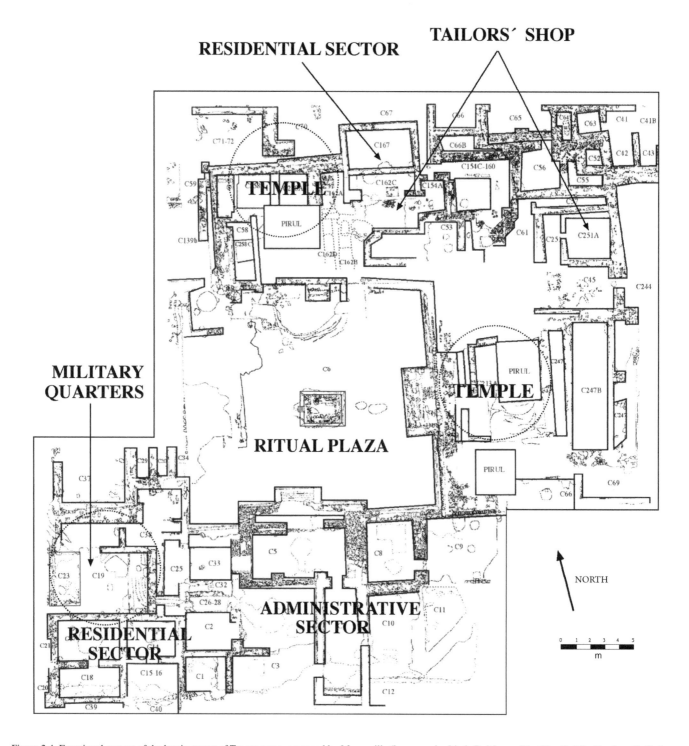

Figure 2.4. Functional sectors of the barrio center of Teopancazco, proposed by Manzanilla (base map by Linda R. Manzanilla, Claudia Nicolás, Agustín Ortiz, and César Fernández). See also Pecci 2000.

Figure 2.5. The ritual component of the barrio center of Teopancazco (Manzanilla 2006a). The main mural painting at Teopancazco (from Starr 1894; redrawn by César Fernández).

the fringes of the main plaza in which marine fish were eaten (identified by Edmundo Teniente [Instituto Politécnico Nacional] in Rodríguez Galicia 2006, 2007).

2. An **administrative** sector (located in the southern portion of the compound as well as the main plaza) where corporate groups, particularly craft representatives, meet with urban administrators to deliver the barrio products. Stamp seals occur here (Fig. 2.6), with iconography related to the main social units—the city, the state deity (the God of Thunder), the fire deity, the foreign groups (perhaps represented by a monkey seal)—and which may be used by different groups to differentiate from others their products or tribute (Fig. 2.7). Administrative devices may be related to round pottery objects called *tejos* as well as small trinkets of clay (Fig. 2.8), known as "game pieces." These may be individual craftsmen identification symbols (most of the rooms, porticoes, and patios at Teopancazco have a set of roundels of the main size groups in different proportions), associated with the hierarchy of the personnel working in them (represented by the variations in size and weight), or measuring units for craft production (the three main sizes are the same as seen with the mica disks manufactured using the roundels as models) (Fig. 2.8). They may not be gaming pieces because they occur in most rooms of the neighborhood center, associated with the pottery roundels.

3. The third element is the specialized **craft** production of costumes and headdresses used by intermediate elites, represented by bone tools such as needles, pins, perforators, and awls (Fig. 2.9) (Padró Irizarri 2002; Padró and Manzanilla 2004; Manzanilla 2006b; Pérez Roldán 2005; Manzanilla et al., forthcoming); the remains of animals such as mammals (rabbit, deer) that provided hair and hide for costumes, as well as faces that could be removed from the animals and made into headdresses; marine fauna such as conch shells, crocodile and turtle plates, and crab fragments (Rodríguez Galicia 2006, 2007) attached to the cotton cloth

coming from the Gulf Coast; and different types of birds that provided feathers for headdresses. Human bodies may also have been processed, as we have found human bones that have been cooked, roasted, nibbled, cut, and transformed into instruments and masks (Torres Sanders et al. 2007). The symbolic codes transmitted by the attire of the nobles were specific to a particular neighborhood as identity symbols. Teopancazco is characterized by the "priest of the ocean" motif (see Kubler 1967).

In Teopancazco, the "tailors' shops" are located in the northeastern and northern sectors between two possible temples, the eastern and northern.

4. The fourth component is a **residential** sector, which we believe houses the nobles that head the neighborhood. This sector is set originally between the two tailors' shops.

5. The fifth are the living quarters for the **military** personnel of the neighborhood (Fig. 2.10), which in Teopancazco may be located in the southwestern portion of the compound, where military iconography (figurines dressed in military outfits accompany the burial of a male child about 8 years in age [Figs. 2.11, 2.12] and mural paintings occur with military males [see drawings in Cabrera Castro 1995]) is clustered.

6. The sixth component is an alignment of **kitchens** and storerooms set in the northern periphery of the barrio center (Pecci et al., in press), and devoted to feeding the craftsmen and military. The grinding stones in this alignment are the only ones that display maize phytoliths; the rest of the metates in the barrio center were devoted to craft production, for grinding masses of stucco, pigment, fibers, and lacquer (Manzanilla, Reyes, and Zurita 2006).

7. A large **open area** for festivities, exchange activities, and ball games (Gómez-Chávez et al. 2004). At Teopancazco, it is situated to the east, the only sector where there is a great wall delimiting the neighborhood center.

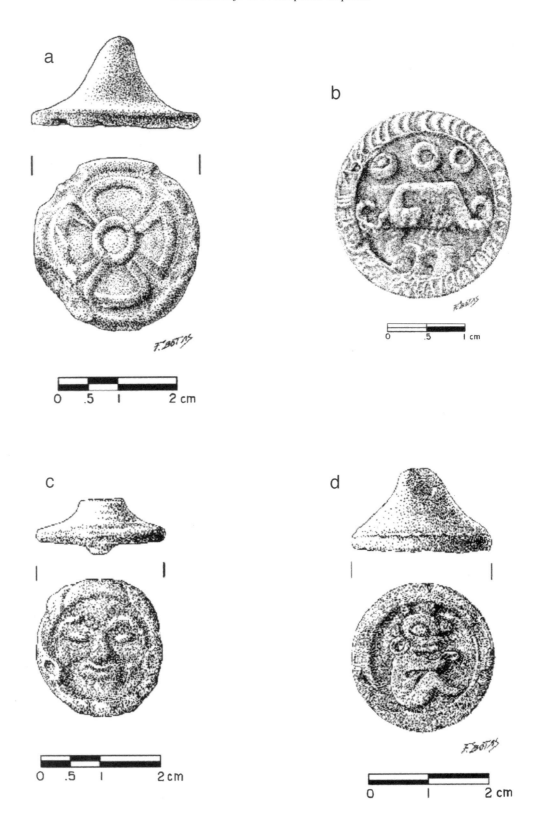

Figure 2.6. The administrative component of the Teopancazco barrio center (Manzanilla 2006a). *a*, four-petaled flower seal, probably the glyph of the city of Teotihuacan; *b*, God of Thunder's emblem seal; *c,* the Fire God seal from Teopancazco; *d*, a seal with a monkey figure, from Teopancazco (drawings by Fernando Botas).

In neighborhood centers located near the civic core of the city, the different functions may occur in separate compounds, as in La Ventilla 92-94. On the other hand, multiethnic neighborhood centers located in the southern periphery, such as Teopancazco, may include all these functions in separate sectors of the barrio center.

At Teopancazco we found evidence of a rite that involved decapitating males. Each head was placed inside a vessel, and then another vessel was placed on top to serve as a lid (Fig. 2.13). Some of the crania had cinnabar (Fig. 2.14), which sets them apart as very important people in this society, but also as part of minority groups (as Gazzola [2004:555] proposed). Most of these funerary vessels were set in pits, while others were set in a former *tablero-talud* temple, crowning the important burials of Tlamimilolpa times. These may have been rituals related to the ball game, perhaps as termination rituals for the Late Tlamimilolpa changes within the barrio center; these rituals involving sets of decapitated heads are not found in apartment compounds. The presence of cinnabar in many of them is important because in the Gulf Coast, some yokes, palms, and axes associated with the ball game and decapitation also have this mineral (Gazzola 2004:557). Thanks to the strontium isotope and stable isotope analyses, we know that most of the craftsmen and decapitated males were migrants from other parts of the central highlands or from the Gulf Coast (Solís-Pichardo et al. 2007; Morales and Cifuentes 2008).

Thus, La Ventilla 92-94, Tepantitla, perhaps the Group Five Prima, Yayahuala, and Teopancazco may have been distinct barrios. These have large congregational courtyards that are much larger than the largest courtyards in residential compounds such as Tetitla or Oztoyahualco 15B:N6W3. They lack food preparation areas typical of multifamily compounds. These barrio centers may have had the leadership of a powerful "house" that organized not only communal rites, but also very special crafts, such as the production of costumes and headdresses for the Teotihuacan elite.

With our extensive excavations at Teopancazco (Manzanilla 2003a, 2003c; Padró and Manzanilla 2004), and due to the interdisciplinary nature of our project, we are able to glimpse a phenomenon not seen before: the increasing disarticulation of the corporate structure of Teotihuacan during Xolalpan times when certain powerful "houses" fostered direct relations with craftsmen of other regions in Mesoamerica, such as the Gulf Coast, without the intervention or mediation of the central authority of the Teotihuacan state or the Merchants' Barrio that housed merchants from the Gulf Coast (Rattray 1988, 1989). The elaboration of elite attire decorated with products from Veracruz allowed these powerful "house" heads unprecedented economic power, and these more liberal actions allowed them to avoid the corporate strategy (Blanton et al. 1996), and instead employ an exclusionary strategy that increasingly pulled apart the fragile corporate tissue of the state until the collapse.

Figure 2.7. Bundle representations in mural paintings (redrawn by Rubén Gómez-Jaimes).

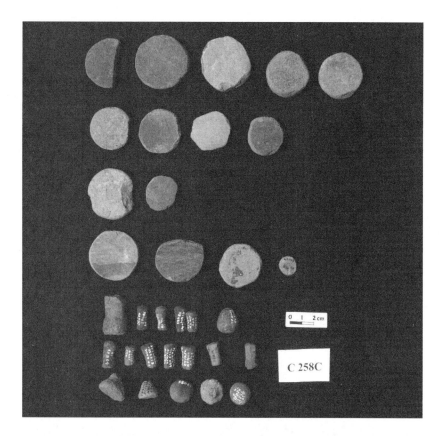

Figure 2.8. Pottery roundels (*tejos*) and trinkets, perhaps "tokens," from Teopancazco (photograph by Rafael Reyes).

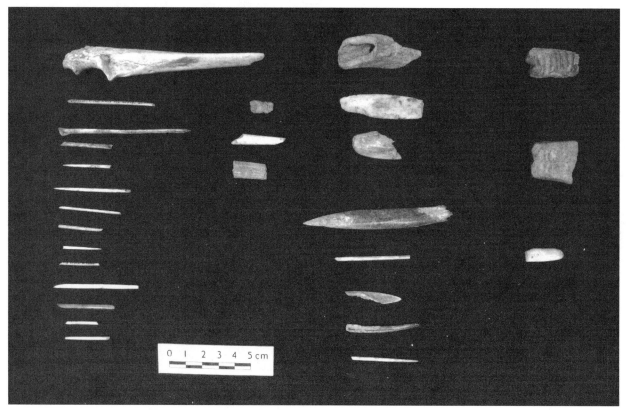

Figure 2.9. Tailors' implements found at the Teopancazco workshop (Pérez Roldán 2005; Padró Irizarri 2002; Padró and Manzanilla 2004; photograph by Rafael Reyes).

Figure 2.10. Military attire of the Teopancazco neighborhood, perhaps the barrio guard (Starr 1894; redrawn by César Fernández).

Indicators of Specialization at Teotihuacan

I see four different scales in which craft production took place (Fig. 2.15):

1. The apartment compounds where everyday needs were met.

2. Extensive craft sectors in the periphery of the site to produce what the urban population needed.

3. Specialized identity markers (such as costumes and head-dresses) crafted in barrio sectors under the supervision of noble "houses."

4. Specific crafts under the control of the rulers in embedded workshops (mica objects, darts, theater-type censer plaques, perhaps jadeite adornments, travertine [*tecali* and *ónix* adornments and sculptures]).

In most apartment compounds, craft activities were developed as part-time tasks. Edge rejuvenation and prismatic blade extraction from obsidian cores were carried out in many compounds.

Most of the craft production sectors for the urban dwellers seem to have been placed on the city's periphery. There is a large obsidian production sector in the northeastern periphery (San Martín de las Pirámides' eastern sector), possibly because the obsidian mines of Otumba and Pachuca lie to the northeast of the city itself. No Classic period obsidian workshop has been

excavated until now, so we know practically nothing about the organization of obsidian production within the city.

In the eastern periphery lie lapidary production areas, such as the one studied by Turner (1987) in Tecópac (N3E5), where jadeite, serpentine, quartz, quartzite, *tecali*, shell, and mica were converted into different small objects, suggesting that most of these raw materials may have come from the east. Basalt grinding stones may have been manufactured in several sectors, except the western (Millon 1973).

Pottery production workshops that seem to be located in the southern periphery, at sites such as Tlajinga 33 (Widmer 1987, 1991; Storey and Widmer 1989), take advantage of the clay sources in this sector. Lime plaster production sectors are placed to the northwest (Manzanilla 1993), presumably because the limestone areas are located in the Tula Valley (Díaz-Oyarzábal 1980).

Some production areas changed with respect to the type of craft produced, as was the case for Tlajinga 33, which was converted from a lapidary production sector in Tlamimilolpa times to a San Martín Orange manufacturing area (bowls and jars) during Late Xolalpan times (Widmer 1987, 1991; Storey and Widmer 1989). These changes occurred perhaps when some elite barrio centers such as La Ventilla took over the organization of specialized lapidary production for elite costumes.

Figure 2.11. High-rank attire of Teopancazco, perhaps a ball game player. Figurine found in Burial 4, a male child (drawing by Fernando Botas).

In multiethnic barrio centers, we seem to have evidence of full-time craftsmen, perhaps of foreign origin, devoted to manufacturing specialized sumptuary goods such as costumes, headdresses, and personal paraphernalia. We view Teopancazco as a site where we have a large variety of raw materials coming from the Gulf Coast:

(a) a great variety of fish from the coastal lagoons: horse mackerel, catfish, bass, shark and others (Teniente 2006; Rodríguez Galicia 2006, 2007).

(b) local birds, such as cardinal (*Richmondena cardinalis*), bobwhite (*Colinus virginianus*), hawk (*Bubo* sp.), duck (*Anas* sp.), waterfowl (*Fulica americana*), and turkey (*Meleagris gallopavo*), as well as some from the Gulf Coast (heron [*Anhinga anhinga*]) (Rodríguez Galicia 2006).

(c) crocodile, armadillo, turtles (*Kinosternon* sp. and *Pseudemys scripta*), crabs, and marine mollusks, these last from the Gulf Coast, the Caribbean, and the Pacific (Rodríguez Galicia 2006; Villanueva 2006).

We also have a large number of bone tools (pins, needles, awls, perforators), as we mentioned before; these implements were concentrated only in two sectors of the compound, together with the animals that provided the feathers, hides, and plaques. Padró Irizarri (2002) proposed that the regular shape and narrow diameter of the eye of the needles suggest they were used to sew with cotton thread or animal hair (particularly rabbits).

At Teopancazco, weasel and some canid crania show signs of having been detached from the facial portion, perhaps to be set in the frontal portion of headdresses (Valadez and Rodríguez 2004).

We also have pottery from the Gulf Coast, particularly Orange lacquer vessels, Potrero cream on brown, and Terrazas lustrous ware. There are examples of complete bowls made with local clays and lacquered with possible *Salvia* seeds (Manzanilla 2006a: Fig. 7) to make them look as if they were coming from the Gulf Coast. There are some examples of complete foreign vessels with red on brown and negative designs, with pastes coming from Ocotelulco in Tlaxcala, according to the neutron activation (Speakman and Glascock 2006; Neff 2006). Riego Ruiz (2005) found an unusual proportion of foreign figurines, particularly from the Gulf Coast, at Teopancazco, which may underscore the presence of two or more ethnic groups living near each other in the same compound.

The six formal burials in one of the "tailors'" sectors of the compound were all adults, and when identified to sex, they proved to be males (Torres and de Angeles, pers. comm.). Some of them (numbers 15 and 17, who were migrants, as seen in the strontium 87/86 ratios) (Schaaf and Solís 2006) had needles and instruments for sewing and attaching objects to the cotton *mantas* brought from the Gulf Coast. We thus have data that they may have been foreign craftsmen specialized in making elite attire.

The manufacture of elite dress may have been a hallmark of barrio centers, and Teopancazco may not have been an exception. Even though Gómez has stressed stone working as the main craft activity at La Ventilla 92-94, the profusion of bone instruments—particularly needles—found there (Terrazas 2007) suggests that other attire was being manufactured, where lapidary platelets/plaques, beads, and pendants were sewn to the cloth.

Indicators of Ethnicity at Teotihuacan

As a result of René Millon et al.'s (1973) mapping project, it has become clear that Teotihuacan had sectors of resident foreigners (Rattray 1987). The Oaxaca Barrio named Tlailotlacan to the southwest (Spence 1990, 1996; Rattray 1993), the Merchants' Barrio housing people from the Gulf Coast, in Mezquititla and Xocotitla to the east (Rattray 1988, 1989), and the Michoacán sector to the west (Gómez-Chávez 1998) were all situated on

Figure 2.12. Figurine representing a warrior with costume, found in the burial of a male child (drawings by Fernando Botas).

Figure 2.13. Extraordinary rituals in barrio centers such as Teopancazco (large displays of decapitated male individuals, some of which were set in this pit together with newborn babies) (photo by Linda R. Manzanilla).

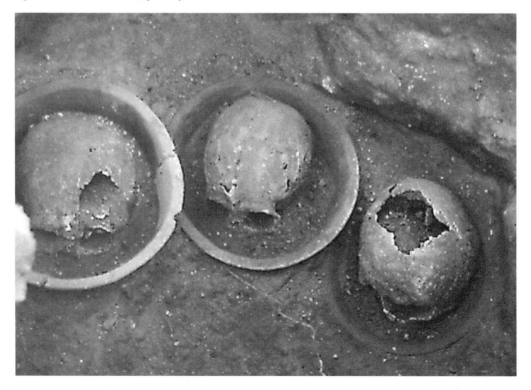

Figure 2.14. Detail of heads in vessels (photograph by Linda R. Manzanilla).

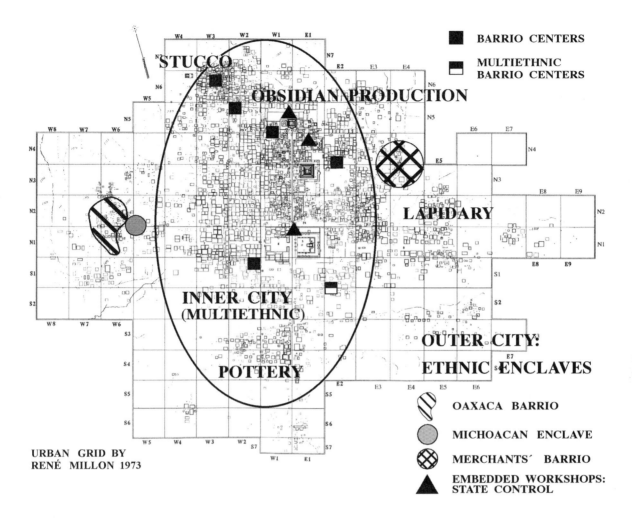

Figure 2.15. Craft production sectors in the city (drawing by Linda R. Manzanilla and Rubén Gómez-Jaimes; base map by René Millon 1973).

the periphery of the site, where incoming people first came into contact with the city. These sectors display either house forms that contrast sharply with the Teotihuacan standard (as seen in the Merchants' Barrio) or funerary and ritual practices that differ from those that characterize the city (for example, urn burials in the Oaxaca Barrio, or multiple burials in shafts in the Michoacán sector). There are probably other differences (see Blanton 1994), such as the way they prepare food and the ingredients they use (different cuisine), the costumes they wear, and perhaps the composition of their households (Manzanilla 2007a).

With strontium isotope analysis, we have proposed that the Merchants' Barrio housed people who came to the city from two sectors of the Gulf Coast and stayed only for a time (while they delivered and procured goods) before returning to their homeland (Price et al. 2000). In contrast, people from the Oaxaca Barrio came originally from the central valleys of Oaxaca; they formed a family that maintained some canonical elements of their culture

of origin, but assimilated the Teotihuacan diet and form of living. In typical Teotihuacan apartment compounds, such as Oztoyahualco 15B:N6W3, we have clear traces of what Teotihuacanos ate, how they prepared food, how they conducted rituals in their ceremonial courtyards, and what their standard funerary practices were (Manzanilla 1993; Manzanilla 1996; Manzanilla and Barba 1990; Barba et al. 2007). With strontium 87/86 analysis (Price et al. 2000), we have also detected one individual living at Oztoyahualco who was not local, someone who may have come from the Gulf Coast. This small multiethnic component in Teotihuacan apartment compounds is enlarged when we look at barrio centers.

The foreign presence in multiethnic neighborhoods may be detected in anomalous offerings or burial practices. At Teopancazco, by AD 350 a large set of termination rituals was practiced to consecrate the end of the Tlamimilolpa period: each of the approximately 25 decapitated males had his cranium placed in

Table 2.1 Courtyard and temple sizes.

	Main Courtyard (m²)	Main Temple Room (m²)
Residential Compounds		
Oztoyahualco 15B	25	10
Tlamimilolpa	ca. 7	
Tetitla	ca. 125	ca. 40
Yayahuala	ca. 168	ca. 54
Possible Barrio Centers		
Teopancazco	ca. 275	ca. 57
Tepantitla	ca. 182	ca. 153
Zacuala	ca. 224	ca. 224
La Ventilla 92-94	ca. 400	ca. 169

a San Martín Orange ceramic basin, topped with a bowl or cover (Manzanilla 2006a: Fig. 9), a practice paralleled only at Cerro de las Mesas, Veracruz (Drucker 1943). Other rites involved breaking a large set of vessels, some of them large polychrome tripods, with symbols drawn from Teotihuacan state iconography (tassel headdresses) (Manzanilla 2006a: Fig. 8), including the capture of a Gulf Coast heron by a serpent (Manzanilla 2000, 2003c, 2006a: Fig. 5), a motif that suggests bringing in a labor force, raw materials, and goods from the Gulf Coast to this particular barrio compound.

These termination rituals may have also marked a change in Teotihuacan society, with less stress on diversity, in the way ethnic groups were woven into the Teotihuacan fabric; a change in urban planning as "urban renewal" took place (the retraction of the Teotihuacan sphere of influence); and possibly increasing tension between the corporate structure of the Teotihuacan government and the network organization of the important houses that ruled the barrios.

Many of the Teopancazco craftsmen, as well as the decapitated male skulls with cinnabar found in the large termination ritual of Late Tlamimilolpan/Early Xolalpan times, were migrants, as shown in the strontium isotope analysis (Solís-Pichardo et al. 2006, 2007; Schaaf and Solís 2006).

Indicators of Hierarchy at Teotihuacan

Following González Licón (2003), we may address the indicators of residential hierarchy by reviewing: access to resources; the location, size, and form of architectural features such as compounds; raw materials, decoration, and provenience of artifact assemblages; differences in sumptuary goods in burials, and energy expenditure and heterogeneity of funerary patterns; and health conditions.

Access to Basic Resources

When we consider the presence/absence of botanical and faunal resources, as well as exogenous raw materials, we conclude that the differences in access are very slight between Teotihuacan compounds. Nearly all have access to maize, squash, beans, amaranth, chenopods, dog, turkey, rabbits, hares, deer, and waterfowl, but an exception is Tlajinga 33, where Storey (1992) has suggested freshwater fish and turkey eggs were consumed as crisis food in Late Xolalpan. Leaving this exception aside, even low-status compounds such as Oztoyahualco 15B:N6W3 have a very balanced diet, as burials and their isotopic values show (Civera 1993; Manzanilla et al. 2000). Some residential compounds may have had access to allochthonous fruits and plants such as tobacco, avocado, and cotton (Manzanilla 1996).

Access to Sumptuary Goods

Nearly all compounds have decorated tripod vessels and mural paintings, but they vary in quantity and quality. Sempowski (1987:117) has compared the number of funerary offerings, the type of objects, and the quantity of exotic goods at La Ventilla B, Zacuala Patios, and Tetitla to understand hierarchy. This approach, as well as a holistic view of access to resources and goods, and functional differences between compounds, should be undertaken to obtain the whole picture.

Architecture

With respect to architecture at Teotihuacan, the large apartment compounds near the Street of the Dead seem to display the best mural paintings. There are exceptions though (particularly Tlamimilolpa). When we differentiate residential compounds and barrio centers, we have to focus on courtyard and temple sizes (Manzanilla et al., forthcoming) (see Table 2.1). Wealthier residential compounds and barrio centers have larger main courtyards and temples, with the exception of Teopancazco's main temple rooms.

Hierarchical Structure

In the apartment compounds, one household seems to have been the most active in bonding the household group to the urban hierarchy. At Oztoyahualco 15B:N6W3, this is seen in Household 3, linked to the God of Thunder cult (Tláloc vases, Tláloc representations on covers with a handle), the richest burials, and foreign fauna (Manzanilla 1993, 1996).

Access to jadeite, mica, and slate seems to have been controlled by the Teotihuacan state. We now know that two compounds in the city—Xalla and the Viking Group—had 90% of the mica (Rosales de la Rosa 2004). Nevertheless, even the poorest apartment compound, such as Oztoyahualco 15B:N6W3, had access to these materials, but in very small amounts. With respect to marine shells, the difference also lies in the quantity and the proportion of Pacific versus Atlantic shell species (Manzanilla 1996).

Certain burials in each compound had very rich offerings. At Oztoyahualco, Burial 8 was exceptional for it contained a male adult (twenty-two years of age with an intentionally deformed skull associated with an impressive theater-type incense burner) who was perhaps a family head (Manzanilla and Carreón 1991).

Theater-type censers were used profusely at Xolalpan (where they are found in the altar and in a western courtyard) and Tlamimilolpa (where they are grouped around Burial 4 and kept in caches, ready for ritual use). Decorated tripods are also common at Xolalpan and Tlamimilolpa (Linné 1934, 1942), but very rare—though present—at Oztoyahualco 15B:N6W3 (Manzanilla 1993). One difference between these compounds lies in the presence of Maya fine wares in the western portion of Xolalpan and in the central part of Tlamimilolpa, possibly due to their proximity to the Merchants' Barrio. Other imported wares, such as Thin Orange and Granular Ware, are present in all compounds.

Stratification in Teotihuacan society has been seen through various datasets (from variables such as room size, use of space, decoration, construction techniques, burials, and offerings), generating a model that sees many levels and clear-cut social distinctions (Millon 1976, 1981; Sempowski 1987, 1994; Cowgill 1992), not having recognized the difference between multifunctional barrio centers (such as Teopancazco) and apartment compounds. Another model sees a whole range of slight socioeconomic differences between social groups that may reflect a variety of statuses within compounds, with multiple opportunities for achievement and thus a more complex panorama than stated before (Manzanilla 1996; see also Pasztory 1988).

Our point is that Teotihuacan society displayed a diversity of elite and non-elite social groups where ethnic, social, and professional differences were woven in a complex fabric, without sharply defined classes (Manzanilla 1996, 2006a).

Final Remarks

Even though the famous Teotihuacan grid may give the impression of a single integrated settlement, the city seems more like a site with multiple nuclei. In this chapter I have stressed a distinction not made before, a distinction between residential compounds and multifunctional barrio centers where intermediate urban elites may have organized specialized elite craft production in a multiethnic environment. The size of the main ritual courtyard and temple, as well as the presence or absence of food preparation activity areas and the profusion of craft activities and special funerary practices and burials, help to distinguish these two types of compounds from each other.

Multiethnicity is present in all the compounds at Teotihuacan, but in different percentages. Foreign supporters are present in Teotihuacan apartment compounds, but migrants to the city are particularly evident in foreign barrios and peripheral barrio centers.

The degree of specialization in craft production may be differentiated in apartment compounds and barrio centers. Some apartment compounds, such as Oztoyahualco 15B:N6W3, show non-specialized craft activities, together with some group specialization such as stucco burnishing and finishing. We suspect that its inhabitants may have had relatives in villages in the northern Teotihuacan Valley and in the Tula Valley, where limestone was procured, and which furnished some of the fauna found in the compound. The relationship between city and villages is yet to be studied.

There are peripheral neighborhoods, such as Tlajinga 33, that may have had full-time specialists, particularly in Late Xolalpan times. Barrio centers such as La Ventilla and Teopancazco may have had full-time craftsmen to craft elite paraphernalia, but at Teopancazco, we have found that this labor force mostly came from the Gulf Coast, and provided many animals and goods directly to the Teotihuacan rich who fostered this barrio (Fig. 2.16). La Ventilla 92-94, near the core of the city, has separate compounds to fulfill diverse functions: the ritual compound, the administrative building, and the craft production and living quarters. Teopancazco, more peripheral, has these three major functions clustered in one compound, adjacent to a vast open space for communal activities.

Hierarchy is best expressed in the location of the structures near the Street of the Dead, the size of the compound and its courtyard, the profusion and complexity of mural paintings, and the proportion of foreign raw materials controlled by the state.

Beyond neighborhoods, there seem to have been four large sectors in the city (Fig. 2.17), as the *campan* in Tenochtitlan. My impression is that the northwestern sector of the city had birds of prey as their emblem; the northeastern sector had jaguars and goggled figures; the southeastern, serpents; and the southwestern, coyotes and canids (Manzanilla 2007b). These emblems are reproduced on the Las Colinas vessel (Linné 1942). Perhaps these were the sectors from which the four principal ruling lineages came (Manzanilla 2001, 2002a, 2002b, 2007b). The two sectors in the south may have a greater multiethnic composition than the northern and more traditional sectors.

Teotihuacan displays a complex web of ethnic and social differences woven originally into a corporate structure that tried to harmonize them. Nevertheless, the increasing detachment of the Teotihuacan state with respect to allochthonous good procurement, and the seizing of this task by the powerful intermediate elites in some barrios, tore down the corporate structure, and enhanced the competition between houses for elite good production. This phenomenon reminds us of what Elson and Covey (2006:14) wrote: "Paradoxically, the intermediate elite enables state administration, while its success and proliferation may promote the breakup of centralized administration into less-integrated political forms."

The presence of a large variety of animals and goods from the Gulf Coast at Teopancazco, but also from Tlaxcala, may show that sooner or later, other centers in these regions escaped from Teotihuacan's control as the corporate structure collapsed.

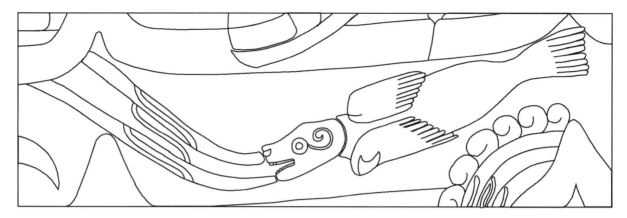

Figure 2.16. The fish as a possible emblem for the noble "house" of Teopancazco (represented in the Mythological Animals' mural painting) (figure redrawn by R. Gómez-Jaimes).

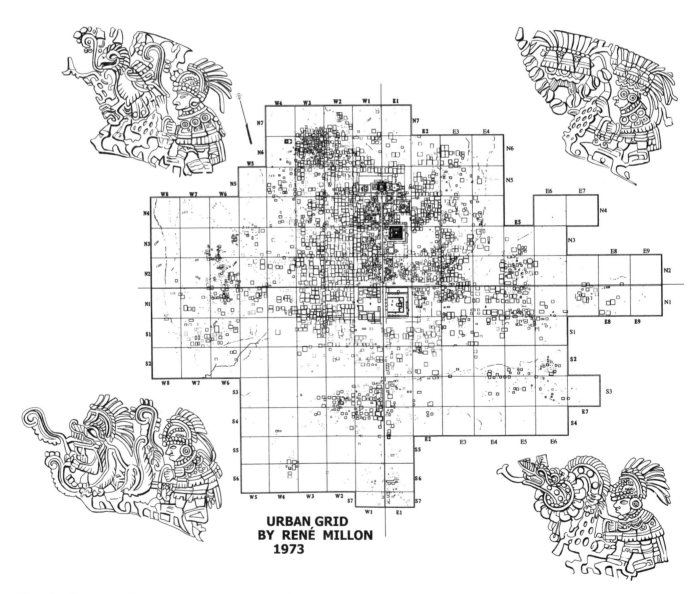

Figure 2.17. The proposed four sectors of the city (involved in the co-rulership) (Manzanilla 2007; base map of Teotihuacan by René Millon 1973; redrawn by L.R. Manzanilla, R. Gómez-Jaimes, and C. Fernández).

Acknowledgments

I thank my collaborators of the projects here cited for their interdisciplinary work, particularly the members of the project "Teotihuacan: Elite and Government"—Diana Martínez, Cristina Adriano, Emilio Ibarra, Judith Zurita, Manuel Reyes, Raúl Valadez, Bernardo Rodríguez, Liliana Torres Sanders, Luis Adrián Alvarado, Johanna Padró, Alessandra Pecci, Agustín Ortiz, Jorge Blancas, Luis Barba, Ana María Soler, Avto Gogichaishvili, Jaime Urrutia, Laura Beramendi, Galia González, Peter Schaaf, Gabriela Solís, Pedro Morales, Edith Cifuentes, Samuel Tejeda, Michael Glascock, Hector Neff, José Luis Ruvalcaba, Emiliano Melgar, Adrián Velázquez, Belem Zúñiga, Norma Valentín, Mauro de Angeles, Claudia López, Claudia Nicolás, Beatriz Maldonado, Marcela Zapata, Sandra Riego, Gilberto Pérez Roldán, Miguel Angel Baez, Edgar Rosales de la Rosa, Alejandra Guzmán, Citlali Funes, Mayra Lazcano, Leila França, Juan Rodolfo Hernández, Laura Bernal, Nidia Ortiz, Enah Montserrat Fonseca, Gabriela Mejía, Berenice Jiménez, Julieta López, Hilda Lozano, Estibaliz Aguayo, Meztli Hernández, Mijaely Castañón, Dinna Esparza, and many others. I thank Rafael Reyes for some of the photographs, and Fernando Botas, César Fernández, and Rubén Gómez-Jaimes for the drawings. I also thank Joyce Marcus for her suggestions to improve the text. This project was made possible thanks to support from UNAM and CONACYT, and to the Consejo de Arqueología of INAH for the permit.

References

Barba, Luis, Agustín Ortiz, and Linda Manzanilla
2007   Commoner ritual at Teotihuacan, central Mexico. In *Commoner Ritual and Ideology in Ancient Mesoamerica*, edited by N. Gonlin and J.C. Lohse, pp. 55–82. University Press of Colorado, Boulder.

Blanton, Richard E.
1994   *Houses and Households: A Comparative Study*. Interdisciplinary Contributions to Archaeology. Plenum Press, New York and London.

Blanton, Richard E., Gary M. Feinman, Stephen A. Kowalewski, and Peter N. Peregrine
1996   A dual-processual theory for the evolution of Mesoamerican civilization. *Current Anthropology* 37(1):1–14.

Cabrera Castro, Rubén
1995   Teopancazco. Casa Barrios o del Alfarero. In *La Pintura Mural Prehispánica en México. I. Teotihuacan*, tomo I. Catálogo, edited by B. de la Fuente, pp. 157–61. IIE-UNAM, México, D.F.

Civera-C., Magalí
1993   Análisis osteológico de los entierros de Oztoyahualco. In *Anatomía de un conjunto residencial teotihuacano en Oztoyahualco*, Vol. II, edited by L. Manzanilla, pp. 832–59. Instituto de Investigaciones Antropológicas, UNAM, México, D.F.

Cowgill, George L.
1992   Social differentiation at Teotihuacan. In *Mesoamerican Elites: An Archaeological Assessment*, edited by D.Z. Chase and A.F. Chase, pp. 206–20. University of Oklahoma Press, Norman.

Díaz-Oyarzábal, Clara Luz
1980   *Chingú: Un sitio clásico del área de Tula, Hgo*. Colección Científica no. 90. Instituto Nacional de Antropología e Historia, México, D.F.

Drucker, Philip
1943   *Ceramic Stratigraphy at Cerro de las Mesas, Veracruz, Mexico*. Bulletin 141. Smithsonian Institution, Washington, D.C.

Elson, Christina M., and R. Alan Covey (editors)
2006   *Intermediate Elites in Pre-Columbian States and Empires*. University of Arizona Press, Tucson.

Gazzola, Julie
2004   Uso y significado del cinabrio en Teotihuacan. In *La costa del Golfo en tiempos teotihuacanos: propuestas y perspectivas. Memoria de la Segunda Mesa Redonda de Teotihuacan*, edited by María Elena Ruiz-Gallut and Arturo Pascual-Soto, pp. 541–69. INAH, México, D.F.

Gillespie, Susan D.
2000a   Beyond kinship: An introduction. In *Beyond Kinship: Social and Material Reproduction in House Societies*, edited by R. Joyce and S.D. Gillespie, pp. 1–21. University of Pennsylvania Press, Philadelphia.
2000b   Lévi-Strauss. Maison and Société à Maisons. In *Beyond Kinship: Social and Material Reproduction in House Societies*, edited by R. Joyce and S.D. Gillespie, pp. 22–52. University of Pennsylvania Press, Philadelphia.

Gómez-Chávez, Sergio
1998   Nuevos datos sobre la relación de Teotihuacan y el Occidente de México. In *Antropología e Historia del Occidente de México. XXIV Mesa Redonda de la Sociedad Mexicana de Antropología*, Vol. III, pp. 1461–93. Sociedad Mexicana de Antropología-UNAM, México.
2000   *La Ventilla. Un barrio de la antigua ciudad de Teotihuacan*. Thesis in Archaeology, Escuela Nacional de Antropología e Historia, México, D.F.

Gómez-Chávez, Sergio, Julie Gazzola, and Jaime Núñez-Hernández
2004   Nuevas ideas sobre el juego de pelota en Teotihuacan. In *La costa del Golfo en tiempos teotihuacanos: propuestas y perspectivas. Memoria de la Segunda Mesa Redonda de Teotihuacan*, edited by M.E. Ruiz-Gallut and A. Pascual-Soto, pp. 165–99. INAH, México, D.F.

González Licón, Ernesto
2003   *Social Inequality at Monte Alban, Oaxaca: Household Analyses from Terminal Formative to Early Classic*. PhD dissertation, University of Pittsburgh, Pittsburgh.

Kubler, George
1967   *The Iconography of the Art of Teotihuacan*. Studies in Pre-Columbian Art and Archaeology no. 4. Dumbarton Oaks, Washington, D.C.

Lévi-Strauss, Claude
1982   *The Way of the Masks*, translated by Sylvia Modelski. University of Washington Press, Seattle.

Linné, Sigvald
1934   *Archaeological Researches at Teotihuacan, Mexico*. Ethnographical Museum of Sweden, Stockholm.
1942   *Mexican Highland Cultures. Archaeological Researches at Teotihuacan, Calpulalpan and Chalchicomula in 1934/1935*. Ethnographical Museum of Sweden, Stockholm.

Maisels, Charles Keith
1990   *The Emergence of Civilization: From Hunting and Gathering to Agriculture, Cities, and the State in the Near East*. Routledge, London and New York.

Manzanilla, Linda
1988   The Economic Organization of the Teotihuacan Priesthood: Hypotheses and Considerations. Paper presented at the Symposium on Art, Polity, and the City of Teotihuacan, Dumbarton Oaks Library and Collections, Washington, D.C., October 9.
1996   Corporate groups and domestic activities at Teotihuacan. *Latin American Antiquity* 7(3):228–46.
1997a   Early urban societies: Challenges and perspectives. In *Emergence and Change in Early Urban Societies*, edited by L. Manzanilla, pp. 3–39. Plenum Series in Fundamental Issues in Archaeology. Plenum Press, New York.
1997b   Teotihuacan: Urban archetype, cosmic model. In *Emergence and Change in Early Urban Societies*, edited by L. Manzanilla, pp. 109–31. Plenum Series in Fundamental Issues in Archaeology. Plenum Press, New York.
1998   Teotihuacan 'Palaces': Social Diversity in an Urban Setting. Paper presented at the Dumbarton Oaks Pre-Columbian Symposium "Ancient Palaces of the New World: Form, Function, and Meaning," Washington, D.C., October 10.
2000   Noticias. Hallazgo de dos vasijas policromas en Teopancazco, Teotihuacan. *Arqueología Mexicana* VIII(44):80.
2001   Agrupamientos sociales y gobierno en Teotihuacan, Centro de México. In *Reconstruyendo la ciudad maya: el urbanismo en las ciudades antiguas*, edited by A. Ciudad, M.J. Iglesias-Ponce de León, and M.C. Martínez, pp. 461–82. Publicaciones de la SEEM 6. SEEM, Madrid.
2002a   Organización sociopolítica de Teotihuacan: lo que los materiales arqueológicos nos dicen o nos callan. In *Memorias de la Primera Mesa Redonda de Teotihuacan*. UNAM-Instituto de Investigaciones Antropológicas-Instituto de Investigaciones Estéticas, INAH, México, D.F.
2002b   Gobierno corporativo en Teotihuacan: una revisión del concepto 'palacio' aplicado a la gran urbe prehispánica. *Anales de Antropología* 35:157–90.
2003a   The abandonment of Teotihuacan. In *The Archaeology of Settlement Abandonment in Middle America*, edited by T. Inomata and R.W. Webb, pp. 91–101. Foundations of Archaeological Inquiry. University of Utah Press, Salt Lake City.
2003b   Social identity and daily life at Classic Teotihuacan. In *Mesoamerican Archaeology: Theory and Practice*, edited by J.A. Hendon and R.A. Joyce, pp. 124–27. Global Studies in Archaeology. Blackwell Publishing Co., Malden, MA.
2003c   Teopancazco: un conjunto residencial teotihuacano. *Arqueología Mexicana. Teotihuacan: ciudad de misterios* XI(64):50–53.
2006a   Estados corporativos arcaicos. Organizaciones de excepción en escenarios excluyentes. *Cuicuilco* 13(36)(enero–abril):13–45. ENAH, Mexico.

2006b   La producción artesanal en Mesoamérica. *Arqueología Mexicana* (La producción artesanal en Mesoamérica) XIV(80) (julio–agosto):28–35.
2007a   La unidad doméstica y las unidades de producción. Propuesta interdisciplinaria de estudio. *Memoria 2007* de El Colegio Nacional, México:415–51.
2007b   Las 'casas' nobles de los barrios de Teotihuacan: estructuras exclusionistas en un entorno corporativo. *Memoria 2007* de El Colegio Nacional, México:453–70.
in press Metrópolis prehispánicas e impacto ambiental: el caso de Teotihuacan a través del tiempo. In *Escenarios de cambio ambiental: Registros del Cuaternario en América Latina*. Volumen especial de la Unión Mexicana de Estudios del Cuaternario, edited by Margarita Caballero and Beatriz Ortega. Universidad Nacional Autónoma de México, México, D.F.

Manzanilla, Linda (editor)
1993   *Anatomía de un conjunto residencial teotihuacano en Oztoyahualco*. 2 vols. Instituto de Investigaciones Antropológicas, Universidad Nacional Autónoma de México, México.

Manzanilla, Linda, and Luis Barba
1990   The study of activities in Classic households, two case studies from Cobá and Teotihuacan. *Ancient Mesoamerica* 1(1):41–49.

Manzanilla, Linda, and Emilie Carreón
1991   A Teotihuacan censer in a residential context: An interpretation. *Ancient Mesoamerica* 2:299–307.

Manzanilla, Linda, Samuel Tejeda, and Juan Carlos Martínez
2000   Implicaciones del análisis de calcio, estroncio y zinc en el conocimiento de la dieta y la migración en Teotihuacan, México. *Anales de Antropología* 33(1996–1999):13–28. Instituto de Investigaciones Antropológicas, UNAM, México.

Manzanilla, Linda, Manuel Reyes, and Judith Zurita
2006   Propuesta metodológica para el estudio de residuos químicos en metates de uso no doméstico: Teopancazco, Teotihuacan. Poster presented at the Congreso Interno del Personal Académico del Instituto de Investigaciones Antropológicas, UNAM, August 29, 2006.

Manzanilla, Linda, Luis Barba, Agustín Ortiz, and Alessandra Pecci
forthcoming Domestic Ritual in the Complex of Courtyards-Altars-Domestic Temples at Teotihuacan. Means of Integration or Control?

Manzanilla, Linda, Raúl Valadez, Bernardo Rodríguez, Johanna Padró, and Gilberto Pérez Roldán
forthcoming Producción de atavíos y tocados en un centro de barrio de Teotihuacan. El caso de Teopancazco. In *Artesanos y especialistas: indicadores arqueológicos*, edited by L.R. Manzanilla and K. Hirth.

Marquina, Ignacio
1922   Arquitectura y Escultura. In *La Población del Valle de Teotihuacan*, Vol. I, Cap. III, edited by M. Gamio, pp. 99–164. Secretaría de Agricultura y Fomento, México, D.F.

Martínez-Yrízar, Diana, and Cristina Adriano-Morán
2006 Exploring Relations between Plants and the Prehispanic Inhabitants of Teotihuacan. Paper presented at the Symposium "The Social Life of Seeds: Paleoethnobotanical Approaches to the Biographies of Plants and People in Ancient Mesoamerica," 71st Annual Meeting of the Society for American Archaeology, San Juan, Puerto Rico, April 26–30, 2006.

Millon, René
1973 *Urbanization at Teotihuacan, Mexico. The Teotihuacan Map. Part One: Text*. University of Texas Press, Austin.
1976 Social relations in ancient Teotihuacan. In *The Valley of Mexico*, edited by E.R. Wolf, pp. 205–48. University of New Mexico Press, Albuquerque.
1981 Teotihuacan: City, state and civilization. In *Handbook of Middle American Indians, Supplement I. Archaeology*, edited by V. Bricker and J.A. Sabloff, pp. 198–243. University of Texas Press, Austin.
1992 Teotihuacan studies: From 1950 to 1990 and beyond. In *Art, Ideology and the City of Teotihuacan*, edited by J.C. Berlo, pp. 339–429. Dumbarton Oaks, Washington, D.C.

Morales, Pedro, and Edith Cifuentes
2008 *Informe técnico sobre los estudios de isótopos estables en 43 muestras de entierros de Teopancazco, Teotihuacan*. Laboratorio de Isótopoes Estables, Instituto de Geología, UNAM, México, D.F.

Neff, Hector
2006 *Technical Report on the Pottery from Teopancazco*. Dept. of Anthropology and IIRMES, California State University-Long Beach, CA.

Ortiz-Butrón, Agustín
1990 *Estudio químico de las áreas de actividad de una unidad residencial teotihuacana*. Thesis in Archaeology, Escuela Nacional de Antropología e Historia, México, D.F.

Ortiz, Agustín, and Luis Barba
1993 La química en el estudio de áreas de actividad. In *Anatomía de un conjunto residencial teotihuacano en Oztoyahualco*, edited by L. Manzanilla, pp. 617–60. Instituto de Investigaciones Antropológicas, UNAM, México, D.F.

Padró Irizarri, Virgen Johanna
2002 *La industria del hueso trabajado en Teotihuacan*. PhD dissertation in Anthropology, Facultad de Filosofía y Letras de la UNAM, México, D.F.

Padró, Johanna, and Linda Manzanilla
2004 Bone and Antler Artifact Analysis. A Case Study from Teotihuacan, Mexico. Paper presented at the Symposium "Craft Production at Terminal Formative and Classic Period Teotihuacan, Mexico," 2004 Annual Meeting of the Society for American Archaeology, Montreal, Canada, April 3, 2004.

Pasztory, Esther
1988 A reinterpretation of Teotihuacan and its mural painting tradition, and catalogue of the Wagner Murals Collections. In *Feathered Serpents and Flowering Trees: Reconstructing the Murals of Teotihuacan*, edited by K. Berrin, pp. 45–77, 135–93. The Fine Arts Museums of San Francisco, San Francisco.

1992 Abstraction and the rise of a utopian state at Teotihuacan. In *Art, Ideology, and the City of Teotihuacan*, edited by J.C. Berlo, pp. 281–320. Dumbarton Oaks, Washington, D.C.

Paulinyi, Zoltan
1981 Capitals in pre-Aztec central Mexico. *Acta Orientalia Academiae Scientiarum Hung* XXXV(2–3):315–50.

Pecci, Alessandra
2000 *Análisis químico de pisos y áreas de actividad: estudio de caso en Teopancazco, Teotihuacan*. Master's thesis in Anthropology, Facultad de Filosofía y Letras de la UNAM, México, D.F.

Pecci, Alessandra, Agustín Ortiz, Luis Barba, and Linda Manzanilla
in press Distribución espacial de las actividades humanas con base en el análisis químico de los pisos de Teopancazco, Teotihuacan. In *VI Coloquio Bosch Gimpera. Lugar, Espacio y Paisaje en Arqueología: Mesoamérica y otras áreas culturales*. Instituto de Investigaciones Antropológicas, UNAM, México, D.F.

Pérez Roldán, Gilberto
2005 *Informe técnico sobre los instrumentos de hueso trabajado de la 'sastrería' de Teopancazco, Teotihuacan*. Instituto de Investigaciones Antropológicas, UNAM, México, D.F.

Plunket, Patricia, and Gabriela Uruñuela
1998 Preclassic household patterns preserved under volcanic ash at Tetimpa, Puebla, Mexico. *Latin American Antiquity* 9(4):287–309.

Pollock, Susan
2002 *Ancient Mesopotamia: The Eden that Never Was*. Cambridge University Press Series: Case Studies in Early Societies. Cambridge University Press, Cambridge.

Price, T. Douglas, Linda Manzanilla, and William H. Middleton
2000 Immigration and the ancient city of Teotihuacan in Mexico: A study using strontium isotope ratios in human bone and teeth. *Journal of Archaeological Science* 27(October):903–13.

Rattray, Evelyn C.
1987 Los barrios foráneos de Teotihuacan. In *Teotihuacan. Nuevos datos, nuevas síntesis, nuevos problemas*, edited by E. McClung de Tapia and E.C. Rattray, pp. 243–76. Instituto de Investigaciones Antropológicas, UNAM, México, D.F.
1988 Nuevas interpretaciones en torno al Barrio de los Comerciantes. *Anales de Antropología* XXV:165–80. Instituto de Investigaciones Antropológicas, UNAM, México, D.F.
1989 El Barrio de los Comerciantes y el conjunto de Tlamimilolpa: un estudio comparativo. *Arqueología* 5:105–29. Dirección de Monumentos Prehispánicos, INAH, México.
1993 *The Oaxaca Barrio at Teotihuacan*. Universidad de las Américas-Puebla, Cholula.

Riego Ruiz, Sandra
2005 *Las figurillas cerámicas de Oztoyahualco 15B:N6W3, Teopancazco y Xalla. Análisis comparativo en tres conjuntos teotihuacanos*. Thesis in Archaeology, Escuela Nacional de Antropología e Historia, México, D.F.

Rodríguez Galicia, Bernardo
2006 *El uso diferencial del recurso fáunico en Teopancazco, Teoti-huacan, y su importancia en las áreas de actividad.* Master's thesis in Anthropology (Archaeology), Facultad de Filosofía y Letras, UNAM, México, D.F.
2007 Ictiofauna encontrada en el sitio arqueológico de Teopancazco, Teotihuacan. (Un análisis por microscopía electrónica de barrido y de rayos X.) Paper for the XXVIII Mesa Redonda de la Sociedad Mexicana de Antropología, Colegio de las Vizcaínas, México, D.F., August 2007.

Rosales de la Rosa, Edgar Ariel
2004 *Usos, manufactura y distribución de la mica en Teotihuacan.* Thesis in Archaeology, Escuela Nacional de Antropología e Historia, México, D.F.

Schaaf, Peter, and Gabriela Solís
2006 *Informe técnico del análisis isotópico de $^{87}Sr/^{86}Sr$ en varios entierros de Teopancazco.* Laboratorio Universitario de Geoquímica Isotópica (LUGIS), UNAM, México, D.F.

Sempowski, Martha L.
1987 Differential mortuary treatment: Its implication for social status at three residential compounds in Teotihuacan, México. In *Teotihuacan. Nuevos datos, nuevas síntesis y nuevos problemas*, edited by E. McClung de Tapia and E. Childs Rattray, pp. 115–31. Instituto de Investigaciones Antropológicas, UNAM, México, D.F.
1994 Part I. Mortuary practices at Teotihuacan. In *Mortuary Practices and Skeletal Remains at Teotihuacan*, edited by M.L. Sempowski and M.W. Spence, pp. 1–314. Urbanization at Teotihuacan, Mexico, no. 3. University of Utah Press, Salt Lake City.

Solís-Pichardo, G., P. Schaaf, T. Hernández-Treviño, P. Horn, and L. Manzanilla
2006 Isótopos de Sr en Teotihuacan: trazadores de migración humana en la antigüedad. Poster presented at the Reunión Anual de la Unión Geofísica Internacional, Puerto Vallarta, October 30–November 3, 2006.

Solís-Pichardo, G., P. Schaaf, L. Manzanilla, and P. Horn
2007 Ancient Human Migration and Sr Isotopes: The Teotihuacan Site (Mexico) as an Example. Poster presented at the 20. Lateinamerika-Kolloquium, Kiel, Alemania, April 11–13, 2007.

Speakman, Jeff, and Michael Glascock
2006 *Technical Report on 12 Pottery Samples from Teopancazco.* Archaeometry Laboratory, University of Missouri Research Reactor Center, Columbia.

Spence, Michael W.
1990 Excavaciones recientes en Tlailotlacan, El barrio oaxaqueño de Teotihuacan. *Arqueología* 5:81–104. Dirección de Monumentos Prehispánicos, INAH, México.
1996 Comparative analysis of ethnic enclaves. In *Arqueología mesoamericana. Homenaje a William T. Sanders*, Vol. I, edited by A.M. Mastache, J.R. Parsons, R.S. Santley, and M.C. Serra Puche, pp. 333–53. INAH-Arqueología Mexicana, México, D.F.

Starr, Frederick
1894 Notes on Mexican archaeology. The painted house at San Juan Teotihuacan. In *Bulletin 1*, pp. 3–16. Department of Anthropology, University of Chicago Press, Chicago.

Storey, Rebecca
1992 *Life and Death in the Ancient City of Teotihuacan: A Modern Paleodemographic Synthesis.* University of Alabama Press, Tuscaloosa.

Storey, Rebecca, and Randolph J. Widmer
1989 Household and community structure of a Teotihuacan apartment compound: S3W1:33 of the Tlajinga Barrio. In *Households and Communities*, edited by S. MacEachern, D.J.W. Archer, and R.D. Garvin, pp. 407–15. Archaeological Association of the University of Calgary, Chacmool, Calgary.

Teniente, Edmundo
2006 Identificación de los peces de Teopancazco, Instituto Politécnico Nacional. In *El uso diferencial del recurso fáunico en Teopancazco, Teotihuacan, y su importancia en las áreas de actividad*, by Bernardo Rodríguez-Galicia. Master's thesis in Anthropology (Archaeology), Facultad de Filosofía y Letras, UNAM, México, D.F.

Terrazas Mata, Alejandro
2007 *Tratamientos mortuorios y organización bio-social en el sitio de la Ventilla 92-94, Teotihuacan.* PhD dissertation in Anthropology, Facultad de Filosofía y Letras, UNAM, México, D.F.

Torres Sanders, Liliana, Raúl Valadez Azúa, Bernardo Rodríguez Galicia, and Linda Manzanilla Naim
2007 *Alteraciones taxonómicas en restos óseos de Teopancazco.* Technical report for the project "Teotihuacan: Elite and Government," headed by Linda R. Manzanilla.

Turner, Margaret Hempenius
1987 The lapidaries of Teotihuacan, Mexico. In *Teotihuacan. Nuevos datos, nuevas síntesis, y nuevos problemas*, edited by E. McClung de Tapia and E.C. Rattray, pp. 465–71. Instituto de Investigaciones Antropológicas, UNAM, México, D.F.

Valadez, Raúl, and Bernardo Rodríguez
2004 *Informe técnico de la identificación de fauna de Teopancazco, Teotihuacan.* Laboratorio de Arqueozoología, Instituto de Investigaciones Antropológicas, UNAM, México, D.F.

Villanueva-García, Gerardo
2006 *Relación biológica del material malacológico. Teopancazco.* Technical report, Sección de Biología, Dirección de Salvamento Arqueológico, INAH, México.

Widmer, Randolph J.
1987 The evolution of form and function in a Teotihuacan apartment compound: The case of Tlajinga 33. In *Teotihuacan. Nuevos datos, nuevas síntesis, y nuevos problemas*, edited by E. McClung de Tapia and E.C. Rattray, pp. 317–68. Instituto de Investigaciones Antropológicas, UNAM, México, D.F.
1991 Lapidary craft specialization at Teotihuacan: Implications for community structure at 33:S3W1 and economic organization in the city. *Ancient Mesoamerica* 2(1):131–47.

3

Household, Workshop, Guild, and Barrio

The Organization of Obsidian Craft Production in a Prehispanic Urban Center

Kenneth G. Hirth

Introduction

Although archaeologists have always been interested in the structure of prehispanic urban centers, their investigation is a difficult and challenging task, due to three reasons. First, because of the high value of urban space and the elevated risk that organic refuse creates for infectious disease in areas of high population density, refuse is often systematically removed from urban areas. This removal significantly reduces the accumulation of refuse in and around domestic and non-domestic structures and restricts investigation of comparative social organization. Second, refuse that does accumulate in cities tends to build up in vacant house lots, creating composite deposits from multiple contributing households and institutions. These deposits often represent palimpsests of whole neighborhoods, and while they may provide insight for studying community-level consumption patterns, they usually cannot be associated with specific households. Third, the premium on space in urban environments often leads to the rapid demolition of abandoned buildings and the recycling of usable construction materials into other structures. The result is that urban structures are often poorly preserved and are swept clean of most associated artifact assemblages.

This study examines the organization of craft production at the household and neighborhood levels in the prehistoric urban center of Xochicalco, Morelos. Xochicalco was the capital of a regional conquest state that grew to power in western Morelos during the Epiclassic period between AD 65 and 900 (Fig. 3.1). It was a mid-sized urban center with impressive civic-ceremonial architecture and a resident population of between 10,000 and 15,000 persons (Hirth 2000a). What is most important is that none of the three constraints mentioned above are found at Xochicalco. Excavations over the past four decades have revealed that the site was attacked and rapidly destroyed around AD 900, resulting in the burning of domestic and non-domestic structures across the site. Although public areas of the site were looted, residential structures were rapidly destroyed. When the houses burned and roofs collapsed, relatively complete assemblages were trapped on the house floors. These conditions permit a more robust reconstruction of household structure and domestic activities than has been possible at other urban centers in Central Mexico.

The goal of this volume is to examine the organization of prehispanic urban centers at three levels of organization: the household, the compound, and neighborhood barrios. I address this question from the perspective of craft specialization and discuss how craft production at Xochicalco was, or was not, organized at the household, compound, and barrio levels. Excavations at Xochicalco between 1992 and 1993 explored workshop areas where evidence was found for the production of obsidian prismatic blades (Fig. 3.2) (Hirth 2006). Four domestic workshops and one public workshop were excavated to explore the scale and

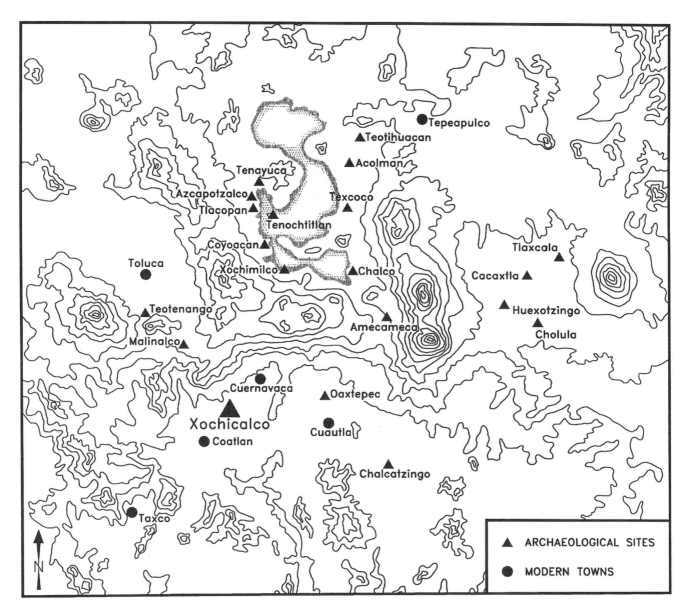

Figure 3.1. The location of Xochicalco in Central Mexico.

organization of obsidian craft production in domestic and public contexts. The results of these investigations provide a model for how obsidian craft production was organized in many mid-sized urban centers across Central Mexico. While obsidian craft production is unique in several ways, I believe the organizational principles of domestic craft production were the same for many types of crafts practiced throughout Central Mexico.

This paper addresses these issues in several steps. First, it examines the saliency of the household, compound, and barrio as organizational structures for comparative socioeconomic analysis in prehispanic Mesoamerica. The conclusion reached is that under normal conditions, compounds do not exist as an intermediary category between household and barrio levels of organization. At Xochicalco and in most other sites in Mesoamerica, compounds

are coterminous with households and only become apparent in unusually large high-density urban centers like Teotihuacan. Second, it discusses the size and structure of households at Xochicalco and how craft production was organized within them. Third and finally, it examines whether craft production was organized at the level of the urban barrio at Xochicalco. Important here is whether craft producers in different households participated in, or were organized into, some form of guild or commercial association as has been suggested for other groups in Central Mexico like the Aztecs. The information suggests that they were not, and that artisan guilds and formal commercial organizations at the community level were not a common feature of Mesoamerican craft production.

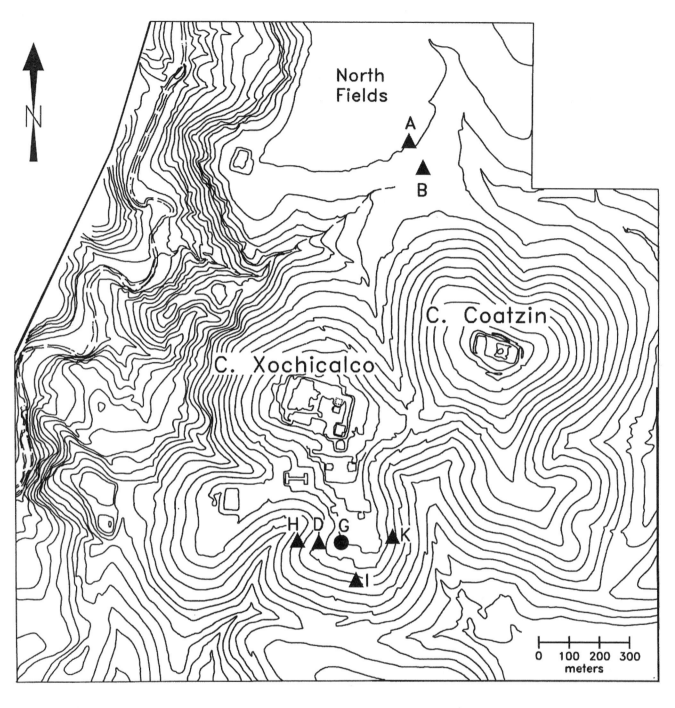

Figure 3.2. The location of obsidian craft areas at Xochicalco.

The Household, Compound, and Barrio as Analytical Units

Robert Santley and I have discussed the relationship between households and compounds as analytical units in several previous publications and I follow that perspective here (Hirth 1993b; Santley and Hirth 1993a, 1993b). In archaeological investigation it is important to distinguish the physical manifestations of what we study from the inferential units we believe they represent. Failure to do so places us in a scientific no-man's-land between the descriptive foundation that we do well in archaeology and the behavioral inferences we hope to draw from them.

Households are an inferential unit that we identify from the physical remains of domestic structures that we record archaeologically. The physical remains of households include buildings, open spaces, storage facilities, refuse deposits, artifact assemblages, and other miscellaneous features associated with normal domestic activities (Winter 1976). Households are often associated with families, although we know this is an oversimplification from the ethnographic record (e.g., Bender 1967). Families are often thought of as groups of individuals linked by kinship relationships, whether they reside together or not. Households, on the other hand, are task-related residential units composed of individuals who reside together for a variety of ends (Hirth 1993b:22–23; Netting et al. 1984: xviii). Households are highly adaptive and can change rapidly in form to fulfill the nurture and nutritional needs of their members. They are a foundational social unit found in all human societies. Perhaps most important for archaeological purposes is the close link between the organization of physical space in households and the social behavior associated with them. Archaeology has linked household organization with architectural and assemblage analysis, changes in household size with the architectural household series, and conceptual views of household with domestic ritual and views of the homestead (Hirth 1993b:24–25; Plunket 1998; Smith 1987).

Compounds, as defined in the introduction to Part I of this volume, are an organizational unit above that of individual households. They are clusters of families that reside together and collaborate in common economic and social activities much like individual households (see Chapter 2). It is here that we encounter conceptual difficulties. This is because compounds are defined largely by archaeological manifestations and have no clear-cut behavioral unit with which we can link them in the anthropological literature. This is due to two circumstances: the flexibility of households to organize themselves in different ways, and our poor understanding of composite residential structures in ancient societies. Compounds are defined in archaeology primarily from the walls, enclosures, and architectural features that group residential and non-residential structures within a built environment. As such, they are derived from archaeological data and their meaning is inferred directly from their associated remains.

Residential compounds have been excavated at a number of archaeological sites in Central Mexico. The list is long, but examples can be found from Ahuitzotla (Tozzer 1921), Cantona (García Cook 2003), Chalcatzingo (Grove 1987), Chiconautla (Vaillant 1935), Chingú (Díaz Oyarzábal 1980), Cihuatecpan (Ev-ans 1988), Cuexcomate (Smith 1992), Loma Torremote (Santley 1977, 1993), Maquixco Bajo (Sanders 1966, 1994), Terremote-Tlaltenco (Serra Puche 1988), Tetimpa (Plunket and Uruñuela 1998), Tula (Healan 1989, 1993), and Xochicalco (Hirth 1993a, 2006), as well as multiple apartment complexes at Teotihuacan (Manzanilla 1993; Séjourné 1966; Storey 1992). In all of these cases, except perhaps for Teotihuacan, the compound is the architectural space designed and built to hold a large, diversified household. The best behavioral correlate for residential compounds in Central Mexico is the large, extended or joint family household. My work at Xochicalco suggests that the household and compound are best thought of as synonymous terms. Compounds do not exist as a *separate* analytical category. Instead, compounds were constructed as housing for integrated households, and vary in size and construction as a result of household growth and differences in social status (Hirth 1993a, 2000a).

Teotihuacan may represent a special circumstance where residential compounds correspond to groups *larger* than individual households. Clearly, its large residential apartment complexes housed multiple family units but it remains unclear how their occupants were linked by kinship, family, and/or economic ties (Spence 1974; Storey 1992). The creation of large compounds organized above the level of extended family households may be a special adaptation to highly nucleated urban areas. The multifloor apartment buildings (*insulae*) of Rome and Ostia, for example, provide extreme examples of large-scale urban residential compounds that were occupied by a range of ethnically diverse and unrelated families. For the most part, however, residential compounds that include more than a single extended or joint family household are rare in Mesoamerica and may be a special adaptation to urban living.

The urban **ward** or **barrio** is a well-recognized level of social organization in Mesoamerica, above the level of individual households. In Central Mexico, urban wards and barrios associated with indigenous social groups are generally referred to as *calpulli* and *tlaxilacalli* in sixteenth-century sources (van Zantwijk 1985). Even here, however, there is variation and ambiguity with respect to the size and composition of these social units. In northern Morelos, the Molotla *calpulli* of 128 households was divided into 9 smaller subdivisions, also called *calpulli* or *chinamitl*, containing from 9 to 32 households (Carrasco 1976). The terms used to characterize these groups varied by geographic location. The *chinamitl* was referred to as a *tequitato* in eastern Morelos and a *barrio pequeño* in the Basin of Mexico (Smith 1993:198). Complicating the picture further, Reyes García (1996:50) has argued that it is unclear whether many of the terms we interpret as wards or barrios actually refer to corporate residential groups. He believes that the term *calpulli* most often refers to a group linked to a patron god or temple, rather than to a residential group. His analysis of legal disputes during the Colonial period suggests that residential clusters are most often referred to by the term *tlaxilacalli*.

What this heterogeneous terminology suggests is that social groupings existed on multiple scales above the level of individual households. What urban barrios represent as social units and how they compare to similar groupings in rural areas is a complex question that we are only beginning to understand (Hirth 2003). Below, I discuss the relationships between households, compounds, and barrios at Xochicalco with respect to the organization of craft production.

Households and Compounds at Xochicalco

Intensive surface mapping established that urban households at Xochicalco were multiple family residences that occupied small compounds ranging from 300 to 800 m² in size (Hirth 2000a: Fig. 6.8; Hirth et al. 2000). At Xochicalco, there was *no* intermediate residential category between the individual households and the larger barrio units in which they were located (Hirth 1995a). Four types of residential structures were identified at Xochicalco: (1) large courtyard residences representing the highest level of elite housing, (2) terrace houses constructed on the wide terraces flanking Cerro Xochicalco, (3) cluster residences consisting of groups of structures built on the slopes between major terraces, and (4) compact residences representing the small isolated domestic structures of the poorest individuals at Xochicalco.

The location of domestic structures across Xochicalco's hillside topography strongly influenced the configuration of their residential floor plans. Courtyard, Terrace, and Cluster residences were all constructed as multifamily residential compounds with different floor plans and degrees of architectural embellishment. On flat terrain, the preferred form of construction was a rectangular compound consisting of room clusters organized around

interior patios. Residential compounds contained two to four interior patios, each of which was occupied by a separate nuclear family within the larger household.

Between 1992 and 1993, two Terrace residences (Operations H and K) and one Cluster residence (Operation I) were excavated to obtain information on household structure and domestic obsidian craft production (Hirth 2006). All three of these households are well-built multifamily compounds that ranged from 210 to 348 m² in size. The usable interior floor space of these three residential compounds are 210 m² in Operation H (Fig. 3.3), 348 m² for Operation I (Fig. 3.4), and 240 m² in Operation K (Fig. 3.5) (Hirth and Webb 2006). Rooms usually had walls fashioned of *tapia* (puddled mud) that were constructed on low stone foundations. Floors were constructed of *tepetate* (sterile hardpan) mixed with crushed stone, *tezontle* (volcanic scoria), and finished with a layer of well-polished stucco. Walls were stucco covered and doorways were often framed with cut stone block. Sleeping benches were found in some rooms and we estimate that the average household at Xochicalco had between 15 and 20 persons.

Structures had two types of roofs. Most buildings had flat roofs constructed of *tapia* poured onto mats that were supported by pole and beam framing. The top surface of flat roofs was finished with a layer of stucco that sealed the roofs from the rain. Some rooms, however, had roofs made of perishable materials, probably using locally available palm thatch. Interior patios were open, and both surface and subsurface drains removed the water that collected in them. Water conservation was important in houses at Xochicalco; drains and ceramic downspouts diverted the runoff from roofs and patios into jars and cisterns.

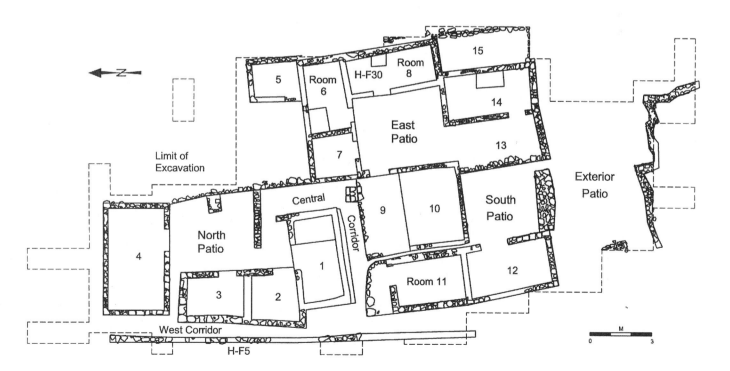

Figure 3.3. The Operation H residential compound.

Household Abandonment and Assemblage Preservation

One of the most important features of Xochicalco's urban landscape is that it was catastrophically destroyed around AD 900 by military conquest and was never reoccupied. Many domestic structures were burned during abandonment, trapping large quantities of domestic refuse on floors when roofs collapsed. Although some looting occurred in residential structures, most of this was focused on the ceremonial zone on the top of the hill. Residential structures below the ceremonial center were not as severely affected by looting, and as a result of rapid site abandonment, large quantities of de facto refuse were recovered from all three excavated households.

The de facto refuse recovered from structure floors consisted of ceramic vessels, ground stone artifacts, flaked stone debitage, and some organic remains. Ceramic vessels were broken directly on the surfaces where they were used and the three domestic compounds each had from 42 to 87 whole vessels on their floors (Fig. 3.6). Ground stone artifacts were usually complete and were found on floors, stacked in caches in or near patios, or distributed along the walls of rooms where they were stored. Celts and axes were most often recovered inside rooms at the base of walls where they may have been stored in bags hung on wall pegs. Flaked stone remains from craft production were recovered in multiple discrete concentrations in rooms, corridors, and patios throughout domestic compounds.

The effects of post-depositional processes on floor assemblages were evaluated using measures of ceramic completeness (Hirth and Webb 2006). Deposit disturbance was evaluated by the number of refits or conjoining pieces found in archaeological contexts (Rice 1987). Although vessels were rarely complete, ceramic refits account for 35–40% of the 10,000–14,000 ceramic sherds recovered from floor contexts in each excavation. While this is a sizeable percentage, the proportion of ceramics from refit vessels is best portrayed by ceramic weight because orphan sherds on floors tend to be small, while refit sherds tend to be large. When examined by weight, the percentage of refit vessels in floor assemblages actually increases from a low of 57.0% in Operation K to a high of 71.5% of floor ceramics in Operation I. Finally, orphan ceramic bodies were typed, weighed, and

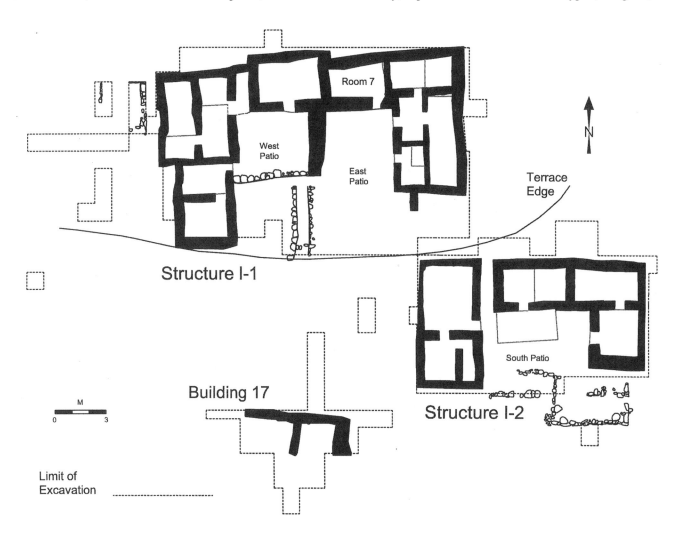

Figure 3.4. The Operation I residential compound.

compared to the estimated weight of the ceramic bodies *missing* from refit vessels to develop a maximal estimate for floor ceramics that can be accounted for by refitted vessels. These comparisons revealed that 83.90% of *all* the potsherds recovered from the floors of the three excavated domestic structures can be accounted for by the vessels broken on them.

The three excavated households and their associated deposits provide an excellent basis for reconstructing activity patterning in Xochicalco's urban households. It is to a discussion of the internal structure of domestic households and how obsidian craft production was organized within them that I turn to now.

The Internal Structure of Xochicalco Households

As mentioned above, the architectural layout of Xochicalco domestic compounds suggests they were joint or extended family households, like those reported from Morelos at the time of the Spanish Conquest (Carrasco 1964, 1968, 1976). We believe that Xochicalco households contained two or more stem or nuclear families occupying adjacent patio groups inside the residence. These patio groups could be connected to one another inside the residential compound like we find in Operations H and I (Figs. 3.3, 3.4) or separated from one another with their own private entrances as in Operation K (Fig. 3.5).

What is most important is that residential compounds at Xochicalco were organized and operated as corporate entities, like we would expect for integrated households. Evidence for corporate behavior is found in shared architectural space, the organization of work, indications of social differentiation, and integration of the residence under a single household head. Evidence for the shared use of space by families within households is found in the layout of sleeping rooms around central patios and in the way patio groups connect to one another. In Operation I, two patio groups (the East and West patios of Structure I-1) are connected by a common patio area on their southern sides, underscoring the corporate nature of residence (Fig. 3.4). At Operation K, a *temazcal* (sweat bath), constructed as an external structure on the south side of the residence, was probably used by all its members (Room 17 in Fig. 3.5). Shared food storage, which would be an excellent indication of corporate activity, was not identified in any of the residential compounds. Water storage, however, was another matter.

Drinkable water was always in short supply at Xochicalco because the only permanent water supply was the Tembembe River, located 1–1.5 km west and 140–150 m below the main residential areas. To minimize the work of hauling water, rainfall was collected and stored communally within many residences. In Estructura 1 Oeste excavated by the Proyecto Xochicalco INAH in 1984, rainfall that fell in one patio was collected and

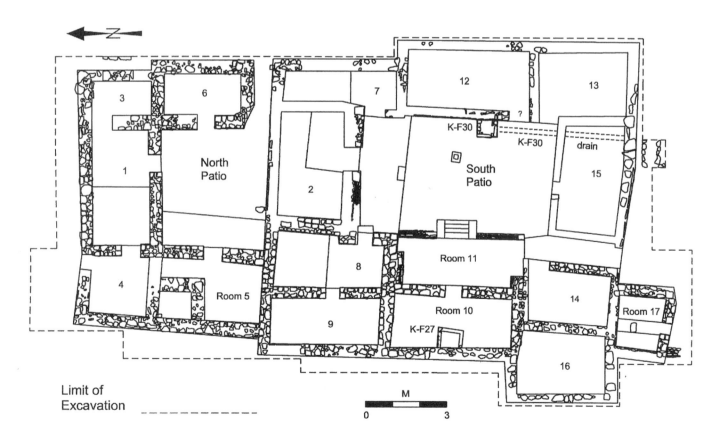

Figure 3.5. The Operation K residential compound.

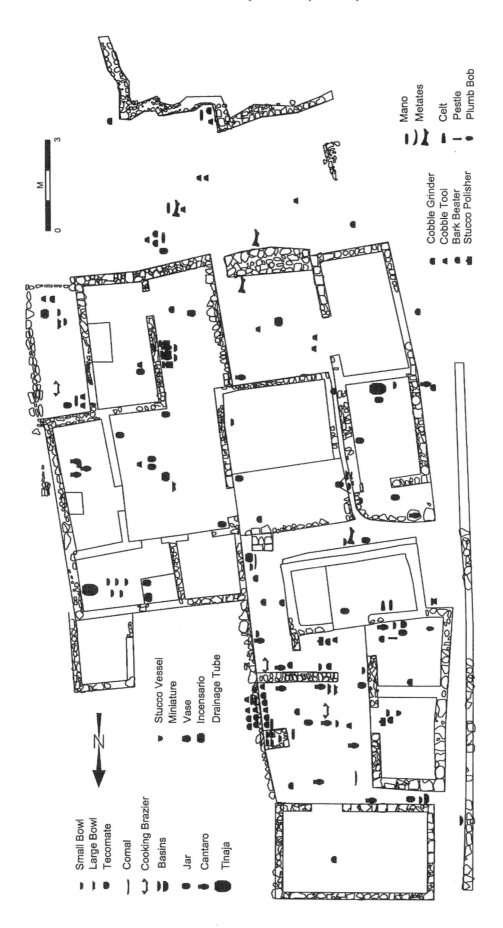

Figure 3.6. Ceramic and domestic ground stone remains recovered from floors in Operation H.

diverted by a subfloor drain into an open cistern in another area of the house (de Vega Nova 1993: Fig. 2; González Crespo et al. 1995). The water in this cistern clearly was shared by all members of the household.

Subfloor cisterns, however, were not constructed in every house. A more common pattern was to collect and store water in large *tinajas* (storage jars) in each household. These storage jars were always located in one area of the house, either in an interior room or in a roofed area where water could stay cool. That storage jars were located centrally, instead of occurring in multiple locations throughout the residence, suggests that water was collected and used jointly by all household members. Operation H deviates slightly from this pattern by having *tinajas* in two areas of the residence (Rooms 6 and 11 in Fig. 3.3).

Additional evidence for corporate behavior can be found in the way work was organized within houses. The distribution of ceramic stoves and cooking vessels, for example, provides information on where food was prepared and distributed to household members. In all three residences, cooking vessels were clustered primarily in one portion of the household. The evidence suggests that instead of each nuclear family preparing its food individually, meals were prepared in one patio group and distributed to all members of the household. These food preparation areas include the North Patio of Operation H (Figs. 3.3, 3.6), the East Patio of Structure I-1 in Operation I (Fig. 3.4), and Room 5 of Operation K (Fig. 3.5). While ceramic stoves were highly portable and easily moved within the domestic residences, no more than two stoves were found inside any residence compound, which is less than we would expect if each nuclear family cooked its food independently. Centralized food preparation would have had the additional benefit of minimizing the expenditure of firewood or charcoal use within households, which, like water, was another scarce resource that required effort to procure in urban settings.

One aspect of food preparation that does not appear to have been a communal activity was grinding corn. Manos, metates, palette grinding slabs, and cobble grinders were found in every patio within the residence. Metates and palette grinding slabs are heavy and appear to have been stored where they were used. This suggests that corn was ground in interior patios throughout the household, with cooking done by the women in one area of the residence.

Special architectural features provide evidence for social differentiation within Xochicalco households. In each residence, one room or cluster of rooms stands out as being better built or more elaborately decorated. The central building in each of these clusters was often better constructed than others and/or had a piece of sculpture marking its special status. Two residences (Operations H and K) had one room that contained a low bench altar on its back wall opposite the doorway. Room 8 in the East Patio of Operation H had a low altar (H-F30) and had two ornaments decorating its roof: a geometrically shaped *almena* and an anthropomorphic sculpture (Fig. 3.7; Becerril 1999). Room 7 in the East Patio of Structure I-1 (Fig. 3.4) had an external

taluded wall decorated with a small stone plaque. Rooms 10 and 11 define a room and portico area in Operation K (Fig. 3.8). This room group is located on an elevated platform connected to the South Patio by a small stairway. Both the east side of this platform and the east wall of Room 10 were constructed in talud. A Huehueteotl sculpture was located in the portico Room 11 and a small altar (Feature K-F27) was located on the back wall of Room 10 opposite the doorway (Fig. 3.5).

I believe these more elaborately decorated buildings were sanctuary rooms used by the household head to conduct rituals important for the corporate integrity of the household. Unfortunately, all three of these rooms were relatively clean and did not contain significant material remains or more than a few items of ceremonial paraphernalia on their floors. Nevertheless, the majority (13 of the 18) of the special ceramic vessels associated with high status or ritual activity in these households (handled censers, figure *incensarios*, ceramic vases, miniature vessels) were located in the patios where sanctuary rooms were located. These differences underscore my suggestion that households were internally differentiated corporate groups where two or more nuclear families resided together under the authority of a household head.

Evidence for Domestic Craft Production

The primary goal of the Xochicalco research was to study the structure and organization of obsidian craft production in a prehispanic urban center. The primary objective of this craft production was to make obsidian prismatic blades, which were the cutting tools of choice in prehispanic Mesoamerica. They were manufactured from specially prepared cores using a combination of both handheld and footheld pressure techniques (Clark 1982; Flenniken and Hirth 2003; Titmus and Clark 2003). What is important about obsidian craft production in these domestic contexts is that each household used and imported raw material from obsidian sources several hundred kilometers away. As a result, obsidian craft production at Xochicalco represents a commercial undertaking that provides insight into the organizational and productive capacity of prehispanic craft specialists at the household level.

Surface reconnaissance and test excavations identified concentrations of obsidian production debitage in seven areas of the site that were manufacturing loci for prismatic blades (Hirth 1995b, 2000a) (Fig. 3.2). Six of these areas were domestic workshops, while one was located in a civic-ceremonial area. Excavations were conducted in four domestic workshops (Operations A, H, I, K) and one civic-ceremonial work area (Operation G) to explore the structure of craft production. In situ production debris was recovered from all these workshops except Operation A, where production surfaces had been destroyed by tractor plowing. Excavations at Operation G indicated that craft production took place in a large open plaza that had been used as a public marketplace (Hirth 2006).

(*upper*) Figure 3.7. Altar in Room 8 of Operation H.

(*lower*) Figure 3.8. Room and portico area (Rooms 10 and 11) of Operation K.

The discussion here focuses on craft production in the four excavated domestic workshops. Rapid household abandonment during Xochicalco's conquest preserved obsidian production debitage *directly* on the floor surfaces where activities were carried out. This Pompeii effect (Binford 1981) is rare in archaeology, but welcome when it occurs since it permits forms of activity analysis that usually cannot be conducted (Schiffer 1985). What it enabled at Xochicalco was a detailed comparative analysis of the scale and organization of obsidian craft production within each of the three domestic workshops.

Analysis revealed that obsidian production was consistently carried out *inside* residential structures. This finding was unanticipated because the manufacture of obsidian flaked stone tools creates a range of hazardous waste that we assumed would be kept away from household residents (Santley and Kneebone 1993). Excavations recovered percussion and pressure debitage in the same areas where daily domestic activities were carried out.

Craftsmen employed several strategies to keep hazardous waste at tolerable levels within households. One of these strategies was to work in a special area or atelier outside the residential compound. Two of the three domestic workshops (Operations H and I) have external ateliers (Area H4 in Fig. 3.9, Building 17 in

Fig. 3.4), although flaked stone production was not restricted to these areas. Craftsmen also worked inside residential compounds within interior patios (TH1, TH2, TH4, I2, TI1, TI2, K3, TK3) as well as in corridors (H3, TH3) and in the doorways of rooms that opened onto lighted areas (HI, I1, Ila, K1) (Figs. 3.9–3.11). Work areas normally contain obsidian production refuse along with the tools used to rejuvenate obsidian cores and to remove prismatic blades.

Although obsidian was worked and debitage was deposited directly on the household floors, there is good evidence that residents of domestic workshops managed hazardous debitage by selectively collecting and removing the largest and most dangerous pieces from floors. Craftsmen reduced the hazards of working obsidian inside the household by confining debitage to small areas, sweeping it against walls, and collecting it in containers for later use or disposal. Despite the hazards presented by production debitage, residents of domestic workshops learned to live with and manage small amounts of obsidian waste within their households. We are thankful that they did so because these remains have been instrumental in the analysis of their production activities.

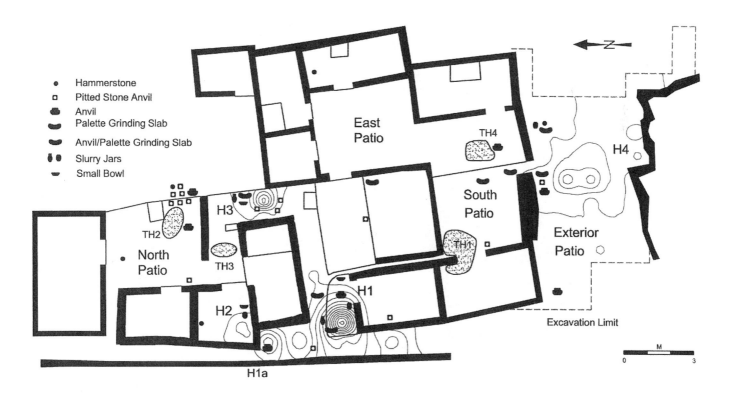

Figure 3.9. Obsidian production areas (HI–H4) and trace production areas (TH1–TH4) recovered on the floors in Operation H.

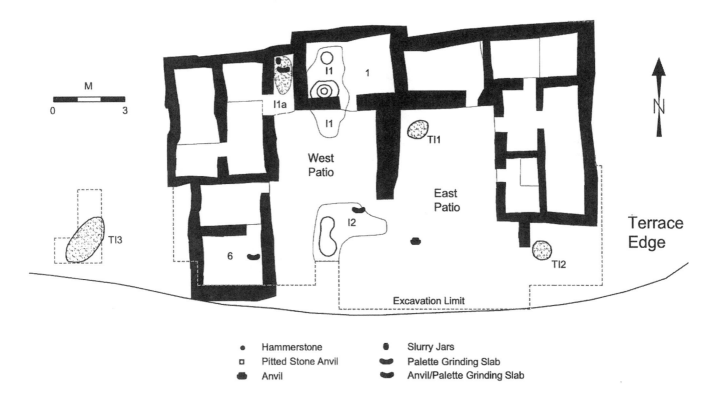

●	Hammerstone		🮲	Slurry Jars
▫	Pitted Stone Anvil		⬳	Palette Grinding Slab
⬢	Anvil		⬳	Anvil/Palette Grinding Slab

Figure 3.10. Obsidian production areas (I1–I2) and trace production areas (TI1–TI3) recovered on the floors of Structure I-1 of Operation I.

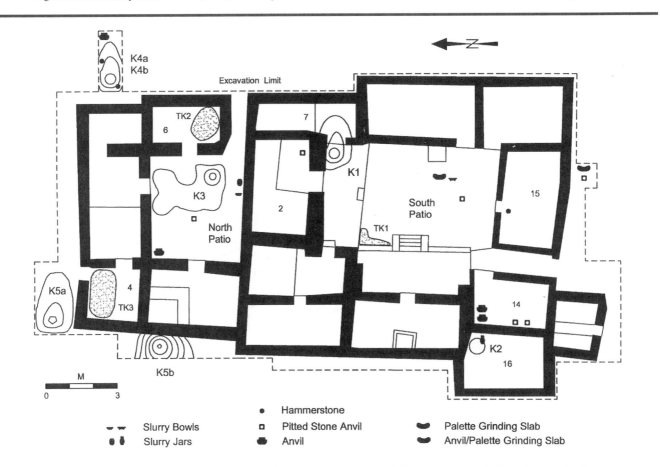

		●	Hammerstone	
⬳ ⬳	Slurry Bowls	▫	Pitted Stone Anvil	⬳ Palette Grinding Slab
● 🮲	Slurry Jars	⬢	Anvil	⬳ Anvil/Palette Grinding Slab

Figure 3.11. Obsidian production areas (KI–K5) and trace production areas (TK1–TK3) recovered on the floors in Operation K.

Table 3.1. Obsidian source analysis for four domestic workshops at Xochicalco.

Workshop	Pachuca*	Otumba		Ucareo		Zacualtipan		Tulancingo		Unknown	
	%	*No.*	%	*No.*	%	*No.*	%	*No.*	%	*No.*	%
Operation A	0.9	0	0.0	34	96.2	1	2.9	0	0.0	0	0.0
Operation H	25.1	1	1.0	16	17.3	51	54.6	1	1.0	1	1.0
Operation I	0.7	1	1.6	57	92.8	2	3.3	1	1.6	0	0.0
Operation K	9.7	1	1.7	35	58.5	15	25.1	1	1.7	2	3.3

(From Hirth et al. 2006: Tables 5.5 and 5.6)
*Percentages of Pachuca obsidian represent the percent in the total lithic assemblage.

The Internal Organization of Domestic Craft Production

Analysis of production residues has provided important information about the organization of craft production in Xochicalco's domestic workshops. Four aspects of production are particularly noteworthy. First, there was no centralized, state control of obsidian procurement at Xochicalco despite the site's location 150–200 km from obsidian sources. Second, although multiple work areas were found in workshops, there was no evidence for internal task specialization or a division of labor between craftsmen. Third, craft production was carried out by multiple part-time craftsmen in each household rather than one, full-time craft specialist. Fourth, craft production was diversified, and households engaged in several different production activities instead of specializing in a single type of production. While a full discussion of production organization is beyond the scope of this chapter, the example of the Operation H workshop illustrates how each of these four features of craft production was represented by and within domestic workshops. A full discussion of production activities in all domestic workshops can be found in Hirth (2006).

Elite Control of Obsidian Procurement

Several investigators have suggested that political control of obsidian was important in the development of complex society and the organization of Mesoamerican political economy (Clark 1987; Pastrana 1998; Santley 1983, 1984; Spence 1981, 1987; Spence et al. 2002). These models usually take one of two forms. In one, obsidian craft production is characterized as taking place under the control of either the state (Spence 1981) or sponsoring elite (Clark 1987). In this argument, direct supervision of production is the key to controlling the flow and distribution of finished goods throughout society. In the second model, the elite or the state are viewed as monopolizing or controlling either the procurement of raw material (Clark 1986; Pastrana 1998; Spence 1981, 1987) or the distribution of finished products (Santley 1983, 1984). In both cases, obsidian and the products manufac-

tured from it are critical commodities in the growth of regional political economies. Neither of these two models is an accurate characterization of obsidian craft production at Xochicalco.

At Xochicalco, craftsmen operated as *independent* craft specialists who were unassisted and unsupported by political institutions in the practice of their craft. Xochicalco craftsmen developed their own, individual networks of resource procurement and supported themselves by producing items for distribution and sale in the public marketplace (Hirth 2006). There is no evidence for centralized or state-supported craft workshops in the site's civic-ceremonial precinct; instead, the majority of the obsidian consumed in the site's elite core appears to have come from the site's domestic workshops (Andrews and Hirth 2006).

In perhaps the purest expression of the independent entrepreneurial spirit, craft specialists at Xochicalco were responsible for procuring their own obsidian, *without* the assistance of centralized state procurement. All four of the excavated domestic workshops were apparently in operation at the moment of site abandonment. What is most significant is that these four workshops did not use the same obsidian sources, which would have been the case if workshops relied on the state for raw material procurement. Operations A and I relied almost entirely on obsidian from Ucareo, Michoacan, while Operation H used obsidian from Zacualtipan and Pachuca, Hidalgo, and to a lesser extent, obsidian from Ucareo, Michoacan (Table 3.1). Operation K likewise relied on obsidian from the three sources of Zacualtipan, Ucareo, and Pachuca, but in notably different proportions from those found in Operation H (Table 3.1). Comparison of floor remains to midden contexts shows that these were stable patterns of obsidian procurement that persisted throughout the Epiclassic period. The only conclusion that can be reached from these data is that each of these contemporary workshops obtained its obsidian independently of the others by developing its own procurement networks (Hirth et al. 2006). The state was not involved in resource procurement; if it had been, all workshops would have obsidian from the same sources in similar frequencies (Hirth et al. 2006).

Internal Division of Labor

Comparative studies of commercial organization have shown that craft production can be intensified through task specialization within the manufacturing sequence (Carrier 1992; Torrence 1986). Two levels of internal task specialization were explored within domestic workshops at Xochicalco. The first considered whether specialized production activities were carried out in workshops that had special ateliers (Santley et al. 1989). The second investigated whether production areas within residences were internally differentiated and linked sequentially in the production process (Sorensen et al. 1989). An example of sequential linkage would be the location of core rejuvenation, blade production, and blade tool manufacture in different areas of the residence.

Analysis revealed *no evidence* for internal task specialization or a division of labor within domestic workshops. As mentioned above, specialized ateliers were found in two of the three well preserved domestic workshops in Operation H (the Exterior Patio) and Operation I (Building 17) (Figs. 3.9, 3.4). What is interesting is that these ateliers did *not* segment or streamline the production process. Instead, the same range of production activities found in these ateliers also occurred within the residence. Analysis of production debitage demonstrated that the same production activities were carried out at different work areas inside the residential compound. No evidence was found for task specialization or the sequential linkage of production tasks. Instead, artisans apparently picked an area in which to work and carried out all production tasks—from core rejuvenation and blade production to the production of tools from prismatic blades—in the same locale. Craftsmen carried out all facets of production without delegating or splitting work with other members of the household.

Full-time or Part-time Craft Specialization

No subject has received more attention in archaeology than the subject of whether craft specialization was a full- or part-time activity. Domestic workshops at Xochicalco were multifamily households that could easily have supported a full-time craft specialist, even under conditions of fluctuating demand for obsidian goods. The presence of multiple work areas within domestic workshops and the multiplicity of tasks carried out within them, however, indicate the presence of *multiple craftsmen* in each domestic workshop. This would be expected in large residential compounds given the Mesoamerican practice of training sons in the economic pursuits of their fathers.

The size of the domestic compounds suggests that each workshop at Xochicalco had a labor force of three to five men who were proficient in obsidian blade production. Likewise, the distribution of production debris indicates that two to three craftsmen were involved in prismatic blade production at the same time. This represents a significant production capacity *if* craftsmen worked simultaneously on a continuous basis. This apparently was *not* the case. Comparison of the number of obsidian

cores reduced in domestic workshops to the number of artisans producing obsidian blades indicates that there was not a full-time craftsman in *any* of the obsidian workshops at Xochicalco! While output levels at Operation H were large enough to have kept one full-time craftsman at work, he would have to have been a restless (and messy) artisan to produce all the production evidence identified in Operation H (Fig. 3.9). This is unlikely, given the low tolerance that other household residents would have to this type of behavior and the fact that it would maximize rather than minimize the contact that children and other family members would have with razor-sharp production wastes. Instead, domestic craft workshops at Xochicalco apparently operated using *multiple part-time* specialists who worked periodically when raw material was available or the demand for finished products required it (Hirth 2006).

Diversified Craft Production

Discussions of craft specialization in Mesoamerica usually focus more on the organization of work (full- or part-time) than on the range of, and relationships between, the items produced. The topic of specialization brings with it the idea of producing a relatively narrow range of items within the same technological industry (for example, ceramics, flaked stone lithics, metallurgy, lapidary, and so on). The evidence from Xochicalco craft workshops does not support this view of craft specialization. Instead, it argues that domestic craft production at Xochicalco followed a model of diversified, rather than specialized, craft activity. Xochicalco domestic craftsmen engaged in a range of craft activities within the same domestic compound. Multi-crafting rather than specialized crafting was the norm at Xochicalco and was a better adaptation to the goals and organization of production within the domestic economy (Hirth 2006).

Operation H shows the greatest diversity of production activities identified in domestic workshops. While prismatic blade production was the primary economic activity within these households, evidence was found for other economic pursuits that included: the manufacture of bifaces in potch opal, the purchase and resale of obsidian bifaces from outside sources, lapidary work in obsidian and other materials, and stucco working and finishing (Hirth and Webb 2006). Add to this the manufacture of obsidian prismatic blades and blade tools, and the likelihood that at least some agriculture was practiced, and we have evidence for six distinct economic activities being carried out within the same household. The other three domestic workshops also practiced diversified economic strategies that included: the manufacture of obsidian prismatic blades, the purchase and resale of obsidian bifaces, lapidary work in obsidian, and the practice of agriculture.

The important point is that *none* of these craft activities was a full-time activity for a single craftsman. Together, however, they represent a multi-crafting strategy where an artisan (or artisans) could be involved in craft production on a full-time basis by providing a range of goods rather than a single commodity

(Hirth 2006). Moreover, I believe that multi-crafting was a common pattern in Mesoamerica that has been overlooked largely because of the emphasis archaeologists place on specialized craft production involving a single commodity. I believe it is this multifaceted dimension of craft production to which Sahagún refers when he says, "*el oficial de cualquier oficio mecánico primero es aprendiz y después es maestro de muchos oficios, y de tantos que de él se puede decir que él es omnis homo*" (the craftsmen of each mechanical craft first is an apprentice and later is a master of many crafts and so many that it can be said that he is a man who knows them all) (Katz 1966:51). That prehispanic craftsmen could be referred to as "masters of several crafts" undoubtedly reflects their practicing a strategy of diversified, rather than specialized, craft production in both domestic and non-domestic contexts (Hirth 2006).

Craft Guilds and Barrio Organization at Xochicalco

Recent research suggests that most craft production took place within domestic workshops by independent craft specialists (Feinman 1999). The question we face is how were these craft specialists organized? Did they operate as small-scale entrepreneurial households independently of one another, or were specialists members of larger corporate economic associations or guilds that protected, supported, and structured the economic production they engaged in? Although investigators have recognized that domestic craft specialists were an important feature of prehispanic societies, most archaeologists have hesitated to characterize them as households of self-sufficient entrepreneurs. Instead, researchers have argued that domestic craftsmen were organized as economic guilds based on ward, barrio, or *calpulli* membership (Berdan 1982; Biskowski 2000:296; Calnek 1978:103; Katz 1966; Mastache et al. 2002; Otis Charlton 1994; Smith 1996; van Zantwijk 1985). These guilds are characterized as corporate groups that provided economic support, labor, and collaboration in production above the level of individual households.

The argument for craft guilds in prehispanic Mesoamerica generally rests on three types of information: (1) the existence of barrios as important components of prehispanic cities, (2) ethnohistoric references to groups of merchants and craftsmen who resided in separate barrios, each with their own barrio temple and patron god (Berdan 1982; van Zantwijk 1985), and (3) the recovery of archaeological evidence for craft production in urban centers that is often interpreted as evidence for barrio-guild forms of organization (Hirth 2006). None of this evidence is compelling or conclusive given the limited amount of stratigraphic investigation that has been conducted.

Frances Berdan argues that among the Aztecs, craftsmen were members of guilds who "were set apart from the rest of Aztec society by virtue of their separate residence, control over membership, internal control over education and ranking, distinct ethnic origins, commitments to particular patron deities and religious ceremonies, and special relations with the state" (Berdan

1982:26). The urban *calpulli* is argued to be the basis of guild organization in prehispanic Central Mexico (Moreno 1962). While this follows the available ethnohistoric literature (Torquemada 1975:1:147), it contains *none* of the critical economic functions that defined craft guilds in Medieval Europe (Smith 1870; Unwin 1963). What ethnohistoric sources agree upon is that craftsmen resided together, worshiped a patron deity, and were organized to meet the needs of the state. But this is true of *every calpulli* whether they contained craftsmen or not!

Monzón (1983:74) rejected the idea that *calpultin* were organized into craft guilds because he felt they lacked the specialized economic structures characteristic of European medieval guilds. Nevertheless, urban *calpultin* do provide a potential structure for the development and organization of craft guilds. The first step in evaluating whether barrios were the basis for craft guild organization is to define them in spatial and residential terms. Then we can investigate whether there is a spatial correlation between craft production and the limits of the barrio in which it is found.

Research at Xochicalco has made it possible to define ward and barrio segments on the slopes of Cerro Xochicalco's central urban core. Intensive site mapping (Hirth 2000a, 2000b) combined with problem oriented site excavation (González et al. 1995) have made it possible to identify internal barrio divisions with a high degree of precision (Hirth 1995b, 2000a). Barrio divisions were defined by prominent boundary architecture in the form of terrace walls, fortifications, walled streets, and visible communication corridors. These features were combined to divide the city into discrete residential segments that could be entered only at key points along transportation corridors.

A total of 14 barrio segments were located on the slopes of the North, West, and South Hills of Cerro Xochicalco (labeled N1–N5, S1–S6, and W1–W4 on Fig. 3.12). Careful mapping made it possible to plot the distribution of domestic and non-domestic architecture throughout these segments and to estimate their resident populations (Table 3.2). If urban barrios were organized similarly to Aztec *calpultin*, then they should show evidence for internal hierarchical organization. In fact, they do. Thirteen of the 14 urban barrio segments contain either a civic-ceremonial structure or an elite residence (Fig. 3.12). Nine of these segments contain both (Hirth 1995b: Table I) (Fig. 3.12).

Population was estimated for each of these segments based on household counts. Preservation was good enough to map the size of individual house compounds and to estimate their residents by counting the number of their respective patio groups (Hirth 2000a). All of these barrio segments had populations that ranged from 100 to 600 persons. In terms of size and internal social composition, these segments are analogous to *chinamitl* or small ward segments referred to in ethnohistoric documents. We believe they reflect the smallest or minimal level of barrio organization in prehispanic urban centers and represent the level that craft guilds would be organized if they existed at Xochicalco.

Figure 3.2 illustrates that all of the obsidian craft workshops are located in two areas of the site: on the South Hill of Cerro

Table 3.2. Population estimates and architectural features of Xochicalco barrios.

	Civic-Ceremonial Structures	Elite Residences	Estimated Population
North Hill			
N1/N2	2	2	540–757
N3	1	2	305–426
N4	0	0	115–161
N5	0	3	165–233
South Hill			
S1	1	4	285–400
S2	2	0	90–126
S3	3	5	250–352
S4	2	3	250–277
S5	3	2	235–329
S6	1	0	85–119
West Hill			
W1	3	7	671–931
W2	1	1	320–448
W3	1	3	115–217
W4	1	0	75–100
Total	*21*	*32*	*3,501–4,876*

(From Hirth 200a: Tables 10.2 and 10.3)

Xochicalco, and in the North Fields on the north side of Cerro Coatzin. Clustering of workshop debris in these two areas could lead investigators to infer that craftsmen were located in two separate barrios at the site. The well-preserved barrio divisions identified on the South Hill, however, indicate this was not the case. The six domestic workshops identified at Xochicalco are located in four different residential areas of the city. While the two workshops in the North Fields (Operations A and B) can be grouped together because of proximity, the four workshops on the South Hill occur in three different barrio segments identified during our field surveys. Operations D and H are situated in sector S1, Operation I is located in sector S5, and Operation K is located in sector S3 (Fig. 3.13).

If domestic workshops were members of an integrated craft guild, we would expect all four workshops on the South Hill to be located within the same barrio segment. That they are not suggests: (1) artisans did not collaborate in corporate craft activities outside the household, and (2) a craft guild did not exist at the barrio level. Instead, craft activity was contained within

the household. In spatial terms, the patterning of workshops at Xochicalco conforms most closely to Hick's (1982, 1984) pattern of dispersed craft production that he credits to community structure.

Decentralized Resource Provisioning and Craft Production

Craft guilds in the Old World were economic organizations that existed for the benefit of their craftsmen. The guilds controlled production processes, ensured quality in production, and protected the livelihood of their members (Epstein 1991; Mackenney 1987; Unwin 1963). Certainly craftsmen at Xochicalco would have benefitted from guild membership for resource procurement. Maintaining access to sufficient quantities of obsidian to practice their craft was fundamental for craftsmen survival. However, the three obsidian sources used in blade production at Xochicalco (Ucareo, Pachuca, Zacualtipan) are all 150–200 km from the site. This gave craftsmen two provisioning options. Either they could travel directly to the source to obtain their obsidian, or they could rely on merchants or itinerant craftsmen to supply them with raw material.

It is here that centralized resource procurement would have favored the formation of an obsidian craft guild. Collective resource procurement by the craft guild would have minimized the cost of procurement to any individual family workshop. Analysis of production debris from domestic workshops makes it clear, however, that this did not occur for two reasons.

First, technological analysis indicates that domestic workshops did not procure or receive obsidian blade cores directly from quarry sources. None of the production debitage associated with core shaping was recovered from domestic workshops as we would expect if craftsmen procured cores directly from quarry locales. Instead, craftsmen at Xochicalco had access only to small, nearly exhausted obsidian cores from which to produce obsidian blades (Hirth et al. 2003). This limited the size and quantity of the blades they could produce, and directly affected their potential livelihood. Xochicalco craftsmen got their blade cores through trade intermediaries, and the fact that raw material was available in limited supplies forced them to modify their production technology to use the material they could get (Hirth et al. 2006).

Second, the source analyses summarized in Table 3.1 demonstrate that resource procurement was a decentralized activity, with each household obtaining the obsidian it needed for blade production independently of one another. Centralized procurement or pooling of resources did not take place. If it had, each domestic workshop would have had access to the same obsidian sources in similar proportions. Instead, households worked to develop their own provisioning networks, and may have even competed with one another to shape independent sources of supply. Although it is easy to see how craftsmen could have benefited from a collaborative procurement strategy, the available information indicates that it did not exist.

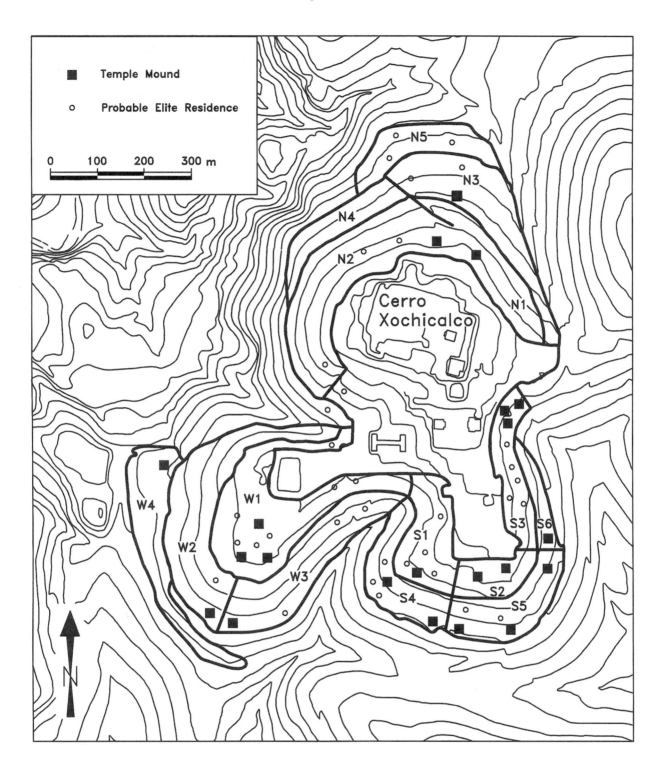

Figure 3.12. The location of barrio segments (N1–N5, S1–S6, and W1–W4) on Cerro Xochicalco.

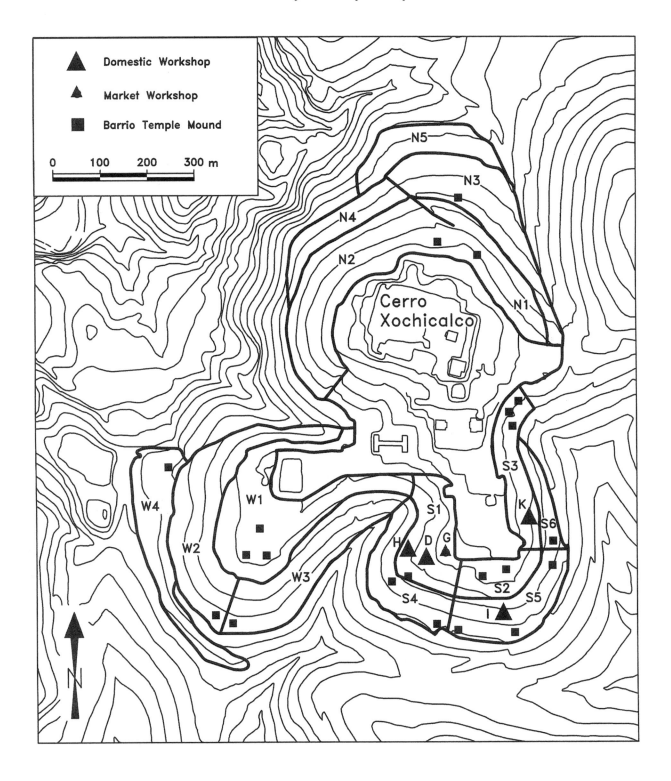

Figure 3.13. The location of domestic workshops by barrio segments (N1–N5, S1–S6, and W1–W4) on Cerro Xochicalco.

Discussion and Conclusions

The organization of craft production is an important topic for two reasons. First, it provides a broad measure of the scale, complexity, and integration of society. Because craftsmen depend on either patrons or broad-based constituencies for their support, craft activity can offer insight into the level of economic interdependency found in prehispanic societies. Second, craft production provides a means to examine structures of organization at both the household and institutional levels. Craft producers are organized to produce a finite task, and the scale and complexity of their work groups provide insight into the type of social structures that the society may employ. For archaeologists, craft production is one of the most visible ways that organizational structures can be studied and it has been used here to examine levels of social organization at the household and neighborhood levels at Xochicalco, Morelos.

Xochicalco was a mid-sized urban center that rose to power between AD 650 and 900. It was one of several independent city-states that developed during the decline of Teotihuacan. Xochicalco grew to integrate western Morelos and much of northeastern Guerrero into a single influential conquest state. Its resident population of 10,000 to 15,000 persons is fairly typical of middle range urban centers found throughout Central Mexican prehistory before the Conquest. What is unique about Xochicalco is the excellent state of preservation of its public and residential architecture. The rapid destruction of the site around AD 900 makes it an excellent location to study obsidian craft production and the organizational structures that allowed it to operate.

The three domestic compounds discussed here have expanded our view of domestic urban life at Xochicalco explored by earlier projects (de Vega Nova 1993; Hirth and Cyphers 1988). Urban residents lived in joint or extended family households composed of two or more nuclear families. These households occupied residential compounds composed of two or more patio groups. The evidence indicates that residential compounds were corporate households whose members were linked by kinship, marriage, common economic motives, work arrangements, and household ritual. Households were organized under the authority of a household head. Well-built sanctuary rooms were identified within residential compounds, and were the focus of household rituals directed by the household head. In general, Xochicalco's urban households are well constructed and adequately provisioned with material goods even though their occupants were not members of the highest social stratum.

Investigation has also clarified how obsidian craft production was organized at the domestic level. What is important is that models that propose centralized control of obsidian production or distribution as the basis for political economy are *not* appropriate for explaining craft production at Xochicalco. Instead, obsidian craft production at Xochicalco was organized entirely as a domestic craft industry. Craftsmen worked independently of one another both inside and outside the household. No evidence was found for task specialization or a division of labor within the household. Analysis of production debitage indicates that craftsmen carried out all production activities in the same locations, beginning with the rejuvenation of in-coming cores and continuing through the manufacture of prismatic blades and blade tools (Hirth 2006). Furthermore, crafting households operated as entrepreneurial entities. They procured their raw material independently of one another and probably competed with each other in the marketplace for the sale of their finished goods.

Pedro Carrasco has argued that full-time craft production was restricted primarily to urban settings with part-time production predominating in rural settings (Carrasco 1977:224). Research at Xochicalco presents a more complex picture. Instead of a simple full- or part-time dichotomy, we find a pattern of multiple craftsmen in urban households operating on a part-time basis within a diversified or multi-crafting production strategy. While the production of obsidian prismatic blades was the most important craft activity carried out in these households, it was not a full-time activity or even the only such activity practiced. The four domestic workshops investigated at Xochicalco show evidence for between four and six different types of economic activities being practiced as part of their household economies. This is not a simple relabeling of the dichotomy between full-time and part-time specialization. Instead, it is a different way of viewing domestic craft production. Artisans engaged in an *array* of economic activities rather than specializing in a single craft on a full- or part-time basis. Examination of craft production elsewhere in Mesoamerica suggests that diversified production strategies and multi-crafting were common economic strategies before the Spanish Conquest (Hirth 2006: Table 12.2).

Finally, this chapter has explored the organization of craft production at levels above that of individual households. The evidence indicates that craft activity was *not* organized at the neighborhood or barrio level at Xochicalco. Good architectural preservation has made it possible to identify barrio segments at the site with a high degree of precision. The fact that obsidian workshops were distributed across multiple barrio segments instead of being concentrated in a single ward suggests that craft production was not organized along barrio lines. Similarly, the development of independent provisioning networks by individual households underscores the absence of cooperative economic interaction between household workshops with similar needs. Given this information, I conclude that craft guilds aimed at fostering economic interaction between artisans did not exist at Xochicalco. Moreover, given the structure of prehispanic craft production, I doubt whether guilds were a common feature of craft production anywhere in Mesoamerica.

This returns us to the general question of social organization in prehispanic urban centers and how populations were grouped at the level of households, compounds, and barrio neighborhoods. The available evidence indicates that both households and barrios are recognizable forms of urban organization at Xochicalco. Evidence for an intermediary level of compound organization, however, is not found. At Xochicalco, the residential compound is synonymous with the household, and economic linkages between craft households are not found. Large high density urban settlements like Teotihuacan represent another problem. If I had to venture a guess as to what Teotihuacan's large residential compounds represent in terms of urban structure, I would say they may be analogous to small *chinamitl* units like those organized as small urban barrios at Xochicalco. That these populations are contained within a single architectural enclosure is probably the product of crowding within Teotihuacan's dense urban nucleus. How urban communities are structured elsewhere in Mesoamerica is a subject for future research.

References

Andrews, Bradford, and Kenneth Hirth
2006   Patterns of stone tool consumption in Xochicalco's civic-ceremonial core. In *Obsidian Craft Production in Ancient Central Mexico*, edited by K. Hirth, pp. 241–57. University of Utah Press, Salt Lake City.

Becerril R., María Esther
1999   *Una unidad habitacional del Epiclásico en Xochicalco, Morelos: El trabajo artesanal de la talla en obsidiana*. Tesis de Licenciatura en Arqueología, ENAH, México.

Bender, D.
1967   A refinement of the concept of household, families, co-residence, and domestic functions. *American Anthropologist* 69:493–504.

Berdan, Frances
1982   *The Aztecs of Central Mexico. An Imperial Society*. Holt, Rinehart and Winston, New York.

Binford, Lewis
1981   Behavioral archaeology and the "Pompeii premise." *Journal of Anthropological Research* 37:195–208.

Biskowski, Martin
2000   Maize preparation and the Aztec subsistence economy. *Ancient Mesoamerica* 1(1):293–306.

Calnek, Edward
1978   El sistema de mercado de Tenochtitlan. In *Economía política e ideología en el México prehispánico*, edited by P. Carrasco and J. Broda, pp. 95–114. Editorial Nueva Imagen, México.

Carrasco, Pedro
1964   Family structure of sixteenth-century Tepoztlan. In *Process and Pattern in Culture*, edited by R. Manners, pp. 185–210. Aldine, Chicago.
1968   Las clases sociales en el México antiguo. Paper presented at the 38th International Congress of Americanists, Stuttgart.
1976   Estratificación social indígena en Morelos durante el siglo XVI. In *Estratificación social en la Mesoamérica prehispánica*, edited by P. Carrasco and J. Broda, pp. 102–17. SEP-INAH, México.
1977   La sociedad Mexicana antes de la conquista. *Historia general de México* 1:165–288.

Carrier, James
1992   Emerging alienation in production: A Maussian history. *Man* 27:539–58.

Clark, John
1982   Manufacture of Mesoamerican prismatic blades: An alternative technique. *American Antiquity* 47:355–76.
1986   From mountains to molehills: A critical review of Teotihuacan's obsidian industry. In *Research in Economic Anthropology. Supplement No. 2. Economic Aspects of Prehispanic Highland Mexico*, edited by B. Isaac, pp. 23–74. JAI Press, Greenwich, Connecticut.
1987   Politics, prismatic blades, and Mesoamerican civilization. In *The Organization of Core Technology*, edited by J. Johnson and C. Morrow, pp. 259–85. Westview Press, Boulder.

de Vega Nova, Hortensia
1993   Interpretación de un conjunto habitacional en Xochicalco, Morelos. *Cuadernos de Arquitectura Mesoamericana* 24:19–28.

Díaz Oyarzábal, Clara Luz
1980   *Chingú. Un sitio Clásico del área de Tula, Hgo*. Colección Científica no. 90. INAH, México.

Epstein, Steven
1991   *Wage Labor and Guilds in Medieval Europe*. University of North Carolina Press, Chapel Hill.

Evans, Susan
1988   *Excavations at Cihuatecpan. An Aztec Village in the Teotihuacan Valley*. Publications in Anthropology no. 36. Vanderbilt University, Nashville.

Feinman, Gary
1999   Rethinking our assumptions: Economic specialization at the household scale in ancient Ejutla, Oaxaca, Mexico. In *Pottery and People*, edited by J. Skibo and G. Feinman, pp. 81–98. University of Utah Press, Salt Lake City.

Flenniken, J. Jeffrey, and Kenneth Hirth
2003   Handheld prismatic blade manufacture in Mesoamerica. In *Mesoamerican Lithic Technology: Experimentation and Interpretation*, edited by K. Hirth, pp. 98–107. University of Utah Press, Salt Lake City.

García Cook, Ángel
2003   Cantona: The city. In *El urbanismo en Mesoamérica. Urbanism in Mesoamerica*, edited by W. Sanders, A.G. Mastache, and R. Cobean, pp. 311–43. INAH, Mexico City; Pennsylvania State University, University Park.

González Crespo, N., S. Garza Tarazona, H. de Vega Nova, P. Mayer Guala, and G. Canto Aguilar
1995   Archaeological investigations at Xochicalco, Morelos: 1984 and 1986. *Ancient Mesoamerica* 6(2):223–36.

Grove, David
1987   *Ancient Chalcatzingo*. University of Texas Press, Austin.

Healan, Dan
1989   *Tula of the Toltecs: Excavations and Survey*. University of Iowa Press, Iowa City.

1993   Urbanism at Tula from the perspective of residential archaeology. In *Prehispanic Domestic Units in Western Mesoamerica*, edited by R. Santley and K. Hirth, pp. 105–19. CRC Press, Boca Raton, Florida.

Hicks, Frederic
1982   Tetzcoco in the early 16th century: The state, the city, and the calpolli. *American Ethnologist* 9:230–49.
1984   Rotational labor and urban development in prehispanic Tezcoco. In *Explorations in Ethnohistory: Indians of Central Mexico in the Sixteenth Century*, edited by H. Harvey and H. Prem, pp. 145–74. University of New Mexico Press, Albuquerque.

Hirth, Kenneth
1993a   Identifying rank and socioeconomic status in domestic contexts: An example from Central Mexico. In *Prehispanic Domestic Units in Western Mesoamerica*, edited by R. Santley and K. Hirth, pp. 121–46. CRC Press, Boca Raton, Florida.
1993b   The household as an analytical unit: Problems in method and theory. In *Prehispanic Domestic Units in Western Mesoamerica*, edited by R. Santley and K. Hirth, pp. 21–36. CRC Press, Boca Raton, Florida.
1995a   Urbanism, militarism, and architectural design: An analysis of Epiclassic sociopolitical structure at Xochicalco. *Ancient Mesoamerica* 6:223–50.
1995b   The investigation of obsidian craft production at Xochicalco, Morelos. *Ancient Mesoamerica* 6:251–58.
2000a   Ancient urbanism at Xochicalco. The evolution and organization of a prehispanic society. *Archaeological Research at Xochicalco*, Vol. I, edited by K. Hirth. University of Utah Press, Salt Lake City.
2000b   The Xochicalco mapping project. In *Archaeological Research at Xochicalco*, Vol. 2, edited by K. Hirth. University of Utah Press, Salt Lake City.
2003   The altepetl and urban structure in prehispanic Mesoamerica. In *El urbanismo en Mesoamérica. Urbanism in Mesoamerica*, edited by W. Sanders, A.G. Mastache, and R. Cobean, pp. 57–84. INAH, Mexico City; Pennsylvania State University, University Park.
2006   *Obsidian Craft Production in Ancient Central Mexico*. University of Utah Press, Salt Lake City.

Hirth, Kenneth G., Bradford Andrews, and J. Jeffrey Flenniken
2003   The Xochicalco production sequence for obsidian prismatic blades: Technological analysis and experimental inferences. In *Mesoamerican Lithic Technology: Experimentation and Interpretation*, edited by K. Hirth, pp. 182–96. University of Utah Press, Salt Lake City.

Hirth, Kenneth, Gregory Bondar, Michael Glascock, A.J. Vonarx, and Thieny Daubenspeck
2006   Supply side economics: An analysis of obsidian procurement and the organization of workshop provisioning. In *Obsidian Craft Production in Ancient Central Mexico*, edited by K. Hirth, pp. 115–36. University of Utah Press, Salt Lake City.

Hirth, Kenneth, and Ann Cyphers Guillén
1988   *Tiempo y asentamiento en Xochicalco*. UNAM, Mexico City.

Hirth, Kenneth, Susan Hirth, and Gyula Pauer
2000   The Xochicalco architectural atlas. In *The Xochicalco Mapping Project. Archaeological Research at Xochicalco*, Vol. 2,

edited by K. Hirth, pp. 197–325. University of Utah Press, Salt Lake City.

Hirth, Kenneth, and Ronald Webb
2006   Households and plazas: The contexts of obsidian craft production at Xochicalco. In *Obsidian Craft Production in Ancient Central Mexico*, edited by K. Hirth, pp. 18–62. University of Utah Press, Salt Lake City.

Katz, Friedrich
1966   *Situación social y económica de los aztecas durante los siglos XV y XVI*. Instituto de Investigaciones Históricas, UNAM, México.

Mackenney, Richard
1987   *Tradesmen and Traders: The World of Guilds in Venice and Europe, c. 1250–1650*. Barnes and Noble Books, Totowa, New Jersey.

Manzanilla, Linda
1993   *Anatomía de un conjunto residencial teotihuacano en Oztoyahualco*. 2 vols. UNAM, Mexico City.

Mastache, Guadalupe, Robert Cobean, and Dan Healan
2002   *Ancient Tollan: Tula and the Toltec Heartland*. University Press of Colorado, Boulder.

Monzón Estrada, Arturo
1983   *El calpulli en la organización de los Tenocha*. Clásicos de la Antropología No. 15. Instituto Nacional Indigenista, Mexico City.

Moreno, Manuel
1962   *La organización política y social de los aztecas*. INAH, Mexico City.

Netting, Robert, Richard Wilk, and Erik Arnould
1984   Introduction. In *Households*, edited by R. Netting, R. Wilk, and E. Arnould, pp. xiii–xxxviii. University of California Press, Berkeley.

Otis Charlton, Cynthia
1994   Plebeians and patricians: Contrasting patterns of production and distribution in the Aztec figurine and lapidary industries. In *Economies and Polities in the Aztec Realm*, edited by M. Hodge and M. Smith, pp. 196–219. Studies on Culture and Society, vol. 6. Institute for Mesoamerican Studies, State University of New York, Albany.

Pastrana Cruz, Alejandro
1998   *La explotación azteca de la obsidiana en la Sierra de las Navajas*. Colección Científica no. 383. INAH, México.

Plunket, Patricia (editor)
1998   *Domestic Ritual in Ancient Mesoamerica*. Monograph 46. Cotsen Institute of Archaeology, University of California, Los Angeles.

Plunket, Patricia, and Gabriela Uruñuela
1998   Preclassic household patterns preserved under volcanic ash at Tetimpa, Puebla, Mexico. *Latin American Antiquity* 9:287–309.

Reyes García, Luis
1996   El término calpulli en documentos del siglo XVI. In *Documentos Nauas de la ciudad de México del siglo XVI*, edited by L. Reyes García, E. Celestino Solís, A. Valencia Ríos, C. Medina Lima, and G. Guerrero Díaz, pp. 21–68. CIESAS, Mexico City.

Rice, Prudence
1987   *Pottery Analysis: A Sourcebook*. University of Chicago Press, Chicago.

Sanders, William
1966   Life in a Classic village. In *Teotihuacan. XI Mesa Redonda*, pp. 123–47. Sociedad Mexicana de Antropología, México.
1994   *The Teotihuacan Valley Project Final Report. Vol. 3. The Teotihuacan Period Occupation of the Valley. Part 1. The Excavations*. Occasional Papers in Anthropology. Department of Anthropology, Pennsylvania State University, University Park.

Santley, Robert
1977   *Intra-Site Settlement Patterns at Loma Torremote and Their Relationship to Formative Prehistory in the Cuautitlan Region, State of Mexico*. PhD dissertation, Department of Anthropology, Penn State University, University Park, Pennsylvania.
1983   Obsidian trade and Teotihuacan influence in Mesoamerica. In *Highland-Lowland Interaction in Mesoamerica*, edited by A. Miller, pp. 69–124. DORLC, Washington, D.C.
1984   Obsidian exchange, economic stratification, and the evolution of complex society in the Basin of Mexico. In *Trade and Exchange in Early Mesoamerica*, edited by K. Hirth, pp. 43–86. University of New Mexico, Albuquerque.
1993   Late Formative society at Loma Torremote: A consideration of the redistribution vs. the great provider models as a basis for the emergence of complexity in the Basin of Mexico. In *Prehispanic Domestic Units in Western Mesoamerica*, edited by R. Santley and K. Hirth, pp. 67–86. CRC Press, Boca Raton, Florida.

Santley, Robert, Philip Arnold, and Christopher Pool
1989   The ceramics production system at Matacapan, Veracruz, Mexico. *Journal of Field Archaeology* 16:107–32.

Santley, Robert, and Kenneth Hirth
1993a Household studies in western Mesoamerica. In *Prehispanic Domestic Units in Western Mesoamerica: Studies of the Household, Compound, and Residence*, edited by R. Santley and K. Hirth, pp. 3–17. CRC Press, Boca Raton, Florida.

Santley, Robert, and Kenneth Hirth (editors)
1993b *Prehispanic Domestic Units in Western Mesoamerica: Studies of the Household, Compound, and Residence*. CRC Press, Boca Raton, Florida.

Santley, Robert, and Ronald Kneebone
1993   Craft specialization, refuse disposal, and the creation of spatial archaeological records in prehispanic Mesoamerica. In *Prehispanic Domestic Units in Western Mesoamerica: Studies of the Household, Compound, and Residence*, edited by R. Santley and K. Hirth, pp. 37–63. CRC Press, Boca Raton, Florida.

Schiffer, Michael
1985   Is there a "Pompeii premise" in archaeology? *Journal of Anthropological Research* 41:18–41.

Séjourné, Laurette
1966   *Arquitectura y pintura en Teotihuacan*. Siglo Veintiuno editores, México.

Serra Puche, Mari Carmen
1988   *Los recursos lacustres de la cuenca de México durante el Formativo*. Colección Posgrado no. 3. UNAM, Mexico City.

Smith, Joshua Toulmin
1870   *English Gilds: The Original Ordinances of More Than One Hundred Early English Gilds*. N. Trübner and Company, London.

Smith, Michael
1987   Household possessions and wealth in agrarian states: Implications for archaeology. *Journal of Anthropological Archaeology* 6:297–335.
1992   *Archaeological Research at Aztec-Period Rural Sites in Morelos, Mexico. Volume I: Excavations and Architecture*. Monographs in Latin American Archaeology no. 4. University of Pittsburgh, Pittsburgh.
1993   Houses and the settlement hierarchy in Late Postclassic Morelos: A comparison of archaeology and ethnohistory. In *Prehispanic Domestic Units in Western Mesoamerica: Studies of the Household, Compound, and Residence*, edited by R. Santley and K. Hirth, pp. 191–206. CRC Press, Boca Raton, Florida.
1996   *The Aztecs*. Blackwell, Oxford.

Sorensen, Jerrel, Kenneth Hirth, and Stephen Ferguson
1989   The contents of several obsidian workshops around Xochicalco, Morelos. In *La obsidiana en Mesoamérica*, edited by M. Gaxiola and J. Clark, pp. 269–75. Colección Científica no. 176. INAH, Mexico City.

Spence, Michael
1974   Residential practices and the distribution of skeletal traits in Teotihuacan, Mexico. *Man* 9:262–73.
1981   Obsidian production and the state in Teotihuacan. *American Antiquity* 46:769–88.
1987   The scale and structure of obsidian production in Teotihuacan. In *Teotihuacan. Nuevos datos, nuevas síntesis, nuevos problemas*, edited by E. McClung de Tapia and E. Rattray, pp. 429–50. UNAM, Mexico City.

Spence, Michael, Phil Weigand, and María de 1os Dolores Soto de Arechavaleta
2002   Production and distribution of obsidian artifacts in western Jalisco. In *Pathways to Prismatic Blades*, edited by K. Hirth and B. Andrews, pp. 61–79. Cotsen Institute of Archaeology, University of California, Los Angeles.

Storey, Rebecca
1992   *Life and Death in the Ancient City of Teotihuacan*. University of Alabama Press, Tuscaloosa.

Titmus, Gene, and John Clark
2003 Mexica blade making with wooden tools: Recent experimental insights. In *Mesoamerican Lithic Technology: Experimentation and Interpretation*, edited by K. Hirth, pp. 72–97. University of Utah Press, Salt Lake City.

Torquemada, Juan de
1975 *Monarquía Indiana*. Editorial Porrúa, Mexico City.

Torrence, Robin
1986 *Production and Exchange of Stone Tools*. Cambridge University Press, Cambridge.

Tozzer, Alfred
1921 *Excavation of a Site at Santiago Ahuitzotla, D.F. Mexico*. Bureau of American Ethnology, Bulletin 74. Smithsonian Institution, Washington, D.C.

Unwin, George
1963 *The Gilds and Companies of London*. F. Cass, London.

Vaillant, George
1935 *Report on the 1935 Excavations at Chiconautla*. On file at the American Museum of Natural History, New York.

van Zantwijk, Rudolf
1985 *The Aztec Arrangement. The Social History of Pre-Spanish Mexico*. University of Oklahoma Press, Norman.

Winter, Marcus
1976 The archaeological household cluster in the Valley of Oaxaca. In *The Early Mesoamerican Village*, edited by K. Flannery, pp. 25–31. Academic Press, New York.

4

Household, Neighborhood, and Urban Structure in an "Adobe City": Tula, Hidalgo, Mexico

Dan M. Healan

Introduction

The present study synthesizes data from survey and excavation that detail the organization and structure of households and larger suprahousehold entities corresponding to neighborhoods at the site of Tula, Hidalgo, a major urban center in Central Mexico during the Early Postclassic period. Excavation data include those recovered from exploration and more extensive exposures of residential structures at numerous localities within the ancient city. Extensively exposed residential complexes provide a remarkably detailed picture of structure and organization at both the household and the neighborhood level at specific localities within the ancient city while less extensive excavations, although lacking in detail, cover a large part of the ancient city and collectively provide a means to evaluate the magnitude of Tula's domestic realm from an entirely different perspective than surface survey. Together with data from mapping and survey of the larger city, these data provide a picture of urban settlement whose scale and complexity have only recently come to be appreciated.

Families, Households, and Their Material Manifestation

The most basic unit of domestic organization consists of at least one but usually a group of individuals who "live together,"

that is, eat, sleep, store property, and perform basic living tasks and functions in close, intimate proximity. Most such groups consist of *families*, although it is probably better not to assume this a priori, especially when dealing with archaeological situations, as Hirth (1993) has admonished. Moreover, "family" is an ambiguous term that subsumes nuclear and variants of supranuclear entities that differ markedly in size and level of organization. Despite these shortcomings (and for lack of an unawkward-sounding alternative), "family," in reality a nuclear family, is used in the present study to refer to the most basic unit of domestic organization.

Although clearly a basic social entity, the family is an economic entity as well, typically the minimal unit of production, distribution, and consumption that exists within a community. Its economic/subsistence aspect is often accentuated by employing alternative terminology, most commonly *household*, although family and household are not necessarily synonymous terms. In our own (Western) society where neolocal residence has been considered the ideal, the two are often used interchangeably, although terms like "single-family households" imply the existence of multifamily versions. Indeed, it appears that ancient Mesoamerican cities overwhelmingly favored a living arrangement involving supranuclear family groups, living in close proximity and sharing facilities and tasks, which we can appropriately consider as a single household. Hence "household," as used here, is a corporate entity composed of people who live together and perform and share various tasks, domestic and otherwise, in close proximity. By "corporate" I mean a group of individuals united by common tasks and goals who interact in a structured fashion, and who share a common identity, usually that of kinship, that distinguishes them from members of other households. In the present paper, therefore, an individual (nuclear) family may comprise a single household or merely one component of a larger, supranuclear family household.

In the present study, "household" and "family" refer to socioeconomic institutions embodying people and relationships rather than the physical facilities they occupy. The material manifestation of a household is a *residence*. More than simply a place where members of a household live, a residence comprises the physical facilities where sleeping, cooking, eating, storage, and other tasks take place. In multifamily household situations where the integrity of each component family is not maintained, it may be difficult or impossible to discern or accurately infer their number and size. Fortunately, at Tula and other Mesoamerican cities, it appears that in multifamily households, each component family maintained a high level of integrity, with its own living area that often clearly included a kitchen or food-cooking area.

The simplest form of residence is a single residence housing a single-family household. From an analytical standpoint, single residences are an especially useful point of departure because they reduce the concept of a residence to its essential elements. A single residence minimally contains some kind of shelter or dwelling (that is, house proper) and an adjacent, peripheral, exterior area or "yard" (e.g., Flannery and Marcus 1994: Fig. 10.2). Minimally, the house is used for sleeping and storage. Other activities, including food preparation and cooking, may take place inside the house or outdoors. Indeed, the yard is often the locus of many activities and may contain special activity-specific facilities, including storage and refuse disposal. Deceased household members are often buried on residential sites as well.

Current data suggest that single residences were not a common form of housing in Mesoamerican cities. Instead, it appears that urban households tended to be multifamily entities living in what can be called compound residences, and whose physical manifestations are commonly called *residential compounds*. Residential compounds are extremely variable in size and form, but all residential compounds share three characteristics: (1) they contain more than one family; (2) each family is associated with a discrete part of the compound residence, thus preserving each family's integrity; and (3) all families within a compound share some of its facilities, making them codependent to some extent. Compound residences thus involve not only agglomeration but integration as well, forming a cofunctioning set of codependent families.

Neighborhoods and Precolumbian Cities

Although a major topic of this volume, "neighborhood" is a rather imprecise term that may apply to patterning at several distinct levels within a city. The lowest level includes patterning immediately above the level of individual households, involving suprahousehold groups typically represented by spatially juxtaposed residences such as those described below for Tula. Other possible examples include clusters of apartment compounds characteristic of the "outskirts" of Teotihuacan. Such groupings seem most likely to involve related households. Many such groupings seem too small to be considered whole neighborhoods unto themselves, although it is not unusual to see anomalous concentrations of diagnostic artifacts involving entities of similar size identified as tentative craft or ethnic "barrios." In the present chapter, such localized suprahousehold groupings are termed "local neighborhoods."

At the other extreme, the highest level entails units immediately below the level of the entire city, such as the division of Tenochtitlan and Teotihuacan into quarters by major thoroughfares, or the division of Tenochtitlan into north-south strips by the network of roads, canals, and *chinampa* plots that pervade the city. Like suprahousehold groups, citywide districts such as these are usually easy to identify, but unlike the former, are probably the product of decision making at the highest level of governance. Most such units seem far too large to represent something comparable to neighborhoods; indeed, their sociopolitical significance is often not readily apparent.[1]

In contrast to these extremes, it seems likely that true urban neighborhoods generally comprise an intermediate level of spatial patterning, larger than a few clustered households but considerably smaller than citywide districts. A case in point is Tenochtitlan, which was subdivided into named neighborhoods or barrios variously called *calpulli* and *tlaxilacalli*, a number of which have been delineated by Calnek (2003) based on Alzate's eighteenth-century map. Three particularly striking aspects of these barrios as delineated by Calnek are (1) considerable variability in size, (2) irregularity of shape, and (3) lack of discernible physical boundaries. Indeed, there would appear to be little outward evidence that would have enabled their detection and delineation by archaeologists.

Site Background

Tula is located in southwestern Hidalgo immediately northwest of the Basin of Mexico, where the preceding Teotihuacan and subsequent Aztec states were situated. The immediate area comprises the southwestern extreme of the Valle del Mezquital, a semiarid region of hills, plains, and valleys that lies between Tula and Pachuca to the east and Ixmiquilpan to the north. In protohistoric times this area was part of the Teotlalpan, a region that sixteenth-century census data and other accounts depict as a prosperous and productive land (Cook 1949).

Mastache et al. (2002) provide a detailed discussion of the geology, present-day and paleoenvironment, and recent land use for the Tula region. Today the local environment is largely semiarid; it is a predominantly xerophytic landscape with localized grassland and mixed forest (Cook 1949:26–28). In many areas the land is heavily eroded with shallow ravines and frequent surface outcrops of *caliche*, characteristic of the region, although it should be noted that much of this erosion is a relatively recent phenomenon that largely postdates Tula's occupation. Cook's (1949) well documented reconstruction of Teotlalpan's ecological history indicates that the region experienced several cycles of extensive erosion and other forms of ecological deterioration, the earliest beginning before the Spanish Conquest. This ecological damage is largely attributed to the effects of overpopulation, with deforestation of hillsides and excessive cultivation of alluvial lands as the principal causes. Cook is careful to distinguish between *climatic* change and human-induced *ecological* change, and maintains that most of the environmental change in the Tula region has been ecological. He suggests that there has actually been little climatic change in the region since Tula's founding and characterizes Teotlalpan at the time of Tula's founding as "a relatively unspoiled but arid area" (Cook 1949:58).

The site itself occupies an exceedingly diverse landscape that includes alluvial valleys and adjacent uplands at the confluence of the Tula and Rosas rivers (Fig. 4.1). To the west, the alluvial valleys are flanked by a series of high hills that form the ancient city's western and southwestern limits. The core of the ancient settlement is situated along a centrally located bluff that forms the eastern and northern flanks of the alluvial valleys. The bluff is partially dissected to form two (north and south) lobes, upon which were constructed the three principal monumental architectural complexes of the city commonly known as Tula Grande, Tula Chico, and the Plaza Charnay. The land east of the bluff is a gently sloping plain that forms the northern and eastern flanks of the Central Valley, and includes a brackish marsh ("El Salitre"). A similar bluff forms the eastern flank of the South Valley and includes a well-defined promontory ("Cerro El Cielito") at its northern end.

Previous Research

Tula's ruins have been known for centuries; indeed, the first systematic excavations date from 1880 as part of Desiré Charnay's explorations of several residential structures as detailed in *Ancient Cities of the New World* (1888). In 1940, Mexico's *Instituto Nacional de Antropología e Historia* (INAH) launched a comprehensive twenty-year program of systematic exploration, under the direction of Jorge Acosta, that principally involved excavation and consolidation of many of the principal structures of Tula Grande (e.g., Acosta 1956–1957). Acosta's work provided a preliminary ceramic chronology that placed Tula's principal occupation within the Early Postclassic period (ca. AD 900–1200). Diehl (1989) provides a detailed account of Acosta's investigations at Tula, and Mastache et al. (2002) provide a comprehensive and detailed description including architectural and iconographic analysis of the principal structures and major monuments excavated by Acosta and others at Tula Grande.

During the 1970s, Tula was the focus of two comprehensive archaeological investigations that ran essentially concurrently. The

first of these was the Proyecto Tula, conducted by INAH under the direction of Eduardo Matos Moctezuma (Matos 1974, 1976), while the second was by the University of Missouri under the direction of Richard Diehl (Healan 1989). Both projects included mapping, surface survey, and excavation within the site proper as well as limited regional survey and excavation, and ethnohistorical research. Two major consequences of these projects were the refinement of Tula's ceramic chronology (Cobean 1990) and, as detailed below, the delineation of Tula's overall extent. More recently, Tula has been the focus of several other research projects that included comprehensive regional survey (Mastache et al. 2002) and excavation of residential complexes at numerous localities within the ancient settlement (e.g., Fernández Dávila 1994; Gómez Serafín et al. 1994; Paredes Gudiño 1992; Healan et al. 1983), some of which are described below.

Tula's initial occupation is associated with Coyotlatelco ceramics, and Tula is one of a number of Coyotlatelco sites that appear in the region during the Epiclassic period (ca. AD 700–900). The Epiclassic period community has been estimated at approximately 5 to 6 km^2 in size and appears to have been centered on the mound/plaza complex known as Tula Chico along the main bluff (Fig. 4.1). The subsequent Early Postclassic period marks a major expansion of the settlement into the adjacent alluvial valleys and plains and construction of the monumental complex known as Tula Grande, which served as the city's primary civic/ceremonial center during its apogee during the Tollan phase (ca. AD 900–1150).

Exploring Tula's Layout and Internal Structure: Three Approaches

It is fortunate that determination of Tula's overall extent and internal structure has been the subject of three independent investigations that employed notably different approaches. The first of these consisted of intensive surface survey conducted by the University of Missouri to delineate the maximum extent of urban settlement based on continuous surface artifact debris (Fig. 4.1). This survey was followed by controlled surface collection involving both random and transect sampling that recovered over 330,000 artifacts, whose surface distributions provide numerous insights regarding Tula's internal structure, as discussed below. The second of these investigations, conducted by INAH's Proyecto Tula, likewise included systematic surface collection as well as the preparation of a photogrammetric topographic map of the site (Yadeun 1975). This map pinpointed some 1,001 surface mounds measuring a meter or more in height, whose spatial distribution is markedly discontinuous, forming distinct clusters of varying size and density (see Fig. 4.9), which likewise shed light upon the city's internal structure. The third investigation examined the aligned linear surface features (discernible on aerial photographs) that are believed to represent roadways, terraces, platforms, or other artificial constructions within the ancient city (Mastache and Crespo 1982). This undertaking revealed the existence of three distinct systems of aligned surface features believed to represent

Figure 4.1. Map of the site of Tula showing the location of excavations of residential compounds depicted in Figures 4.2 and 4.3. *i*, Daini; *j*, *El Corral*; *e*, *f*, *h*, *Canal*; *c*, U98; *a*, *g*, *l*, *museo*; *n*, Toltec House; *k*, *Vivero*; *b*, U27-28; *m*, Malinche; *d*, Tultengo. Dash-dot line delineates the urban limits as defined by the Missouri project survey.

temporally distinct episodes of planned development during the city's history, as discussed below.

These various investigations collectively indicate a city that at its height covered an area of up to 16 km², a strikingly diverse topography of hills, plains, and alluvial valleys (Fig. 4.1) that contrasts sharply with the relatively level terrain of cities like Teotihuacan and Tenochtitlan. Like Teotihuacan, Tula is somewhat cruciform in plan with its principal monumental zone located near the center. Unlike Teotihuacan, however, there is no evidence of major thoroughfares located along Tula's cruciform extremities, which instead appear to represent the extension of settlement along the alluvial valleys on the north, south, and west sides. There is, however, other possible evidence of streets and thoroughfares, as discussed below. Each of the above investigations also produced evidence of heterogeneous features within the ancient city that may indicate neighborhoods or other localized residential entities. Some of this evidence, including that which has been corroborated by excavation, will be considered below.

Types of Residential Structures at Tula

Tula's rich legacy of archaeological investigation includes numerous excavations of residential remains at widespread locations within the urban settlement (Fig. 4.1*a–m*; see also Paredes 1992). These include some of the earliest residential excavations conducted in Mesoamerica (Charnay 1887), although most date from the last several decades. Collectively, these excavations provide a rather diverse picture of residential patterns in a number of respects, including the following:

Construction. All residential structures excavated to date were built of stone to some degree, in most cases restricted to low (about 1 m) stone foundations overlain by courses of adobe that comprised the bulk of the exterior walls. The stone portion was constructed of cobbles of limestone and/or basalt and other volcanic rock consolidated with mud rather than lime mortar, despite the common use of lime plaster as a floor and wall covering. Most interior walls were constructed in a similar fashion, although less substantial partitions were occasionally formed of clay or mud. The widespread use of mud and adobe in residential construction is probably responsible in large part for the general absence of visible architectural remains on the surface of the site today.

Spatial Orientation. All structural remains, residential and otherwise, that have been exposed to date at Tula exhibit one of three spatial orientation schemes with respect to magnetic north, including: (a) approximately due north, (b) approximately 17 degrees east of north, and (c) approximately 18 degrees west of north. Despite the variability in orientation at the site level, it should be noted that all structural remains that have been exposed by excavation within a single locality exhibit the same orientation, suggesting adherence to a particular scheme on the local level. More recently, surface features discernible in aerial

photographs have shed considerable light upon these different orientation schemes, as discussed below.

Form. Many of the residential excavations at Tula were exploratory and involved limited exposure, but most if not all are almost certainly compound rather than single residences given the pervasive pattern of multiple rooms or buildings flanking open spaces suggestive of courtyards or patios (e.g., Figs. 4.2, 4.3). The most extensively excavated residences comprise two distinct forms of residential compounds: house compounds and apartment compounds.

House Compounds

A house compound is a form of compound residence in which the families making up the household are housed in separate dwellings, usually clustered together and facing inward to form a closed or semiclosed unit. Besides the buildings themselves, open space is typically incorporated into the compound to serve as a yard or common space for the component families. This is often a well-defined, centrally located area partially or completely enclosed by the surrounding houses, and commonly referred to as a *solar* or courtyard. Completely enclosed house compounds formed of contiguous houses and freestanding walls between houses may have the appearance of being a single building, although patterns of wall abutments should reveal their true nature. Even seemingly open house compounds could have been enclosed by perishable fences or screens of vegetation, as was often the case for Aztec house compounds.

House compounds have been identified at many urban sites in Mesoamerica, including Tenochtitlan, where Calnek's (2003) extensive study of archival documents and plans indicates that house compounds were the most common form of residence. At Tula, remains of house compounds have been identified at a number of localities (Fig. 4.2). Most of these were sufficiently exposed to reveal the characteristic arrangement of houses and one or more open areas, interspersed among the structures, that represent exterior courtyards. The most extensively exposed house compounds come from a single locality (Canal) where excavation completely exposed the remains of two juxtaposed compounds and partially exposed a third (Fig. 4.2*e*, *f*, *h*; see also Fig. 4.4).

The various house compounds depicted in Figure 4.2 exhibit considerable variability in terms of construction quality, materials used, regularity of plan, and relative spaciousness, at least some of which may reflect variation in the occupants' relative status. Equally noteworthy is the variability seen *within* some of the compounds, which, as described below, may reflect internal differences in status and the accommodation of new members over time.

Apartment Compounds

In contrast to house compounds, apartment compounds are a form of compound residence in which the various families

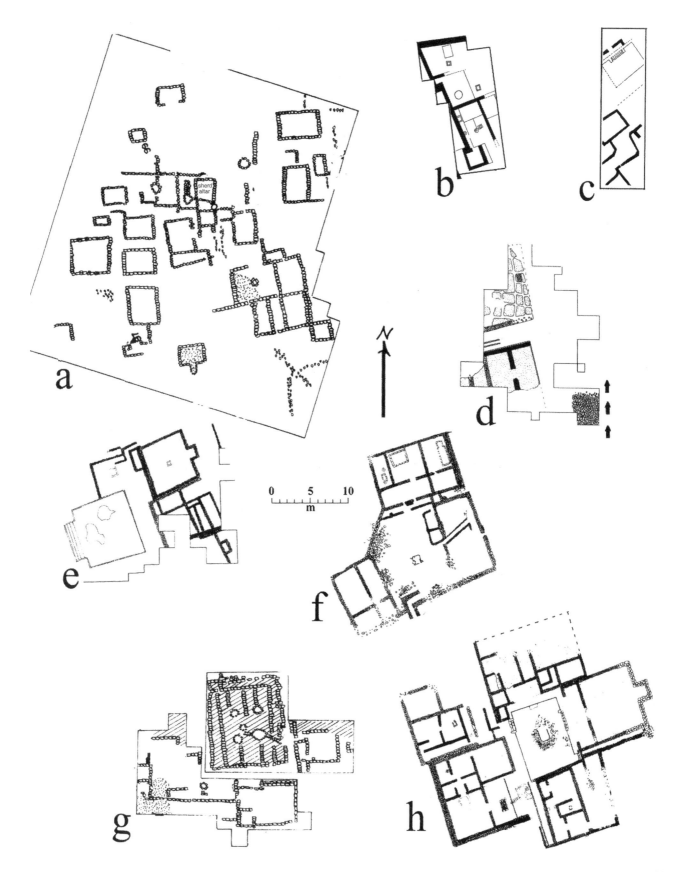

Figure 4.2. Plans of excavated residential structures identified as house compounds in Figure 4.1. Sources: *a, g*, Paredes 1992; *b, c*, Mastache et al. 2002; *e, f, h*, Healan 1989; *d*, Healan et al. 1983. Arrows indicate thoroughfare.

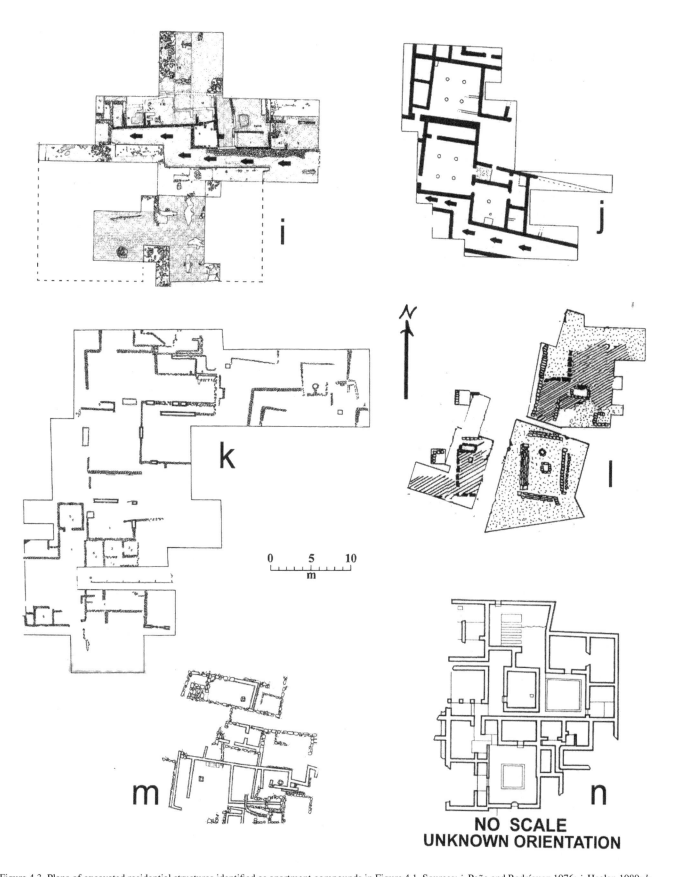

Figure 4.3. Plans of excavated residential structures identified as apartment compounds in Figure 4.1. Sources: *i*, Peña and Rodríguez 1976; *j*, Healan 1989; *k*, Fernández 1994; *l*, *m*, Paredes 1992; *n*, Charnay 1887. Arrows indicate passageways.

Figure 4.4. Plan of the West, Central, and East house compounds and adjacent structural remains in the Canal locality. Arrows indicate thoroughfares.

within the household are housed within a single building rather than in separate houses. Each family occupies a distinct cluster of rooms, which compose an individual apartment or suite, within the building. Like house compounds, apartment compounds contain open, common space in the form of unroofed interior courtyards or patios, which would have been a major source of light for interior and other rooms lacking windows.

Apartment compounds are a particularly characteristic feature of Teotihuacan, where in fact they compose a near exclusive mode of housing during the city's Middle Classic apogee. Outside Teotihuacan, apartment compounds appear to have been a common form of housing for rulers and elite families in many if not most Precolumbian cities, where buildings identified archaeologically and ethnohistorically as palaces generally have this form. This is true of Tula, where buildings interpreted as palaces have been encountered in excavation around Tula Grande. These include Charnay's so-called "Toltec Palace" along the southwest periphery of Tula Grande and the recently excavated Building 4, situated at the northeast corner of the colonnade between Pyramids B and C (Mastache et al. 2006).[2]

Outside Tula's monumental core, structural remains that appear to represent apartment compounds have been encountered in excavation at five other localities (Fig. 4.3), several of which enjoyed relatively extensive exposure. Like the house com-pounds, apartment compounds exhibit notable variation in spaciousness and overall architectural quality; hence, the two forms of compound residence do not appear to have housed different social classes. Moreover, excavated apartment compounds have a widespread distribution that in some cases placed them in close proximity to possibly contemporaneous house compounds.

House Compounds and Household Patterns in the Canal Locality

One of the most extensively exposed systems of residential structures at Tula are those from the Canal Locality (*e, f, h* in Figs. 4.1 and 4.2), where excavations undertaken by the University of Missouri exposed three juxtaposed house compounds (designated the East, Central, and West compounds) and portions of one or more nearby compounds (Fig. 4.4). The well-preserved state of the remains and abundant associated artifacts and features shed considerable light upon various activities, domestic and otherwise, that were performed; they also permit us to make several inferences regarding household size, composition, and other characteristics.

All structures exposed in the Canal Locality were oriented approximately 18 degrees west of magnetic north. These remains have been extensively described in previous publications (Healan 1977, 1989; Mastache et al. 2002), and can be summarized as follows: each compound consists of two or more houses or other structures arranged around a centrally located courtyard, each containing a centrally located rectangular structure believed to have been an altar. Each compound is a closed entity, employing abutting houses and freestanding walls, with access controlled by a single, L-shaped entrance. The West and Central compounds are the largest, containing three and six houses, respectively, whose remains provide evidence for a number of different activities, as discussed below.

Domestic Activity

In general, the large quantities of utilitarian pottery, spindle whorls, cutting and scraping tools, and other artifacts of a primarily domestic nature strongly support the premise that the structures labeled as houses in Figure 4.4 were indeed residential in function. A more concrete picture of the nature and distribution of domestic activity is offered by the spatial distribution of various nonportable or semiportable artifacts and features. To begin with, six possible cooking areas were tentatively identified in the West and Central compounds on the basis of firecontaining features interpreted as hearths (A–F in Fig. 4.5). It should be noted that all but one of these were rather insubstantial affairs, usually shallow, hard-burned depressions in earthen floors, some of which contained small amounts of ash. Most were associated with complete but broken vessels, and three had the neck portion of a large olla resting upside down on the floor, possibly improvised pot stands. Possible cooking areas were identified in five of the nine houses (the other four houses had lost a large portion of their floors to erosion). At least one house (IV) contained two such areas, in separate rooms (B, C in Fig. 4.5).

Five possible areas of food preparation (G–K in Fig. 4.5) were identified principally by whole metates, two of which were accompanied by elongated (cigar-shaped) manos. Four were associated with complete but broken ceramic vessels including plates, bowls, and large spherical ollas, one of which was embedded up to its neck in the floor.

In most cases, possible cooking and food preparation areas did not occur in close proximity. All six possible cooking areas were located *inside* houses while four of five possible food preparation areas were situated in or immediately adjacent to *outdoor* areas, including three around the periphery of the courtyard of the Central compound. Noting that roofed-over space within these residential compounds appears to have been private (family-specific) space while unroofed space was largely accessible to all families in the household, the spatial *and* contextual segregation of these two activities may provide some insight into family-level versus household-level activities and how they were structured. Assuming that cooking of food will usually occur in close proximity to where it will be eaten, the location of cooking (and presumably eating) activities inside individual houses suggests that the partaking of food was largely a private (family-specific) rather than public (household-level) activity. Food preparation, on the other hand, is probably not an activity engaged in by all family members; hence, it is likely to be regarded not as a private family-specific activity but rather as one that may be performed in public space in the company of members of other families in the compound who were involved in the same activity.

Four of the five houses with possible cooking areas each contained one such area, suggesting they housed single families. The fifth house (IV) contained two such areas (B, C in Fig. 4.5), each in its own room that enjoyed its own access from the outside, suggesting this house may have housed two families. Ironically, this is one of the two smallest houses and, as noted below, was apparently a later addition.

Non-Domestic Activity

Several houses were associated with distinctive features suggestive of specialized activities of a non-domestic nature. Adjacent to House VIII was a structure that appears to have been a kiln for firing the large ceramic tubes used for drainage in and around the houses and courtyards, as described elsewhere (Healan 1989). The presence of a single kiln and the absence of large quantities of wasters suggest a pattern of sporadic use.

Several of the houses contained subfloor pits and above-floor enclosures that may have had a primarily domestic (storage) function. Two houses had large pits found to contain caches of exotic vessels, one of which (L in Fig. 4.5) held four Tohil Plumbate vessels and five Central American polychrome vessels, which had apparently been hidden beneath a false bottom floor. Most of the vessels had a worn appearance, suggesting they were used rather than simply hoarded (Diehl et al. 1974). Other exotic pottery includes a surprisingly large number of Plumbate sherds (nearly 1,000), suggesting that the occupants of these house groups had the wherewithal to acquire such items on a regular basis.

Ritual Activity

There are numerous indications that these compounds were the sites of various ritual activities. Most obvious are the ubiquitous sherds from handheld censers and spiked braziers, known to have been used in ritual activity in prehispanic Mesoamerica. Equally abundant were moldmade ceramic figurines, virtually all of them fragmentary, which have been linked to domestic ritual activity in other parts of Mesoamerica (e.g., Marcus 1998). The large number and widespread distribution of these various artifacts in and around the compounds suggest their use at the individual family rather than the household level.

Both ethnographic and ethnohistorical sources frequently mention the existence of household shrines in Mesoamerica, and at least three niche-like extensions in the rear walls of Houses VI and X and inside House VIII may represent such features. It may be more than coincidence that these features are located inside the three largest rooms in the house compounds, and that

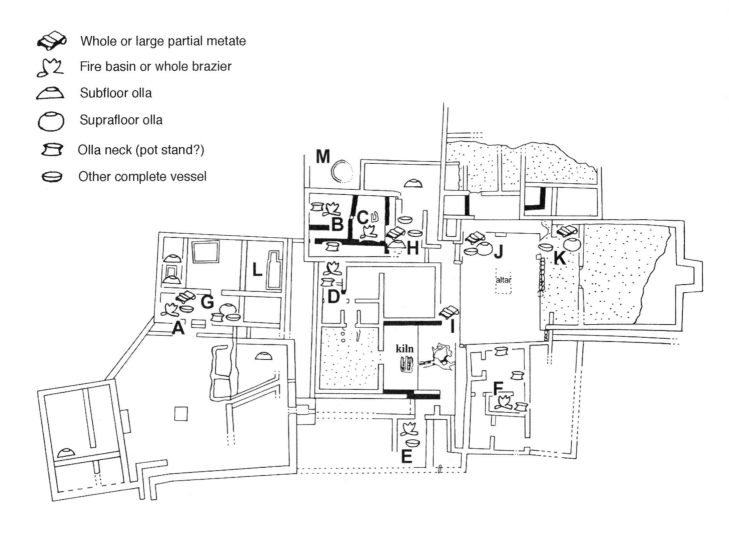

Figure 4.5. Distribution of nonportable, semiportable, and selected portable artifacts and features possibly indicative of various activity areas discussed in text.

all three rooms were floored with lime plaster. Again, their occurrence inside individual houses may indicate ritual activity at the level of individual families.

On the other hand, the presence of structures interpreted as altars in the courtyards of all three compounds suggests ritual activity at the household level. All three altars were badly damaged, but were rectangular in plan. The best-preserved altar, in the courtyard of the Central compound, had sloping sides faced with tabular stone and a top constructed of worked stone blocks and slabs that had been dismantled and the rubble strewn in a circle around it (Fig. 4.6). Among the rubble were ten tenoned stone replicas of human skulls, which had apparently adorned the altar's sides.[3] The interior contained an intrusive pit with loose human teeth, presumably the remnants of a burial that had been removed. Similar altars, some containing burials, have been encountered in other residential compounds at Tula.

Additional evidence of household-level ritual is suggested by the remains of circular stone structures that may have been sweat baths, comparable to Aztec *temazcales*, known to have had ritual connotations. Two such structures were encountered along the northern periphery of the Central compound, one immediately north of House IV (*M* in Fig. 4.5) and the other in the same area but associated with an earlier construction phase. Both were slightly more than a meter in diameter and were constructed of volcanic stones, many blackened by fire, enclosing a burned clay floor and an ashy, charcoal-flecked fill. Traces of stone and adobe walls suggest these circular structures may have been part of a larger enclosed feature, and as such are remarkably similar to two facilities identified as *temazcales* in Structure 6 at Cihuatecpan (Evans 1988: Fig. 7).

Certainly the most salient evidence of ritual activity is the small temple on the west side of the East compound, although

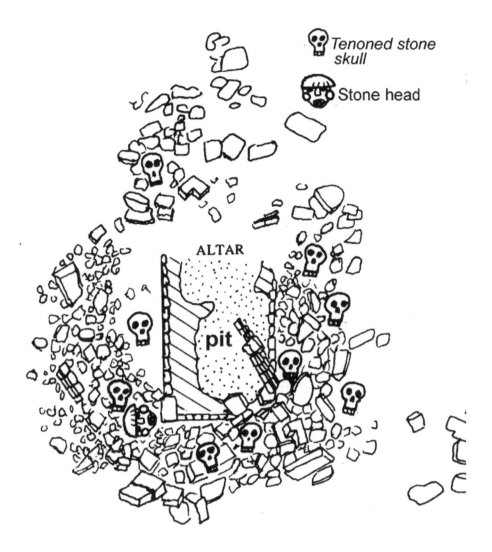

Figure 4.6. Plan of the altar in the Central compound courtyard as encountered in excavation.

its focus appears to have been at the level of the local neighborhood, as discussed below. In contrast to the West and Central compounds, the East compound appears to have contained only two buildings, one of which was a small temple and supporting platform on its western side. The platform was about a meter in height, atop which were the remains of a two-room superstructure, a common configuration for structures interpreted to be temples in Mesoamerica (Marquina 1964; Marcus 1978). Thus, the East compound apparently contained only one house proper (X), which closely resembles House VI in form, including the niche-like extension of the rear wall, its spacious, plaster-covered interior room, and its west-facing location. Like the other two compounds, the East compound had a small courtyard and altar, accessed from the outside by an L-shaped entrance. While the East Group is a one-house compound whose occupant or occupants are presumed to have been associated with the temple,

it should be noted that the temple faces outward toward House VII, which in turn faces the temple, across a small open area or plaza. Thus, the temple is linked to two houses in two different compounds.

Discussion

It seems probable that the families within each compound were related to each other since we are dealing with a society whose social organization was almost certainly based on kinship. Indeed, it is hard to imagine that the degree of intimacy and interaction that must have existed within these compounds, including group domestic and ritual activity in the centrally located courtyards, could have involved non-related families. Moreover, the burial of an individual inside a centrally located altar suggests common bonds, presumably bonds of kinship. Thus it appears that each compound contained a suprafamily household whose component families generally enjoyed their own sleeping and cooking areas. Moreover, it would appear that the West and Central compound households were related to each other, both because of their physical juxtaposition and because they were connected by a system of narrow alleys or passageways that were closed to the outside world but that provided direct access to each other.

Stratigraphic and architectural data indicate several episodes of construction presumed to accommodate an increase in the number of component families in the West and Central compounds over time. For example, it appears that Houses IV and IX (situated on the northwest and southwest corners of the Central compound) were later additions, presumably built to accommodate new families. Both are small, modestly constructed affairs, which, along with their peripheral location, suggest a relatively low status that may be expected of newly emergent families. As noted above, at least one (House IV) contains two separate possible cooking areas, suggesting that it may have housed *two* families.[4] Furthermore, as detailed below, stratigraphic data reveal that the West compound was constructed some time after the Central compound, most likely to accommodate other families from the expanding Central compound household.

The Canal Locality as a Local Neighborhood

The remains exposed in the Canal locality provide evidence of household and suprahousehold patterning at the level of what may be termed a "local neighborhood." Generally speaking, a local neighborhood is a sufficiently localized portion of a city's residential sector that its inhabitants probably would have interacted face-to-face with great regularity, if not daily.

Settlement History

Stratigraphic data and patterns of architectural superposition indicate a complex history of occupation for the Canal locality, beginning with evidence of quarrying and other exploitation that apparently preceded actual settlement of the immediate area of excavation. This includes the extensive removal of soil and underlying *caliche* in the northwest portion of the locality, followed by the deposition of thick layers of refuse. The earliest structural remains date to the latter half of the Tollan phase, and comprised early versions of the Central and East compounds (Fig. 4.7*a*), characterized by a smaller, simpler version of the temple platform in the East compound and a four-house configuration in the Central compound, which partially overlay the earlier quarry and refuse deposits. A particularly notable characteristic of the Central compound is its uniform "footprint," occupying a nearly square block of land measuring approximately 30 m on a side. During this period, refuse deposition continued in the northern, southern, and western peripheries of the Central compound.

At some point the West compound (Fig. 4.7*b*) was constructed, partially overlying these refuse deposits; its later date suggests it may have been constructed to accommodate additional families of the expanding Central compound.

To summarize, settlement of the Canal locality follows a progression beginning with non-resident exploitation followed by settlement, initially on a relatively small scale and expanding in scope over time. It is interesting that a large component of the initial exploitation included dumping of refuse, a practice that continued in the unoccupied periphery after the locality was settled. From the beginning, the Central compound possessed an orderly plan consisting of a nearly square template to which it adhered for its duration. The configuration of the four initial houses left open corners that formed the small plaza between House VII and the neighboring temple and the sites for the later Houses IV and IX (Figs. 4.4, 4.7). Finally, it should be noted that all structural remains encountered in excavation, from the earliest to the latest, exhibited the same spatial orientation.

Neighboring Compounds

While these three compounds dominate the area exposed in excavation, there is evidence of other structures in the neighboring areas (Fig. 4.4). Immediately east of House V was a badly eroded system of walls pertaining to at least two superposed structures whose form and temporal relationship to House V could not be determined. Further east, excavation encountered several well preserved structures immediately north and south of House X; they appear to be parts of other house compounds whose bulk lay beyond the limits of excavation. Additional structural remains were also encountered in the extreme southern limits of excavation approximately 10 m south of House VII. As shown in Figure 4.4, all of these remains exhibit the same spatial orientation as the East, Central, and West compounds.

Roadways

Some of these neighboring structures directly abut those of the Central and West compounds, while others are separated from the latter compounds by passageways that form part of a larger system of thoroughfares linking the various compounds (arrows in Fig. 4.4). In addition, remains of a cobblestone pavement presumed to be a public (that is, open) thoroughfare were encountered along the southwestern limits of the excavation (Figs. 4.4, 4.8). The pavement, which measured approximately 2 m wide, extended east-west along the southern flank of the West and Central compounds and terminated near the southwest corner of the small plaza fronting the East Group temple. The northwest corner of this same plaza is at the termination of a narrow passageway running along the north flank of the East Group that, like the paved roadway, extended beyond the limits of excavation. Thus, the temple is situated at the nexus of two thoroughfares linking it to areas beyond the immediate locality, suggesting that it served a larger area than the three house compounds exposed

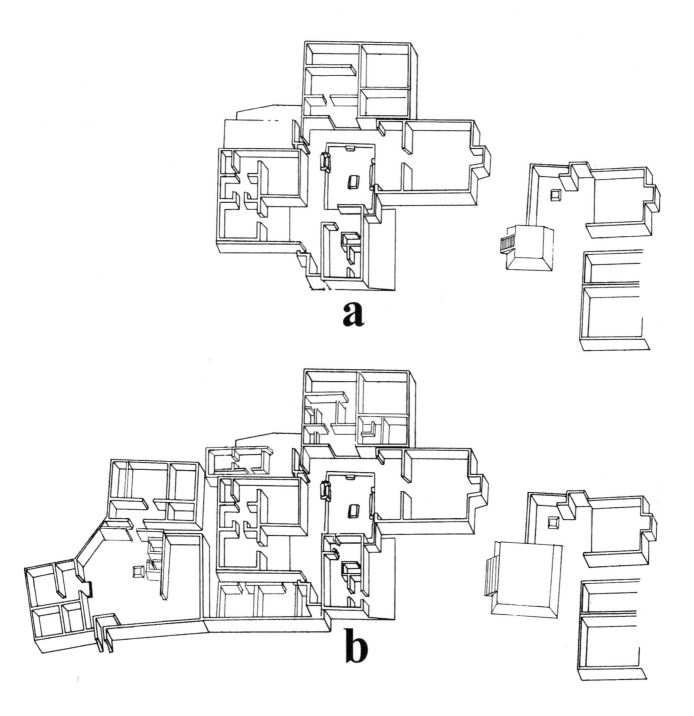

Figure 4.7. Postulated sequence of construction in the Canal locality based on stratigraphic data. *a*, initial settlement; *b*, later growth.

Figure 4.8. Area immediately south of House IX in the Canal locality, showing the east end of the paved thoroughfare (foreground). View is to the northwest. Note that the southeastern portion of the pavement was damaged during its re-exposure.

in excavation. The record of expansion of both the platform and the surmounting temple (Fig. 4.7) presumably reflects an increase in the population that it served over time.

Other Local Neighborhoods

The local neighborhood that was partially exposed at the Canal locality exhibited the following characteristics: (1) a clustered rather than uniform distribution of residential compounds, probably closely-related households formed by expansion of one or more "founding" households over time; (2) existence of public (that is, open) thoroughfares in the intervening areas, including narrow passageways that wind through the clustered compounds and at least one cobblestone "street"; (3) presence of a small-scale temple that provided a mode of interaction and integration among the various households and between households and local

representatives of a higher order (city-level) institution; and (4) a common structural orientation that persisted over time. The ability to discern the structure of local neighborhoods in other excavated localities at Tula is hampered by limited exposure; nevertheless, there is some evidence for similar patterns in other parts of the city. Particularly notable are the Daini and El Corral localities (Fig. 4.3*i*, *j*), both of which include remains of juxtaposed compounds (in both cases apartment compounds), flanked or separated by narrow, "dog-legged" passageways (indicated by arrows), suggesting a similar pattern of clustered residences interspersed with winding passageways. These data suggest there may have been local neighborhoods consisting of apartment compounds, comparable to those consisting of house compounds, or, in general, that clusters rather than uniform distributions of residential compounds were a widespread characteristic of Tula's residential sector.

The paved thoroughfare extending along the southern edge of the Canal locality raises the intriguing prospect of paved streets within the ancient city, and in fact a nearly identical stretch of tabular stone pavement oriented roughly north-south was encountered immediately southeast of a house compound in an obsidian core/blade workshop excavated in the Tultengo locality (Fig. 4.2*d*). Other possible evidence of citywide streets and planning is discussed below.

Beyond the Local Neighborhood: Higher-Order Patterns

All three survey projects previously undertaken at Tula provided evidence for internal patterning at a higher level than what a local neighborhood would entail, although the nature of the patterning is not clear. This evidence includes the following:

Mound Clusters

As noted above, Yadeun's (1975) photogrammetric mapping project identified some 1,001 surface mounds, measuring at least a meter in height, whose distribution is markedly discontinuous, forming distinct clusters of varying size and density (Fig. 4.9). The Canal locality described in the preceding section is situated within one of the larger mound clusters (Fig. 4.9*a*); indeed, two mounds more than 3 m in height are situated immediately northwest and southeast of the excavation (as seen in Fig. 4.10). Yadeun's map does not include mounds less than a meter in height, which he noted comprised the vast majority of mounds identified on the photogrammetric images (1975:15); hence, it cannot be assumed that these clusters coincide with the areas of densest occupation within the ancient city. Indeed, the distribution of surface artifact densities from the Missouri project survey show numerous "hot spots" in areas with few such mounds. Moreover, in the Canal locality there was relatively little if any topographic indication of any of the structures exposed by excavation (Fig. 4.10).

Mastache et al. (2002:171–72) have suggested that the largest mounds in Yadeun's three-tiered size category may represent the principal politico/religious units of entities comparable to the *barrios grandes* of Tenochtitlan, although this cannot be evaluated without knowing the specific location of these particular mounds.[5] Except for the northern portion of the alluvial valley, the largest and densest clusters of mounds occur in the higher areas of the city, particularly around the three monumental plazas (Fig. 4.9). It should be noted that the higher elevations also comprise the longest-settled portions of the city, while much of the area characterized by low mound density appears to have been settled relatively late, as discussed below. Thus it seems likely that these clusters are largely temporal composites, in essence the "accumulation" of mound construction over time.

Structural Orientation

In a previous study, Mastache and Crespo (1982) identified numerous aligned, linear surface features on aerial photographs of Tula, which they interpreted as surface manifestations of man-made features. In fact, three distinct systems of alignments were delineated (Fig. 4.11), each of which corresponds to one of three schemes of orientation exhibited by extant architectural remains at the site. In examining Figure 4.11, two principal configurations are noted: (1) *lines*, some more than a kilometer in length, possibly traces of ancient roadways, walls, or canals; and (2) full or partial *rectangles*, smaller instances of which may represent platforms or terraces, while larger instances enclosing areas as large as approximately 850 × 850 m defy interpretation.

Based on their correspondence to the orientation of structural complexes of known age, the three orientation schemes were interpreted by Mastache and Crespo as diachronic in nature, each representing a policy of orientation that was followed during a particular period of Tula's history. The earliest, a generally north-south orientation, is centered around and includes Tula Chico, the monumental center of Tula's initial (Prado/Corral phase) settlement. The second, oriented about 17 degrees east of north (the orientation of Middle Classic Teotihuacan), covers much of the same area, but is centered around and includes Tula Grande, the city's monumental center during its Tollan phase apogee. The final pattern, the 18 degrees west of north orientation seen in the Canal locality, is far more extensive and presumably represents the city at its maximum extent during the latter half of the Tollan phase.

Evidence that Tula possessed internal planning — indeed, that the city possessed *three* such plans — is as enigmatic as it is intriguing. Their interpretation as diachronic phenomena may explain how such systems could occur in the same area, even overlapping in some cases. However, additional field research including "ground-truthing" of such features is clearly needed before firm conclusions can be drawn. It is a fact, however, that all structural remains encountered to date at Tula correspond to one of these three orientation schemes, and that architectural remains with differing orientation schemes occasionally occur in close proximity to each other, as in the *museo* locality (Figs. 4.2*a*, *g*, 4.3*l*; see also Mastache et al. 2002: Fig. 6.10). It is also the case that within any given locality, all structural remains, from earliest to latest, exhibit the same orientation, perhaps an indication that some policy of orientation was followed at a local (neighborhood) level. It may simply reflect convenience on the part of individual builders or rebuilders, although this seems unlikely to account for the persistence of a common orientation scheme through time in all localities excavated to date. Given the preceding, it would appear that the orientation of a particular structure indicates not when the structure itself was built, but rather *when the locality was settled*. This would explain why extensive surface traces of all three schemes, rather than only the latest of the three, are visible today.

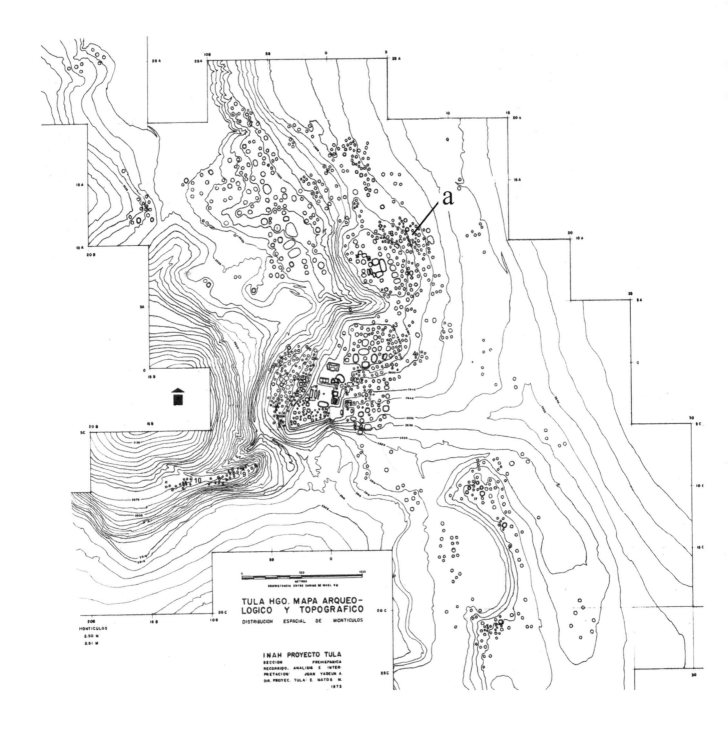

Figure 4.9. Topographic map of the site of Tula showing the distribution of mounds greater than 1 m in height, and the location of the Canal locality (*a*). Source: Yadeun 1975.

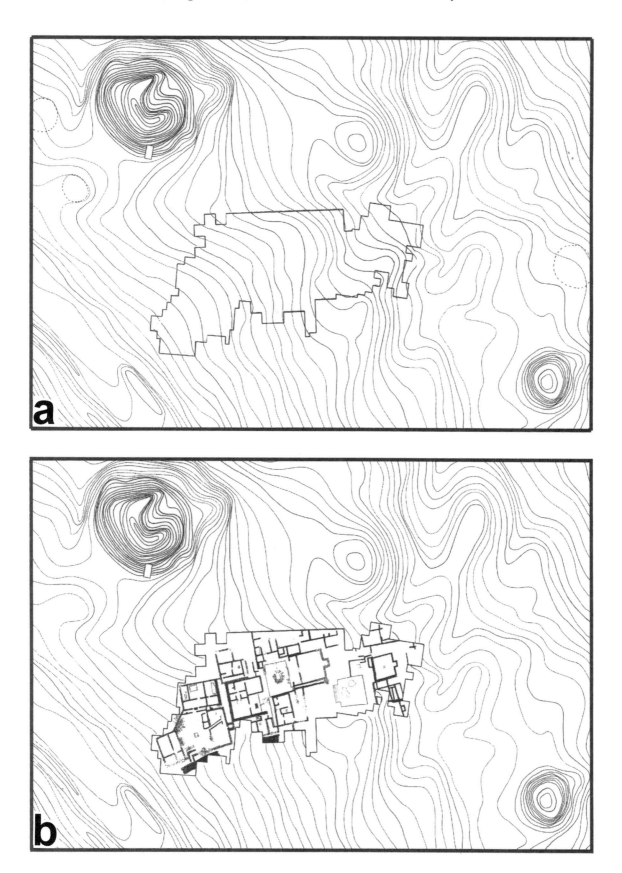

Figure 4.10. Topographic map of the greater Canal locality. *a*, before excavation; *b*, after excavation. Contour interval = 20 cm.

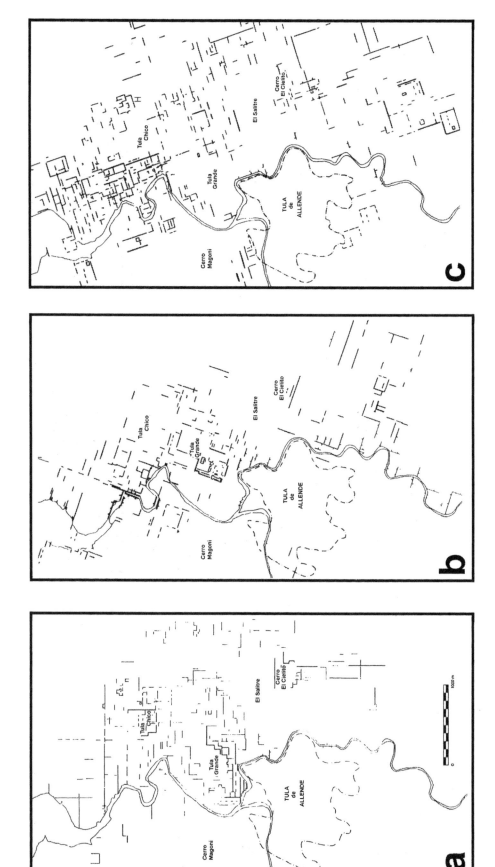

Figure 4.11. Spatial distribution of linear surface features visible on aerial photographs corresponding to three spatial orientation schemes of architectural remains seen at Tula. *a,* north-south; *b,* ca. 17 degrees east of north; *c,* ca. 18 degrees west of north.

Conclusions

Certainly one of the most salient conclusions that can be drawn from the present study is that Tula's urban households were generally multifamily affairs housed in two distinct forms of compound residence: house compounds and apartment compounds. The predominance of compound residences at Tula agrees with evidence from other sites that single-family residences were not a common form of housing in Mesoamerican cities. To some extent, the paucity of single-family residences may simply reflect a bias towards excavating visible surface mounds, which are more likely to represent larger entities than single residences. On the other hand, at sites such as Teotihuacan and Xochicalco where surface survey conducted under near ideal surface conditions permitted the identification of large numbers of residential structures, the vast majority of remains clearly comprised larger entities than single residences. Archival data suggest a similar pattern for Aztec Tenochtitlan, where multifamily residences appear to have been the most common form of residence inside the city (Calnek 2003). The predominance of compound residence in Mesoamerican cities probably reflects their greater efficiency with respect to the use of limited urban space as well as the primary role played by kinship in structuring relationships and activities in these societies.

A particularly salient characteristic noted in several localities is the tendency for both house compounds and apartment compounds to occur in clusters. Such "clusters of clusters" are believed to comprise local neighborhoods where the bulk of the residents' interaction and daily activities probably took place. The Canal locality provides a particularly detailed perspective on the organization of domestic and other activities at both the household and local neighborhood levels, and provides evidence to suggest that clustered compounds may have largely been the product of growth over time. In this way the organization of the residential sector into clusters of kin-based households could easily have been the result of actions taken at the local level rather than some overall, high-level policy; indeed, I believe that this is largely a "bottom up" process that may indicate a looser or less centralized system of urban governance than may have existed at other cities. In this regard it is interesting to note that similar clusters of apartment compounds occur at Teotihuacan but are almost entirely restricted to compounds in the city's periphery, while the city core exhibits a uniform, almost gridlike, arrangement of apartment compounds.

On the other hand, Mastache and Crespo's (1982) evidence of widespread aligned surface features certainly implies the existence of citywide planning, and I hope that future investigation will shed additional light on both the veracity and the nature of these intriguing surface features. Certainly the existence of paved thoroughfares in two different localities suggests that some of these features could represent roadways. Above all, the existence of these surface features and their interpretation as diachronic phenomena provide one explanation for the existence of three different orientation schemes among the extant structural remains at Tula, one that involves conscious planning rather than random events.

The existence of two forms of compound residence at Tula is curious since there seems to be little distinction between the two in terms of their occurrence: both forms are found throughout the city, sometimes in close proximity to one another, and both exhibit a tendency to occur in clusters. One strikingly consistent difference is that all of the structural complexes identified as house compounds in Figure 4.2 exhibit the west of north orientation, while none of the complexes identified as apartment compounds do (that is, four exhibit the north-south scheme and one the east of north scheme). Assuming that most of these remains were correctly identified as to type, the correlation between compound type and spatial orientation is particularly important if, as suggested by Mastache and Crespo, each orientation is temporally specific. This would suggest that apartment compounds were the predominant form of housing in the city prior to its rapid growth during the Tollan phase, when the predominant form of housing shifted to house compounds. One possible explanation for such a shift is a citywide change in housing from the top down, comparable to what appears to have occurred at Teotihuacan during the Tlamimilolpa phase. At Tula, however, there is no evidence of citywide demolition of preexisting housing comparable to what Millon (1973:56) characterized as "urban renewal" at Teotihuacan, which would have obliterated evidence of earlier orientations rather than leaving the multiple orientations seen at the site today (Fig. 4.11). Hence, the shift from apartment to house compounds may have been piecemeal, the result of decisions made at the local level.

The later possibility is particularly interesting given indications, noted in the preceding section, of a heterogeneous internal structure suggestive of well-defined local neighborhoods. This in turn raises the question of the role of ethnicity in ancient Tula—more specifically, whether the heterogeneous aspects of its internal structure are indications of a multiethnic composition. To be sure, the view of Tula as a multiethnic city is a pervasive theme among the ethnohistorical sources, and the settlement history of the Tula region raises the intriguing possibility of a multiethnic founding population (Mastache et al. 2003:61–76; Healan and Cobean, in press).[6]

Additional archaeological evidence for possible ethnic diversity among Tula's neighborhoods is seen in the distribution of certain artifacts recovered by the Missouri project survey. A case in point is Mazapa Red on Brown,[7] a pottery type that is rare throughout all except the southeastern extreme of the site; no other pottery type exhibits this distribution. Cobean has previously noted that Mazapa pottery is most common in Terminal Classic and Early Postclassic sites in the Basin of Mexico, particularly the Teotihuacan Valley where it was first identified,[8] and suggested that "it is at least possible that the sections of Tula's urban zone with the highest amounts of Mazapa Red on Brown were inhabited by a different social or ethnic group from the rest of the urban zone" (1978:391).

It is interesting to note that this (southeastern) portion of the site also contains high surface concentrations of obsidian core/blade debitage, where excavation partially exposed a core/blade workshop in the Tultengo locality (Fig. 4.2*d*). Indeed, the workshop ceramic assemblage contained unusually large amounts of Mazapa ceramics that, citing Cobean's observations, led Healan et al. (1983:144) to suggest that the locality may have been settled by immigrants from the Basin. Stratigraphic data revealed that at the time the workshop was initially settled during the Early Tollan phase, the locality was barren terrain whose marginal character and location outside the early Tollan phase city may have made it a suitable place for working obsidian. If indeed this locality was initially settled by immigrant obsidian workers, it should be noted that during the late Tollan phase, the locality was incorporated into the growing city and the Mazapa pottery of the workshop ceramic assemblage was gradually replaced by more common Tollan phase types, suggesting the incorporation of these peoples into Tula's cultural mainstream.

Aside from obsidian working, there is other evidence for craft production at specific localities within the ancient city, including ceramic figurines (Healan and Stoutamire 1989:213) and ceramic vessels (Hernández et al. 1999). At the present time, however, relative little is known about these localities, and it must not be assumed a priori that these were associated with distinct ethnic entities. Indeed, one must be wary in general of assuming that heterogeneity in settlement-wide archaeological assemblages represents ethnic diversity rather than other factors, such as status.

Finally, it should be noted that despite all the evidence for dense, urban settlement at Tula based on excavation, there is in fact relatively little corroborating surface evidence. This is forcefully illustrated by the paucity of discernible topographic evidence for the extensive subsurface remains excavated in the Canal locality (Fig. 4.10). Tula was, above all, an "adobe city," and the lack of association between surface and subsurface features is undoubtedly a product of the inherently unstable nature of mud and stone construction that inspired Covarrubias' often-cited observation that Toltec architecture "was meant to impress but not to last" (1957:273). Whatever the reason, however, it is wrong to perpetuate the characterization of Tula as a modest settlement in light of the considerable body of evidence to the contrary.

Endnotes

1. For example, Calnek (2003:157–61) notes that each of the four named quarters of Tenochtitlan had a ruler, although the place of these particular rulers in the overall governance of the city is unclear, nor is it clear what kinds of activities took place at the level of the individual quarters.

2. It should be noted, however, that other so-called "palaces" at Tula Grande, including the well-known *Palacio Quemado* complex, are more likely public buildings than residences, as others (e.g., Kristan-Graham 1993) have also suggested.

3. Beneath rubble was a replica of a human head, carved from limestone, which had been placed on the courtyard floor at the southwest corner of the altar (Fig. 4.6). The head measured about 16 cm in width and its neck had been broken off a larger piece of sculpture, which was not encountered in excavation; its placement by the altar may have been part of the activity associated with its destruction. The facial features and hair treatment are quite similar to "standard bearer" statues at the circular pyramid in the nearby El Corral locality excavated by Acosta (1974: Fig. 13).

4. Another possibility is that House IV, and perhaps House IX as well, housed servants who were attached to the household, although this seems less likely.

5. Yadeun distinguished three classes of mounds by height: (1) less than 1 m, (2) 1 to 2.5 m, and (3) greater than 2.5 m. As noted, mounds less than 1 m in height were not included on the map, and the latter two classes of mounds are delineated by light versus bold outlines that cannot be reliably distinguished given the map's small size.

6. Regional survey revealed the existence of two distinct settlement systems in the Tula region during the Classic period. The first of these appears to have been a wholesale colonization of the region by Teotihuacan, which included a regional center with a layout and internal structure like that of Teotihuacan (Díaz 1980). The second of these consisted of a number of hilltop settlements in the periphery of the region that appear to overlap in time with the Teotihuacan settlements but were associated with Coyotlatelco ceramics and exhibited architectural and other ties to northern and western Mexico. The subsequent Epiclassic period saw the abandonment of both of these settlement systems and the appearance of Tula's initial settlement, whose inhabitants may have derived entirely or in part upon these previous settlements.

7. Ironically, Mazapa was once thought to be a common and diagnostic pottery type of Tula during its apogee, prior to Cobean's (1990) comprehensive study of ceramics that demonstrated this was not the case.

8. Mazapa ceramics were quite common in recent excavations in the tunnels behind the Pyramid of the Sun at Teotihuacan, including assemblages containing Mazapa ceramics along with Blanco Levantado and other ceramics associated with Tula's Early Postclassic Tollan phase (Manzanilla, pers. comm.).

References

Acosta, Jorge R.
1956   Interpretación de algunos datos obtenidos en Tula relativos a la 1957 época tolteca. *Revista Mexicana de Estudios Antropológicos* 14:75–110.
1974   La pirámide de El Corral de Tula. In *Proyecto Tula, Primera Parte*, edited by E. Matos, pp. 27–56. Colección Científica no. 15. Instituto Nacional de Antropología e Historia, Mexico, D.F.

Calnek, Edward
2003   Tenochtitlan-Tlatelolco: The natural history of a city. In *Urbanism in Mesoamerica*, edited by W.T. Sanders, A.G. Mastache, and R.H. Cobean, pp. 149–203. Instituto Nacional de Antropología e Historia, Mexico City; Pennylvania State University, University Park.

Charnay, Desiré
1887   *Ancient Cities of the New World*. Harper and Brothers, New York.

Cobean, Robert
1978   *The Pre-Aztec Ceramics of Tula, Hidalgo, Mexico*. PhD dissertation, Department of Anthropology, Harvard University.
1990   *La Cerámica de Tula, Hidalgo*. Serie Arqueología, no. 215. Instituto Nacional de Antropología e Historia, México.

Covarrubias, Miguel
1957 *Indian Art of Mexico and Central America*. Knopf, New York.

Cook, Sherburne F.
1949 *The Historical Demography and Ecology of the Teotlalpan*. Ibero-Americana 33. University of California Press, Berkeley.

Díaz, Clara
1980 *Chingú: Un sitio clásico del área de Tula, Hidalgo*. Colección Científica no. 90. Instituto Nacional de Antropología e Historia, México, D.F.

Diehl, Richard A.
1989 Previous investigations at Tula. In *Tula of the Toltecs: Excavations and Survey*, edited by D.M. Healan, pp. 13–29. University of Iowa Press, Iowa City.

Diehl, Richard, R. Lomas, and J. Wynn
1974 Toltec trade with Central America: New light and evidence. *Archaeology* 27:182–87.

Evans, Susan (editor)
1988 *Excavations at Cihuatecpan, An Aztec Village in the Teotihuacan Valley*. Publications in Anthropology no. 36. Vanderbilt University, Nashville.

Fernández Dávila, Enrique
1994 La producción de artefactos líticos en Tula, Hidalgo. In *Simposium Sobre Arqueología en el Estado de Hidalgo*, edited by E. Fernández, pp. 47–79. Colección Científica no. 282. Instituto Nacional de Antropología e Historia, México, D.F.

Flannery, Kent V., and Joyce Marcus
1994 *Early Formative Pottery of the Valley of Oaxaca, Mexico*. Memoirs, no. 27. Museum of Anthropology, University of Michigan, Ann Arbor.

Gómez Serafín, Susana, F. Sansores, and E. Fernández Dávila
1994 *Enterramientos humanos de la época prehispánica en Tula, Hidalgo*. Colección Científica no. 276. Instituto Nacional de Antropología e Historia, México, D.F.

Healan, Dan M.
1977 Architectural implications of daily life in ancient Tollan, Hidalgo, Mexico. *World Archaeology* 9:140–56.

Healan, Dan M. (editor)
1989 *Tula of the Toltecs: Excavations and Survey*. University of Iowa Press, Iowa City.

Healan, Dan M., and R.H. Cobean
in press La Interacción Cultural entre el Centro y el Occidente de México Vista desde la Región de Tula. In *Las Sociedades Complejas del Occidente de México en el Mundo Mesoamericano*, edited by E. Williams, L. López Mestas, and R. Esparza. El Colegio de Michoacán, Zamora.

Healan, Dan M., and J. Stoutamire
1989 Surface survey of the Tula urban zone. In *Tula of the Toltecs: Excavations and Survey*, edited by Dan M. Healan, pp. 203–36. University of Iowa Press, Iowa City.

Healan, Dan M., J. Kerley, and G.J. Bey III
1983 Excavation and preliminary analysis of an obsidian workshop at Tula, Hidalgo, Mexico. *Journal of Field Archaeology* 10:127–45.

Hernández, Carlos, R.H. Cobean, A.G. Mastache, and M.E. Suárez
1999 Un taller de alfareros en la antigua ciudad de Tula. *Arqueología* 22:69–88, INAH, México, D.F.

Hirth, Kenneth G.
1993 The household as an analytical unit: Problems in method and theory. In *Prehispanic Domestic Units in Western Mesoamerica*, edited by R. Santley and K. Hirth, pp. 21–36. CRC Press, Boca Raton, Florida.

Kristan-Graham, Cynthia
1993 The business of narrative at Tula: An analysis of the vestibule frieze, trade, and ritual. *Latin American Antiquity* 4:3–21.

Marcus, Joyce
1978 Archaeology and religion: A comparison of the Zapotec and Maya. *World Archaeology* 10:172–91.
1998 *Women's Ritual in Formative Oaxaca*. Memoirs, no. 33. Museum of Anthropology, University of Michigan, Ann Arbor.

Marquina, Ignacio
1964 *Arquitectura prehispánica*. Instituto Nacional de Antropología e Historia, México, D.F.

Mastache, Alba Guadalupe, and Ana María Crespo
1974 La ocupación preshispánica en el área de Tula, Hgo. In *Proyecto Tula, Primera Parte*, edited by E. Matos, pp. 71–103. Colección Científica no. 15. Instituto Nacional de Antropología e Historia, México, D.F.
1982 Análisis sobre la traza general de Tula, Hgo. In *Estudios sobre la Antigua Ciudad de Tula*, pp. 11–38. Colección Científica no. 121. Instituto Nacional de Antropología e Historia, México, D.F.

Mastache, Alba Guadalupe, Robert H. Cobean, and Dan M. Healan
2002 *Ancient Tollan: Tula and the Toltec Heartland*. University Press of Colorado, Boulder.
2006 Four Hundred Years of Cultural Continuity in Epiclassic and Early Postclassic Tula. Paper presented in the Dumbarton Oaks Conference on the Art of Urbanism, México, D.F., October 2006.

Matos Moctezuma, Eduardo (editor)
1974 *Proyecto Tula, Primera Parte*. Colección Científica no. 15. Instituto Nacional de Antropología e Historia, Mexico, D.F.
1976 *Proyecto Tula, Segunda Parte*. Colección Científica no. 33. Instituto Nacional de Antropología e Historia, Mexico, D.F.

Millon, René
1973 *Urbanism at Teotihuacan*, Vol. 1. University of Texas Press, Austin.

Paredes Gudiño, Blanca
1992 *Unidades Habitacionales en Tula, Hgo*. Serie Arqueología, no. 210. Instituto Nacional de Antropología e Historia, México, D.F.

Peña, Agustín, and María Carmen Rodríguez
1976   Excavaciones en Dainí, Tula, Hgo. In *Proyecto Tula, Segunda Parte*, edited by E. Matos, pp. 85–90. Colección Científica no. 33. Instituto Nacional de Antropología e Historia, México, D.F.

Yadeun Angulo, Juan
1975   *El estado y la ciudad: el caso de Tula, Hgo.* Colección Científica no. 25. Instituto Nacional de Antropología e Historia, México, D.F.

5

Tikal: Evidence for Ethnic Diversity in a Prehispanic Lowland Maya State Capital

Marshall Joseph Becker

Introduction

The role of Tikal, as the regional capital of an impressive lowland Maya state, has become more clearly defined since the decipherment of numerous texts relating to this city. Confirmation of the premier role of Tikal's kings also derives from texts recovered from nearby dependencies and from other state capitals throughout the region. Modern excavations at Tikal provide impressive sets of evidence for the complex social structure that existed during the Classic period, with the presence of a written language best reflecting this complexity. Discovery of a wide range of types of ritual and domestic structures as well as a large market area further document Tikal's role as a major Maya city (cf. Smith 2003:8–11). However, the physical arrangement of the approximately 2,500 structures of central Tikal (Carr and Hazard 1961) has long been recognized as distinct from that of obviously urban Teotihuacan. At Tikal, the dispersed 690 clusters of residential and civic buildings and the significance of differences in architectural patterning offer clues to ethnic diversity that has long been postulated for the site.

The meaning of variations among the distinct and predictable configurations of building arrangements (architectural grammars) used for residential groups of structures at Tikal has been considered for more than forty years. Both residential and non-residential group patterns, or "plaza plans," have been recognized at Tikal (Fig. 5.1), with most of these patterns also identified at other sites. Only four (Plaza Plan 2 through Plaza Plan 5) of the dozen plaza plans defined to date relate to residential architecture.[1] Each example of these four plans represents a single type of "house" (residential complex for a single extended family):

Plaza Plan 2. A residential group with a temple or shrine centered on the eastern margin of its main plaza (Fig. 5.2; Becker 1971a, 1972b, 1999, 2003a:258–62).

Plaza Plan 3. A residential group composed of rectangular structures neatly or "formally" arranged around the margins of a plaza, often with ancillary structures (Becker 2003a:262; Haviland, forthcoming).

Plaza Plan 4. A residential group similar in plan to Plaza Plan 3, but including a central courtyard shrine (see Fig. 5.3; Becker 2003a:262–64).

Plaza Plan 5. A residential group with an "informal" and apparently random clustering of residential structures around and near one or more small plazas (Haviland et al. 1985; Becker 2003a:264).

The several types of residential or civic groups, each sharing the same architectural pattern (plaza plan), reflect the social complexity expected within an urban society. Each house type that conforms to a single and specific architectural grammar

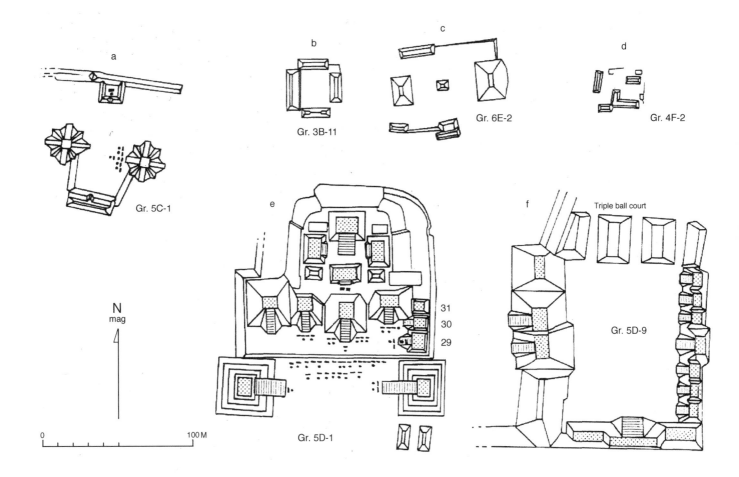

Figure 5.1. Six of the dozen plaza plans now identified at Tikal. *a*, Plaza Plan 1; *b*, Plaza Plan 3; *c*, Plaza Plan 4 (see also Fig. 5.3*B*); *d*, Plaza Plan 5; *e*, Plaza Plan 6; *f*, Plaza Plan 7. (See Fig. 5.2 for Plaza Plan 2.)

(plaza plan) reflects a form of non-verbal communication. The wide variety of these plans at Tikal provides evidence suggesting the presence of people representing ethnic groups not native to that city, or even to the Maya lowlands. Families living in houses with the same plaza plan may be inferred to share kinship relations, or to represent cultural traditions reflecting their ethnic origins. Ethnic variations within the state capital of Tikal may be best revealed by examining plaza plan data as well as the ritual behaviors found to be specific to one of these architectural patterns. These data also may indicate when specific ethnic groups arrived at Tikal, from whence they came, and how these populations multiplied or changed over time. Factors leading to major social and political shifts also may be detectable. In turn, the presence of ethnic differences at Tikal strongly indicates the multicultural variations characteristic of complex states and their sociopolitical dynamics.

At Tikal during the Classic period, the complexity of architecture (variations in building types, size, and so on) plus the number of monuments with texts and calendrical-astronomical data indicate this polity's central position as a major capital of a regional state. Tikal's domestic economy, involving a wide range of occupational or craft specializations, provides yet another indicator of social complexity. While we still know very little about Maya craft specialization in general (see Cowgill 2003a:40), at Tikal the presence of ceramic specialists, masons, "dentists," flint and obsidian knappers, stoneworkers, and other craft specialists can be demonstrated (Becker 1971a, 1973a, 1973b, 1999, 2003b). Inomata's (2001) inference that craft specialization is a form of elite production that may be a kind of "attached specialization" may apply to smaller sites, but at Tikal, production was in the hands of families of independent specialists living in widely distributed residential groups. The distribution of these residential groups at Tikal, and the important differences in their architectural patterns, provide a basic indication of diversity within this regional capital (see also Webster et al. 2007).

In recent decades, as the residential, ritual, or market functions have been recognized for each specific plaza plan, the potential for using these architectural patterns to reconstruct aspects of

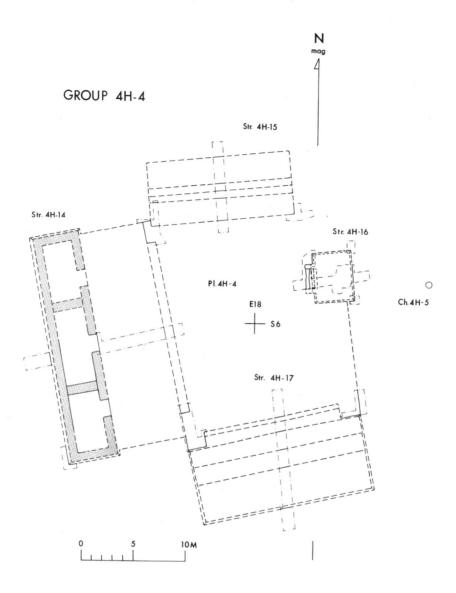

Figure 5.2. An example of Plaza Plan 2 at Tikal (Gr. 4H-IV). The overall size of this group, at 875 m², is slightly larger than that of Gr. 7F-XV (Fig. 5.3*D*), the smallest known example of Plaza Plan 4 at Tikal.

culture contact and culture history has improved. Continuing research relating to architectural groups at Tikal has added new examples of plaza plans, and has identified plaza plans of similar configurations at sites beyond Tikal. Presumably, architectural groups of the same form reflect similar functions, providing new opportunities to examine the spatial as well as temporal distribution of parallel examples. The distribution and dating of specific plaza plans among the ancient cities of the Maya lowlands, and far beyond, suggest that regional and possibly ethnic differences may be linked to each of these architectural grammars and their associated traits, revealed only through excavation.

Ethnic variations among the peoples resident at Tikal were suggested during early excavations, based solely on the presence of an unusual clustering of Plaza Plan 2 groups along the eastern margin of the "urban" center (Becker 1971a). These contiguous residential groups, each characterized by a "temple" on the eastern margin, were interpreted as representing an immigrant community whose distinct ritual activities were reflected in this specific architectural pattern (Becker 1999). The only other cluster of residential groups conforming to Plaza Plan 2 at Tikal is located along the southern margin of the site core, although a few isolated cases of Plaza Plan 2 are distributed throughout the site. Since most of the Plaza Plan 2 groups at Tikal are found in two clusters, they might be barrios, or possibly represent enclaves of outsiders (Becker 2003b). In fact, only 15% of all architectural groups in and around Tikal conform to Plaza Plan 2, while at Caracol, as many as 80% of the residential groups conform to Plaza Plan 2 (Chase and Chase 2004:139).

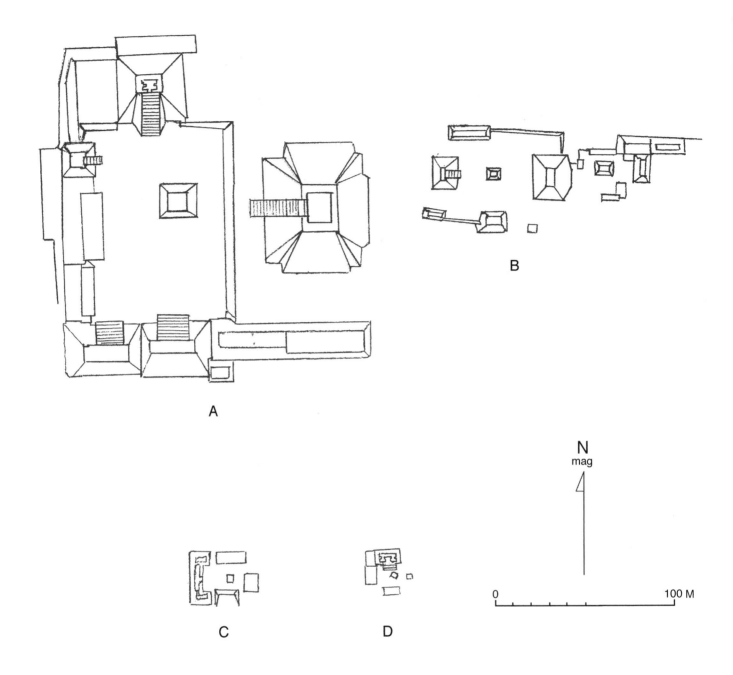

Figure 5.3. Five examples of Plaza Plan 4 at Tikal, all at the same scale to indicate variations in house size (from Becker 2005:86, Fig. 1). *A*, Gr. 5C-III; *B*, Groups 6E-II and 6E-III; *C*, Gr. 6F-I; *D*, Gr. 7F-XV.

Plaza Plan 4 at Tikal

The study of other residential plaza plans may enable us to reconstruct processes of culture change through time and space in this part of the Maya realm and to understand aspects of the written histories now available. A focus on Plaza Plan 4 at Tikal (Fig. 5.3), and its diagnostic traits, provides indications of critical contact among the Maya and with cities to the north. Note that all the known Plaza Plan 4 groups at Tikal are located along the southern tier of the site center, an area in which Laporte identified an unusual "buried" group of structures. This enormous cluster of buildings, Tikal Gr. 6C-XVI, and the unique "burial" of this entire area under deep fill merited considerable attention by the Proyecto Nacional Tikal (PNT). These ninety structures are arranged around five contiguous patios (Laporte 2003a:202–14; for plans see Laporte 2003b:295–300, Fig. 10.4). Some artifacts recovered from within this group were made in Teotihuacan (Iglesias 2003:194), but whether they were trade items or "brought" as personal goods is not known. The implication is that this entire locale, later buried in a fashion unknown elsewhere at Tikal, represented an effort to bury the memory of a residential enclave that served people who came from Mexico. The peculiar absence of burials associated with Gr. 6C-XVI (see Haviland 2003b) prevents any application of modern skeletal analyses that might answer important questions regarding biological origins (cf. Price et al. 2000; Wright 2005; also Wright et al. 2002).

The presence in the southeastern corner of Tikal's Great Plaza of a small structure (Str. 6E-144) with *talud-tablero* architecture had been believed to reflect influence from Teotihuacan (see also Str. 5C-53, Coe 1965:382) or indicate that some residents of Tikal were Teotihuacanos (see also Cowgill 2003b). Epigraphic evidence suggests that the child of a Teotihuacan ruler had been installed as the ruler of Tikal in AD 379 (Martin and Grube 2000; Stuart 2000). Other architectural evidence at Tikal that appears to indicate influence from central Mexico is a series of residential groups scattered throughout the southern portion of the site. This small number of residential groups each consists of rectangular structures arranged around one or more courtyards, similar to Plaza Plan 3, but characterized by a low, square platform in the principal plaza. These were termed Tikal "Plaza Plan 4" and associated with Mexican influences (Becker 1984, also 1991a; Manzanilla and Ortiz 1990).

At Tikal, the small size of the centrally located Plaza Plan 4 platforms (relative to the principal surrounding structures) now identified within residential groups (Fig. 5.3) suggests their use as altars or shrines (see also Chase 1985:116). These low platforms have been identified as "central courtyard shrines." Plaza Plan 4 groups were among the first structure arrangements or plaza plans identified at Tikal when it was proposed that this specific plan could be used to examine influences from the central Mexican highlands on the Maya lowlands (Becker 1971a; see Fig. 5.1). Plunket and Uruñuela (2002:31) were the first to explore at length the history of studies relating to the distribution of central courtyard shrines, which they suggest are relatively "common

features of Mesoamerican residential architecture." They trace the first published observations on central courtyard shrines to the work of Séjourné (1966: Fig. 1) and Sanders (1966:137–38), while noting five other scholars who, between 1979 and 2000, made at least passing reference to this subject. In the identification of residential plaza plans, focus tends to be on the forms of the structures surrounding the plaza, or enclosing the principal courtyard of the group. Plaza Plan 4, however, is defined by the presence of a central courtyard shrine situated in the center of the plaza. As Kidder (2004:514) suggests, "plazas are not just simply empty spaces that developed because architecture enclosed an open area; they must be understood as the central design elements of community planning and intra-site spatial organization." Each of the Plaza Plan 4 groups at Tikal includes rectangular structures in an orderly pattern, but never includes the "temple" (or "shrine") on the east that is characteristic of Plaza Plan 2.

Most of the Plaza Plan 4 groups now identified at Tikal are relatively large, both in the number of structures included as well as the area covered by each (see Table 5.1). Possibly we recognize the diagnostic platforms more easily in large groups because the central courtyard shrines, like all the other structures in large groups, are easily visible during mapping (cf. Becker 2004a, 2004b). If some small groups now identified as "Plaza Plan 3" have undetected platforms at the center of their plazas, such small structures might be invisible except through careful excavation (cf. Group 7F-XV). Only 8 of the approximately 690 architectural clusters on the map of central Tikal (Carr and Hazard 1961) have been identified as Plaza Plan 4 groups (Becker 1982). Plaza Plan 4 groups are notably absent from the mapped transects extending out beyond central Tikal and at Uaxactun (Puleston 1983: Figs. 3d, 3l), suggesting that Plaza Plan 4 is an urban phenomenon. The possibility that the Tikal Plaza Plan 4 groups are all Terminal Classic in date (ca. AD 825–950; see Valdés and Fahsen 2004) need not indicate that these residential groups were initiated during that period. All of the structures forming each of the known Plaza Plan 4 groups at Tikal may have begun as Plaza Plan 3 groups at an earlier date, perhaps being "cognitively" altered by the addition of a central courtyard shrine after AD 800.

At Tikal, these central courtyard shrines include one or more cached skulls (see Table 5.1). Rodríguez (1997) associates skull caches with Early Classic Teotihuacan, where Manzanilla indicates that central altars are the rule, and commonly are *also* associated with a temple on the east (Manzanilla 2002). The emergence of Plaza Plan 4 groups at Tikal and elsewhere in the Maya lowlands appears to have been strongly influenced by cultural rules from Teotihuacan, perhaps being modified in these Maya contexts. The origins of altars placed in the center of patios (plazas) at Tikal and elsewhere in the Maya lowlands may be sought in the Valley of Mexico.

In the Mexican highlands, there is evidence for central courtyard shrines at much earlier dates than at Tikal. The village of Tetimpa, Puebla, situated just northeast of Popocatépetl

Table 5.1. Identified Plaza Plan 4 groups at Tikal (N = 8).

Group	Structure Number	Number of Structures	Area (m²)	Skull Present
5C-III	5C-48/54, 6C-23/25	10	38,000	+
6C-XVI-Sub	6C-Sub-23, 26-27, etc.	5 or more[a]	3,500 (est.)	?
6D-I	6D-50/66	17	10,625	+
6D-X	6D-33/37	5	2,000	+
6E-II	6E-143/146, 133/135	7	6,300	?
6E-III	6E-147/156	10	2,700	+
6F-I	6F-47/51	5	1,400	+
7F-XV[b]	7F-45/49	5	750	+

[a]This is a deeply buried group of structures, and only partially excavated.
[b]Originally identified as a Plaza Plan 2 (see Becker 1982:129).

in the central Mexican highlands, has been sealed in volcanic ash since about AD 100. Tetimpa provides Preclassic examples of a pattern not yet well known from an early date in the Maya lowlands. Plunket and Uruñuela (1998a:81–83, Figs. 4, 5, also 1998b) identify a number of "central courtyard shrines" at Tetimpa, but these are not platform-like such as those associated with Tikal Plaza Plan 4 residential groups. Uruñuela and Plunket (2002:21) discuss data from twenty-one domestic compounds of the Late Tetimpa period (50 BC–AD 100). Within these domestic compounds, at the center of the courtyard, "there is often a small shrine" (central courtyard shrine), six of which have been identified (Uruñuela and Plunket 2002:21, 33–34). Uruñuela and Plunket (2002:21) state that "even in those exceptional cases that lack a formal shrine, this center is marked with a stone. . . . " Uruñuela and Plunket (2002:26) specifically note that they have not yet identified burials associated with central courtyard shrines from the Late Tetimpa period. They did find a skull within one of the central courtyard shrines that may provide important biological links to populations of a later date in the Maya lowlands, an area they have not reviewed. What, if anything, is covered by or contained within any central courtyard shrine at Tetimpa (and elsewhere) may be an essential archaeologically recoverable feature by which ethnic group identity may be traced. Note should be made of Manzanilla's (2002) observation that "[t]he central altars of ritual courtyards often house important burials that include offerings of jadeite, slate, marine shells, miniature vases, and *floreros*, among other items (Sánchez 1989:373–75)."[2] The "central altars" that appear in ritual groups may be unrelated to those central courtyard shrines found at Tikal and elsewhere. Jones (1996) uses the term "central courtyard shrine" for platforms associated with ballcourts, platforms that have no

demonstrated relationship to those central courtyard shrines in residential groups.

Teotihuacanos

In the city of Teotihuacan, every aspect of urban development is impressively evident, on a scale far beyond the level achieved anywhere in the Maya lowlands. Most evident in Teotihuacan's urban landscape is the wide array of self-contained residential compounds, some of which include large temples while others have small examples or no evident temples. Variations in temple size, as well as their presence or absence, reflect the vast cultural differences present within this city. Residential groups at Teotihuacan are organized more like those at ancient Pompeii than the residential groups at Tikal. Manzanilla (2004:128) deftly summarizes the complexity and variations among the structures at Teotihuacan, and gives a history of excavations at that site.

Manzanilla indicates that several features associated with specific apartment compounds at Teotihuacan merit detailed study, including a search for evidence of funerary cults, abandonment rites, and domestic rituals conducted in courtyards. She points out that several compounds at Teotihuacan "may involve a central altar, a small temple or sanctuary, and the adjacent rooms" (Manzanilla 1993, also 2002:43). Manzanilla (2004:51, Fig. 5.14; following Linné 1934) also points out a possible platform in the center of the apartment compound of Xolalpan. For example, the Oztoyahualco 15B:N6W3 apartment compound courtyard C41, occupied by a relatively poor family, is "the only one with a central altar in its earliest construction level" (Manzanilla 2002:46, 2004:136). More importantly, other courtyards with evidence for rituals had portable temple models serving in lieu of altars, rather than constructed platforms (Manzanilla 1996). A more extensive and detailed review of these data may provide clues regarding the evolution of this central altar pattern at Teotihuacan. These groups may be antecedents, and direct ancestors, of the Plaza Plan 4 groups of later date seen at Tikal and possibly elsewhere in the Maya lowlands.

Manzanilla (2004: Table 5.1) lists ten of the "apartment compounds" at Teotihuacan and some associated features. The presence of a courtyard-centered altar within specific groups at Teotihuacan may reflect a pattern that appears at an even earlier date among the Zapotec, one that was exported to Teotihuacan. At Teotihuacan at least two barrios, *Comerciantes* and Tlailotlacan, include "foreign" architecture, mortuary patterns, and artifacts, suggesting that these residences may represent ethnic or cultural groups from outside the city. Biological data are discussed below. Of approximately fifteen courtyard groups at Tlailotlacan, also called the "Oaxaca Barrio" (also see Manzanilla 2004:125, Fig. 5.1), five have been excavated and found to reflect "standard Teotihuacan apartment compounds, though with Zapotec tombs in them" (Spence 2002:55). Spence (2002:56, also 65–67) describes the courtyard altar within TL6 and its long history. The earliest of these courtyard altars dates from the Early Tlamimilolpa period, approximately AD 300, and includes a seated subadult burial within it. While subadult burials elsewhere have been associated with sacrifice, high mortality rates in this age group should be noted. Spence (2002:57) indicates that the construction covering the early TL6 altar was preceded by a cut into a tomb located within the early altar to deposit objects near the skull of that burial. This behavior resembles activities related to some Plaza Plan 2 constructions at Tikal. At Tikal, when a non-Plaza Plan 2 group was converted to a Plaza Plan 2 group, the construction of a "temple on the east" was initiated by the penetration of any previous structure and into the bedrock for a burial. The Plaza Plan 2 structure was built over the preexisting structure. Each succeeding construction required a penetration of the previous structure by a burial before new construction began.[3]

Spence provides important information from Tlailotlacan, at the western edge of Teotihuacan. At Tlailotlacan, Spence (2002:59, Fig. 6.3) identifies an altar, covering a burial, in the center of the compound. That altar is surrounded by six ritual deposits and the burial of a subadult. He suggests Tlailotlacan was settled originally around AD 200 by Zapotec immigrants from the Valley of Oaxaca and that these people retained their ethnic identity until the city was abandoned some 450 years later! Despite centuries of culture change, these Zapotec people were still identifiable in the archaeological record (cf. Rattray 1987). Spence (2002:53) suggests that Zapotec residents at Teotihuacan "accepted" the apartment compound as a residential form, but developed "larger courtyards (usually with central altars)." Comparisons with possible altars at the Zapotec capital of Monte Albán or central altars at Tetimpa may reveal, as Manzanilla suggests, that this is a general central Mexican phenomenon. Thus, the Tikal versions of the central courtyard shrine may de-

rive from the north, but Plaza Plan 4 may not have originated at Teotihuacan (see review by Manzanilla 2002; also Winter 2002). Spence (2002) offers evidence that "patio altars" were a Zapotec introduction to Teotihuacan, and later were directly or indirectly exported to Tikal during the middle to late Late Classic period.

An important observation is that careful excavation of the centers of courtyards at Teotihuacan, Monte Albán, and other sites in Mexico is far more common than at lowland Maya sites (e.g., Manzanilla and Barba 1990:44, Fig. 2). The known percentage of residential groups at Teotihuacan with patio altars, or a shrine-stone equivalent, remains unknown. On the other hand, excavations in residential areas at Tikal have rarely extended beyond the structures surrounding the plazas, and rarely into the plazas themselves. Test excavations at Tikal may find that Plaza Plan 4 groups began as Plaza Plan 3 (regular grouping of residential structures around a plaza) and were "converted" to Plaza Plan 4 by the addition of a platform, or shrine-with-skull(s), in the center of the open space. Several conversions of residential plaza plan types at Tikal are well documented (Becker 1999:144–45, 153, Table 114; e.g., Str. 6C-41 began as Plaza Plan 3, see Fig. 105).

The Plaza Plan 4 architectural format at Tikal may represent an ideological shift made by the residents of some Plaza Plan 3 groups through the addition of a central courtyard shrine. Unlike Teotihuacan, at Tikal and elsewhere in the Maya realm the traits diagnostic of Plaza Plan 2 (temple on the east, containing axial burials) (Fig. 5.2) and Plaza Plan 4 do not overlap, with two possible exceptions. The map of Chunchucmil (Dahlin and Mazeau 2001) reveals extremely orderly household and other groups, many of which conform to Plaza Plan 2. However, many of the apparent "Plaza Plan 2" groups at Chunchucmil also appear to have small platforms in the centers of their plazas, platforms of the type that are diagnostic of Plaza Plan 4 at Tikal. At Monte Albán, Oaxaca, Joyce Marcus (1999:69) describes "adoratories" (platforms) located in the center of the *Patio Hundido* on the North Platform, dated to AD 150–500. These large platforms, measuring up to 15 m on a side, are not single foci for a residential group, but may have some relationship to those platforms diagnostic of Plaza Plan 4 at Tikal. Marcus also notes "a rectangular oratory," measuring about 3 × 4 m, within Building S on the Main Plaza at Monte Albán. How, or if, these various Early Classic examples relate to Tikal Plaza Plan 4 remains unknown (see also Deal 1988 for family altars associated with residences in Chiapas).

The general absence of Plaza Plan 4 at Maya sites such as Cobá, Palenque, Piedras Negras, Yaxhá, and Copán suggests that those at Tikal are specific to people from Teothuacan playing a role at Tikal *because* it was a major capital. The households of Cobá and Teotihuacan have been discussed by Manzanilla and Barba (1990). The site map (Folan et al. 1983), however, does not reveal obvious regularities or patterns. The limited distribution of Plaza Plan 4 elsewhere in the Maya realm may be indicative of a cultural pattern as yet not known, but its presence at Tikal strongly suggests an important relationship with Teotihuacan.

Skulls Deposited in Central Courtyard Shrines: Burials, Caches, or Problematical Deposits?

Only recently have human remains become the focus of major research projects in Central America (e.g., Tiesler-Blos and Cucina 2003). Surveys of burials recovered from excavations in the Maya area began with Ricketson's (1925) overview, which noted an incredible array of mortuary forms, even within a single Maya site. The range of variation throughout Mesoamerica is overwhelming. The only regularity appears to be an absence of communal cemetery areas anywhere in the Maya realm. The many studies of mortuary practices (Ruz 1965, updated in 1968; Welsh 1988; see also Carr 1995) point out many of the difficulties faced by Mayanists (cf. Duncan 2005a:32–39, 84). These include determining what constitutes a "normal burial" (cf. Becker 1991b, 1992; Duncan 2005a:58, also 2005b). Adding to this complexity are the number of cases in which skulls are found to have been altered, removed, and/or relocated (Becker 2008).

Archaeological evidence for human decapitation or skull removal in ancient Mesoamerica (see Ricketson 1925; Blom 1954; Moser 1973; Boone 1984; cf. Becker 1986b) generally lacked detailed data until recently (Duncan 1999; see also Sugiyama and López 2007). Of particular interest in the study of Plaza Plan 4, and in particular the human skulls found within central courtyard shrines, is the work of Vera Tiesler-Blos (2002, 2003; also Duncan 2007). These studies provide important evidence for decapitation, as distinct from post-decomposition removal of a skull for ritual purposes. The considerable diversity of body parts selected to be used in caches or other "ritual" deposits throughout the Maya lowlands suggests that ethnic, as well as economic, differences may be identifiable in this aspect of the archaeological record (see also Iglesias 2003). To determine origins for skulls that are found in unusual contexts, DNA may be used more effectively than a series of iconographic depictions of "foreigners" (Marcus 2003:339–41; see also Martin 2003). Burials, or even pieces of people, aid in determining if someone interred at the site came from afar. If mortuary patterns within a site differ, do they correlate with different architectural patterns? Can we predict which mortuary pattern will be associated with a specific architectural grammar, as in plaza plan research, or do burial customs within a site vary only through time?

Spence (2002:59–60) examined data relating to crania and other buried human parts from various contexts in Tlailotlacan at Teotihuacan and urges caution regarding conclusions of human sacrifice (cf. Ricketson and Ricketson 1937:55–58, 145, Plate 48). Manzanilla observed that skulls separated from the skeleton, and often located within a vessel, are more common than generally recognized. Manzanilla (2006) reports examples of such skulls from excavations at Teopancazcoa and Teotihuacan, and also notes many from Veracruz sites (cf. Mock 1998:113–14; also Mock 1994; Massey and Steele 1997; Massey 1994).

At Tikal, excavations in six of the eight identified central courtyard shrines diagnostic of Plaza Plan 4 have found human skulls within cache vessels; two remain to be tested (Laporte, pers. comm., 2007). These finds were predicted only from an evaluation of maps of Tikal. These detached skulls, sometimes termed "trophy heads," serve as diagnostic artifacts within these central courtyard shrines, providing an archaeologically recognizable trait diagnostic of Plaza Plan 4 at Tikal. Thus, we have the architectural feature of a central platform that defines Plaza Plan 4 plus a prediction of ritual behavior in the form of a skull cache/burial that can be verified only through archaeology. The sources of these skulls at Tikal, and elsewhere (Robin 1989), have yet to be confirmed (see Tiesler-Blos 2002). "Cached" skulls at Tikal may have been relocated from other contexts, presumably burials, or from recently deceased persons (see Tiesler-Blos and Cucina 2003, also 2007; also Tiesler-Blos 2003; cf. Becker 1996, Ms. A).[4]

The significance of these cached or deposited skulls at Tikal and elsewhere remains uncertain. Can we determine the meaning of ritual activities that involve the placement of one or more skulls, detached from their bodies, in a formalized, archaeologically recognizable pattern and demonstrate the cognitive continuities in regional "belief" systems? The important studies of the actual human bones, such as those using strontium isotope ratios to determine possible immigration patterns (Price et al. 2000; also Wright 2005), and the non-metric skeletal trait analysis used by Duncan, point the way toward resolving some of these basic issues.

Underlying this study of Plaza Plan 4 is the demonstration that we can predict, and thus "understand," the past through the recognition and exploration of architectural grammars. In his excellent summary of Aztec provincial sites in Morelos, M.E. Smith (2002) presents a perceptive summary of the *great* and *little* traditions, as they evolved in the 1950s (Redfield 1952), an idea effectively reviewed and put into current context by McAnany (2002). Smith (2002:93) uses this concept to examine the relationship between peasant or village culture and the "dominant 'high' culture of their encompassing civilizations." The identification of regularities or patterns within large sites enables us to examine recognizable units and how they compare through time and space. For example, the mortuary program long associated with Plaza Plan 2 at Tikal became replicated among the ruling class only with the burial of the ruler in Temple I, and also in Temple VI (Becker 1999). At Tikal, one of several "little" traditions became equivalent to, or incorporated into, the great tradition at the site. The historical literature, or texts, from Tikal and other sites provides information relevant to this Tikal "king," and should be reviewed for clues to, or confirmation of, these shifts in social organization.

Tainter's (1978) early discussion of prehistoric mortuary patterns and their relationships with social systems provided a basic format for integrating the archaeological evidence with anthropological processes. Manzanilla (2002:49–50) indicates that differing patterns of funerary ritual at Teotihuacan served as "markers of social identity" for different ethnic groups. She believes these differences also reflect hierarchy within and among the apartment compounds at Teotihuacan. In effect, Manzanilla points the way toward using these "markers" to recognize population movements and/or cultural influences in areas at considerable distances from Teotihuacan. Travis Stanton recently analyzed this subject from a Yucatecan perspective by examining Teotihuacan influences on the northern Maya lowlands during the period AD 550–700. Stanton's (2005) review of the literature led him to conclude that the pre-1980s "ideas such as enclaves of Teotihuacanos living in the Maya area" has now shifted to either of two other views: (1) either the Maya appropriated and innovated Mexican cultural ideas, or (2) there were Middle Classic period enclaves that can be identified, as at the site of "Chac II." Both views may be correct, since we are examining independent states within which various organizational systems may have existed. Stanton, however, finds no evidence for permanent residents at Chac II who came from Teotihuacan, reinforcing the view that contacts need not be accompanied by migrants or emissaries. To demonstrate Teotihuacano presence at Tikal, we must do more than document contact via trade and exchange of ideas, as in art or architecture. Identification of influences in the form of an architectural grammar, such as a specific plaza plan form, should lead us to two predicted trait assemblages that are related: (1) specific mortuary patterns that are highly culture specific; and (2) studies of the actual skeletons that can confirm if some of the residents of these groups were born or raised at Teotihuacan, or descended from Teotihuacanos (e.g., Marcus 2003).

Plaza plans can be used to examine Rapoport's (1993) assumptions that architecture can be used to define a capital, and to differentiate among several capitals in a region. If we can identify architectural diagnostics, Rapoport's ideas can be applied to the Maya lowlands. The architectural configurations within a regional capital probably had an "inside-out" influence. The dominant form of plaza plan in the capital city, or power center, spreads to areas that are under the suzerainty of that particular center. The skeletal evidence may reveal if the diffusion results from a population that actually relocates and recreates their architectural forms, or if the forms reflect only cultural influences that alter behaviors in subject populations. In the former case, analysis of the bones may confirm population movement. In the latter case, we might expect sharp boundaries where the spheres of influence end. R. Glaab and C. Taylor (2005) suggested that differences in percentages of Plaza Plan 2 (frequencies) might reveal such boundaries, or limits to the respective areas of influence, between Tikal and Caracol. This would be an innovative approach to the use of maps to explore the territorial extent of the political power so loudly proclaimed on many Maya monuments.

Meaning of Plaza Plans

Recognizing a mortuary or architectural pattern does not tell us what that pattern means. The possible "meaning" of platforms that include "caches" of skulls or other materials remains to be decoded. Mapping a site may offer important clues to architectural grammars, but focused excavations are needed to define or recognize the existence of archaeological attributes. Both offer a window to understanding past behaviors (see Robin 2003). Extending Tainter's mortuary pattern research to architectural groups provides another means by which we may relate various aspects of cultural attributes within a city, as well as helping to demonstrate transfers or "diffusion" among other cities. Implicit in Tainter's approach, as with studies of various aspects of lowland Maya architectural groups, are questions regarding the fundamental goals of archaeologists studying the ancient Maya. The epistemology of Maya archaeology rarely is made explicit, allowing scientific methods to be subordinated to treasure hunting within the many sites, large and small, throughout the lowlands. Sites are difficult to understand if they, or clusters of their component structures, are seen only in terms of size and associated wealth (Becker 2004a).[5] Many excavations now seek to answer specific questions, or to test hypotheses.

Examination of the biological evidence now complements the rich archaeological data being assembled. Responding to Marcus's (2003:354–55) call for the "sourcing of skeletons," Duncan (2005b:3) sought to infer meaning from the special postmortem placement of skulls as well as the distribution of skull deposits and the biology of the skulls themselves. Veneration would be suggested if the skulls belonged to members of the burying group, and humiliation if they are the skulls of outsiders. We have yet, however, to determine if skull placement patterns alone may reveal ethnicity.

What do differences in the absolute size of the groups in which we find Plaza Plan 4 platforms (numbers of structures, surface area of all platforms, and so on) mean? The majority of Plaza Plan 4 groups recognized at Tikal appear along a strip at the central and eastern portions of the southern mapped region. This "distribution" may relate to the unusually large average size of the groups in this zone (more than 8.4 structures). In general, Plaza Plan 4 groups (like Plaza Plan 2 groups) are not limited to any specific size (see endnote 5). The configuration of a group, however, may be altered at any point in its history. Revealing this process requires that large portions of a plaza be stripped. The search for the addition of a central courtyard shrine and determining when it may have been added to a group's architectural pattern are simple tasks highly suitable for a small project. The identification of ethnic origins of Plaza Plan 4, however, may be revealed by clues regarding the first appearance of Plaza Plan 4 at Tikal, and determining the identity of the people of the diagnostic skulls.

Despite the extensive testing of various "components and spatial distribution of domestic ritual" (Manzanilla 2002:45) at Teotihuacan, we need to gather further data on this subject. George Cowgill (2003a:40–41, also 2003b), in discussing cosmology at Teotihuacan, notes that we know very little about craft specialization at Teotihuacan, or even how the people in this huge city were fed. The human skeletal remains associated with central courtyard shrines at Teotihuacan and elsewhere remain to be identified and tabulated, with the data used to verify patterning. Also needed are data on the astronomical orientations of the central courtyard shrines, or platforms, at sites where they are identified. Orientation of each structure is another feature that helps us decode architectural meanings and detect patterns. The alignments of these small structures may reveal connections among various sites, and help to reinforce ideas regarding ethnicity and its spread. For example, Winter (2002:69) notes that at Monte Albán in Oaxaca, the central courtyard shrines, or platforms, are "oriented 8 degrees north of east, the Olmec orientation present at later dates at La Venta."

Discussion

Examination of the various elements of settlement pattern and social organization that existed among the ancient Maya has long been focused on ceramics (Culbert 1993) and artifacts (Moholy Nagy 2008). As we gather information on variations in settlement pattern, within a single city or between cities and regions, we also can decipher aspects of social organization. Taken together, these data enable us to understand life at a capital such as Tikal, and how it differs from life in peripheral towns and villages. The small platforms diagnostic of Tikal Plaza Plan 4, and their distribution within the Maya area, may indicate the degree of influence from Mexico. Is this part of a continuum reflecting a gradation of influence that is higher to the north and declines as one approaches Tikal (cf. Houk 1996; cf. Hammond et al. 1998), or did influences from Central Mexico have affects primarily in lowland Maya capitals such as Tikal?[6] I suspect that Teotihuacan's influences in the Maya lowlands were strongest in capitals such as Tikal, where economic as well as cultural ties were important. Marcus (2003) points out, however, that the few texts and imported vessels reflecting Teotihuacan "influence" actually may reveal more about a leader's need to legitimize his claim to the throne at Tikal and elsewhere. She believes that gaps in the succession of Maya rulers could explain the timing of increased interaction with the highlands (Marcus 2003:353).

The political and social systems at the enormous site of Teotihuacan are a challenge to decode. Manzanilla (2002:42), in examining domestic ritual at Teotihuacan ca. AD 1–600, makes the important observation that, oddly, the site *lacks* dynastic iconography. The absence of written texts, a trait commonly correlated with "kingship," is addressed by Manzanilla in her discussion of theories of "corporate rulership." Manzanilla offers a model for Teotihuacan, where later rulership reflects the duality or division of power between internal (domestic) and external (ritual) "leaders." She also holds that co-rulers, who are heads of noble houses in the four sectors of the city, are most often represented in their priestly capacities (Manzanilla 2006), an aspect of dual leadership that characterizes all "urbanized" cultures (Becker 1975). Manzanilla's explanation may relate to cross-cultural rules relating to moiety leaders, and the duality that are parts of systems of rulership (cf. Becker 1983, 1988, and so on).

The decline in Teotihuacan's power left state capitals such as Tikal without the economic or other support needed to maintain sociopolitical organization. The internal changes that mark the Late Classic period at Tikal reflect internal reorganization, and economic stimuli derived from massive construction programs. Changes, marked by the decline in the use of written languages during the period ca. AD 850–1000, reflect the decline and decentralization of sociopolitical structure. Powerful kings, such as those ruling Tikal, gradually lost control of their dependencies. Their power weakened as the towns and cities that once were part of their realm devolved to the control of local "chiefs" who maintained order only within their chiefdoms. They may have retained many trappings or material culture of the Classic period, but as craft production and economic exchange declined, so did the material evidence of chiefly power. The introduction of copper and other metals as prestige goods into these sociopolitical systems may have helped to stabilize chiefdoms rather than enabling low-level kingdoms to survive. This process of political devolution may not have been rapid or uniform, but it was irreversible, and it set the stage for the impressive changes in the Maya realm that were to take place over the next 1,000 years.

Conclusions

1. Architectural as well as several other archaeological lines of evidence strongly support the belief that Tikal was a regional capital, or major city-state, with complex ethnic diversity characterizing its inhabitants.

2. The diversity in plaza plans at Classic period Tikal, and the rituals that are specific to each of them, provide the strongest reflection of the presence of ethnic differences within this ancient Maya capital.

3. Plaza Plan 4 groups at Tikal, characterized by the presence of a small platform in the center of the principal plaza of each residential cluster, reflect a ritual pattern that arrived in this city during the Late Classic period. A Plaza Plan 4 origin at Teotihuacan is suggested by comparative data, but as with iconographic and ceramic evidence, does not confirm an ideological shift at Tikal.

4. Excavations conducted in six of the eight platforms defining Plaza Plan 4 groups at Tikal have revealed diagnostic skull "placements," possibly representing fertility rites of a specific ethnic population.

5. The correlation of specific occupational specializations (crafters) with those residential groups at Tikal that conform to Plaza Plan 2 has not been found in Plaza Plan 4 groups. The specific place in Tikal society occupied by residents of Plaza Plan 4 groups remains unknown.

6. Plaza Plan 4 may be a late introduction to Tikal, representing a distinct ethnic group that continued to grow in influence and have a wider distribution within this capital during the Postclassic period.

Acknowledgments

Sincere thanks are due Dr. Linda R. Manzanilla for her kind invitation to present these data at the 2006 meeting of the Society for American Archaeology. Her significant editorial efforts, together with those of Claude Chapdelaine, brought this paper into focus. Thanks also are due to Jon Hageman, Ricardo Encalada, William Folan, K. Geesey, Rigden Glaab, Kathryn Goodley, Jeannie Carpenter, Patti Hite, Christopher Jones, Roberto Mejilla, Richard Swain, Gair Tourtellot, and all the others who provided suggestions and comments on various aspects of this research. Special thanks are due to Joyce Marcus for her important suggestions and editorial efforts; to William N. Duncan, Michael E. Smith, and Timothy Pugh for providing information critical to this line of research; and to Jill Rheinheimer for editorial work. My thanks also are due to Prof. Asif Agha (Department Chair) and to Dr. Richard Hodges (Director of The University Museum) for their encouragement of this research. All of the ideas presented, as well as any errors of interpretation or presentation, are the responsibility of the author alone.

Endnotes

1. Both residential and non-residential group patterns (plaza plans) have been recognized at Tikal, and most also can be found at other sites in the Maya realm and beyond. Seven were easily identified (Becker 1971a) and three others were delineated by 1980. Recognition that the lowland Maya city of Tikal incorporated a wide range of forms of residential and political building clusters was a factor in concluding that Maya society was socially complex and was divided into a number of city-states (Becker 1982:117–20, 2001). Laporte's solar observatory (2003b:287) may be an eleventh plaza plan. Tikal Plaza Plan 1 has been described at length (Jones 1969). The various Plaza Plans identified at Tikal, and elsewhere, are listed here. Numbers 1 through 10 are described at length elsewhere (Becker 2003a); the page numbers to that publication are included below.

Plaza Plan	Page Numbers*	Notes
1	258	Twin-Pyramid Complex. See Jones 1969.
2–5		Residential plaza plans, described in this chapter.
6	264–65	"Temple Triad" that includes temples at the east, west, and north of a plaza (also called North Acropolis Plan; cf. Folan et al. 2001).
7	265	"Seven Sisters": a set of 7 temples on the east of a plaza.
8	265	Ball courts (possibly related to "skull racks"?).
9	265–66	Markets.
10	266–67	E-Groups (astronomical rituals?). Possible antecedents of Plaza Plan 2.
11		"New" round structures.
12		Proposed ritual group with two (unpaired) temples on the east, one on the west, a "statue shrine" in the plaza area, etc. (see Pugh 2001:18, Figs. 1–4; Pugh 2002, 2002–2004, 2003a, 2003b; Duncan 2005a: Fig. 15.6).

*From Becker 2003a.

2. Manzanilla's important inference regarding ritual (non-domestic) architecture derives from the limited sample of excavations reviewed in Sánchez's thesis (1989). The key word here is "ritual." The elaborate Tikal Burial 85 was placed in front and to the south of a temple, then sealed with an altar-like platform. That platform is not a central courtyard shrine, nor is it in a domestic context. Non-domestic also describes Winter's (2002:71, Fig. 7.6) plan of the Main Plaza at Monte Albán in the Valley of Oaxaca, where there are at least three altars of note, probably dating from ca. AD 700–800, that are similar to the Tikal Burial 85 situation. Referring to the "Great Tradition," Winter (2002:73) suggests that in the Main Plaza, "Temples in the middle of the plaza are analogous to household patio altars." In addition, in a late Period II level at *Palacio del Ocote* (ca. AD 300–350) on the northeastern part of the "North Platform," there is an altar in the center of the patio covering a seated burial (González Licón et al. 1992:122). Winter adds a discussion of the "TPA compound" that he (2002:79, Fig. 7.6d) notes includes a temple on the north of a central patio with an altar in it, and an entryway on the south. Winter notes that the temple-patio-altar (TPA) becomes common in the nuclear area of sites dating from ca. AD 450 and later, and a largely standardized plan for site centers (foci), but apparently is not common (or even present?) in residential groups.

3. Tikal's 690 architectural groups are largely residential compounds, each being occupied by a family of varied size (cf. Becker 1986a). These "houses" are randomly interspersed with civic or ritual architectural groups (Becker 1982). One barrio-like cluster consisting only of Plaza Plan 2 groups (Becker 1999, 2003b) suggests a neighborhood grouping. Possible antecedents to Tikal Plaza Plan 2 also can be found at Teotihuacan, where eastern temples are common within residential compounds and in barrio centers, such as Teopancazco and possibly at Yayahuala. Manzanilla (2006:23–24) points out there is a structure within the Yayahuala compound that "was large enough to be interpreted as a neighborhood temple (Séjourné 1966:213)." This pattern is similar to Tikal Str. 5G-8 within Gr. 5G-2, a Plaza Plan 2 group (Becker 1971a, 1999). Manzanilla (2002:45, Fig. 5.3) also provides evidence for a possible Plaza Plan 2 in her depiction of a residential compound at Zacuala measuring about 50 by 60 m, with a square temple on the east having a base of about 17 m on a side.

4. Forty years ago, Ruz (1965, also 1968) noted that adult phalanges often were associated with infant and child burials (see also Duncan 2005a:79). Such deposits of finger bones, reported to be common at Caracol, may represent a regional variant of the skull cache "pattern" (e.g., A. Chase 1994:166–69; D. Chase 1994:124, 129; Chase and Chase 2004:141).

5. At Tikal, the surface area covered by the substructures of the oratorios, or "temples on the east," of Plaza Plan 2 groups ranges from 22.04 to 184.90 m^2, and even the five smallest examples range from 22.04 to 48.50 m^2 (Becker 1999:153, Table 115). This considerable variation reflects enormous differences in wealth among groups of people sharing a ritual behavior that involved only 15% of the people at Tikal. We may infer, therefore, that heterarchical variation was an important feature of social organization at Tikal.

Vast variations in size are found *within* each type or category of residential groups (plaza plans), leading us to ask other questions regarding social organization at Tikal. Some type of "hierarchy," or vertical ranking of power, has been assumed because economic strata, if not social (societal) differences, are inferred from the size variations in residential groups (Becker 2004a). Most scholars view Classic period Maya society as hierarchical. While the Tikal polity may have been hierarchical, organization within the city may have been heterarchical, as suggested by variations in size and wealth found within each specific plaza plan. Confusing economic variations (access to resources) with social ranking limits our ability to understand Classic Maya society and blurs our understanding of the actual societal transitions that mark both ends of the Classic period (cf. Becker 1988). While variations in plaza plan may reflect ethnic differences, variations in size (economic expenditure) among groups conforming to the same plaza plan lead me to suggest that the structure and organization of power within lowland Maya society during the Classic period may include modes not yet understood (cf. Manzanilla 1989; cf. Haviland 2003a:133–34; Becker 2004a). The variations found within a *single* plaza plan type also may be used to infer a heterarchical social structure, or one in which the organization of power may include vertical systems along with other, horizontal (or lateral, non-hierarchical) modes (Crumley 1987, 1995, especially 2003; also Becker 2003a, 2003b, 2004a). Heterarchy also might explain fragile patterns of social organization tied to lowland Maya kingship, patterns that might explain the evolution as well as the devolution of Maya states, replaced by Maya chiefdoms in the Postclassic period (Becker 1983, see also 1988).

M.E. Smith (2007) describes a new model for urban planning that considers coordination among buildings and spaces to be specific to a city and its dependencies. Within "standardization among cities" he includes architectural inventories and orientations as well as spatial patterning and metrology. The ability of a population to construct a city with multiple plaza plans, or what M.E. Smith terms architectural "inventories," may also provide evidence for heterarchy. Such inventories and orientations are aspects of architecture that we have long since applied to the evaluation of the construction of specific plaza plans; however, now we can demonstrate that the same plan is used for residential groups reflecting vastly differing levels of wealth. In the case of residential plaza plans at Tikal, we are seeing an internal origin, deriving from within an extended family, rather than a top-down orientation, such as that of a "king" to his subjects. In fact, we can demonstrate that Plaza Plan 2 at Tikal was long used for private residences before the entire conceptual pattern was employed in the burial of a king beneath Tikal's Temple I, thus representing a bottom-up process, with a "little" residential tradition becoming "great." The change in mortuary programs associated with the burial in Temple I may reflect the rise to power of the lineage of a specific ethnic group.

6. Frequency differences between the Plaza Plan 2 frequencies at sites in eastern Belize and the Tikal realm (Glaab and Taylor 2005) noted above need to be determined for Plaza Plan 4. In each case, they may reflect cultural and/or political influences.

References

Becker, Marshall Joseph

1971a *The Identification of a Second Plaza Plan at Tikal, Guatemala and Its Implications for Ancient Maya Social Complexity.* PhD dissertation in Anthropology, University of Pennsylvania. University Microfilms, Ann Arbor.

1971b Plaza plans at Quirigua, Guatemala: The use of a specific theory regarding cultural behavior in predicting the configuration of group arrangements and burial patterns in a yet untested community settlement pattern. *Katunob* VIII(2):47–62.

1973a Archaeological evidence for occupational specialization among the Classic period Maya at Tikal, Guatemala. *American Antiquity* 38:396–406.

1973b The evidence for complex exchange systems among the ancient Maya. *American Antiquity* 38:222–23.

1975 Moieties in ancient Mesoamerica: Inferences on Teotihuacan social structure. Parts I and II. *American Indian Quarterly* 2:217–36, 315–30.

1982 Ancient Maya houses and their identification: An evaluation of architectural groups at Tikal and inferences regarding their functions. *Revista Española de Antropología Americana* XII:111–29.

1983 Kings and classicism: Political change in the Maya lowlands during the Classic period. In *Highland-Lowland Interaction in Mesoamerica: Interdisciplinary Approaches*, edited by A.G. Miller, pp. 159–200. Dumbarton Oaks Research Library and Collection, Washington, D.C.

1984 The development of polity in Mesoamerica as interpreted through the evolution of plaza plans: Suggested influences of the central Mexican highlands on the Maya lowlands. *Revista Española de Antropología Americana* 14:47–84.

1986a Household shrines at Tikal, Guatemala: Size as a reflection of economic status. *Revista Española de Antropología Americana* 16:81–85.

1986b An ethnographical and archaeological survey of unusual mortuary procedures as a reflection of cultural diversity: Some suggestions for the interpretation of the human skeletal deposits from excavations at Entella, Sicily, Italy. *La Parola del Pasato: Rivista di Studi Antichi* 226:31–56.

1988 Changing views of the changing Maya: Evolution and devolution in an ancient society. *Revista Española de Antropología Americana* 18:21–35.

1991a Plaza plans at Tikal, Guatemala, and at other lowland Maya sites: Evidence for patterns of culture change. *Cuadernos de Arquitectura Mesoamericana* 14:11–26.

1991b Earth offerings among the Classic period lowland Maya: Burials and caches as ritual deposits. In *Perspectivas Antropológicas en el Mundo Maya*, edited by M. Josefa Ponce de León and F. Perramon, pp. 45–74. Publicaciones del SEEM, Vol. 2. Seminario Español de Estudios Mayas, Barcelona.

1992 Burials as caches, caches as burials: A new interpretation of the meaning of ritual deposits among the Classic period lowland Maya. In *New Theories on the Ancient Maya*, edited by Elin C. Danien and Robert J. Sharer, pp. 185–96. Symposium Series Vol. 3, University Museum Monograph 77. University Museum, University of Pennsylvania, Philadelphia.

1996 Medieval mortuary customs in Italy: Skull relocations and other unusual burial procedures. *Archeologia Medievale* 23:699–714.

1999 *Tikal Report No. 21: Small Structure Excavations and the Definition of Plaza Plan 2.* University Museum Monograph 104. University Museum, University of Pennsylvania, Philadelphia.

2001 Houselots at Tikal, Guatemala: It's what's out back that counts. In *Reconstruyendo la Ciudad Maya: El Urbanismo en las Sociedades Antiguas*, edited by Andrés Ciudad Ruiz, M. Josefa Iglesias Ponce de León, and M. Carmen Martínez Martínez, pp. 427–60. Publicaciones de la SEEM no. 6. Sociedad Española de Estudios Maya, Madrid.

2003a Plaza plans at Tikal: A research strategy for inferring social organization and processes of culture change at lowland Maya sites. In *Tikal: Dynasties, Foreigners, & Affairs of State: Advancing Maya Archaeology*, edited by Jeremy A. Sabloff, pp. 253–80. School of American Research Press, Santa Fe.

2003b A Classic period barrio producing fine polychrome ceramics at Tikal, Guatemala: Notes on ancient Maya firing technology. *Ancient Mesoamerica* 14:95–112.

2004a Maya heterarchy as inferred from Classic-period plaza plans. *Ancient Mesoamerica* 15:127–38.

2004b Plaza Plan 4 en Tikal, Guatemala: The 'Central Altar Group Plan' como influido por contactos con México. Paper presented at the XIV Encuentro Internacional de Cultura Maya, Universidad Autónoma de Campeche, Campeche, México, November 10–13.

2008 Skull rituals and plaza plan 4 at Tikal: Lowland Maya mortuary patterns. *The Codex* 17(1–2):12–41, University Museum, University of Pennsylvania, Philadelphia.

forthcoming Beheadings or Skull Relocations in Medieval Prague?: Seven Examples of Decapitation from the Cerninski Palace Excavations, Loretanske namesty.

Blom, Frans
1954 Ossuaries, cremation, and secondary burials among the Maya of Chiapas, Mexico. *Journal de la Société des Américanistes* 43:123–37.

Boone, Elizabeth H. (editor)
1984 *Ritual Human Sacrifice in Mesoamerica*. Dumbarton Oaks, Washington, D.C.

Carr, C.
1995 Mortuary practices: Their social, philosophical-religious, circumstantial, and physical determinants. *Journal of Anthropological Method and Theory* 2(2):105–200.

Carr, Robert F., and J.E. Hazard
1961 *Tikal Report No. 11: Map of the Ruins of Tikal, El Peten, Guatemala*. Museum Monograph. University Museum, University of Pennsylvania, Philadelphia.

Chase, Arlen F.
1994 A contextual approach to the ceramics of Caracol, Belize. In *Studies in the Archaeology of Caracol, Belize*, edited by D.Z. Chase and A.F. Chase, pp. 157–82. Monograph 7. Pre-Columbian Art Research Institute, San Francisco.

Chase, Diane Z.
1985 Ganned but not forgotten: Late Postclassic archaeology and ritual at Santa Rita Corozal, Belize. In *The Lowland Maya Postclassic*, edited by Arlen F. Chase and P.M. Rice, pp. 104–24. University of Texas Press, Austin.
1994 Human osteology, pathology, and demography as represented in the burials of Caracol, Belize. In *Studies in the Archaeology of Caracol, Belize*, edited by D.Z. Chase and A.F. Chase, pp. 123–35. Monograph 7. Pre-Columbian Art Research Institute, San Francisco.

Chase, Diane Z., and Arlen F. Chase
2004 Archaeological perspectives on Classic Maya social organization from Caracol, Belize. *Ancient Mesoamerica* 15:139–47.

Coe, William R.
1965 Current research: Southeastern Mesoamerica. *American Antiquity* 30(3):374–83.

Cowgill, George
2003a Teotihuacan: Cosmic glories and mundane needs. In *The Social Construction of Ancient Cities*, edited by Monica L. Smith, pp. 37–55. Smithsonian Books, Washington, D.C.
2003b Teotihuacan and Early Classic interaction: A perspective from outside the Maya region. In *The Maya and Teotihuacan: Reinterpreting Early Classic Interaction*, edited by Geoffrey E. Braswell, pp. 315–35. University of Texas Press, Austin.

Crumley, Carole L.
1987 A dialectical critique of hierarchy. In *Power Relations and State Formation*, edited by T.C. Patterson and C.W. Gailey, pp. 155–69. American Anthropological Association, Washington, D.C.

1995 Heterarchy and the analysis of complex societies. In *Heterarchy and the Analysis of Complex Societies*, edited by Robert M. Ehrenreich, Carole L. Crumley, and Janet E. Levy, pp. 1–6. Archaeological Papers no. 6. American Anthropological Association, Arlington.
2003 Alternate forms of social order. In *Heterarchy, Political Economy and the Ancient Maya*, edited by Vernon Scarborough, Fred Valdez, Jr., and Nicholas Dunning, pp. 136–45. University of Arizona Press, Tucson.

Culbert, T. Patrick
1993 *The Ceramics of Tikal*. Tikal Reports no. 25, University Museum Monograph 81. University Museum, University of Pennsylvania, Philadelphia.

Dahlin, Bruce, and Daniel Mazeau (editors)
2001 *The Pakbeh Regional Economy Program: Report of the 2001 Field Season*. Sociology-Anthropology Department, Howard University, Washington, D.C.

Deal, Michael
1988 Recognition of ritual pottery in residential units: An ethnoarchaeological model of the Maya family altar tradition. In *Ethnoarchaeology among the Highland Maya of Chiapas*, edited by Thomas A. Lee and Brian Hayden, pp. 61–89. Paper No. 56. New World Archaeological Foundation, Provo.

Duncan, William N.
1999 Postclassic Mortuary Practices in Civic-Ceremonial Contexts in Petén, Guatemala. Paper presented at the 64th Annual Meeting of the Society for American Archaeology, Chicago.
2005a *The Bioarcheology of Ritual Violence in Postclassic El Petén, Guatemala (AD 950–1524)*. PhD dissertation in Anthropology, Southern Illinois University, Carbondale.
2005b Understanding veneration and violation in the archaeological record. In *Interacting with the Dead: Perspectives on Mortuary Archaeology for the New Millennium*, edited by Gordon F.M. Rakita, Jane E. Buikstra, Lane A. Beck, and Sloan R. Williams, pp. 207–27. University of Florida Press, Tallahassee.
2007 Human remains from surface collections and features in structures. In *Excavations at Cerro Tilcajete: A Monte Albán II Administrative Center in the Valley of Oaxaca*, by Christina M. Elson, pp. 119–20. Memoirs, no. 42. Museum of Anthropology, University of Michigan, Ann Arbor.

Folan, William J., Joel D. Gunn, and María del Rosario Domínguez Carrasco
2001 Triadic temples, central plazas and dynastic palaces: A diachronic analysis of the royal court complex, Calakmul, Campeche, Mexico. In *Royal Courts of the Ancient Maya, Volume 2: Data and Case Studies*, edited by Takeshi Inomata and Stephen D. Houston, pp. 223–65. Westview Press, Boulder.

Folan, William J., Ellen R. Kintz, and Laraine A. Fletcher
1983 *Coba: A Classic Maya Metropolis* [with maps]. Studies in Archaeology. Academic Press, New York.

Glaab, Rigden A., and Chrissy Taylor
2005 Dos Hombres-Gran Cacao intersite research: The 2004 mapping season. In *Programme for Belize Archaeological Project: Report of Activities from the 2004 Field Season*, edited by Fred Valdez, Jr., pp. 35–44. Occasional Papers no. 4. Mesoamerican Archaeological Research Laboratory, University of Texas, Austin.

González Licón, Ernesto, Lourdes Márquez, and Raúl Matadamas
1992   Exploraciones arqueológicas en Monte Albán, Oaxaca, durante la temporada 1990–1991. *Boletín del Consejo de Arqueología* 1991. Instituto Nacional de Antropología e Historia, México, D.F.

Hammond, Norman, Gair Tourtellot, Sara Donaghey, and Amanda Clark
1998   No slow dusk: Maya urban development and decline at La Milpa, Belize. *Antiquity* 72:831–37.

Haviland, William A.
2003a   Settlement, society, and demography at Tikal. In *Tikal: Dynasties, Foreigners, and Affairs of State*, edited by Jeremy A. Sabloff, pp. 111–42. SAR Press, Santa Fe.
2003b   Tikal, Guatemala: A Maya Way to Urbanism. Paper prepared for the Third INAH-Penn State Conference on Mesoamerican Urbanism; revised version of manuscript presented Nov. 2003. Copy on file in the M.J. Becker Archives, West Chester University.
forthcoming   *Tikal Report. Excavations in Residential Groups of Tikal.* University Museum, University of Pennsylvania, Philadelphia.

Haviland, W.A., M.J. Becker, A. Chowning, K.A. Dixon, and K. Heider
1985   *Tikal Report No. 19. Excavations in Residential Groups of Tikal: Groups 4F-1 and 4F-2.* University Museum, University of Pennsylvania, Philadelphia.

Houk, Brett A.
1996   *The Archaeology of Site Planning: An Example from the Maya Site of Dos Hombres, Belize.* PhD dissertation in Anthropology, University of Texas, Austin.

Iglesias Ponce de León, María Josefa
2003   Problematical deposits and the problem of interaction: The material culture of Tikal during the Early Classic period. In *The Maya and Teotihuacan: Reinterpreting Early Classic Interaction*, edited by Geoffrey E. Braswell, pp. 167–98. University of Texas Press, Austin.

Inomata, Takeshi
2001   The power and ideology of artistic creation: Elite craft specialists in Classic Maya society. *Current Anthropology* 43(3):321–45.

Jones, Christopher
1969   *The Twin-Pyramid Group Pattern: A Classic Maya Architectural Assemblage at Tikal, Guatemala.* PhD dissertation, Department of Anthropology, University of Pennsylvania, Philadelphia.
1996   *Tikal Report 16. Excavations in the East Plaza of Tikal.* Museum Monographs 92. University Museum, University of Pennsylvania, Philadelphia.

Kidder, Tristram R.
2004   Plazas as architecture: An example from the Raffman Site, northeast Louisiana. *American Antiquity* 69(3):514–32.

Laporte Molina, Juan Pedro
2003a   Thirty years later: Some results of recent excavations at Tikal. In *Tikal: Dynasties, Foreigners, and Affairs of State*, edited by Jeremy Sabloff, pp. 281–318. SAR Press, Santa Fe.

2003b   Architectural aspects of interaction between Tikal and Teotihuacan during the Early Classic period. In *The Maya and Teotihuacan: Reinterpreting Early Classic Interaction*, edited by G.E. Braswell, pp. 199–216. University of Texas Press, Austin.

Linné, Sigvald
1934   *Archaeological Researches at Teotihuacan, Mexico.* V. Petterson, Stockholm. Reprint, with an introduction by George L. Cowgill, University of Alabama Press, Tuscaloosa, 2003.

Manzanilla, Linda
1989   Niveles de análisis en el estudio de unidades habitacionales. *Revista Española de Antropología Americana* 20:9–18.
1993   Arquitectura y áreas de actividad. Banco de datos. In *Anatomía de un conjunto residencial teotihuacano en Oztoyahualco*, edited by Linda Manzanilla, pp. 98–189. Instituto de Investigaciones Antropológicas, Universidad Nacional Autónoma de México, México, D.F.
1996   Corporate groups and domestic activities at Teotihuacan. *Latin American Antiquity* 7(3):228–46.
2002   Living with the ancestors and offering to the gods: Domestic ritual at Teotihuacan. In *Domestic Ritual in Ancient Mesoamerica*, edited by Patricia Plunket, pp. 43–52. Monograph 46. University of California, Los Angeles.
2004   Social identity and daily life at Classic Teotihuacan. In *Mesoamerican Archaeology: Theory and Practice*, edited by Julia A. Hendon and Rosemary A. Joyce, pp. 124–47. Blackwell Publishing, Bodmin, Cornwall.
2006   Estados corporativos arcaicos. Organizaciones de excepción en escenarios excluyentes. *Cuicuilco* 13(36):13–46.

Manzanilla, Linda, and Luis Barba
1990   The study of activities in Classic households: Two case studies from Cobá and Teotihuacan. *Ancient Mesoamerica* 1:41–49.

Manzanilla, Linda, and Agustín Ortiz
1990   Los altares domésticos en Teotihuacán. Hallazgos de dos fragmentos de maqueta. *Cuadernos de Arquitectura Mesoamericana* 13:11–13.

Marcus, Joyce
1999   Early architecture in the Valley of Oaxaca 1350 B.C.–A.D. 500. In *Mesoamerican Architecture as a Cultural Symbol*, edited by Jeff Karl Kowalski, pp. 59–75. Oxford University Press, New York.
2003   The Maya and Teotihuacan. In *The Maya and Teotihuacan: Reinterpreting Early Classic Interaction*, edited by G.E. Braswell, pp. 337–56. University of Texas Press, Austin.

Martin, Simon
2003   In line of the founder. In *Tikal: Dynasties, Foreigners, and Affairs of State*, edited by Jeremy Sabloff, pp. 3–45. SAR Press, Santa Fe.

Martin, Simon, and N. Grube
2000   *Chronicle of the Maya Kings and Queens: Deciphering the Dynasties of the Ancient Maya.* Thames and Hudson, London.

Massey, Virginia K.
1994   Osteological analysis of the skull pit children. In *Continuing Archaeology at Colha, Belize*, edited by T. Hester, H. Shafer, and J. Eaton, pp. 209–20. Studies in Archaeology 16. Texas Archaeological Research Laboratory, University of Texas, Austin.

Massey, Virginia K., and D. Gentry Steele
1997 A Maya skull pit from the Terminal Classic period, Colha, Belize. In *Bones of the Maya: Studies of Ancient Skeletons*, edited by Stephen L. Whittington and David M. Reed, pp. 62–77. Smithsonian Institution Press, Washington, D.C.

McAnany, Patricia
2002 Rethinking the great and little tradition paradigm from the perspective of domestic ritual. In *Domestic Ritual in Ancient Mesoamerica*, edited by Patricia Plunket, pp. 115–20. Monograph 46. Cotsen Institute, University of California, Los Angeles.

Mock, Shirley Boteler
1994 Destruction and denouement during the Late-Terminal Classic: The Colha skull pit. In *Continuing Archaeology at Colha, Belize*, edited by T. Hester, H. Shafer, and J. Eaton, pp. 221–31. Studies in Archaeology 16. Texas Archaeological Research Laboratory, University of Texas, Austin.
1998 The defaced and the forgotten: Decapitation and flaying/mutilation as a termination event at Colha, Belize. In *The Sowing and the Dawning: Termination, Dedication, and Transformation in the Archaeological and Ethnographic Record of Mesoamerica*, edited by Shirley Boteler Mock, pp. 112–33. University of New Mexico Press, Albuquerque.

Moholy Nagy, Hattula
2008 *The Artifacts of Tikal. Tikal Report 27A: Ornamental and Ceremonial Artifacts and Unworked Material.* University Museum, University of Pennsylvania, Philadelphia.

Moser, Christopher L.
1973 *Human Decapitation in Ancient Mesoamerica.* Studies in Pre-Columbian Art and Archaeology, No. 11. Dumbarton Oaks, Trustees for Harvard University, Washington, D.C.

Plunket, Patricia, and Gabriela Uruñuela
1998a The quick and the dead: Decision-making in the abandonment of Tetimpa. *Mayab* 13:78–87.
1998b Preclassic household patterns preserved under volcanic ash at Tetimpa, Puebla, Mexico. *Latin American Antiquity* 9(4):287–309.
2002 Shrines, ancestors, and the volcanic landscape at Tetimpa, Puebla. In *Domestic Ritual in Ancient Mesoamerica*, edited by Patricia Plunket, pp. 31–42. Monograph 46. Cotsen Institute, University of California, Los Angeles.

Price, T. Douglas, Linda Manzanilla, and William D. Middleton
2000 Immigration and the ancient city of Teotihuacan in Mexico: A study using strontium isotope ratios in human bone and teeth. *Journal of Archaeological Science* 27:903–13.

Pugh, Timothy W.
2001 *Architecture, Ritual, and Social Identity at Late Postclassic Zacpetén, Petén, Guatemala: Identification of the Kowoj.* PhD dissertation in Anthropology, Southern Illinois University, Carbondale.
2002 Remembering Mayapán: Kowoj domestic architecture as social metaphor and power. In *The Dynamics of Power*, edited by Maria O'Donovan, pp. 301–23. Occasional Paper no. 30. Center for Archaeological Investigations, Board of Trustees, Southern Illinois University, Carbondale.

2002–2004 Activity areas, form, and social inequality in residences at Late Postclassic Zacpetén, Petén, Guatemala. *Journal of Field Archaeology* 29(3/4):351–67.
2003a The exemplary center of the Late Postclassic Kowoj Maya. *Latin American Antiquity* 14(4):408–30.
2003b A cluster and spatial analysis of ceremonial architecture at Late Postclassic Mayapán. *Journal of Archaeological Science* 30:941–53.

Puleston, Dennis E.
1983 *Tikal Report 13: The Settlement Survey of Tikal.* University Museum Monograph 48. University of Pennsylvania, Philadelphia.

Rapoport, Amos
1993 On the nature of capitals and their physical expression. In *Capital Cities/Les Capitales: Perspectives Internationales, International Perspectives*, edited by J. Taylor, J.G. Lengellé, and C. Andrew, pp. 31–67. Carleton University, Ottawa.

Rattray, Evelyn C.
1987 Los barrios foráneos en Teotihuacan. In *Teotihuacan. Nuevos datos, nuevas síntesis, nuevos problemas*, edited by Emily McClung de Tapia and Evelyn Rattray, pp. 243–73. Instituto de Investigaciones Antropológicas, Universidad Nacional Autónoma de México, México, D.F.

Redfield, Robert
1952 The natural history of folk society. *Social Forces* 31:224–28.

Ricketson, Oliver G., Jr.
1925 Burials in the Maya area. *American Anthropologist* 27:381–401.

Ricketson, Oliver G., Jr., and E.G. Ricketson
1937 *Uaxactun, Guatemala. Group E 1926-31.* Publication no. 477. Carnegie Institution of Washington, Washington, D.C.

Robin, Cynthia
1989 *Preclassic Maya Burials at Cuello, Belize.* BAR International Series 480. BAR, Oxford.
2003 New directions in Classic Maya household archaeology. *Journal of Archaeological Research* 11:307–56.

Rodríguez Meléndez, Yasha N.
1997 *Elite Caches and Caching Practices in the Maya Lowlands.* Master's thesis in Anthropology, Arizona State University, Tempe, Arizona.

Ruz Lhuillier, A.
1965 Tombs and funerary practices of the Maya lowlands. In *Handbook of Middle American Indians. Vol. 2, Archaeology of Southern Mesoamerica*. Robert Wauchope, general editor, pp. 441–61. University of Texas Press, Austin.
1968 *Costumbres funerarias de los antiguos mayas.* Universidad Nacional Autónoma de México, México, D.F.

Sánchez, José I.
1989 *Las unidades habitacionales en Teotihuacan: el caso de Bidasoa.* Tesis de Licenciatura, Escuela Nacional de Antropología e Historia, México, D.F.

Sanders, William T.
1966   Life in a Classic village. In *Teotihuacan. XI Mesa Redonda*, pp. 123–47. Sociedad Mexicana de Antropología, México, D.F.

Séjourné, Laurette
1966   *Arquitectura y pintura en Teotihuacán*. Siglo XXI Editores, México, D.F.

Smith, Michael E.
2002   Domestic ritual at Aztec provincial sites in Morelos. In *Domestic Ritual in Ancient Mesoamerica*, edited by Patricia Plunket, pp. 93–114. Monograph 46. Cotsen Institute, University of California, Los Angeles.
2003   A quarter century of Aztec studies. *Mexicon* 25(1):4–10.
2007   Form and meaning in the earliest cities: A new approach to ancient urban planning. *Journal of Planning History* 6(1):3–47.

Spence, Michael W.
2002   Domestic ritual in Tlailotlacan, Teotihuacan. In *Domestic Ritual in Ancient Mesoamerica*, edited by Patricia Plunket, pp. 53–66. Monograph 46. Cotsen Institute, University of California, Los Angeles.

Stanton, Travis
2005   Horizontal excavations at the Muuch Group. In *The Pakbeh Regional Economy Program: Report of the 2001 Field Season*, edited by Bruce Dahlin and Daniel Mazeau, pp. 82–107. Sociology-Anthropology Department, Howard University, Washington, D.C.

Stuart, David
2000   The arrival of strangers: Teotihuacan and Tollan in Classic Maya history. In *Mesoamerica's Classic Heritage: From Teotihuacan to the Aztecs*, edited by David Carrasco, Lindsay Jones, and Scott Sessions, pp. 465–513. University Press of Colorado, Boulder.

Sugiyama, Saburo, and Leonardo López Luján
2007   Dedicatory burial/offering complexes at the Moon Pyramid, Teotihuacan: A preliminary report of 1998–2004 explorations. *Ancient Mesoamerica* 18:127–46.

Tainter, J.
1978   Mortuary practices and the study of prehistoric social systems. In *Advances in Archaeological Method and Theory*, Vol. 1, edited by M. Schiffer, pp. 105–41. Academic Press, New York.

Tiesler-Blos, Vera
2002   Un caso de decapitación prehispánica de Calakmul, Campeche. *Antropología física latinoamericana* 3:129–42. UNAM–Asociación Latinoamericana de Antropología Biológica.

2003   Sacrificio, tratamientos póstumos y disposición del cuerpo humano entre los Mayas de Calakmul: una visión osteotafonómico. *Los Investigadores de la Cultura Maya* 11, Tomo I (10):116–23. Universidad Autónoma de Campeche.

Tiesler-Blos, Vera, and Andrea Cucina
2003   Sacrificio, tratamiento y ofrenda del cuerpo humano entre los mayas del Clásico. Una mirada bioarqueológica. In *Antropología de la Eternidad: La muerte en la cultura maya*, edited by Andrés Ciudad-Ruiz, Mario Humberto Ruz-Sosa, and Josefa Iglesias Ponce de León, pp. 337–53. Sociedad Española de Estudios Mayas (Centro de Estudios Mayas), Madrid.

Uruñuela, Gabriela, and Patricia Plunket
2002   Lineages and ancestors: The Formative mortuary assemblages of Tetimpa, Puebla. In *Domestic Ritual in Ancient Mesoamerica*, edited by Patricia Plunket, pp. 20–30. Monograph 46. Cotsen Institute, University of California, Los Angeles.

Valdés, Juan Antonio, and Federico Fahsen
2004   Disaster in sight: The Terminal Classic at Tikal and Uaxactun. In *The Terminal Classic in the Maya Lowlands*, edited by A. Demarest, P. Rice, and D. Rice, pp. 140–61. University of Colorado Press, Boulder.

Webster, David L., Timothy Murtha, Kirk D. Straight, Jay Silverstein, Horatio Martínez, Richard E. Terry, and Richard Burnett
2007   The great Tikal earthwork revisited. *Journal of Field Archaeology* 32(1):41–64.

Welsh, W. Bruce M.
1988   *An Analysis of Classic Lowland Maya Burials*. BAR International Series 409. British Archaeological Reports, Oxford.

Winter, Marcus
2002   Monte Albán: Mortuary practices as domestic ritual and their relation to community religion. In *Domestic Ritual in Ancient Mesoamerica*, edited by Patricia Plunket, pp. 67–82. Monograph 46. Cotsen Institute, University of California, Los Angeles.

Wright, Lori E.
2005   Identifying immigrants to Tikal, Guatemala: Defining local variability in strontium isotope ratios of human tooth enamel. *Journal of Archaeological Science* 32:555–66.

Wright, Lori E., T. Douglas Price, J.H. Burton, and Peter Rank
2002   Teotihuacanos at Tikal and Kaminaljuyu? Paper presented at the 67th Annual Meeting of the Society for American Archaeology, Denver, Colorado, March 20–24.

—6—

Maya Home Life

Daily Practice, Politics, and Society in Copan, Honduras

Julia A. Hendon

Introduction

Over a century of archaeological work in the Copan Valley, Honduras, has developed an increasingly fine grained picture of the complexity of the prehispanic society that reached its peak during the Late Classic period (Marcus 2004). One way to bring this complexity into sharper focus and to consider its impact on the experience of living in such a society is to look at a particular social and spatial context, that of the domestic space of residential compounds. In this chapter, I consider what the study of life at home can tell us about the ways that this complex society was made more complicated and more cosmopolitan by "a social life characterized by flux, uncertainty, [and] encounters with difference" (Piot 1999:23). Drawing on research that has studied the people themselves, their patterns of settlement and built environment, and the social practices in which they regularly engaged, I argue that domestic space contributes to a sense of shared identity and history that creates a dynamic and contested social and political landscape.

Settlement History in the Copan Valley

The Copan River has created a series of small alluvial valleys or pockets as it flows southwestward through the mountains of western Honduras into Guatemala (Fig. 6.1). Archaeologists have discovered the remains of settlement in Copan dating back to at least 1400 BC (Fash 2001:63; Hall and Viel 2004). Early researchers posited that the "Maya-ness" of Copan was introduced as a whole by immigrants from the Maya lowlands who established a kingdom that may have incorporated the indigenous, possibly non-Maya-language speaking, residents (Longyear 1947, 1952; Willey 1986). Epigraphic, iconographic, and biological research now suggest that Ruler 1, the founder of the Copan ruling dynasty in the fifth century AD, may indeed have come from elsewhere. Strontium isotope analysis and stable oxygen isotope analysis of the skeleton from the tomb believed to be that of Ruler 1 indicate that the individual lived in the central Maya lowlands as a child and only came to Copan later (Buikstra et al. 2004), while text and imagery underscore an important Teotihuacan connection (Marcus 2004; Stuart 2005).

Recent research on the Formative occupation of the valley suggests that Ruler 1's origins may have been distinct from that of his subjects. Pottery and sculpture found in early contexts demonstrate the exchange of materials and ideas with the southwestern highland area of Guatemala and the Pacific Coast (Fash 2001:63–71, 2005; Fash and Stuart 1991; Viel 1998; Viel and Hall 1997, 2000). Ceramic ties with Honduras and El Salvador have also been noted. This evidence of diverse and far-ranging connections has been interpreted as the result of more than just economic

Figure 6.1. Western Honduras with the location of major archaeological sites and regions indicated.

ties. It has been argued that groups from the Maya highlands and the Pacific coastal area moved into the valley during the Early Formative period. Who these immigrants encountered when they reached the Copan Valley remains an open question.

A cluster of Early Formative burials found deep below one of the largest residential compounds in the valley (Fash 1985, 2001) provides evidence that people in the Copan Valley lived in a society with a long history of social differentiation, even longer than the establishment of dynastic royal rule. During the Classic period, the alluvial pockets along the river were organized into a single political entity. Copan's political ties extended as far west as Quirigua, with whom it had a contentious history that reached its nadir with Quirigua's capture of the thirteenth ruler of Copan in AD 738 (Looper 1999). Its eastern reach was more limited. Although the region around the modern town of La Entrada was closely linked to Copan culturally and economically and may have been politically subordinate (Nakamura et al. 1991), other well-populated areas such as the Naco, lower Ulúa, Comayagua,

and Sulaco Valleys remained culturally distinct and politically separate (see Ashmore 1987; Ashmore et al. 1987; Hirth 1988; Joyce 1988b, 1991; Schortman and Urban 1994, 2004).

It has been suggested that the last confirmed ruler, the sixteenth, found it necessary to share power and privilege more widely among members of high-status Copan families in order to secure their continued support in the face of declining standards of living and resources (Fash 2005; Fash and Stuart 1991). Competition for authority and privilege predated this particular ruler's tenure, however. René Viel (1999) has argued that more than one royal dynasty existed and that, over time, rulership shifted, perhaps to some extent in a patterned fashion, among at least two and possibly more noble houses who had legitimate but contested claims on the kingship and other political offices. Based on the occurrence of similar pectorals worn by human figures depicted on sculpture in the Main Group and in surrounding residences, Viel has further argued that these houses were associated with particular areas of settlement. The early ninth century saw the

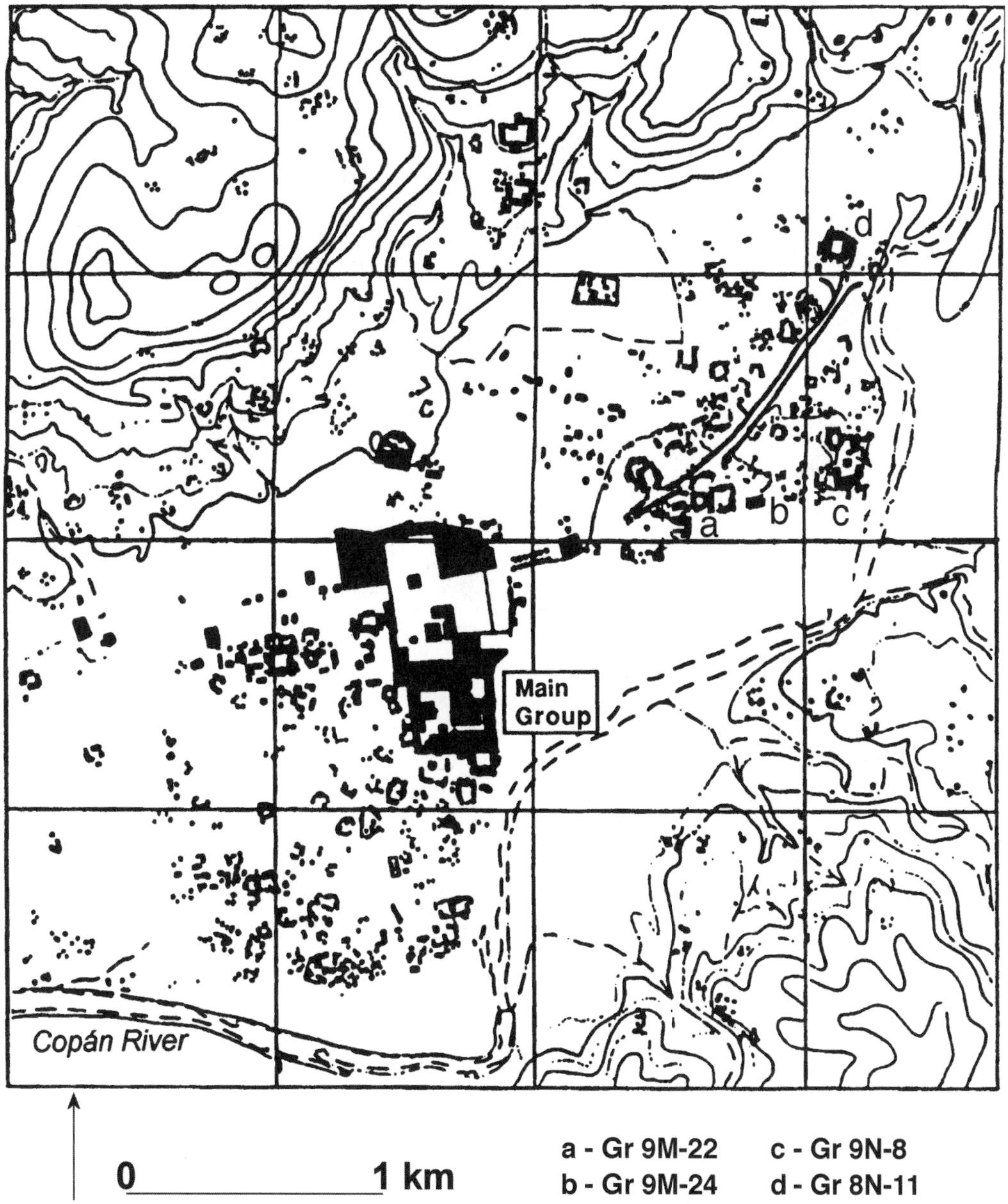

a - Gr 9M-22   c - Gr 9N-8
b - Gr 9M-24   d - Gr 8N-11

Figure 6.2. Settlement around the Main Group with the location of four excavated urban residential compounds discussed in the chapter.

Copan kingdom fall apart, in part due to local circumstances including environmental degradation, the effects of population growth, and possibly political factionalism among the ruling elite, and in part due to economic and political realignments affecting Mesoamerica as a whole. Although dynastic political control did not survive, the valley was not immediately abandoned nor did all forms of social difference disappear (Fash et al. 2004; Webster et al. 2004).

The Main Group, the collection of monuments and religious, governmental, and residential buildings built for and used mainly by the rulers of the Copan polity, sits on the valley floor of one

of the most densely populated alluvial pockets (Fig. 6.2). A large open plaza takes up the northern part of the area where most of the freestanding monuments are located (Fig. 6.3). The plaza is enclosed by buildings and, on the south, bounded by the rise of the Acropolis. The top of the Acropolis is divided into two enclosed courtyards, the East and West Courts. In the area at the foot of the Acropolis is the main ballcourt and the Hieroglyphic Staircase (see Ashmore 1991; Fash 2001; Longyear 1952). The massive and elaborate nature of the architecture throughout the Main Group tempts one to perceive it as something permanent and immutable (Fig. 6.4). What we see now, however, is only a

Figure 6.3. Monumental architecture and stelae in the open plaza of the Main Group (photo by the author).

moment in what was a long-term and ongoing process of rebuilding individual structures, relocating monuments, and redesigning whole areas of the complex—the moment when this process of movement and change came to a halt as political authority broke down in the early ninth century AD. Early structures that go back to a period between AD 100 and 400, based on radiocarbon dates and ceramic types recovered by archaeological excavations (Sharer et al. 2005), lie within the walls and beneath the floors of the ballcourt, the Hieroglyphic Staircase, and the Acropolis.

Spaces like the Main Group are closely connected to the effort on the part of some members of society to centralize and concentrate political authority in the hands of the few. Such authority cannot be separated from the person of the ruler or the royal house, making these spaces a kind of domestic space writ large. The royal family inhabits the entire complex even though their living quarters occupy only a small portion of the area. The location of early residences lies under the Acropolis. By the time of the last ruler, Ruler 16 (ruled AD 763–820/822?) (Fash 2001; Fash and Agurcia Fasquelle 2005; Looper 1998;

Martin and Grube 2000), the royal family was living behind the Acropolis, in an area much lower in elevation, separated from the large plaza and ballcourt by the bulk of the Acropolis itself (Andrews and Bill 2005; Andrews and Fash 1992).

The Copan Valley floor and sides are dotted with the remnants of groups of low stone platforms supporting residential structures, many rebuilt more than once. Sylvanus Morley, one of the earliest archaeologists to work in the valley, remarked that "every available spot in the valley was intensively occupied [by the Late Classic period]. Wherever one strays from the beaten tracks, one encounters the vestiges of former occupation: fallen buildings, fragments of elaborate sculptural mosaics, pyramids, platforms, terraces, and mounds" (Morley 1920:14). Systematic survey of the valley, including all the alluvial pockets, the foothills, and the tributary drainages, has confirmed this impression, with over 4,000 structures mapped (Canuto 2002; Fash 1983c; Fash and Long 1983; Freter 1988; Leventhal 1979). While many of the residential sites consist of a set of structures grouped around and facing onto a central open area, referred to here as the courtyard

Figure 6.4. The main ballcourt at Copan (photo by the author).

or patio, other sites are made up of several such groupings. The density of buildings reaches a maximum in an area extending approximately 2 km around the Main Group. About 2,000 remains of buildings have been located and mapped in this area and a smaller number excavated (Fash and Long 1983).

Our most informative body of information on Late Classic daily life comes from horizontally extensive excavations in two different parts of the settlement that were occupied during the period of maximum population size and greatest political centralization. One is the eastern part of the more densely settled area around the Main Group, known as the Sepulturas zone. My discussion is based primarily on three residential compounds from this zone, which provide one of the most complete recoveries of information about the Late Classic occupation (see Figs. 6.2, 6.5–6.7). Group 9N-8 has at least fourteen patios, each surrounded by a set of buildings, mostly residences but also kitchens, work platforms, and religious structures. The patios have been designated A–M. Patios A and B share a raised artificial platform that puts them at a slightly higher elevation than the adjoining

patios. Of these, Patios A–F, H–K, and M have been excavated. Group 9M-22 is a three-patio compound, two of which (Patios A and B) were excavated. Group 9M-24 is a single patio group (see Diamanti 2000; Gerstle and Webster 1990; Gonlin 1985; Hendon 1987, 1991; Hendon et al. 1990; Hendon et al. 1990; Sheehy 1991; Webster et al. 1986; Widmer 1997).[1] All three groups were slated for restoration to expand the tourist park. This made it possible to clear off the entire final construction phase of the buildings and excavate the full depth of the deposits of trash behind them. The restorers dismantled the surviving walls in order to reset them to vertical, giving the excavators a chance to explore the earlier phases of construction and to locate burials and caches.

Excavation (rather than test-pitting and survey) of residential sites outside this inner zone spans a range of site sizes and locations (see Fash 1983c). I draw on the most fully documented of these excavations, based on published research on seven[2] smaller residential groups in the less densely settled portion of the valley further away from the Main Group (Fig. 6.8). These

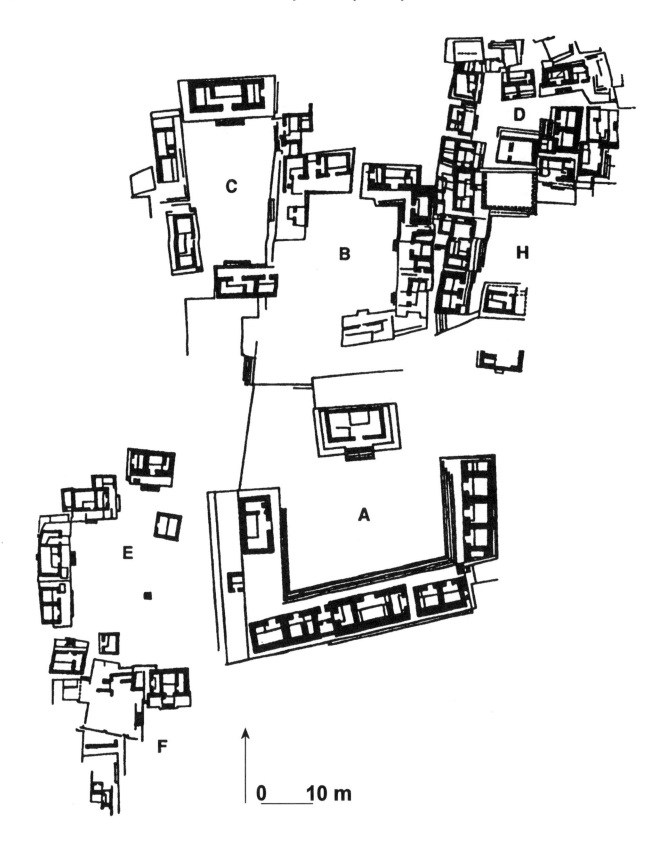

Figure 6.5. Group 9N-8, one of the largest compounds and home to an important noble house. Patios A-E and H have been excavated.

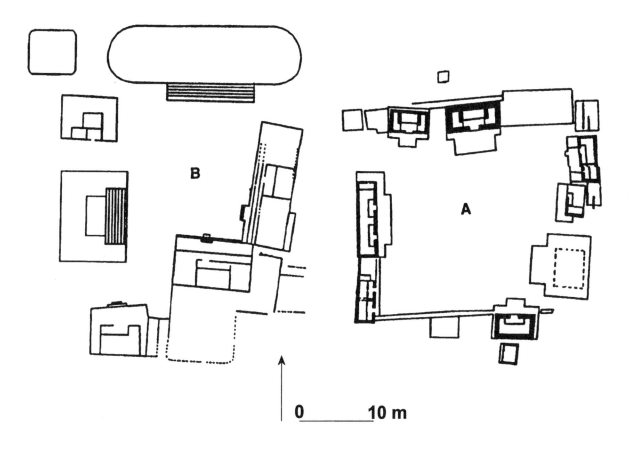

Figure 6.6. The two excavated patios (A, B) of Group 9M-22.

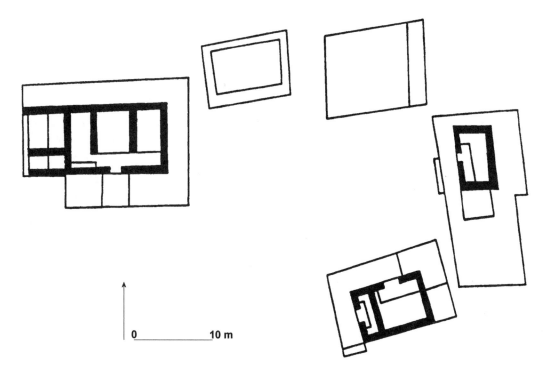

Figure 6.7. Group 9M-24, a small residential compound in the urban zone. It is a single patio group.

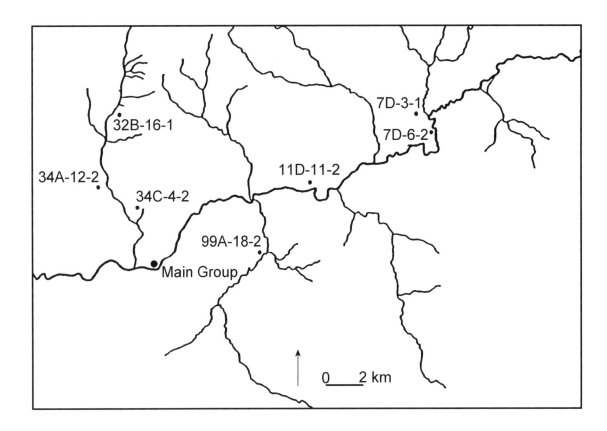

Figure 6.8. The Main Group and seven rural sites in the Copan Valley (redrawn from Gonlin 1993: Fig. 3.1).

sites provide a look at daily life among the less wealthy sector of the population that lived further away from the center of power (Gonlin 1993, 1994; Webster and Gonlin 1988). The seven sites are 11D-11-2, 7D-6-2, 7D-3-1, 34A-12-2, 32B-16-1, 99A-18-2, and 34C-4-2. Although most of these sites do not have enough structures to create a four-sided arrangement, they do share a consistent practice of orienting all buildings toward a central space or patio, sometimes paved, sometimes not. Site 11D-11-2 is the largest of the seven and most resembles the smaller groups in the inner zone, such as Group 9M-24, in its use of worked stone and architectural features. These rural and urban groups provide a comparable sample based on similar excavation strategies and methods.

Archaeologists working at Copan view the densely settled area around the Main Group, including the Sepulturas zone, as a more urban settlement occupied by members of an elite class (e.g., Fash 2001; Sanders 1989; Webster 1999). On the whole, the houses are larger and better built, there is more sculpture, some spectacularly well furnished burials have been found here, and the residents were better endowed with worldly goods. The largest number of aggregated groupings of courtyards are found here, as well as the tallest supporting platforms, and the most labor-intensive forms of construction using cut stone blocks, rubble fill, and stucco plaster. The Early Formative cemetery and an even earlier

house were found below the Patio of Group 9N-8, indicating a very long sequence of residential occupation. Nevertheless, it is important to keep in mind that significant variation exists within this area that undercuts a model of social difference as a simple division between monolithic or undifferentiated groups of elites and commoners (Gonlin 1985, 2004; Hendon 1989, 1991, 1992a, 1992b). Nor is a simple urban/rural distinction between large and dense settlement around the Main Group and small and dispersed settlement elsewhere an entirely accurate generalization, given the occurrence of large residential compounds with multiple patios in the foothills (Fash 1983b; Maca 2002; Whittington and Zeleznik 1991). Smaller centers with monumental architecture that developed in some of the eastern pockets and along tributary streams were incorporated into the expanding Copan polity as well (Canuto 2004; Morley 1920; Pahl 1977; Saturno 2000). Even the small residential patios containing only one, two, or three structures show evidence of multigenerational occupation and rebuilding over time (Gonlin 1993); they are smaller-scale examples of the same processes operating in the inner settlement area and the Main Group itself.

The tendency has been to compare sites as a whole to one another (e.g., Group 9N-8 to 9M-24), or to categorize sites into a typology having four or more levels (see Fash 1983a; Fash and Long 1983; Willey and Leventhal 1979; Willey et al. 1976). The excavation of residences, however, makes us aware that quite noticeable differences can exist even within a single compound in terms of number of structures, areal extent, architecture, and work effort or energetics (Hendon 1992b). Take, for example, the quantity and location of the two kinds of stone most commonly used for building: faced river cobbles, and blocks of quarried tuff. There is a greater and more consistent use of block masonry in the inner or urban zone and in the larger compounds, but not all buildings are built this way. Residents of these compounds made a consistent set of choices when deciding which parts of the building should be built out of blocks and which of cobbles. If one is going to use only some blocks, then they should be used for the front wall rather than the back, the staircase on the front of the foundation platform, the doorjambs into the main room of the residence, or the stone bench built inside those rooms. Some quite impressive looking structures from the front become much less so as one moves around the sides to the back, where one also finds much of the household trash (Hendon 1987, 1991, 1992a). Furthermore, the small group 9M-24 has some very nicely shaped masonry architecture, as do the small foothill sites of 11D-11-2 and 7D-6-2 (Gonlin 1985, 1994).

The Materialization of Social Difference

Characteristics that may indicate differences in status—such as treatment in death, energetics of housing, permanent modification of the body, depiction in sculpture, memorialization in text, access to resources, and so on—do not come together to form a single pattern, providing an illustration of the complicated social landscape of Late Classic society. The large sample of burials excavated in the valley over the last century has been subjected to numerous studies of diet and health. These studies demonstrate that the social, biological, and ecological stresses that could result in interruptions in childhood growth, infant mortality, and diseases such as anemia and tooth decay were widespread among men and women, rural and urban dwellers, and people of lesser and greater social status (based on burial treatment or residence) during the period of peak occupation (Gerry and Chesson 2000; Gerry and Krueger 1997; Lee 1995; Padgett 1996; Reed 1998, 1999; Storey 1992, 1997, 1998, 1999; Whittington 1999; Whittington and Reed 1997). The overall conclusion revealed by this research is that "during periods of childhood and adulthood all individuals had impaired nutritional status" (Storey 1999:178). Individuals believed to be of higher status, based on how they were buried, may have eaten a somewhat better diet but their bodies still show evidence of disease. Even rulers were not immune from the stresses of life at Copan. Examination of the bodies from tombs under the Acropolis, believed to be those of members of the Copan dynasty, exhibit similar patterns of childhood malnutrition or diseases, although these individuals seem to have been somewhat healthier and better nourished as adults (Storey 2005).

Body modification, often taken as another sign of individual status, also fails to follow the expected pattern. The use of den-

tal inlays (circular pieces of jade, other green-colored stone, hematite, or other materials set into a person's front teeth) or dental filing, notching teeth, or otherwise physically altering their shape indicates that these forms of beautification were not restricted to residents of large residential compounds, to those buried in elaborate graves, or even to those living in the urban area (Rhoads 2002:74, 225–34). Ornaments for ears and lips are found in the small rural sites as well as at the three Sepulturas compounds.

Burial treatment itself is variable within compounds. While it is true that richly endowed burials have been found in Sepulturas and other areas around the Main Group, other burials in the same residential compounds are simpler in how the body was treated, what was included in the grave, and whether a formal grave was even provided. Residences in Sepulturas contain a spectrum of methods of interment, ranging from stone-walled, vaulted tombs with niches that look very much like ones in the Main Group to smaller, unvaulted and stone-lined crypts placed in building platforms or below the paved floor of the central patio. In other cases, a grave was dug in building fill, subsoil below the courtyard along the fronts and sides of buildings, or in the middens behind the residential structures. Other individuals were deposited in the middens or building fill with no evidence of formal placement. Tombs and crypts contain a similar range of offerings, including polished brown ware (Surlo) and polychrome vessels, objects for personal adornment made of shell or jade/greenstone as well as stingray spines, obsidian blades, clay figurine-whistles, and *Spondylus* shells. The burials in graves usually lack pottery or more elaborate sorts of jewelry but do include ceramic beads, bone tools, or obsidian blades as well as figurine-whistles (Hendon 1991, 2003c). This mortuary variation has been used to argue for at least two levels of status among residents of Sepulturas compounds but statistically significant variation between these levels in terms of health and diet has not been documented (Storey 1998).

Only two of the seven rural residential sites I am using here yielded burials (Gonlin 1993). At 34A-12-2, the graves most likely date from early in the Late Classic period and contained decorated or polychrome pottery and metates. At the other site, 99A-18-2, the burials did not have any obvious funerary offerings but metates were used as part of the stones delimiting the graves. A third site, 7D-3-1, lacks burials but has a cist inside one of the structures containing two polychrome vessels, a chert biface, an obsidian eccentric, and a jade or greenstone ornament. A polished mirror, possibly made of pyrite, was also found at this site, although not in the cache.

Distribution of resources based on archaeological remains also suggests that the use of valued or imported materials was not restricted to those living in the Main Group or immediately around it. Obsidian from Guatemala and Honduras, for example, is the material of choice throughout the valley to make sharp cutting implements, and is used to make objects of personal adornment. Obsidian objects are also placed in burials or ritual caches (Aoyama 1995, 2001; Freter 1988; Hendon et al.

1990:151–55, 185; Mallory 1984). In addition to the obsidian eccentric mentioned above (from site 7D-3-1), Gonlin (1993) reports an obsidian cylindrical ornament from 11D-11-2 as well as nineteen green obsidian blades from the late site of 7D-6-2. The locally produced polychrome pottery types, the most common of which is known as *Copador*, is used everywhere (Beaudry 1984; Bishop et al. 1986; Viel 1993a, 1993b; Webster et al. 2004). Painted vessels known collectively as Ulúa polychromes, coming from central and southern Honduras, found their way into rural household inventories in small quantities (Fash 1983c; Freter 1988; Gonlin 1993). Jade and shell were used for jewelry and to embellish clothing. Objects made of these materials have been found in the Main Group and Sepulturas excavations but also in some small rural sites including 11D-11-2, 7D-3-1, and 34C-4-2 (Fash 2001; Hendon 1991; Gonlin 1993).

Social Houses

Modeling Late Classic Copan social organization as structured by social houses that crosscut status or class distinctions provides a better way to understand this variation (Hendon 2002b, 2003b, 2007). Social houses represent an important locus of identity in Mesoamerica (see Chance 2000; Gillespie 2000a, 2000b; Joyce 2000; Monaghan 1995:244–46). Copan social houses, like those in other Mesoamerican societies, rely heavily on connections between people, physical houses, and material objects for their perpetuation.

People become house members through various means. These can include descent from other members but, unlike in a lineage model, descent through a particular line, such as that of males, is only one of several possible ways to use relatedness as the basis for a claim of membership. Other ways include marriage to someone already part of the social house, adoption, capture, or living in the same area. Membership thus brings people together through genealogy and alliance, kinship and locality, to create a flexible but enduring social group of variable size that encompasses people of differing wealth, status, and role as well as of different ages, genders, and family ties. Although social house members often use kinship as a way of referring to one another, this is as much a rhetorical strategy as a reflection of what we would call actual blood relationships (Waterson 1995). Membership is really oriented around common investment in the house estate, an investment embodied in shared participation in ritual and day-to-day interactions, and combines material possessions with intangible property or wealth (Lévi-Strauss 1982; Weiner 1992). The latter might include what we would think of as rights, such as the right to perform certain ceremonies, produce particular items (often regalia used in such ceremonies), or employ specific names and titles. If Viel's analysis of Copan kingship is correct, some noble houses in the Sepulturas area were also in a position to make a claim on the position of ruler.

The Continual Recreation of Social Difference

The differences in the sets of data I have just described, including health and diet, body modification, burial treatment, and access to valued materials, suggest that we are dealing with categories that were continually recreated through practice to accomplish both the reinforcement of group solidarity at the level of the social house and differentiation within and among houses. These forms of differentiation and integration do not "exist in some sense in a state of virtuality, not as something given but as *something to be done*," something that is relational and that people "construct, individually and especially *collectively*, in cooperation and conflict" (Bourdieu 1998:12, original emphasis). Because the important process is the continual creation or reaffirmation of difference and distance (how groups differentiate themselves to create social difference), the particular markers of distinction cannot remain stable even though stability, or its appearance, is one way to make such processes and relations seem immutable.

This desire to fix that which is not stable helps explain why the built environment emerges as the most consistent marker of social difference at Copan during the Late Classic (Fig. 6.9). As the most enduring and visible element of the social house's estate—an element, moreover, that stands for generational continuity—dwellings, temples, or other buildings provide an important means to express this desire. First, the size, material, and scale of residences are among the most visible and enduring expressions of the control of resources and energy needed to build, renovate, and maintain them (Abrams 1987, 1994; Carrelli 2004; Fash 2005; Hendon 1991, 1992a, 2002b). Second, buildings and more broadly residential places provide a focal point for practices that turn these structures into tangible historical referents for their residents that span generations and speak to multiple actors (Pred 1990; Rodman 2003; Soja 1985). These practices, including building renovation, the placement of caches of polychrome serving vessels or even more domestic objects such as grinding stones or storage jars, the burying of people, and the incorporation of sculpture and hieroglyphic texts, turn these dwellings into "memory machines" (Douglas 1993:268), the enduring manifestation of the social group that inhabits them (Hendon 1991, 2000, 2003a; Willey and Leventhal 1979).

The materialization of social difference achieved and indeed created through the investment in the built environment results, on the whole, in less accessible spaces. The layout of Copan monumental space places walls around the largest open space (the main plaza with most of the sculptured monuments and the ballcourt) and interposes a substantial barrier, in the form of the Acropolis, between this plaza and the dwellings of Ruler 16 and his family. In other words, taller buildings and enclosed unroofed spaces become more and more private in the sense that they are more closely connected to groups of people who control how these spaces are used, viewed, and developed (Birdwell-Pheasant and Lawrence-Zúñiga 1999). This increasing difficulty of access and of opportunities for control provide other means by which

Figure 6.9. Group 9N-8 Patio B (foreground) and Patio A (background) after restoration. Structure 9N-82, with its hieroglyphic bench and ancestral sculpture, is visible under the thatched roof protecting it from the elements (photo by the author).

people, especially members of noble inner zone houses, differentiate and perpetuate their own histories. This is the control not only of what people may experience but of what people know (Hendon 2000).

For people living around the Main Group, increasing one's living space while maintaining the central open space of the patio or courtyard could really be achieved only by rebuilding existing structures or by filling in the corners of the group with new buildings set between older ones. Expanding a building's footprint was made difficult by the use of tall foundation platforms whose square footage limited the degree to which the actual residence, sitting on top of the platform, could be extended horizontally. Although some Sepulturas residences had two stories (Hohmann 1995), their construction posed engineering problems in an earthquake-prone area that were only partially resolvable given existing technology, building materials, and engineering knowledge. Thus, this zone became more built up over time until the largest group (9N-8), made up of many contiguous courtyards, becomes very difficult to enter.

Only one or two entrances exist, and entering through what was probably the main one still challenges a visitor with the task of passing through several compounds in order to reach others. The difference in elevation between Patios A and B, on their raised platform, and the other patios exacerbates this issue of access from one patio to another.

Rural residents rebuilt their living areas, sometimes renovating existing buildings, sometimes adding new ones and abandoning older ones. Unlike the royal and noble houses in and around the Main Group, rural dwellers in the small sites considered here were less likely to build over an existing structure and were more likely to add on to it or to leave it standing as they expanded the size of the residential group by adding new structures. The more dispersed nature of settlement outside the inner zone makes a more expansive building pattern possible, but it is interesting to note that these rebuilding episodes maintain the orientation toward the patio space.

The tighter arrangement of residential space in the Sepulturas zone has a pragmatic relationship to density and length of occupation but the resulting spatial enclosure is no less capable of being meaningful because it is to some extent dictated by circumstances. Because urban compounds have relatively few entry points and the stone houses are raised on platforms, the resulting exterior is mostly that of plain back walls rising high above a passerby. If one stood on one of the building platforms of the Acropolis, the highest part of the Main Group, one would be above the surrounding urban residences built on the valley floor. However, the close spacing and high walls of these residences would impede such a bird's-eye view into the courtyards and counter the hierarchy immanent in these differences in height and point of view (Hendon 2002b).

In terms of the residential compounds themselves, spaces inside buildings are less visible than the patio area or wide exterior terrace (Joyce and Hendon 2000). This would also be mediated by construction materials. Stone walls are less permeable to sound and light, confining what is said or done inside them more effectively than walls of wood or clay. At the same time, stone walls limit the occupants' observation of people's comings and goings to what can be seen through the doorway (if not closed off by a mat or curtain). The more permeable wood and clay walls change the experience of inside and outside and afford greater opportunity for continued interaction between people working outside and inside the house (Robin 2002). People inside the wattle-and-daub houses in rural and urban Copan, such as those found at practically all groups considered here, would have been able to note what was happening outside more readily than their neighbors in stone buildings.

People used sculpture and hieroglyphic inscriptions to further endorse a sense of historically constituted identity (Handler 1994). The small compounds in the foothills do not have evidence of architectonic sculpture but the residents of 34C-4-2 possessed a small freestanding sculpture in the shape of a house or bench. Stone images of a frog were found at two other sites, 7D-3-1 and 11D-11-2 (Gonlin 1993). Inner zone and some of the larger compounds and centers away from the Main Group display sculpture or texts in ways that help them become an embodiment of continuing group identity tied to the materialization of the continuity of the social house as well as sources of differential knowledge and experience (Hendon 2002b, 2007).

Inscriptions provide the most specific and individualized information about a social group or individual. Rulers clearly expended more effort on recording information because the bulk of hieroglyphic inscriptions, both freestanding and architectonic, are found in the Main Group. Such texts make permanent those events and attributes of the lives of the ruling house that the rulers want to establish as historical record, making concrete a particular history by providing a focus for social memory. A few examples of hieroglyphic writing are found set into the exterior walls of elite residences (Ashmore 1991; Hendon 1992a). On one building in Patio C of Group 9N-8 (Str. 9N-69), the builders divided the text between the upper and lower registers of the façade, placing an abbreviated form of the date in the upper and a short text dedicating the building itself in the lower (Hendon

2002b). Separating the glyph blocks for the date from those for the subject and event portion of the text means that the date would be the most visible part and what a potential viewer/reader would encounter first. The physical house becomes fixed in time, providing a way to anchor house identity to historical as well as generational time.

Most hieroglyphic inscriptions in the inner area, including the residential compounds in the Sepulturas zone, are found inside buildings. Like such texts in the Main Group, which are associated with buildings on the Acropolis, the least accessible area, the majority of texts displayed by the noble houses in the context of their domestic space are hidden in the interior of their houses. Exact knowledge of the content of these inscriptions is shared with only those people allowed access to the intimate interior spaces of the household. Such inscriptions generally take the form of long and detailed texts carved on the face of benches in the main room of the best built and most elaborate residence in the compound (see Webster 1989; Willey et al. 1978). Such seats of authority (Gillespie 1999) affiliate inner zone noble houses with the centralized political structure but because the emphasis is on recording temporally fixed action by members of the social group living in the residential compound, they memorialize events of significance to the resident social house and only indirectly to the polity as a whole.

Sculpture placed on the outside of residences may be set into both the upper and lower registers of the building (Fig. 6.10; see Andrews and Fash 1992; Ashmore 1991; Baudez 1989, 1994; Fash 1992; Hendon 1992a; Webster et al. 1998). Such figures would have been visible from at least some vantage points outside the confines of the compound itself, even in densely settled Sepulturas. Two residences, one in Group 9N-8 and the other in Group 8N-11, display seated human figures that wear pectorals affiliating them with one of Viel's royal lines. Inner zone residences draw on a common set of motifs and rules about their placement that are also used, on an even larger scale, on the monumental buildings in the Main Group itself (see Fash 1992), creating a kind of parallelism between the space controlled by the ruling authority and that controlled by noble or elite houses (Hendon 1992a; Bachand et al. 2003).

Foreign Relations

During the Late Classic period, the presence of foreigners in one residential patio of the largest group in the Sepulturas zone (Patio D of Group 9N-8) has been suggested based on what seem to be higher amounts of imported material culture, especially Ulúa polychromes and figurine-whistles (Gerstle 1988). These foreigners, usually identified as Lenca-speaking,[3] have been seen as an enclave with some sort of special function (perhaps economic, perhaps political) and of relatively high social status.

As noted earlier, pieces of imported Ulúa polychrome pottery have turned up in excavations and test pits of rural sites. Their presence attests to the fact that eighth- to tenth-century Copanecos were involved in exchange relations with the com-

Figure 6.10. One of the ancestral figures on the façade of Structure 9N-82, after restoration (photo by the author).

signals more than the persistence of enduring exchange relationships. Cassandra Bill (1997) has suggested that the excavations in Patio D recovered more bits of foreign pottery because it was occupied late in the history of Group 9N-8 when, presumably, interest in these imported wares was greatest. What I find more relevant is the fact that Patio D's excavators recovered a greater amount of pottery overall than was found in the other patios of Group 9N-8. Compiling information from Tables 5.5 and 5.6 of Gerstle's dissertation (1988:124–25), it becomes clear that there are 27,387 pieces in her sample, 10,049 of which come from Patio D. In other words, Patio D contributes more than one-third (36.69%) of the potsherds to the total number from Group 9N-8. No other patio comes close to this. As Table 6.1 indicates, this dominance extends to the frequency of Ulúa polychromes. But knowing that 0.81% of all Ulúa polychromes excavated in Group 9N-8 were found in Patio D does not establish a greater preference for these types of vessels by Patio D residents unless we can find a way to factor out the influence of the larger total amount of material from that patio.

An alternate way to look at how much imported pottery was being consumed by the residents of the different patios does exist. Table 6.2 contains the results of calculating the frequency of Ulúa polychromes as a percentage of the total number of sherds from each patio rather than of the overall number of sherds from all patios combined. This seems preferable because it provides a useful, albeit imperfect, measure of consumption and, indirectly, of the ability to satisfy this desire to have foreign polychrome vessels available for serving and eating food. What emerges from the figures in Table 6.2 is that Patios A, D, and H are all similar, with slightly more than 2% of their pottery classified as Ulúa polychromes. It is now Patio B that stands out with 5.07%. Extending the analysis to the other groups discussed in this chapter, Patio A of Group 9M-22 also shows a notable presence with 3.01% of the pottery excavated belonging to the Ulúa polychrome category (175 out of 5,805).

Yet another way to consider this question would be to look at just the fancy serving and table ware, thus removing pottery that served a different purpose, such as cooking, storage, and so on. Some time ago I noted that when comparing the frequency of imported polychromes in each patio of Group 9N-8 as a percentage of the total number of fancy sherds from that patio (including locally produced polychromes and carved brown wares), we find that Patio A has the highest proportion of imports, at almost 12%, and that Patios B, C, and D are comparable to one another at about half that of Patio A (Hendon 1991). What these comparisons suggest is that in addition to the residents of Patio D, several noble houses in Group 9N-8 (and at least one in Group 9M-22) valued the acquisition and use of Ulúa polychromes.

The possibility of foreign enclaves also does not find support from studies of biological data. Megan Rhoads has analyzed the distribution of genetically inherited dental traits by studying Late Classic burials from the inner zone and foothills "as a proxy to determine biological distance between or among groups" (Rhoads 2002:44). Her work reveals that regardless of its pos-

plex societies to their east and south (see Gerstle 1988; Hendon 1991; Joyce 1986; Maca 2002; Viel 1993a, 1993b). Produced throughout the Late Classic period, this pottery varies regionally and changes through time (Beaudry-Corbett et al. 1993; Joyce 1993). The most important areas of production and use have been identified as the lower Ulúa River valley, the area around Lake Yojoa, and the Comayagua Valley. The types of Ulúa vessels found at Copan suggest they mostly came from Comayagua (Viel 1993a, 1993b). Imported moldmade figurine-whistles and similarities between Copan Valley and central Honduran storage vessels further show that the Copan people maintained important connections with their eastern neighbors (Hendon 2003b; Joyce 1993; Longyear 1952; Schortman and Urban 2004; Tercero 1996; Viel 1993a, 1993b).

The question that has been asked (most intensively by Andrea Gerstle [1987, 1988]) is whether the presence of these pots and figures, foreign both in terms of their origin and their style,

Table 6.1. Distribution of Ulúa Polychrome pottery in Group 9N-8.

Patio	Number of Sherds from each Patio	Percent of all Sherds (N = 27,387)	Number of Ulúa Polychromes from each Patio	Percent of Ulúa Polychromes
A	3,282	11.98	78	0.28
B	946	3.45	48	0.18
C	1,986	7.25	31	0.11
D	10,049	36.69	222	0.81
E	1,794	6.55	12	0.04
F	1,539	5.62	17	0.06
H	5,116	18.68	120	0.44
K	2,543	9.29	49	0.18
M	132	0.48	0	0.00

Table 6.2. Distribution of Ulúa Polychrome pottery in each patio of Group 9N-8.

Patio	Number of Ulúa Polychromes from each Patio	Number of Sherds from each Patio	Percentage that are Ulúa Polychromes
A	78	3,282	2.38
B	48	946	5.07
C	31	1,986	1.56
D	222	10,049	2.21
E	12	1,794	0.67
F	17	1,539	1.10
H	120	5,116	2.35
K	49	2,543	1.93
M	0	132	0.00

sible ethnically, linguistically, and geographically diverse origins, the Copan population was remarkably homogeneous in terms of biological relatedness by the time of the Late Classic period. Only one clear distinction emerged from a range of analyses: that two biological lineages can be differentiated (Rhoads 2002:215–21). Rhoads notes that these two lineages, called here for convenience A and B, crosscut the spatial and status categories derived from other archaeological data. In other words, members of both biological lineages were found in burials in the Main Group, in the dense and conventionally elite residential area around it, and out in the more dispersed foothill settlements.

In those cases where it is possible to consider the burials from one particular residential patio or from agglomerations of such patios as found in the urban zone, it turns out that men and women from the same domestic setting most often belong to the same biological lineage. Furthermore, no genetically foreign or distinct enclaves could be identified. Take the three groups from the Sepulturas area mentioned earlier. Group 9M-24, the smallest, was occupied by people belonging to Lineage A. Group 9M-22's two excavated patios contained burials belonging entirely or mostly to Lineage B. Both lineages were found in the largest group, 9N-8. Patios A, B, C, D, E, F, and H have more burials belonging to Lineage B while those from Patio J are members of Lineage A. Even the residents of Patio D are biologically indistinguishable from their close neighbors in the adjacent patios and the rest of the Copan pocket. The distribution of lineages does not correspond to sex in any regular way, suggesting that people frequently married members of their own biological lineage. Other excavated groups in this area are occupied by Lineage A (9N-5, 9N-6, 9M-18, and 9M-27) (Rhoads 2002: Table 7.8).

These biological data do not mean that people in the Copan Valley necessarily had no sense of different degrees of relationship or thought of themselves as divided into two generally endogamous groups. Kinship may be defined in ways that emphasize smaller scale or shorter-term connections, and of course is not directly dependent on shared descent. These data do suggest that over time the residents of the alluvial pocket around the Main Group built up a wide-ranging and long-lasting set of relations and connections that were both biological and social. These connections may have complicated the construction of clearly defined social difference based on location, wealth, or descent. The several royal houses that Viel (1999) suggests supplied rulers over the course of the Copan dynasty were allied with other houses whose members resided in Sepulturas and other parts of the inner zone. These noble houses have both a social and a physical presence, being made up of living members and ancestors bound together through multiple means of asserting connection, including descent, marriage, shared residence, and shared rights in the house estate, the most substantial part of which is the compound itself.

Daily Life and Domestic Space

The excavated compounds in Sepulturas and their smaller counterparts in the foothills provide evidence of the importance of domestic space to social reproduction and identity. People did not spend all their time within the confines of their dwellings. They would have left to travel, farm, gather resources, visit, arrange marriages, hunt, participate in religious ceremonies, attend on the ruler, go to war, and so on. Nevertheless, the volume and range of materials recovered as well as the degree of architectural renovation and elaboration leave the impression of an intensive sociality and productivity that must have occupied much of people's time and creative energies. Reviewing the evidence from these residential areas, three clusters of productive action and sociality emerge as important: crafting, storing, and feasting.

Productive Action at Home

The economic interdependence of people living together in Late Classic Copan comes through in the consistent association between domestic space and evidence for a range of productive action over time. Given the size of some of the residential groupings discussed here, some domestic groups were large indeed yet they display a similar pattern of activities conventionally defined as economic. In all cases, analysis of the architecture of these residences, the artifacts found, and their contextual associations (including where and with what they are found) allows us to see the kinds of daily living activities that took place there. Pottery jars, plates, bowls, and basins for mixing, cooking, and serving; basalt or rhyolite manos and metates for grinding corn; sharp cutting tools made out of obsidian; and bones from deer and other animals all demonstrate that food preparation, food consumption, and storage took up people's time. But daily life during this time period included more than just making sure everyone was fed and housed. People made things while at home. Thread, cloth, jewelry, cutting tools, and bark paper were the kinds of objects that might be manufactured, based on recovered artifacts.

Perhaps the most domestic of domestic activities are those connected with preparing and cooking food. These quintessential activities of daily life took place in outdoor locations in the patio, on the terraces, or in roofed areas that were not fully enclosed rooms. Many residential compounds possess more than one cooking or food preparing area. The artifacts associated with these areas include a brazier with a shallow plate that formed a kind of portable stove for heating food (Gonlin 1993; Hendon 1987, 1988) or outdoor hearths (Gonlin 1993); manos and metates for grinding maize; bowls and basins for mixing and cooking; jars for holding water or other ingredients; animal bones; and obsidian or chert tools for cutting, scraping, sawing, grooving, slicing and other kinds of processing of hard and soft materials, such as wood, leather, shell, bone, antler, plants, and meat (Aoyama 2001; Mallory 1984). All of the cooking and food preparation activities that used these objects did not necessarily take place simultaneously; maize grinding might be done at one point in the day, cooking at another. Both maize grinding and cooking require water, which would have been carried into the compound in jars from reservoirs or rivers. These necessary and repetitive activities—the movement of people, the rasp of the grinding stones, the crackle of the fire, the smell of food cooking, the noise of water being poured, and people's conversations—contributed both to the rhythm of the day and the sensory experience of living.

Forms of production requiring training and the development of skills and abilities are implied by the kinds of material culture found in Copan residential sites. Evidence for textile production in Sepulturas comes from spindle whorls, centrally-perforated clay disks, and bone tools, specifically needles, pins, and weaving picks (Hendon 1997, 1999b; see also McMeekin 1992). Spinning weights have also been found in rural sites (Gonlin 2000). Both spindle whorls and centrally-perforated clay disks served as weights for spindles used to spin thread of different weights and from different raw materials. Bone tools for sewing or weaving include needles of various sizes, pins (identical to the needles but lacking an eye), and brocade picks. Needles and pins vary considerably in length, suggesting their use on a variety of materials. These implements may be used both for sewing and in weaving. Brocade picks (often labeled awls) are usually made of deer bone. Twice as long as they are wide, they taper to a sharp point and are used to lift warp threads when creating brocade design (see O'Neale 1945). These tools were recovered from excavations of Group 9N-8 and 9M-22, with the greatest concentration coming from Patios B, D, and H of Group 9N-8.

Spinning and weaving are often described as women's work in prehispanic Mesoamerica and a great deal of evidence exists to support an association between female gender and these particular forms of production that created highly valued materials (Hendon 1997, 1999a, 1999b). The strong associations between productive action and gender in indigenous Mesoamerican societies today do not create a closed or exclusive approach to knowledge and work (Hendon 2006). Participation by people of a different gender is not prohibited by social sanctions or stigma yet at the same time is not common (Asturias de Barrios 1998; Chamoux 1993). The difficulty of learning to weave—the lengthy apprenticeship, the physical skills and expertise with the technology required, the mental skills that must be developed over time—and the home-based structure of the training process tend to reproduce a particular form of gendered involvement over time (Greenfield 2004). At the same time, it is important to realize that textile production may require the assistance of other household members, including adult men and boys (Hicks 1994), just as other forms of specialized production typically associated with men by Spanish accounts also relied on the assistance of women (Hendon 2006).

Making useful or decorative objects from shell and bone has been documented from several areas of urban Copan. The most complete contexts, and by implication, the most intensive involvement in these crafts, come from Patios D and H of the large multi-patio complex of Group 9N-8. Structure 110B on the western side of Patio H is a building with four rooms. Three of them (Rooms 1–3) form a suite, with the only door to the outside in Room 1. A range of tools, objects, and raw materials were recovered from inside Room 2, at least some of which were used for making shell ornaments (Widmer 1997; see also Hendon 1987:227–32, 389–90). These include obsidian blades, cut and drilled pieces of marine shell, and stone work tablets. Some of these artifacts had been stored inside pottery vessels or on a shelf. One of the pots contained a broken star-shaped ornament, more of which was found on the floor along with other pieces of shell. Two other vessels were full of dirt and burned material. Room 4 of the same structure as well as rooms in Structure 9N-115A and Structure 9N-61A (in Patio D) contained raw materials and finished objects of shell or bone (Gerstle and Webster 1990:62–71, 114–21, 168–70; Hendon 1987:184–87, 221–23, 389–90). All of these rooms could be entered from the outside directly through a doorway that gave access to the large terraces of the foundation platform.

Worked shell and bone that had been cut, drilled, scraped, or otherwise processed have been found in contexts suggesting working on terraces and platforms in other areas of Group 9N-8 (see Hendon 1987). The shell working in Copan's Structure 9N-110B Room 2 takes place in the most enclosed and least visible location considered here. It is the most private location, in the sense of being the most controllable by the participants and the least subject to intrusion by others. This privacy, which suggests a desire to keep hidden what was being produced or the process of production itself, comes at a cost: the only natural light comes from the doorway into Room 1, which in turn has only one doorway onto the terrace. Artificial light may have been provided by burning material in the two pots, but the amount of illumination would not be great. Thus, this was not an easy place to cut, scrape, and shape brittle shells into complicated shapes and objects. The other rooms, with their direct access to the outside, would have been better lit and still fairly private if the workers stayed inside and did not take advantage of the large terrace, but not nearly as conducive to secrecy.[4]

When thinking about action, especially that subsumed under craft production, the tendency is to focus on either the end product or the tasks carried out. Crafting things also entails interaction between people, the material at hand, and the setting. The spatial concentration of cooking and food preparation suggests this activity was somewhat separated from other things people were doing in the course of a day, such as making cloth or shell ornaments, gathering in rooms, and eating. Its location on terraces, next to foundation platforms, or on small platforms kept it visible and allowed the people grinding maize, cutting up meat, preparing vegetables, and stirring the pot to not only be seen but to be aware of what others were doing around them. The sights, sounds, and smells that accompanied the movement of people as they went about their tasks constructed a temporal rhythm to the day.

Responsibilities for these and other actions of daily life become integral to intersubjective identities that are overlapping and to a certain extent situational, given that people did not devote all their time to making things such as shell ornaments. How would these identities relate to the axes of variation commonly associated with social identity, such as age, gender, or class? Let me focus here on gender and age. Such associations suggest that many of the people in these cooking areas were women and girls. It is very easy, for example, to imagine that older children and adolescents were responsible for bringing water from streams or reservoirs in the early mornings and as needed during the day. It may seem an appropriate application of the symmetry of the sexual division of labor to imagine male shell workers crouched over *Spondylus* and *Olivella* shells in smoky, dimly lit Room 2 while their female relatives and fellow residents congregate in the cooking areas to get meals ready or sit on the wide terraces spinning and weaving. I think a more reasonable interpretation, one that is respectful of the ambiguities in the textual and visual sources that attribute gender to tasks, is that some dividing up of responsibilities was necessary, and that this led to different associations between some people and some practices, opening the way for multiple identities through what was done, where, and with whom (see Hendon 2006).

Storing

Given the widespread and long-standing custom of interring people, objects, and buildings in residential places, it seems reasonable to infer that a general understanding prevailed among Late Classic Copanecos that being in a residential compound put one in the presence of the dead as well as the living. Burials and caches combine the material with the moral. They are loci where items, and sometimes people, of material and symbolic value are not only deposited and guarded, but also altered. Noble and royal houses at Copan revisited tombs and other graves, in the process adding objects or people (or individual bones) as well as removing part or all of the contents (Bell et al. 2004; Hendon 2000, 2003a). These practices may be fruitfully considered to be a form of storage, allowing comparison with what we usually assume is a utilitarian or practical activity.

Based on the distribution of storage jars and other kinds of artifacts, I have argued that the smaller residential groups in Sepulturas (Groups 9M-24 and 9M-22) used separate platforms behind or next to their residences to support storage structures while residents of Group 9N-8 preferred to keep their resources in side rooms inside their dwellings where they would have been much less obvious to people not inside the house itself (Hendon 1987, 1991, 2000). The occurrence of such spaces, their number, and their location would be something that was well known to the residents of a community. People would know that other people have things stored, but they would not all know the same thing or have access to the same knowledge equally. Through the type of fixed storage container used, people create differences in visibility. While the powerful noble house in Group 9N-8 worked to make certain kinds of places or actions less visible by controlling movement and observation through the physical and symbolic barriers its members constructed, other social houses put on display their material resources by making their location, albeit not their quantity or type, obvious. The difference in more and less visible formal storage space relates to differences in the application of an idea of storage, which reflects another way that people tried to fix the mutable issue of status (Hendon 2000).

Feasting

Storage, the built environment, and productive action of food and valued objects such as textiles and shell ornaments relate directly to feasting, which emerges as one important way in which noble houses and the royal house of the sixteenth ruler worked to reiterate claims to status and importance. In a study of the distribution of functional classes of pottery vessels (food serving, food preparation, storage, and those used for ritual), grinding stones, and other ceramic objects used in ritual (such as figurine-whistles and *candeleros*), I found that the most elaborate dwelling in a patio was a focus of feasting activity (Hendon 2003b). The difference between this dwelling and others in the same patio is one of degree rather than absolutes. In other words, these dominant structures (Hendon 1991) do not monopolize food serving, ritual, and preparation for their compound, but they are the setting for preparing and serving food to the exclusion of other activities practiced elsewhere in the compound, such as crafting. Moreover, the patios with the greatest investment in the built environment (Patios A of Groups 9N-8 and 9M-22)— which indicates a wealthier, more successful, and longer-lived

social house—have less evidence of food preparation and serving than their neighbors in the same group. While it is possible that the residents of both Patio As hosted less, I think it more likely that they relied on their associated patios to provide the food and drink for feasts occurring in the large courtyards of Groups 9N-8 and 9M-22 Patio A. The success of these events, both as reproducers of existing social relations and as a way to alter such relations, depends heavily on the labor and contributions of all house members or allies. Women's participation in particular was crucial to these events. Not only would they have had primary responsibility for food preparation but they would also have produced at least some of the items used as gifts, particularly textiles (Hendon 1997, 1999a, 1999b, 2002a, 2003b).

At the same time, the densities in Patio A of Group 9M-22 are greater than those for Patio A of Group 9N-8. Excavations in Group 9M-22 provide a basis to suggest that residents of smaller houses were as eager, if not more so, to participate visibly in status enhancing feasting activities as residents of larger, wealthier households. Food preparation and food serving vessels are associated with a number of structures or open areas in each patio of Group 9M-22, suggesting that the social house was involved in as much, if not more, feasting as their larger neighbors in Group 9N-8, who were potential rivals and allies but who were also wealthier and of higher rank, making direct competition difficult.

Group 9M-22 is connected to a raised and paved walkway that runs from the Main Group (to the west) into the elite residential area, terminating in a large, walled courtyard that forms part of Group 8N-11, another elaborate residential compound with sculpture and a carved bench (Webster et al. 1998). A small spur leading toward Group 9M-22 juts off the main walkway (see Fig. 6.2). This physical connection may represent social ties between Group 9M-22 and its more impressive neighbor to the north, Group 8N-11, or directly to the Main Group. Such ties could have included the provision of food to support the Group 8N-11 noble house in its feasting of important rivals such as Group 9N-8, participation in such feasts, and the hosting of return feasts back in the Group 9M-22 compound.

The residents of Patio A of Group 9N-8 were able to draw on a wide circle of house members to prepare and supply food and materials, but they did not enjoy exclusive rights to the role of host. Reciprocal feasting within the large compound of Group 9N-8 may have been important as a way for the noble house as a whole to compete with other houses in the potentially fluid and unstable domain of social status. With so many patios, the Group 9N-8 house was both larger and more diverse than most of the other high-ranking houses around the Main Group, such as Group 8N-11, making the retention of group solidarity especially challenging. Sponsoring feasts in celebration of life cycle events or as part of a temporal religious cycle may therefore have been equally important for the renewal of internal social ties.

Rural dwellers also used polychrome serving vessels and ritual objects such as censers. Their presence as part of the domestic assemblage at all seven of the sites discussed here suggests that ritual and commensal events were not restricted to richer or higher ranking sectors of society. Residents of these small sites may also have been involved in larger-scale feasting events through their social connections to the more substantial residential groups in the foothills or with residents of the inner zone (Hendon 2003b).

Feasting serves to reinforce hierarchy within noble houses in a spirit of mutual help and cooperation, as well as between the ruling house and all others. Evidence from the area south of the Acropolis where Ruler 16 lived indicates that he and fellow members of the royal house were also committed to hosting feasts (Andrews and Bill 2005). The recovery of a deposit of obsidian tools, animal bone, potsherds, and marine shell from an area in front of Temple 16 on the Acropolis may indicate that such events also took place here. Use-wear analysis demonstrates that the obsidian tools were heavily used both to work shell and to process meat, hide, wood, and other plant materials (Aoyama 1999:169).

Concluding Remarks

From heterogeneous beginnings, possibly the result of more than one migration of people into the valley, the Late Classic Copan polity emerges as a biologically homogeneous but socially differentiated population. Evidence for a foreign enclave is not supported by the analysis of the large sample of skeletal remains or the distribution of pottery, but the importance of exchange relationships with societies living east and south of the valley is demonstrated by the presence of imported Ulúa polychrome pottery. Study of how Copan's people differentiated themselves reveals the importance of social houses that crosscut status and wealth. At the same time, research on variation in health and diet, distribution of valued or imported resources, architectural elaboration, memorialization in text or image, body modification, and burial patterns argue for the continual recreation of social difference through practice. The physical house itself—its form, decoration, materials, and contents—emerges as a particularly powerful means to produce social difference and alternative histories that emphasize non-royal action and materiality.

The study of domestic life in large and small residences located near the center of political power and located far away provides a perspective on the Late Classic Copan sociopolitical order that suggests it was a dynamic one, reflecting the complicated, uncertain, and cosmopolitan nature of society. While the political relations encoded in hieroglyphic texts carved on behalf of the royal houses seem to record the existence of an enduring and unchanging system revolving around a single ruling dynasty, with all aspects of political power or status defined solely in relationship to that dynasty, the activities in the surrounding residential compounds suggest that social and political relations were negotiated, contested, and enacted through practices of daily life, extending even to storage and special events.

The location of the ballcourt and the many monuments argues that events sponsored by royalty in the Main Group played an important role in the social and political landscape of the Late Classic Copan polity. It is striking, however, the degree to which non-royal living areas discussed here provided an alternative social space for the construction of identity and the reproduction of social difference. People not only lived at home but were buried there as well (see Gillespie 2001; McAnany 1998). They engaged in ongoing and intense kinds of social interaction in the buildings and open spaces of their dwellings. Specialized abilities and knowledge were deployed in the creation of a range of objects, including textiles, shell ornaments, and bark paper. No less important endeavors doubtless took place that left little archaeological trace—such as music-making, oratory, writing, training for the ball game, and dance. Feasting served to reinforce internal hierarchies within houses while allowing more and less prominent noble houses to compete with one another.

The long-term and large-scale research in the Copan Valley, carried out by many different scholars and specialists using a range of analytical approaches and theoretical perspectives, has produced an impressive body of material with which to address questions of social, economic, and political relations. The combination of settlement pattern survey and excavation of residential patio compounds provides an important body of data that complements and challenges the information derived from the study of monumental architecture and hieroglyphic texts. Although, as this chapter makes clear, studying these complementary datasets has produced many significant insights into Copan society and the polity that it supported, productive research avenues remain to be explored.

The nature of settlement in the rural areas, outside the urban core, has been addressed through a number of different excavations and surveys. This work has allowed us to recognize the variety of settlement in the foothills and other pockets of the valley, which ranges from small-scale farmsteads to impressive multi-patio compounds comparable to those around the Main Group. No synthesis of the social and economic variety underlying this settlement variation has been put forward yet. Such a synthesis would allow a greater understanding of the complicated nature of Copan society as well as augment our understanding of the creation and reproduction of social difference. It would also give us a more nuanced understanding of the complexities of political relationships and the exercise of political authority.

The relationship between the Copan polity and other societies in Honduras also emerges as an area of research that needs further research and better theorizing. The material markers of connections with groups to the east and north are present in abundance. The imported polychrome pottery and figurines discussed in this chapter would benefit from a much more detailed analysis, one that takes into account what has been learned about temporal and regional differences in style by researchers working in the Naco, Ulúa, and Comayagua Valleys. Compositional analysis would further clarify questions of origins and trade routes. These and other kinds of studies not mentioned here can draw on the extensive body of information already gathered to produce increasingly detailed and subtle reconstructions of this ancient civilization.

Endnotes

1. Research on other residential compounds in Sepulturas and in other parts of the inner zone of settlement may be found in Andrews and Bill (2005), Andrews and Fash (1992), Ashmore (1991), Manahan (2004), Webster et al. (1998), Willey and Leventhal (1979), and Willey et al. (1994).

2. Nancy Gonlin discussed eight sites in her dissertation but concluded that one of them (34A-12-1) was not occupied full-time as a residence but was most probably a temporary or seasonal shelter. Since I want to concentrate on dwellings (places used year round and over at least one generation as residences), I have decided not to include 34A-12-1 in my discussion.

3. Ethnographic research and the study of early Spanish documentary sources do suggest that Lenca speakers were distributed over much of western and southern Honduras during the sixteenth century, as far east as the lower Ulúa Valley (Chapman 1985; Sheptak 2005). Archaeological investigation of these areas has reported a fair amount of material cultural diversity across this wide area of southwestern and central Honduras, making the identification of an archaeological signature for "Lenca-ness," whether thought of as a strictly linguistic category or a more diffuse cultural identity, less than straightforward (see Ashmore 1987; Ashmore et al. 1987; Hendon and Lopiparo 2004; Hirth 1992; Joyce 1988a, 1988b, 1991; Lopiparo 2003; Robinson 1989; Schortman and Urban 1994, 1995; Stone 1941).

4. It may be asked if shell ornaments were actually being made in Room 2 or if the archaeological features there are better interpreted as evidence for the storage of tools and materials that would have been brought into Room 1 or even onto the terrace for working. I would agree that some of the objects found there may have been in storage; certainly not all of them were connected to the production of shell objects. It is the presence of fragments of shell in the floor area that is most indicative of actual processing in the room. These fragments had been cut or scraped off in the process of shaping the material and would not be present if all working took place elsewhere.

References

Abrams, Elliot M.
1987 Economic specialization and construction personnel in Classic period Copan. *American Antiquity* 52:485–99.
1994 *How the Maya Built Their World: Energetics and Ancient Architecture.* University of Texas Press, Austin.

Andrews, E. Wyllys, and Cassandra R. Bill
2005 A Late Classic royal residence at Copan. In *Copan: The History of an Ancient Maya Kingdom*, edited by E. Wyllys Andrews and William L. Fash, pp. 239–314. School of American Research Press, Santa Fe.

Andrews, E. Wyllys, and Barbara W. Fash
1992 Continuity and change in a royal Maya residential complex at Copan. *Ancient Mesoamerica* 3:63–88.

Aoyama, Kazuo
1995 Microwear analysis in the southeast Maya lowlands: Two case studies at Copan, Honduras. *Latin American Antiquity* 6:129–44.
1999 *Ancient Maya State, Urbanism, Exchange, and Craft Specialization: Chipped Stone Evidence from the Copan Valley and the La Entrada Region, Honduras/Estado, urbanismo, intercambio, y especialización artesanal entre los Mayas antiguos: Evidencia de lítica menor del valle de Copán y la región de La Entrada, Honduras.* Memoirs in Latin American Archaeology 12. Department of Anthropology, University of Pittsburgh, Pittsburgh.
2001 Classic Maya State, urbanism, and exchange: Chipped stone evidence of the Copan Valley and its hinterland. *American Anthropologist* 103:346–60.

Ashmore, Wendy
1987 Cobble crossroads: Gualjoquito architecture and external elite ties. In *Interaction on the Southeast Mesoamerican Frontier: Prehistoric and Historic Honduras and El Salvador*, edited by Eugenia J. Robinson, pp. 28–48. BAR International Series 327. British Archaeological Reports, Oxford.
1991 Site-planning principles and concepts of directionality among the ancient Maya. *Latin American Antiquity* 2:199–226.

Ashmore, Wendy, Edward M. Schortman, Patricia A. Urban, Julie C. Benyo, John M. Weeks, and Sylvia M. Smith
1987 Ancient society in Santa Barbara, Honduras. *National Geographic Research* 3(2):232–54.

Asturias de Barrios, Linda
1998 Weaving and daily life. In *The Maya Textile Tradition*, edited by Margo Blum Schevill, pp. 65–87. Harry Abrams, New York.

Bachand, Holly, Rosemary A. Joyce, and Julia A. Hendon
2003 Bodies moving in space: Ancient Mesoamerican human sculpture and embodiment. *Cambridge Archaeological Journal* 13:238–47.

Baudez, Claude F.
1989 The house of the Bacabs: An iconographic analysis. In *The House of the Bacabs, Copan, Honduras*, edited by David Webster, pp. 73–81. Dumbarton Oaks, Washington, D.C.
1994 *Maya Sculpture of Copan: The Iconography.* University of Oklahoma Press, Norman.

Beaudry, Marilyn P.
1984 *Ceramic Production and Distribution in the Southeastern Maya Periphery: Late Classic Painted Serving Vessels.* BAR International Series 203. British Archaeological Reports, Oxford.

Beaudry-Corbett, Marilyn, Pauline Caputi, John S. Henderson, Rosemary A. Joyce, Eugenia J. Robinson, and Anthony Wonderly
1993 Lower Ulúa region. In *Pottery of Prehistoric Honduras: Regional Classification and Analysis*, edited by John S. Henderson and Marilyn Beaudry-Corbett, pp. 65–135. Monograph 35. Institute of Archaeology, University of California, Los Angeles.

Bell, Ellen E., Robert J. Sharer, Loa P. Traxler, David W. Sedat, Christine W. Carrelli, and Lynn A. Grant
2004 Tombs and burials in the Early Classic acropolis at Copan. In *Understanding Early Classic Copan*, edited by Ellen E. Bell, Marcello A. Canuto, and Robert J. Sharer, pp. 131–57. University of Pennsylvania Museum of Archaeology and Anthropology, Philadelphia.

Bill, Cassandra R.
1997 *Patterns of Variation and Change in Dynastic Period Ceramics and Ceramic Production at Copan, Honduras.* PhD dissertation, Dept. of Anthropology, Tulane University. UMI, Ann Arbor.

Birdwell-Pheasant, Donna, and Denise Lawrence-Zúñiga
1999   Introduction: Houses and families in Europe. In *House Life: Space, Place and Family in Europe*, edited by Donna Birdwell-Pheasant and Denise Lawrence-Zúñiga, pp. 1–35. Berg, Oxford.

Bishop, Ronald L., Marilyn P. Beaudry, Richard M. Leventhal, and Robert J. Sharer
1986   Compositional analysis of Copador and related pottery in the southeastern Maya area. In *The Southeast Maya Periphery*, edited by Patricia A. Urban and Edward M. Schortman, pp. 143–67. University of Texas Press, Austin.

Bourdieu, Pierre
1998   *Practical Reason: On the Theory of Action.* Stanford University Press, Stanford.

Buikstra, Jane E., T. Douglas Price, Lori E. Wright, and James A. Burton
2004   Tombs from the Copan acropolis: A life history approach. In *Understanding Early Classic Copan*, edited by Ellen E. Bell, Marcello A. Canuto, and Robert J. Sharer, pp. 191–212. University of Pennsylvania Museum of Archaeology and Anthropology, Philadelphia.

Canuto, Marcello A.
2002   *A Tale of Two Communities: Social and Political Transformation in the Hinterlands of the Maya Polity of Copan.* PhD dissertation, University of Pennsylvania. UMI, Ann Arbor.
2004   The rural settlement of Copan: Changes through the Early Classic. In *Understanding Early Classic Copan*, edited by Ellen E. Bell, Marcello A. Canuto, and Robert J. Sharer, pp. 29–50. University of Pennsylvania Museum of Archaeology and Anthropology, Philadelphia.

Carrelli, Christine W.
2004   Measures of power: The energetics of royal construction at Early Classic Copan. In *Understanding Early Classic Copan*, edited by Ellen E. Bell, Marcello A. Canuto, and Robert J. Sharer, pp. 113–27. University of Pennsylvania Museum of Archaeology and Anthropology, Philadelphia.

Chamoux, Marie-Noëlle
1993   La difusión de tecnologías entre los indígenas de México: una interpretación. In *Semillas de industria: Transformaciones de la tecnología indígena en las Américas*, edited by Mario Humberto Ruz, pp. 123–44. Centro de Investigaciones y Estudios Superiores en Antropología Social, Mexico City; Smithsonian Institution Center for Folklife Programs and Cultural Studies, Washington, D.C.

Chance, John K.
2000   The noble house in colonial puebla, Mexico: Descent, inheritance, and the Nahua tradition. *American Anthropologist* 102:485–502.

Chapman, Anne
1985   *Los hijos del copal y la candela: ritos agrarios y tradición oral de los lencas de Honduras.* Universidad Nacional Autónoma de México, México, D.F.

Diamanti, Melissa
2000   Excavaciones en el conjunto de los Patios E, F, y M, Grupo 9N-8 (Operación XV). In *Proyecto Arqueológico Copán: Segunda Fase: excavaciones en el área urbana de Copán, Tomo IV*, edited by William T. Sanders. Secretaría de Cultura, Artes y Deportes, Instituto Hondureño de Antropología e Historia, Tegucigalpa, Honduras.

Douglas, Mary
1993   The idea of a home: A kind of space. In *Home: A Place in the World*, edited by Arien Mack, pp. 261–81. New York University Press, New York.

Fash, Barbara W.
1992   Late Classic architectural sculpture themes in Copan. *Ancient Mesoamerica* 3:89–104.

Fash, William L.
1983a   Introducción. In *Introducción a la arqueología de Copán, Honduras, Tomo III*, edited by Claude F. Baudez, pp. 5–22. Proyecto Arqueológico Copán, Secretaría de Estado en el Despacho de Cultura y Turismo, Tegucigalpa, Honduras.
1983b   *Maya State Formation: A Case Study and Its Implications.* PhD dissertation, Dept. of Anthropology, Harvard University.
1983c   Reconocimiento y excavaciones en el valle. In *Introducción a la arqueología de Copán, Honduras, Tomo 1*, edited by Claude F. Baudez, pp. 229–469. Proyecto Arqueológico Copán, Secretaría de Estado en el Despacho de Cultura y Turismo, Tegucigalpa, Honduras.
1985   La secuencia de ocupación del Gr 9N-8. *Yaxkin* 8:135–49.
2001   *Scribes, Warriors and Kings*, 2nd ed. Thames and Hudson, London.
2005   Toward a social history of the Copan Valley. In *Copan: The History of an Ancient Maya Kingdom*, edited by E. Wyllys Andrews and William L. Fash, pp. 73–101. School of American Research Press, Santa Fe.

Fash, William L., and Ricardo Agurcia Fasquelle
2005   Contributions and controversies in the archaeology and history of Copan. In *Copan: The History of an Ancient Maya Kingdom*, edited by E. Wyllys Andrews and William L. Fash, pp. 3–32. School of American Research Press, Santa Fe.

Fash, William L., E. Wyllys Andrews, and T. Kam Manahan
2004   Political decentralization, dynastic collapse, and the Early Postclassic in the urban center of Copan, Honduras. In *The Terminal Classic in the Maya Lowlands: Collapse, Transition, and Transformation*, edited by Arthur A. Demarest, Prudence M. Rice, and Don S. Rice, pp. 260–87. University Press of Colorado, Boulder.

Fash, William L., and Kurt Z. Long
1983   Mapa arqueológico del valle de Copan. In *Introducción a la arqueología de Copán, Honduras, Tomo III*, edited by Claude F. Baudez. Secretaría de Estado en el Despacho de Cultura y Turismo, Tegucigalpa, Honduras.

Fash, William L., and David S. Stuart
1991   Dynastic history and cultural evolution at Copan, Honduras. In *Classic Maya Political History: Hieroglyphic and Archaeological Evidence*, edited by T. Patrick Culbert, pp. 147–79. Cambridge University Press, Cambridge.

Freter, AnnCorinne
1988 *The Classic Maya Collapse at Copan, Honduras: A Regional Settlement Perspective*. PhD dissertation, Dept. of Anthropology, Pennsylvania State University. UMI, Ann Arbor.

Gerstle, Andrea I.
1987 Ethnic diversity and interaction at Copan, Honduras. In *Interaction on the Southeast Mesoamerican Frontier: Prehistoric and Historic Honduras and El Salvador*, edited by Eugenia J. Robinson, pp. 328–56. BAR International Series 327, vol. 2. British Archaeological Reports, Oxford.
1988 *Maya-Lenca Ethnic Relations in Late Classic Period Copan, Honduras*. PhD dissertation, Dept. of Anthropology, University of California, Santa Barbara. UMI, Ann Arbor.

Gerstle, Andrea I., and David L. Webster
1990 Excavaciones en 9N-8, conjunto del patio D. In *Proyecto Arqueológico Copán Segunda Fase: excavaciones en el área urbana de Copán, Tomo III*, edited by William T. Sanders, pp. 25–368. Secretaría de Estado en el Despacho de Cultura y Turismo, Instituto Hondureño de Antropología e Historia, Tegucigalpa, Honduras.

Gerry, John P., and Meredith S. Chesson
2000 Classic Maya diet and gender relationships. In *Gender and Material Culture in Archaeological Perspective*, edited by Moira Donald and Linda Hurcombe, pp. 250–64. St. Martin's Press, New York.

Gerry, John P., and Harold W. Krueger
1997 Regional diversity in Classic Maya diets. In *Bones of the Maya: Studies of Ancient Skeletons*, edited by Stephen L. Whittington and David M. Reed, pp. 196–207. Smithsonian Institution Press, Washington, D.C.

Gillespie, Susan D.
1999 Olmec thrones as ancestral altars: The two sides of power. In *Material Symbols: Culture and Economy in Prehistory*, edited by John E. Robb, pp. 224–53. Occasional Paper 26. Center for Archaeological Investigations, Southern Illinois University, Carbondale.
2000a Maya "nested houses": The ritual construction of place. In *Beyond Kinship: Social and Material Reproduction in House Societies*, edited by Rosemary A. Joyce and Susan D. Gillespie, pp. 135–60. University of Pennsylvania Press, Philadelphia.
2000b Rethinking ancient Maya social organization: Replacing "lineage" with "house." *American Anthropologist* 102:467–84.
2001 Personhood, agency, and mortuary ritual: A case study from the ancient Maya. *Journal of Anthropological Archaeology* 20:73–112.

Gonlin, Nancy
1985 *The Architectural Variation of Two Small Sites in the Copan Valley, Honduras: A Rural/Urban Dichotomy?* Master's thesis, Dept. of Anthropology, Pennsylvania State University. UMI, Ann Arbor.
1993 *Rural Household Archaeology at Copan, Honduras*. PhD dissertation, Pennsylvania State University. UMI, Ann Arbor.
1994 Rural household diversity in Late Classic Copan, Honduras. In *Archaeological Views from the Countryside: Village Communities in Early Complex Societies*, edited by Glenn M. Schwartz and Steven E. Falconer, pp. 177–97. Smithsonian Institution Press, Washington, D.C.

2000 Lo que las mujeres y los hombres hacen: investigaciones recientes en hogares antiguos en Copán, Honduras. *Yaxkin* 13:23–39.
2004 Methods for understanding Classic Maya commoners: Structure function, energetics, and more. In *Ancient Maya Commoners*, edited by Jon C. Lohse and Fred Valdez, pp. 225–54. University of Texas Press, Austin.

Greenfield, Patricia Marks
2004 *Weaving Generations Together: Evolving Creativity in the Maya of Chiapas*. School of American Research Press, Santa Fe.

Hall, Jay, and René Viel
2004 The Early Classic Copan landscape: A view from the Preclassic. In *Understanding Early Classic Copan*, edited by Ellen E. Bell, Marcello A. Canuto, and Robert J. Sharer, pp. 17–28. University of Pennsylvania Museum of Archaeology and Anthropology, Philadelphia.

Handler, Richard
1994 Is "identity" a useful cross-cultural concept? In *Commemorations: The Politics of National Identity*, edited by John R. Gillis, pp. 27–40. Princeton University Press, Princeton.

Hendon, Julia A.
1987 *The Uses of Maya Structures: A Study of Architecture and Artifact Distribution at Sepulturas, Copan, Honduras*. PhD dissertation, Dept. of Anthropology, Harvard University. UMI, Ann Arbor.
1988 Discusión preliminar del estudio de áreas de actividad en Las Sepulturas, Copán: forma, función y distribución de las vasijas de barro. *Yaxkin* 11(1):47–82.
1989 Elite household organization at Copan, Honduras: Analysis of activity distribution in the Sepulturas zone. In *Household and Communities*, edited by S. MacEachern et al., pp. 371–80. Proceedings of the 21st Annual Chacmool Conference, Archaeological Association of the University of Calgary, Calgary.
1991 Status and power in Classic Maya society: An archeological study. *American Anthropologist* 93:894–918.
1992a Architectural symbols of the Maya social order: Residential construction and decoration in the Copan Valley, Honduras. In *Ancient Images, Ancient Thought: The Archaeology of Ideology*, edited by A. Sean Goldsmith, Sandra Garvie, David Selin, and Jeannette Smith, pp. 481–95. Proceedings of the 23rd Annual Chacmool Conference, Archaeological Association of the University of Calgary, Calgary.
1992b The interpretation of survey data: Two case studies from the Maya area. *Latin American Antiquity* 3:22–42.
1997 Women's work, women's space and women's status among the Classic period Maya elite of the Copan Valley, Honduras. In *Women in Prehistory: North America and Mesoamerica*, edited by Cheryl Claassen and Rosemary A. Joyce, pp. 33–46. University of Pennsylvania Press, Philadelphia.
1999a Multiple sources of prestige and the social evaluation of women in prehispanic Mesoamerica. In *Material Symbols: Culture and Economy in Prehistory*, edited by John E. Robb, pp. 257–76. Occasional Paper 26. Center for Archaeological Investigations, Southern Illinois University, Carbondale.
1999b Spinning and weaving in pre-Hispanic Mesoamerica: The technology and social relations of textile production. In *Mayan Clothing and Weaving through the Ages*, edited by B. Knoke de Arathoon, N.L. González, and J.M. Willemsen Devlin, pp. 7–16. Museo Ixchel del Traje Indígena, Guatemala City.

2000   Having and holding: Storage, memory, knowledge, and social relations. *American Anthropologist* 102:42–53.
2002a   Household and state in prehispanic Maya society: Gender, identity, and practice. In *Ancient Maya Gender Identity and Relations*, edited by L. Gustafson and A. Trevelyan, pp. 75–92. Greenwood Publishing Group, Westport, CT.
2002b   Social relations and collective identities: Household and community in ancient Mesoamerica. In *The Dynamics of Power*, edited by Maria O'Donovan, pp. 273–300. Occasional Paper 30. Center for Archaeological Investigations, Southern Illinois University, Carbondale.
2003a   El papel de los enterramientos en la construcción y negociación de la identidad social en los mayas prehispánicos. In *Antropología de la eternidad: la muerte en la cultura maya*, edited by A. Ciudad Ruiz, M.H. Ruz Sosa, and M.J. Iglesias Ponce de León, pp. 161–74. Sociedad Española de Estudios Mayas, Centro de Estudios Mayas, Instituto de Investigaciones Filológicas, Universidad Nacional Autónoma de México, Madrid and Mexico City.
2003b   Feasting at home: Community and house solidarity among the Maya of southeastern Mesoamerica. In *The Archaeology and Politics of Food and Feasting in Early States and Empires*, edited by Tamara L. Bray, pp. 203–33. Kluwer Academic/Plenum Publishers, New York.
2003c   In the house: Maya nobility and their figurine-whistles. *Expedition* 45(3):28–33.
2006   Textile production as craft in Mesoamerica: Time, labor, and knowledge. *Journal of Social Archaeology* 6:354–78.
2007   Memory, materiality, and practice: House societies in southeastern Mesoamerica. In *The Durable House: House Society Models in Archaeology*, edited by Robin Beck, pp. 292–316. Occasional Paper 35. Center for Archaeological Investigations, Southern Illinois University, Carbondale.

Hendon, Julia A., Ricardo Agurcia F., William L. Fash, Jr., and Eloísa Aguilar Palma
1990   Excavaciones en 9N-8, Conjunto del Patio C. In *Proyecto Arqueológico Copán Segunda Fase: Excavaciones en el área urbana de Copán, Tomo II*, edited by William T. Sanders, pp. 11–109. Secretaría de Estado en el Despacho de Cultura y Turismo, Instituto Hondureño de Antropología e Historia, Tegucigalpa, Honduras.

Hendon, Julia A., William L. Fash, Jr., and Eloísa Aguilar Palma
1990   Excavaciones en 9N-8, Conjunto del Patio B. In *Proyecto Arqueológico Copán Segunda Fase: Excavaciones en el área urbana de Copán, Tomo II*, edited by William T. Sanders, pp. 110–293. Secretaría de Estado en el Despacho de Cultura y Turismo, Instituto Hondureño de Antropología e Historia, Tegucigalpa, Honduras.

Hendon, Julia A., and Jeanne Lopiparo
2004   Investigaciones recientes en Cerro Palenque, Cortés, Honduras. *Memoria VII Seminario de Antropología de Honduras "Dr. George Hasemann,"* pp. 187–95. Instituto Hondureño de Antropología e Historia, Tegucigalpa, Honduras.

Hicks, Fredric
1994   Cloth in the political economy of the Aztec State. In *Economies and Polities in the Aztec Realm*, edited by Mary G. Hodge and Michael E. Smith, pp. 89–111. Institute for Mesoamerican Studies, State University of New York, Albany.

Hirth, Kenneth G.
1988   Beyond the Maya frontier: Cultural interaction and syncretism along the central Honduran corridor. In *The Southeast Classic Maya Zone*, edited by Elizabeth Hill Boone and Gordon R. Willey, pp. 297–334. Dumbarton Oaks, Washington, D.C.
1992   Interregional exchange as elite behavior: An evolutionary perspective. In *Mesoamerican Elites: An Archaeological Assessment*, edited by Diane Z. Chase and Arlen F. Chase, pp. 18–29. University of Oklahoma Press, Norman.

Hohmann, Hasso
1995   *Die Architektur der Sepulturas-Region von Copán in Honduras*. Akademische Druck und Verlagsanstalt, Graz.

Joyce, Rosemary A.
1986   Terminal Classic interaction on the southeastern Maya periphery. *American Antiquity* 51:313–29.
1988a   Ceramic traditions and language groups in prehispanic Honduras. *Journal of the Steward Anthropological Society* 15:158–86.
1988b   The Ulúa Valley and the coastal Maya lowlands: The view from Cerro Palenque. In *The Southeast Classic Maya Zone*, edited by Elizabeth H. Boone and Gordon R. Willey, pp. 269–95. Dumbarton Oaks, Washington, D.C.
1991   *Cerro Palenque: Power and Identity on the Maya Periphery*. University of Texas Press, Austin.
1993   The construction of the Mesoamerican frontier and the Mayoid image of Honduran polychromes. In *Reinterpreting Prehistory of Central America*, edited by Mark Miller Graham, pp. 51–101. University Press of Colorado, Niwot, CO.
2000   Heirlooms and houses: Materiality and social memory. In *Beyond Kinship: Social and Material Reproduction in House Societies*, edited by Rosemary A. Joyce and Susan D. Gillespie, pp. 189–212. University of Pennsylvania Press, Philadelphia.

Joyce, Rosemary A., and Julia A. Hendon
2000   Heterarchy, history, and material reality: "Communities" in Late Classic Honduras. In *The Archaeology of Communities: A New World Perspective*, edited by Marcello-Andrea Canuto and Jason Yaeger, pp. 143–59. Routledge, London.

Lee, Carla S.
1995   *A Bioarchaeological Study of Differential Food Access and Activity Type at an Elite Classic Maya Site, Copan, Honduras*. Master's thesis, Dept. of Anthropology, University of Houston. UMI, Ann Arbor.

Leventhal, Richard M.
1979   *Settlement Patterns at Copan, Honduras*. PhD dissertation, Dept. of Anthropology, Harvard University, Harvard.

Lévi-Strauss, Claude
1982   *The Way of the Masks*, translated by Sylvia Modelski. University of Washington Press, Seattle.

Longyear, John M.
1947   *Cultures and Peoples of the Southeastern Maya Frontier*. Theoretical Approaches to Problems 3. Division of Historical Research, Carnegie Institution of Washington, Cambridge, MA.
1952   *Copan Ceramics: A Study of Southeastern Maya Pottery*. Publication 597. Carnegie Institution of Washington, Washington, D.C.

Looper, Matthew G.
1998 A note on the carved bone from Copan Temple 11. *Glyph Dwellers Report 4.* http://nas.ucdavis.edu/NALC/R4.pdf (accessed January 4, 2006)
1999 New perspectives on the Late Classic political history of Quirigua, Guatemala. *Ancient Mesoamerica* 10:263–80.

Lopiparo, Jeanne L.
2003 *Household Ceramic Production and the Crafting of Society in the Terminal Classic Ulúa Valley, Honduras.* PhD dissertation, Dept. of Anthropology, University of California, Berkeley. UMI, Ann Arbor.

Maca, Alan L.
2002 *Spatio-Temporal Boundaries in the Classic Maya Settlement Systems: Copan's Urban Foothills and the Excavations at Group 9J-5.* PhD dissertation, Dept. of Anthropology, Harvard University. UMI, Ann Arbor.

Mallory, John K.
1984 *Late Classic Maya Economic Specialization: Evidence from the Copan Obsidian Assemblage.* PhD dissertation, Dept. of Anthropology, Pennsylvania State University. UMI, Ann Arbor.

Manahan, T. Kam
2004 The way things fall apart: Social organization and the Classic Maya collapse of Copan. *Ancient Mesoamerica* 15:107–25.

Marcus, Joyce
2004 Primary and secondary state formation in southern Mesoamerica. In *Understanding Early Classic Copan*, edited by Ellen E. Bell, Marcello A. Canuto, and Robert J. Sharer, pp. 357–73. University of Pennsylvania Museum of Archaeology and Anthropology, Philadelphia.

Martin, Simon, and Nikolai Grube
2000 *Chronicle of the Maya Kings and Queens: Deciphering the Dynasties of the Ancient Maya.* Thames and Hudson, London.

McAnany, Patricia
1998 Ancestors and the Classic Maya built environment. In *Function and Meaning in Classic Maya Architecture*, edited by Stephen D. Houston, pp. 271–98. Dumbarton Oaks, Washington, D.C.

McMeekin, Dorothy
1992 Representations on pre-Columbian spindle whorls of the floral and fruit structure of economic plants. *Economic Botany* 46:171–80.

Monaghan, John
1995 *The Covenants with Earth and Rain: Exchange, Sacrifice, and Revelation in Mixtec Sociality.* University of Oklahoma Press, Norman.

Morley, Sylvanus G.
1920 *The Inscriptions at Copan.* Publication 219. Carnegie Institution of Washington, Washington, D.C.

Nakamura, Seiichi, Kazuo Aoyama, and Eiji Uratsuji (editors)
1991 *Investigaciones arqueológicas en la región de la Entrada, Primera Fase.* Servicio de Voluntarios Japoneses para la Cooperación con el Extranjero y el Instituto Hondureño de Antropología e Historia, San Pedro Sula.

O'Neale, Lila M.
1945 *Textiles of Highland Guatemala.* Publication 567. Carnegie Institution of Washington, Washington, D.C.

Padgett, Paige M.
1996 *The Effects of Social Status and Residency Patterns on Infection among the Late Classic Maya at Copan, Honduras.* Master's thesis, Dept. of Anthropology, University of Houston. UMI, Ann Arbor.

Pahl, Gary W.
1977 The inscriptions of Rio Amarillo and Los Higos: Secondary centers of the southeastern Maya frontier. *Journal of Latin American Lore* 3:133–54.

Piot, Charles
1999 *Remotely Global: Village Modernity in West Africa.* University of Chicago Press, Chicago.

Pred, Allan
1990 *Making Histories and Constructing Human Geographies: The Local Transformation of Practice, Power Relations, and Consciousness.* Westview Press, Boulder.

Reed, David M.
1998 *Ancient Maya Diet at Copan, Honduras.* PhD dissertation, Dept. of Anthropology, Pennsylvania State University. UMI, Ann Arbor.
1999 Cuisine from Hun-Nal-Ye. In *Reconstructing Ancient Maya Diet*, edited by Christine D. White, pp. 183–96. University of Utah Press, Salt Lake City.

Rhoads, Megan L.
2002 *Population Dynamics at the Southern Periphery of the Ancient Maya World: Kinship at Copan.* PhD dissertation, Dept. of Anthropology, University of New Mexico. UMI, Ann Arbor.

Robin, Cynthia
2002 Outside of houses: The practices of everyday life at Chan Noohol, Belize. *Journal of Social Archaeology* 2:245–68.

Robinson, Eugenia J.
1989 *The Prehistoric Communities of the Sula Valley, Honduras: Regional Interaction in the Southeast Mesoamerican Frontier.* PhD dissertation, Dept. of Anthropology, Tulane University. UMI, Ann Arbor.

Rodman, Margaret C.
2003 Empowering place: Multilocality and multivocality. In *The Anthropology of Space and Place: Locating Culture*, edited by Setha M. Low and Denise Lawrence-Zúñiga, pp. 204–23. Blackwell, Malden, MA.

Sanders, William T.
1989 Household, lineage, and state at eighth-century Copan, Honduras. In *House of the Bacabs, Copan, Honduras*, edited by David Webster, pp. 89–105. Studies in Pre-Columbian Art and Archaeology 29. Dumbarton Oaks, Washington, D.C.

Saturno, William A.
2000   *In the Shadow of the Acropolis: Rio Amarillo and Its Role in the Copan Polity*. PhD dissertation, Dept. of Anthropology, Harvard University. UMI, Ann Arbor.

Schortman, Edward M., and Patricia A. Urban
1994   Living on the edge: Core/Periphery relations in ancient southeastern Mesoamerica. *Current Anthropology* 35:401–30.
1995   Late Classic society in the Rio Ulúa drainage, Honduras. *Journal of Field Archaeology* 22:439–57.
2004   Marching out of step: Early Classic Copan and its Honduran neighbors. In *Understanding Early Classic Copan*, edited by Ellen E. Bell, Marcello A. Canuto, and Robert J. Sharer, pp. 319–35. University of Pennsylvania Museum of Archaeology and Anthropology, Philadelphia.

Sharer, Robert J., David W. Sedat, Loa P. Traxler, Julia C. Miller, and Ellen E. Bell
2005   Early Classic royal power in Copan: The origins and development of the Acropolis (ca. A.D. 250–600). In *Copan: The History of an Ancient Maya Kingdom*, edited by E. Wyllys Andrews and William L. Fash, pp. 201–36. School of American Research Press, Santa Fe.

Sheehy, James J.
1991   Structure and change in a Late Classic Maya domestic group at Copan, Honduras. *Ancient Mesoamerica* 2:1–19.

Sheptak, Russell N.
2005   The Continuity of Social Practices in the Colonial Period Ulúa Valley, Northern Honduras. Presented at the 70th Annual Meeting of the Society for American Archaeology, Salt Lake City, Utah.

Soja, Edward W.
1985   The spatiality of social life: Towards a transformative retheorisation. In *Social Relations and Spatial Structures*, edited by Derek Gregory and John Urry, pp. 90–127. St. Martin's Press, New York.

Stone, Doris
1941   *Archaeology of the North Coast of Honduras*. Memoirs of the Peabody Museum of Archaeology and Ethnology, Harvard University, vol. 9, no. 1. Peabody Museum of Archaeology and Ethnology, Cambridge.

Storey, Rebecca
1992   The children of Copan: Issues in paleopathology and paleodemography. *Ancient Mesoamerica* 3:161–67.
1997   Individual frailty, children of privilege, and stress in Late Classic Copan. In *Bones of the Maya: Studies of Ancient Skeletons*, edited by Stephen L. Whittington and David M. Reed, pp. 116–26. Smithsonian Institution Press, Washington, D.C.
1998   The mothers and daughters of a patrilineal civilization: The health status of females among the Late Classic Maya of Copan, Honduras. In *Sex and Gender in Paleopathological Perspective*, edited by Anne L. Grauer and Patricia Stuart-Macadam, pp. 133–48. Cambridge University Press, Cambridge.
1999   Late Classic nutrition and skeletal indicators at Copan, Honduras. In *Reconstructing Ancient Maya Diet*, edited by Christine D. White, pp. 169–79. University of Utah Press, Salt Lake City.

2005   Health and lifestyle (before and after death) among the Copan elite. In *Copan: The History of an Ancient Maya Kingdom*, edited by E. Wyllys Andrews and William L. Fash, pp. 315–43. School of American Research Press, Santa Fe.

Stuart, David
2005   A foreign past: The writing and representation of history on a royal ancestral shrine at Copan. In *Copan: The History of an Ancient Maya Kingdom*, edited by E. Wyllys Andrews and William L. Fash, pp. 373–94. School of American Research Press, Santa Fe.

Tercero, Geraldina
1996   *Figurines from the Ulúa Valley, Honduras: A Preliminary Study of their Distribution and Uses*. Master's thesis, Dept. of Anthropology, Arizona State University, Tempe.

Viel, René
1993a   Copan Valley. In *Pottery of Prehistoric Honduras: Regional Classification and Analysis*, edited by John S. Henderson and Marilyn Beaudry-Corbett, pp. 13–29. Monograph 35. Institute of Archaeology, UCLA, Los Angeles.
1993b   *Evolución de la cerámica de Copán, Honduras*. Instituto Hondureño de Antropología e Historia, Tegucigalpa, Honduras.
1998   La interacción entre Copan y Kaminaljuyu. In *XI Simposio de investigaciones arqueológicas en Guatemala 1997*, edited by Juan Pedro Laporte and Héctor L. Escobedo, pp. 427–30. Ministerio de Cultura y Deportes, Instituto de Antropología e Historia, Asociación Tikal, Guatemala City.
1999   The pectorals of Altar Q and Structure 11: An interpretation of the political organization at Copan, Honduras. *Latin American Antiquity* 10:377–99.

Viel, René, and Jay Hall
1997   El período formativo de Copan en el contexto de Honduras. *Yaxkin* 16:40–48.
2000   Las relaciones entre Copan y Kaminaljuyu. In *XIII Simposio de investigaciones arqueológicas en Guatemala 1999*, edited by Juan Pedro Laporte, Héctor L. Escobedo, Ana Claudia de Suásnavar, and Bárbara Arroyo, pp. 127–30. Ministerio de Cultura y Deportes, Instituto de Antropología e Historia, Asociación Tikal, Guatemala City.

Waterson, Roxana
1995   Houses and hierarchies in island southeast Asia. In *About the House: Lévi-Strauss and Beyond*, edited by Janet Carsten and Stephen Hugh-Jones, pp. 47–68. Cambridge University Press, Cambridge.

Webster, David
1999   The archaeology of Copan, Honduras. *Journal of Archaeological Research* 7:1–53.

Webster, David (editor)
1989   *The House of the Bacabs, Copan, Honduras*. Studies in Pre-Columbian Art and Archaeology 29. Dumbarton Oaks, Washington, D.C.

Webster, David, Barbara Fash, Randolph Widmer, and Scott Zeleznik
1998   The Skyband Group: Investigation of a Classic Maya residential complex at Copan, Honduras. *Journal of Field Archaeology* 25:319–43.

Webster, David, William L. Fash, and Elliot Abrams
1986   Excavaciones en el conjunto 9N-8, Patio A (Operación VII). In *Proyecto Arqueológico Copán Segunda Fase: excavaciones en el área urbana de Copán, Tomo I*, edited by William T. Sanders, pp. 155–317. Secretaría de Estado en el Despacho de Cultura y Turismo, Tegucigalpa, Honduras.

Webster, David, AnnCorinne Freter, and Rebecca Storey
2004   Dating Copan culture-history: Implications for the Terminal Classic and the collapse. In *The Terminal Classic in the Maya Lowlands: Collapse, Transition, and Transformation*, edited by Arthur A. Demarest, Prudence M. Rice, and Don S. Rice, pp. 231–59. University Press of Colorado, Boulder.

Webster, David, and Nancy Gonlin
1988   Household remains of the humblest Maya. *Journal of Field Archaeology* 15:169–90.

Weiner, Annette B.
1992   *Inalienable Possessions: The Paradox of Keeping-While-Giving*. University of California Press, Berkeley.

Whittington, Stephen L.
1999   Caries and antemortem tooth loss at Copan: Implications from commoner diet. In *Reconstructing Ancient Maya Diet*, edited by Christine D. White, pp. 151–67. University of Utah Press, Salt Lake City.

Whittington, Stephen L., and David M. Reed
1997   Commoner diet at Copan: Insights from stable isotopes and porotic hyperostosis. In *Bones of the Maya: Studies of Ancient Skeletons*, edited by Stephen L. Whittington and David M. Reed, pp. 157–70. Smithsonian Institution Press, Washington, D.C.

Whittington, Stephen L., and Scott Zeleznik
1991   History and Functions of a Pair of Neighboring Rural Elite Residential Compounds in the Ostuman Pocket, Copan, Honduras. Presented at the 56th annual meeting of the Society for American Archaeology, New Orleans.

Widmer, Randolph J.
1997   Especialización económica en Copán. *Yaxkin* 15:141–60.

Willey, Gordon R.
1986   Copan, Quirigua, and the southeast Maya zone: A summary. In *The Southeast Maya Periphery*, edited by Patricia A. Urban and Edward M. Schortman, pp. 168–75. University of Texas Press, Austin.

Willey, Gordon R., William R. Coe, and Robert J. Sharer
1976   Un proyecto para el desarrollo de investigación y preservación arqueológica en Copán (Honduras) y vecindad 1976–81. *Yaxkin* 1:10–29.

Willey, Gordon R., and Richard M. Leventhal
1979   Settlement at Copan. In *Maya Archaeology and Ethnohistory*, edited by Norman Hammond and Gordon R. Willey, pp. 75–102. University of Texas Press, Austin.

Willey, Gordon R., Richard M. Leventhal, Arthur A. Demarest, and William L. Fash
1994   *Ceramics and Artifacts from Excavations in the Copan Residential Zone*. Papers of the Peabody Museum of Archaeology and Ethnology 80. Harvard University, Cambridge, MA.

Willey, Gordon R., Richard M. Leventhal, and William L. Fash
1978   Maya settlement in the Copan Valley. *Archaeology* 31(4):32–43.

—7—

Beyond Capitals and Kings

Domestic Organization and Ethnic Dynamics at Chac-Sayil, Yucatan

Michael P. Smyth

Introduction

Archaeological research has shown that Chac and Sayil, in the heart of the Puuc hills region, were two successive capitals with complex and differing patterns of ethnicity. Mortuary remains, residential architecture, and activity patterns from intensive survey and excavation indicate foreign influence and interaction with ethnic groups both Maya and non-Maya.

In Mesoamerican archaeology, there has been much debate over the degree of foreign influence in the Maya lowlands during the Early Classic period. The limitations of core/periphery approaches such as World System's Theory as an explanatory framework for ancient complex societies has caused some Mesoamericanists to rethink the nature of relationships between Teotihuacan in particular and the Maya area. The current view sees a complex two-way regional interaction between ethnic groups of diverse origin, identity, and social status. Regional interactions have become the subject of renewed interest in the northern Maya lowlands because data now show that this area was not outside the sphere of Teotihuacan influence during the Classic period, as previously believed. Because discussions of Teotihuacan-Maya interactions have focused almost exclusively on elite relationships, few researchers have attempted to explore the impact of ethnic dynamics on the domestic sphere of organization in the Maya area.

Two decades of research at Chac (II) and Sayil have provided valuable comparative data on two successive central places, or capitals, with complex and contrastive patterns of ethnicity (Fig. 7.1). Both settlements were relatively large Maya centers in the Middle-Late (AD 500–750) and Terminal Classic (AD 800–1000) periods, respectively. Chac, including the Grotto of Chac, or Chac I, was a large settlement and likely a political capital that controlled a substantial hinterland at a time of low densities of regional population. Sayil appears to have been one of Chac's satellite settlements to the southeast that later grew, perhaps at the expense of its overlord, to become the new capital of a far more populated subregion in the ninth century. Sayil's rise to preeminence was likely due to political factors and not normal settlement expansion because Chac's decline as a major center occurs about the same time that Sayil becomes a capital city.

Residential architecture, artifact and activity patterns, and mortuary remains from intensive survey and excavation are employed here to show that Chac experienced foreign interactions with non-Maya ethnic groups, especially at the domestic-residential level. Sayil, in contrast, shows Maya ethnic and domestic characteristics that are more typical for the region. This chapter will discuss the changes in domestic organization and ethnic interactions between Middle Classic Chac and Terminal Classic Sayil and will examine the broader implications for understanding the role of the Puuc region in Mesoamerican prehistory.

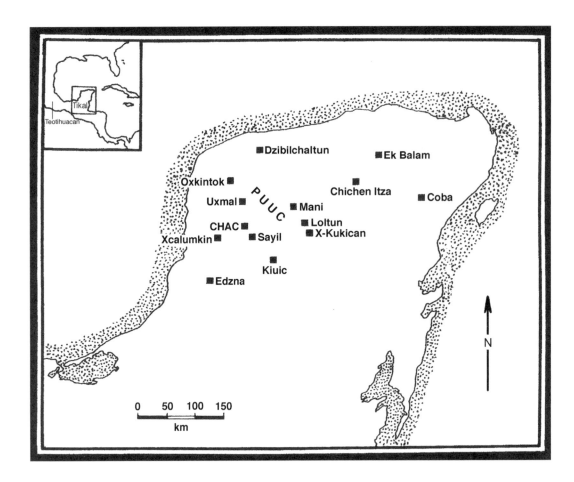

Figure 7.1. The Yucatan Peninsula, showing the locations of Sayil, Chac, and other sites mentioned in the text.

Research Background

Settlement pattern surveys, including architectural mapping and systematic surface collection, were carried out at Chac and Sayil between 1983 and 2004 (Fig. 7.2). The results of these investigations suggest that Sayil covered more than 4.5 km² and was among the largest sites in the Puuc region during the Terminal Classic florescence, and was inhabited by an estimated urban population of almost 10,000, with perhaps an additional 6,000 people residing at outlying satellite communities (Carmean 1991; Dunning 1989; Killion et al. 1989; Sabloff and Tourtellot 1991; Smyth and Dore 1992, 1994; Smyth et al. 1995; Tourtellot et al. 1989, 1990; Tourtellot and Sabloff 1994). Chac is located 1.7 km northwest of the North Palace at Sayil and approximately 500 m west of the modern *Ruta* Puuc highway. Classified by the Archaeological Atlas as a relatively small rank IV settlement, survey work has determined that Chac II is actually much larger, covering an area greater than 3 km² with an estimated population of 6,000 that includes the Chac cave and associated settlement approximately 2 km to the north (Fig. 7.3; Smyth et al. 1998; Smyth 1999).

Excavations at Sayil in the 1980s documenting patterns of Terminal Classic residential site structure concentrated on a settlement cluster known as the Miguel T hectare, located within the central-east portion of the site (Fig. 7.4). This domestic group is believed to represent a fairly typical ethnic Maya farming homestead or head household of a multifamily kin group with allied houselots organized in close proximity for the production of infield gardens, water storage within *chultuns* (underground water cisterns), and other domestic activity in and around perishable foundation brace buildings.

A comprehensive program of excavation at both monumental and residential contexts took place at Chac II beginning in 1995 (Fig. 7.5). Architectural excavation at the Great Pyramid and Grecas Plazas sampled and consolidated a number of buildings including the Great Pyramid itself, which shows five construction episodes beginning in the Early Classic period. The finding of Teotihuacan-like icons in the form of stone sculpture and early-style pottery vessels, green obsidian, and the incorporation of *talud-tablero*-like decorative elements into building façades strongly suggest some form of significant central Mexican influence. The recovery of twenty-three human burials beneath

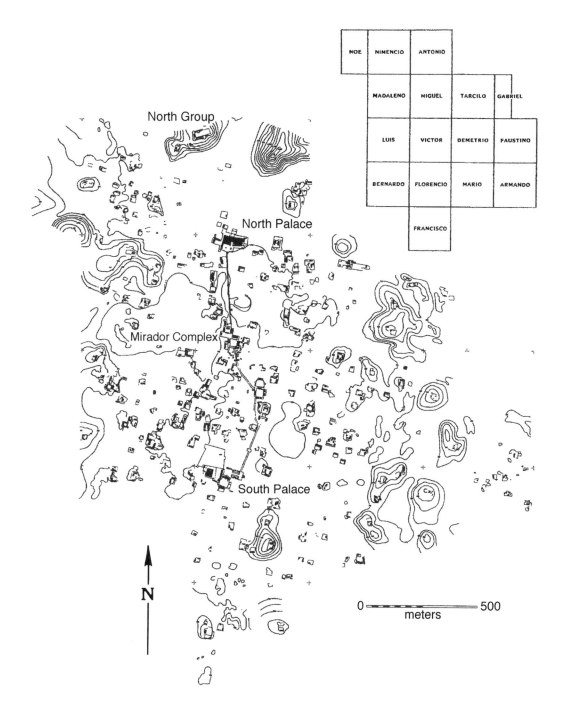

Figure 7.2. Architectural and topographic map of Sayil showing the 3.5 km² survey area and the location of the Miguel T hectare.

the floors of three large multiunit residential substructures resembling apartment compounds shows domestic architecture and mortuary patterns that strongly suggest central Mexican traditions. High quantities of gray obsidian and the presence of green obsidian, numerous biface projectile dart points, and pottery incorporating Teotihuacan forms and icons all indicate the presence of resident foreigners. The combined data from both monumental and especially domestic contexts suggest ethnic patterns of interaction with foreigners affiliated with central Mexican peoples. Although elite emulation of highland Mexican cultural patterns cannot be ruled out for the Early Classic and Late Classic periods at Chac, Middle Classic non-elite contexts show foreign-style domestic architecture and utilitarian artifacts that strongly indicate the presence of Mexican foreigners or their surrogates (Smyth 2006, 2008).

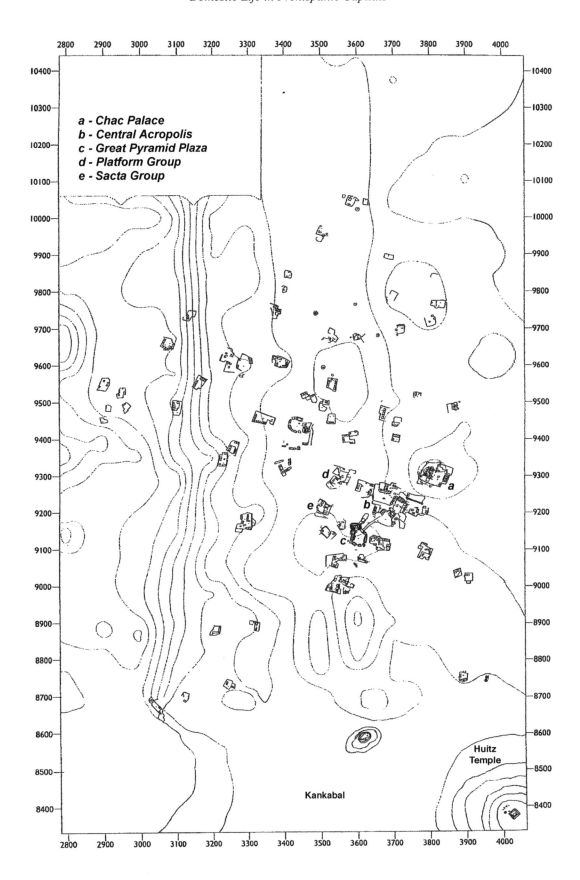

Figure 7.3. Architectural and topographical map of Chac II showing the 2 km² area of survey. North is at the top.

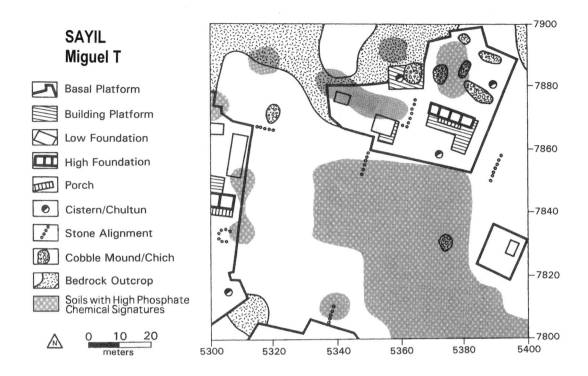

Figure 7.4. Schematic map of the Miguel T hectare from Sayil.

Ethnic Identity and Archaeological Correlates

Much research in archaeology has shown that material style, particularly in regard to ceramics, can express social and ethnic group affiliation (DeBoer 1990; Dietler and Herbich 1998; Holland et al. 1998; Schortman 1989; Shennan 1989; Upham 1990; Wiessner 1983). The approach here does not rely on artifact style alone to indicate ethnic identity, but employs the entire material assemblage from stratigraphic and architectural contexts emphasizing spatial organization as a frame of reference.

Fredrik Barth (1969:9) defines ethnic groups as "categories of ascription and identification by the actors themselves." Ethnic groups are almost always in contact with other ethnic groups, particularly in frontier situations. Boundaries between different ethnic groups often determine and signal membership to a particular group, and criteria may include language, dress, geographical location, or even economic roles (Barth 1969:16; Siverts 1969:104). Group boundaries are dynamic and there is normally tremendous pressure for one group to assimilate. The persistence of ethnic groups in contact situations requires interaction that is structured to allow for the continuation of differences (Barth 1969:16). The relative size of the ethnic groups in situations of contact is also important; usually a larger group will absorb a smaller one. Unequal power relations also affect the survival of group identity. Additionally, the sex ratio of an ethnic group is a factor in determining the degree of interaction and assimilation. Resident foreign males who marry into another ethnic group may increase the likelihood that the wives' cultural traits will be incorporated into their group (Cohen and Middleton

1970:13–21). Even the maintenance of a group boundary over time does not ensure that the character of the boundary remains the same since boundaries need not be expressed by the same idioms over the centuries (Siverts 1969:105).

In Mesoamerican archaeology, ethnic enclaves have been studied in relation to Teotihuacan. An enclave is composed of an ethnic group living in a foreign land, typically in an urban setting, and serving special functions such as garrisons, embassies, or trade centers (Spence 1996:334). Maintaining ethnicity in enclaves is usually more difficult than in a "simple" frontier situation; the residents are far from home and under extreme pressure to assimilate. Because ethnic enclaves can be difficult to detect archaeologically, Michael Spence (1996:335–36) has suggested several criteria that may be present:

- Distinctive traits should be pervasive in the structure or area. This would indicate the wide participation of most of the residents in a different cultural tradition.

- Mortuary patterns will often differ significantly from local traditions. Caution must be exercised because burial information may signal social class rather than a different ethnicity. Likewise, different burial practices may not explicitly signal ethnicity, but may serve to reinforce hierarchy.

- The inhabitants of an enclave may be physically distinct. Differences may exist due to both biology and culture. Cranial and dental modification may be useful in this

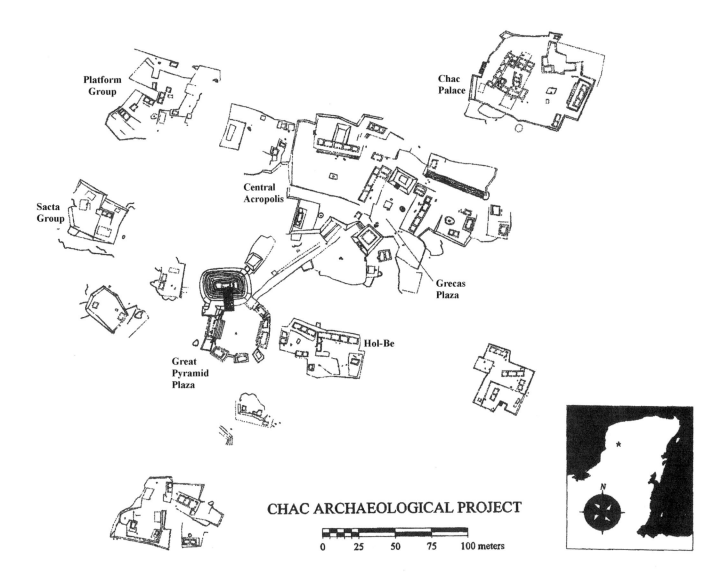

Figure 7.5. Map of the central zone of Chac, showing the locations of the Platform and Sacta Groups in relation to major monumental architecture.

regard, but again with the caveat that differences could be from status differences rather than ethnicity. Biology can also be complex. The residents of enclaves may be expected to differ somewhat from the homeland population due to the founder effect and subsequent genetic isolation. Intermarriage between the host population and the enclave population will further contribute to ethnic differentiation from the homeland population.

- Foreign artifacts should be present. These may be either actual imports or locally made copies done in a foreign style (Santley et al. 1987). It is difficult to separate the use of artifacts for promoting ethnicity from artifacts used to enhance local status (the elite emulation hypothesis) (Demarest and Foias 1993); foreign or foreign-style utilitarian objects are often better indicators.

- Architecture may be distinct. Spence notes that this is the most nebulous criterion due to widespread similarities in domestic architecture across most of Mesoamerica. He notes, for example, that Teotihuacan-style residences may have been acceptable to foreign groups living in the city. Whether native groups built and lived in foreign-style residences is more doubtful and debatable.

Approaching ethnic boundaries as dynamic entities that change diachronically requires examining why enclaves persist, why they dissolve, and why they become acculturated by the host culture. Therefore, ethnic dynamics must be considered over a long period of time. What may start out as an enclave may not persist as such; that is, the residents may become acculturated and assimilated into the host culture after a few generations or they may leave and return home after a short time.

Domestic Patterns at Sayil: Miguel T Hectare

Investigations at the Miguel T hectare focused on the basal platform at N7860/E5350 (Fig. 7.4; Sabloff and Tourtellot 1991). Domestic vernacular architecture, *chultuns*, and the predominance of utilitarian ceramics and other domestic artifacts at this platform suggest residential occupation spanning less than 200 years during the Terminal Classic period (Tourtellot et al. 1989). The possible exception to residential occupation involves the northern half of the platform, which may have served some separate function given the number, organization, and orientation of several oddly shaped cobblestone mounds (*bak ch'ich'*) commonly found at other northern lowland Maya centers. One possibility is that the northern half of the platform was engaged in craft production such as ceramic manufacturing, given the high densities of surface ceramics (Dore, pers. comm., 1994), a pattern often associated with kiln areas or the places where ceramic vessels are fired (Arnold 1991; Smyth et al. 1995; Santley et al. 1989). The remains of *chultuns* to the east and west are consistent with ceramic-making activities that require a sizable supply of water.

The principal building of the house compound is a southward-facing, four-room, double-stone-lined foundation that had mostly perishable walls and a thatched roof. The easternmost room may have been a later addition or was an existing informal room that became formalized shortly thereafter. Other associated features include a well-defined porch or patio activity area south of the room block that also serves to border a rainwater catchment area for the residential *chultun*. Constructed of local limestone blocks, the north wall extended up to 18 m long, forming a faced-stone wall up to four courses backing the entire structure. Along the wall was a small midden with several partial vessels and a fragmentary and poorly preserved burial, which, like all other burials here, appears to have been some form of dedicatory offering to one of the last levels of the basal platform. Two typical Terminal Classic vessels, including an inverted dish covering the head of Burial 1, were recovered. Burial 2 was found below the floor in the northwest corner of the formal central room. The skeleton was in a flexed position, and was by a large Yocat Striated water jar that was complete and upright but which contained only sub-floor construction fill (Tourtellot et al. 1989:10–13). Off to the west was a third burial, perhaps female, and a poorly preserved skeleton in a flexed position, but no significant goods were found in association (Tourtellot et al. 1989:17).

The residential architecture of the Miguel T hectare shows no unusual characteristics for Puuc settlement other than the on-platform *ch'ich'* mounds that are normally found off-platform and are so ubiquitous at Sayil and throughout the region. The small burial sample is fairly typical with a tendency for flexed burial position but no formal chambers and minimal burial goods accompanying the interment. Indeed, there appears to be similarity between the Sayil burials and the Late Classic burials from Chac in Structure 5 of the Platform Group, a time when the Chac site as a whole seems to have reasserted its Maya ethnic identity (see below; Smyth 2006). The ceramic assemblage from surface collections, excavations, and complete vessels is overwhelmingly the local Terminal Classic Cehpech complex dominated by striated and slate ware pottery. The lithic assemblage shows nothing out of the ordinary either. Overall, while this group exhibits potential evidence for some level of occupational specialization, there are no clear indications of anything but a local farming group of Maya ethnic identity and likely commoner social status.

Domestic Patterns of Ethnicity at Chac

In contrast to Sayil, evidence of foreign ethnicity at Chac was obtained from excavations at two residential platforms called the Sacta and Platform Groups, located to the west and northwest of the Great Pyramid Plaza. The objective was to document patterns related to domestic activity, both early and late, and to investigate the possibility of an ethnic enclave of foreign origin.

The Platform Group Architecture

Surface mapping showed unusual spatial arrangement and orientation for numerous perishable buildings located upon different surface levels (Fig. 7.6) but showed no stone vaulted roof buildings, which is unusual considering the close proximity to the monumental core of Chac. Immediately below Late Classic constructions were boulder foundations; excavation revealed large modular and multi-room substructures integrated with corridors and walled interior patios. These substructures are oriented about 15 degrees east of north and show spatial conventions and organization similar to central Mexican domestic architecture at this time, especially the apartment compounds found at Teotihuacan (Smyth and Rogart 2004).

The room interiors of five stone foundations (braces) for perishable buildings (Structures 1, 2, and 3) were exposed horizontally. A Round Structure and two additional foundation braces (4 and 5) were also tested. Based on ceramics, radiocarbon assays, and architectural stratigraphy, all surface structures except the Round Structure are dated to the Late Classic period. Horizontal exposures beneath and around Structures 1 and 2, however, revealed a substantial substructure that was leveled and filled with large stones (Fig. 7.7). The substructure was then used as the building platform for later construction. This explains the spatial orientation of the more typical Maya houses of the later phase; the last occupants used the substructure to build upon and thus were restricted to its general form and placement. The substructure shows the remains of multiple rooms, interior corridors, and a possible interior patio area with a relatively thick stucco floor and boulder wall foundation. In fact, the lower building's large, rough-cut boulders likely were used as foundation walls for a perishable roof. There was no evidence for upright posts or vault stones. The substructure was built upon a layer of relatively sterile construction fill used to level the bedrock. The most intriguing aspect of the substructure was that it did follow

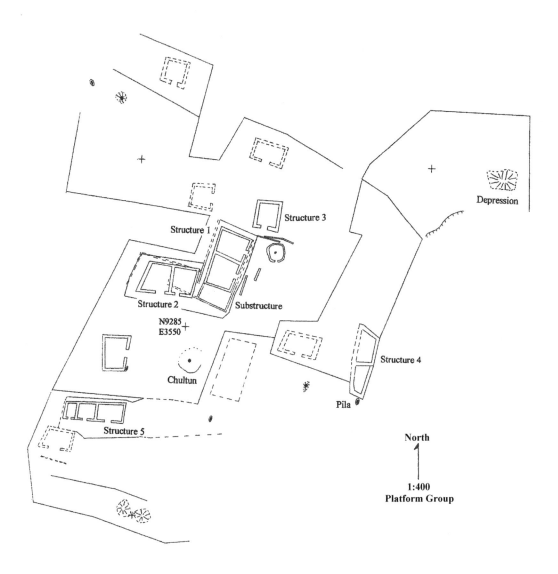

Figure 7.6. Planimetric map of the Platform Group at Chac.

traditional Maya spatial conventions consisting of small house foundations (like those found in the late phase of the Platform Group and at Sayil's Miguel T) oriented along cardinal directions around a central plaza area.

Based upon architectural stratigraphy, there appears to have been two phases of occupation in the Platform Group. The later phase, still visible on the surface, consists of a series of two-room range structures aligned on the edges of plaza areas. The Platform Group substructure clearly predates the superimposed Late Classic structures. Numerous carbon samples were taken in the hope of chronometrically dating the substructure but results were mostly spurious, probably due to recently burned roots. Many of the ceramic forms discovered in the lower stratigraphic levels, however, are from early-style vessels, with substantial quantities of Maya Thin Orange wares, polychromes, and early slate wares believed to be diagnostic of Early-Middle Classic

occupation. Based upon similarities in architecture, burial patterns, and ceramics, the early occupation in the Platform Group is almost certainly contemporaneous with the early phase of the Sacta Group that has been terminally or postdated to AD 660 ± 40 (see below).

The Sacta Group Architecture

Situated atop a high hill 100 m west of the Great Pyramid (Figs. 7.3, 7.5, 7.8), the Sacta Group exhibits a typical Maya two-room foundation brace (Structure 1) below which was a sizable substructure extending over most of the platform surface. As with the Platform Group substructure, it appears that the buildings of the late phase of occupation were constructed upon the early structure after it had been filled and leveled. Despite the leveling process, the Sacta substructure remains more intact

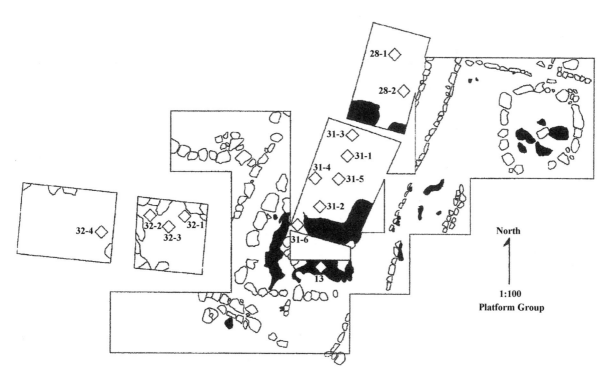

Figure 7.7. Plan drawing of the substructure excavations, stucco floors (dark shading), and burial locations (numbered diamonds) from the Platform Group at Chac.

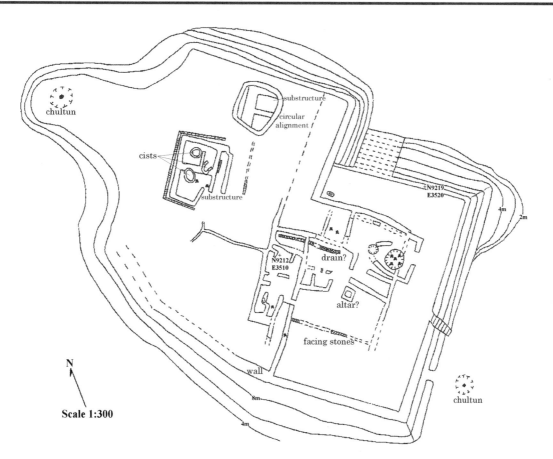

Figure 7.8. Planometric map of Sacta Group showing the layout of the modular-style substructure, burials, and contours.

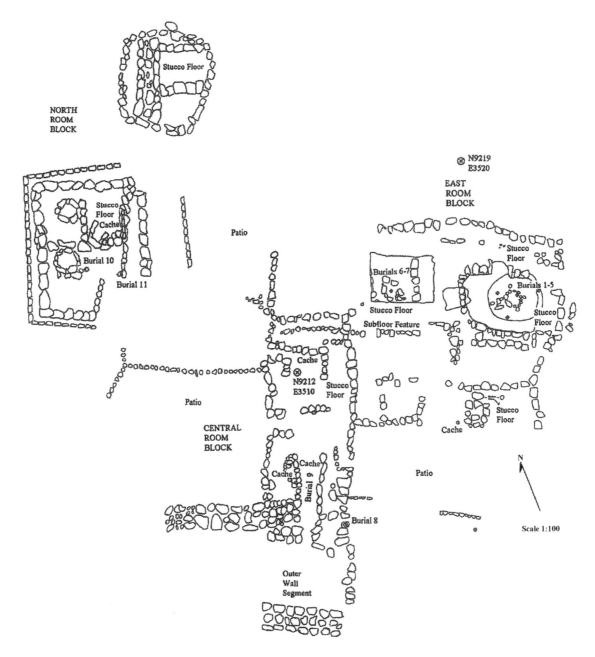

Figure 7.9. Detailed plan of the remains of the Sacta substructure after excavation and consolidation.

(Fig. 7.9). The substructure was constructed from large, rough-cut boulders and a small step or platform edge on the south side of smaller, well-faced stones underlying the large, rough-cut walls. Therefore, it seems to be associated with the early structure rather than any late occupation. The inclusion of chinking stones (*cuñas*) does, however, differentiate the smaller faced-stones from the later faced-walls, leading to the conclusion that this feature is a step or platform edge that split the interior patio area into two levels. A second stone alignment to the northwest is similarly constructed and appears to be a remnant of some kind of drainage system because it follows the downhill slope of the

bedrock and leads in the general direction of two stucco basins and a *chultun* (below).

Preserved stucco floor sections were associated with the substructure. The most intact area was underneath the east room of Structure 1—a thick, unbroken stucco floor similar to the one found in association with the Platform Group substructure. Two unusual subfloor features were found under the substructure floor and walls and consisted of two pits in the bedrock plastered with stucco to form subfloor basins. One of them (Stucco Basin #2) was rather small and contained mostly rocks and debris. The other (Stucco Basin #1) was a very large feature, both in diameter (approximately 2 m) and in depth (about 1 m), and contained three circular stone cists and the remains of five subadult burials (Sacta Burials 1–5). The floor of the substructure laid over the basins was notably thick (about 10 cm) and intact, possibly indicating that the basins were carefully sealed.

The west half of the Sacta Group included a Late Classic-style platform built upon bedrock outcrops. This sector was one of three connected room blocks or apartment clusters adjacent to three interior patio spaces. The entire complex appears to have been surrounded by a high stone wall about one meter thick, based on the finding of footing stones on the south platform edge and numerous boulder stones now lying off-platform around the perimeter. There were also possible entryways or wall openings aligned with staircases on the north and east sides and another opening leading to a large *chultun* on the west. On the northwest edge of the platform, a circular stone alignment was cleared of boulders and tested. At 50 cm below the surface, a one-meter thick boulder wall with adobe-like mortar was encountered running north-south and connected to the nearby substructure. About 20 cm further down, two perpendicular boulder walls running east appeared and defined two adjacent room areas. At 1.5 m below the surface, a red-brown stucco floor was found in the north room area; it continued east toward the platform edge. These rooms (and likely others unexcavated) are part of a larger room block integrated with the nearby substructure to form an L-shaped building wing and adjacent patio area.

The Sacta substructure possesses very unusual spatial and physical characteristics more typical of contemporaneous central Mexican domestic structures than those from the northern Maya area. Oriented between 15 and 20 degrees east of north, the substructure shows interior space organized as multiple rooms or room blocks with the remains of stucco floors, interior patios, corridors, a rectangular altar, and a subfloor drain conduit. Covering nearly the entire surface area of the Sacta platform, the sheer size and non-Maya residential characteristics, the early pottery diagnostics like Thin Orange and polychrome ware sherds, and a terminal or post occupation C-14 date of AD 660 ± 40 (calibrated two sigma, 96% probability, AD 660–790) strongly suggest a foreign-style residential compound constructed and occupied by AD 550 if not earlier (Linné 1934; Millon 1973; Manzanilla 1993).

In summary, in the Middle Classic (approximately AD 550 or earlier), stucco basins are constructed (built either first or at the same time as the larger structure) and then utilized in a ritual manner. The interment of four, or perhaps five, child burials is probably a dedicatory offering for the construction of the building or just the overlying room, since the subfloor drain conduits seem to be associated. Immediately after, the substructure was either constructed or expanded by using large, rough stone walls at least three courses high and some form of perishable superstructure. The large interior space of this building is divided into multiple rooms, articulating onto patio areas. In the Late Classic, the substructure was ritually terminated and leveled. As part of this event, an adult female accompanied by a dog (Burial 8) was

buried in a stone cist, and the cist was sealed with a thick stucco mixture. From this mix, a charcoal sample has yielded a C-14 date of AD 660. Subsequently, most walls (including the surrounding wall) were collapsed, and typical Maya foundation braces and a bare platform were constructed upon the construction debris. The large boulder walls from the substructure were then used as retaining walls for building platforms across the surface of this hilltop group.

The Platform Group and Sacta Group Artifacts

A number of early-style and foreign-style vessels were recovered in burials and caches; most were early slate wares associated with Early Classic polychrome sherds (Fig. 7.10). Virtually all vessels were stucco-coated with many showing resist painting, a decorative technique typical of Teotihuacan ceramics. One early slate ware vessel exhibits a stylized image of a fanged deity with a flowing headdress and goggle-eyes that resembles the central Mexico storm god (Tlaloc). This image was painted in red specular hematite. Another unusual vessel is an incised thin-walled (less than 5 mm), black-ware (Ekpedz *inciso*) cylindrical vase with an outflaring rim that is similar to vessel forms from Teotihuacan.

A stucco-coated, black and brown-on-orange, single-chambered, boxlike ceramic receptacle, apparently for burning incense, in the form of a temple with a three-part cornice molding and sloping lower wall is identified as a *candelero*, interred with a adult male (Burial 3) seated inside a circular stone-lined

Figure 7.10. Foreign-style vessels recovered from the Platform Group burials and caches at Chac II (clockwise left to right): *a*, a Chemax early slate ware tripod dish exhibiting a stylized image of a fanged deity with a flowing headdress and goggle-eyes that resembles the central Mexico storm god (Tlaloc), painted in red specular hematite; *b*, an incised black-ware tripod cylinder vessel with nubbin supports (unidentified) showing Teotihuacan-style decoration; *c*, an incised thin-walled, black-ware (Ekpedz *inciso*) cylindrical vase with an outflaring rim; *d*, a stucco-coated, black and brown-on-orange, single-chambered, boxlike ceramic receptacle or *candelero* (unidentified), apparently for burning incense, in the form of a temple with a three-part cornice molding and sloping lower wall.

cist. I have argued that these boxlike, chambered receptacles (which have been found at centers like Oxkintok, Xcambó, and Dzibilnocac) are *candeleros* that were manufactured as Maya renderings of this distinctive central Mexican culture diagnostic (Smyth and Rogart 2004).

An incised tripod cylinder vessel with nubbin supports (unidentified) shows incised triangles and skull-like appliqué decoration similar to mural paintings from the Atetelco compound at Teotihuacan (Martin and Grube 2000:185). Also, a partial Fine Orange tripod plate with hollow rattle supports and mica inclusions is similar to Fine Buff (Code 30) from Matacapan, dated to the Middle Classic period, with incised skull and sun motifs found on grater (*molcajete*) vessels from central Mexico. Interestingly, the form of the tripod plate is characteristic of the southern Gulf Coast, not the Maya lowlands. In fact, both of these vessels appear to be foreign imports and must have been heirlooms ritually broken and deposited within a Late Classic building (Smyth and Rogart 2004:33).

In the Stucco Basin #1, subadult burials were sandwiched between partially complete Early-Middle Classic vessels. One tripod dish shows negative resist painting with stylized speech scrolls. Based upon context, I have argued that these burials might be sacrifices to a rain deity. At Teotihuacan, for instance, children were sacrificed to the *tlaloque* and infants that died at birth were often placed on large pottery fragments (Cabrera Castro 1999a, 1999b:529; Sánchez Alaniz and González Miranda 1999:402–3; Serrano and Lagunas 1975; Smyth and Rogart 2004). Other

10 cm

Figure 7.11. The base of a bifacially worked obsidian dart point (atlatl?), recovered from early contexts of the Sacta substructure, showing workmanship typical of Teotihuacan, and an atlatl dart point of probable Mexican obsidian and workmanship, from the Chac Plaza; both appear to be from a highland Mexican source, possibly Otumba or Zaragoza obsidian.

Early Classic pottery included a cached Thin Orange ware bowl placed over a red ware bowl (Cache 1), both identified as Kinich Naranja and that show surface finishing similar to San Martín Orange ware from Teotihuacan (Rattray 2001:265).

The residential groups contain a high percentage of obsidian prismatic blades (n = 92, 52% of site total), some of which are from highland Mexican sources. One particular obsidian biface point shows Teotihuacan workmanship. Many other chert biface projectiles are identified as dart points (n = 31) that were found in association with both substructures (Fig. 7.11; Smyth and Rogart 2004). According to Rovner and Lewenstein (1997:27–28), arrow and spear points from Becán and Dzibilchaltún with a mean maximum thickness of 8 mm can be classified as dart points. Given that dart points are typically found in Late or Terminal Classic period contexts in the region (Rovner and Lewenstein 1997:28, 79), their appearance in earlier contexts at Chac might be significant, particularly if they were for atlatls, because Teotihuacan warriors are almost always depicted as wielding spear-throwers. These data suggest a foreign group of merchant-warriors living at Chac.

Twenty-one obsidian samples were tested by elemental neutron activation in 1996, which indicated that twenty were from El Chayal and one was from San Martín Jilotepeque; both sources are Guatemalan (Smyth 1998: Table 2). However, since this analysis, seven gray samples appear to be non-Guatemalan obsidians (based on color, opacity, and textures) and are most likely of highland Mexican origin (following Braswell et al. 2000). In addition, the base of a bifacially worked obsidian dart point recovered from early contexts of the Sacta substructure shows workmanship typical of Teotihuacan (Spence, pers. comm., 2003) and is likely a highland Mexican source, possibly Otumba or Zaragoza obsidian. Also, another dart point of probable Mexican obsidian and workmanship and seven green Pachuca obsidian blade fragments were recovered from the Pyramid Plaza. These data as well as the finding of numerous chert dart points, virtually all from the Platform and Sacta Groups, support the presence of resident foreigners who were familiar with central Mexican lithic traditions.

A pyrite encrusted slate disk with two perforations was recovered with one of two seated burials (Burials 10 and 11) in the room areas of the northwest Sacta substructure. This pyrite encrusted slate disk and numerous worked and perforated marine shells, including large bivalve shells for a necklace, are often considered to be central Mexican-related status items and costume accessories (Stone 1989:157). Two caches of seashell were also recovered. The first consisted of a single large shell pierced for suspension and worn around the neck, typical of the regalia of a Teotihuacan warrior as depicted in Maya art. The other was recovered at the base of the central altar within an inverted globular jar filled with thirty-seven small shells. It is clear that the residents of the Sacta Group had access to coastal resources. Other unusual burial elements include red cinnabar found either as small nodules or as paintings on the stones of burial cists, small flakes of mica, and awls of worked animal bone.

The Platform Group and Sacta Group Burials

Mortuary patterns support a foreign presence at these early residential compounds but not at the level of elite social status. Twenty-three human burials were found within subfloor contexts. All burials were in seated or flexed positions placed into circular to oval-shaped (round) stone-lined cists or between pottery vessels in tight fetal positions. The latter were infant-perinatal burials including five apparently interred as ritual offerings within a large circular, stuccoed depression below the east wing of the Sacta substructure. These "round" burials and child offerings show striking similarities to central Mexican mortuary customs practiced during the Middle Classic period.

Eleven definite and two possible subfloor burials (P28-1A, P28-2, P32-1, P32-2, P32-3, P32-4, P31-1, P31-2, P31-3, P31-4, P31-5, P31-6, and Burial 13) were associated with the Platform Group substructure (Fig. 7.7). All were found sealed below the substructure's stucco floor and therefore must date to the Early to Middle Classic periods. With one exception, all burials were primary, interred in seated or tightly flexed positions (perhaps as part of burial bundles) within circular to oval-shaped, stone-lined cist chambers. Skeletal analysis of eleven individuals with preserved diagnostic attributes identified six adult males, four adult females, and one adult whose sex is indeterminate (Tiesler 1999b, 2000).

Three burials in particular present unusual mortuary characteristics that exemplify patterns of possible foreign ethnic identity. Burial P32-3 consisted of a robust adult male placed in an oval mortuary space in a flexed position, lying on his right side (Fig. 7.12). While erosion and rodent activity make the identification of pathologies very difficult, fragments of the cervical vertebrae show notable evidence of arthritis and the frontal bone of the cranium shows a healed blunt trauma and some degree of cultural flattening. The occipital fragments, however, exhibit no signs of cultural modification. Four out of ten teeth show evidence of caries and the enamel of all three canines were affected by hypoplasia, indicating some episodes of nutritional stress during the life of this particular individual. Trace element analysis performed on eight of the burials revealed a different nutritional profile for P32-3, possibly indicating a foreign origin or residency (Tiesler 1999a:13). Burial P32-3 also included two worked seashells (*Spondylus americanus*), complete early-style ceramic vessels, and a partially worked animal bone.

Burial P31-2 was an adult female of medium to gracile build. The surviving teeth show signs of light wear, with two out of ten exhibiting signs of advanced caries and no evidence of cultural modification. Burial architecture is a round cist made from large stones. This individual was interred with three early-style vessels, most notably a tripod dish (Chemax) with divergent sides, an enlarged outflaring rim, and a figure in red specular hematite painted on the bottom portraying the central Mexican rain god Tlaloc. Additionally, this vessel was "killed" by punching a hole through the middle of the painted design.

Burial P31-3 was an adult of robust build, most likely a male (Fig. 7.13). The surfaces of the bones were partially covered

Figure 7.12. Burial P32-3 consisted of a robust adult male placed in an oval mortuary space in a flexed position, lying on his right side. Trace element analysis revealed a different nutritional profile for P32-3, possibly indicating a foreign origin or residency. This burial sample, unfortunately, could not be tested by strontium isotope analysis. The trowel is 23 cm.

with a red ochre patina. Rodent activity and erosion make the determination of pathologies nearly impossible but there is little or no evidence for cultural modification visible on the cranium fragments. This individual was buried in a seated position within a round cist, and grave goods included a piece of deer antler, a worked piece of animal bone, a pair of jade ear flares, and the single-chambered Mayanized version of a *candelero* discussed above.

Of the eight human burials in the Sacta Group (Figs. 7.8, 7.9), three show the strongest evidence of non-Maya ethnic patterns;

all were found within Stucco Basin #1 (described above). Burial 1 was of a child of one to three years in age. Notably lacking in the skeletal inventory are elements of the upper extremities, trunk, and head; the long bones were concentrated in a small area (10 cm by 10 cm). Based upon these data, one can reasonably interpret this burial as a secondary deposition (Tiesler 2001). The bones were found on a tripod plate decorated with a stylized Tlaloc face and a bird of prey headdress, covered with a large portion of a Chimbote Cream polychrome bowl from Campeche. Burial 5 is the fourth perinatal burial in Stucco Basin #1, found in a tightly flexed position between two ceramic vessels: a tripod dish covered by a large Chemax water jar fragment. On the bottom of the tripod dish, a decoration was painted in resist, representing a stylized speech scroll (Smyth and Rogart 2004:36). These mortuary patterns strongly suggest a ceremonial offering that may have involved ritual sacrifices, perhaps dedicated to the central Mexican rain gods.

Although foreign mortuary patterns suggestive of central Mexican traditions are strongly implied, the early burial patterns for the Puuc region are poorly known. The available data from Oxkintok and Xcambó do suggest that extended body position was the preferred manner of interment (López Vázquez and Fernández Marquínez 1987:42–43; Rivera Dorado and Fernández Martín 1989:69–70; Reindel 1997:203, 237). The largest prehispanic burial population for northern Yucatan comes from the northern coastal site of Xcambó, where more than 500 burials were recovered between 1996 and 2000 (Sierra Sosa and Martínez Lizarraga 2001). Xcambó had a significant population in the Early Classic period, and the most common methods of burial interment at this time were flexed in a fetal position and fully extended (Sierra Sosa and Martínez Lizarraga 2001:8). Burial patterns at Dzibilchaltún seem to favor extended burials, especially during the Early Phase II (Andrews and Andrews 1980:319, Table 8). At Chac, in contrast, there are no extended burials; most are seated, and some are flexed in a tight fetal position, mostly on the left side, within circular stone-lined cists. Perhaps not coincidentally, seated and flexed burials within circular pits (*fosas*) are the most common form of skeletal position at Teotihuacan (Cabrera Castro 1999b:506–7).

A strontium isotope analysis was completed on thirteen Chac burials to determine biological origin. While none of the samples run show any direct biological affiliation with central Mexico, the two burials that were most likely to have been of foreign origin (P31-3 and P32-3), unfortunately, could not be tested. The average values for the tested individuals, however, show close correspondence with expectations for the region but are identical with Xcambó (Fig. 7.14), a site that had significant occupations during the Early Classic period and important long-distance contacts with the Gulf Coast and the Petén area when Teotihuacan was strongly active at Tikal. Recent trace element composition analysis of tooth enamel from Xcambó burials suggests there were indeed foreigners in the burial population (Cucina 2008).

Figure 7.13. Burial P31-3 was an adult of robust build, most likely a male, buried in a seated position within a round cist; there were multiple grave goods including the single-chambered Mayanized version of a *candelero* pictured in the center. The trowel is 23 cm.

Discussion

The differences between Sayil and Chac can be attributed to their variable settlement histories and patterns of ethnic identity. Sayil was a relatively large central place in this part of the Puuc region during the Terminal Classic and is typical in terms of its settlement layout and patterns of domestic organization when compared to other known sites in the vicinity. The evidence from the Miguel T hectare shows a Maya farming homestead perhaps also engaged in some limited form of occupation specialization related to ceramic manufacture. The standard houselot arrangement of foundation brace buildings arranged around a central patio with nearby water sources such as *chultuns*, utilitarian ceramics (Cehpech), local lithic artifacts, and informal mortuary patterns are pretty much what one would expect for Terminal Classic Maya farming populations. There is no reason to believe that the ethnic identity of the people who occupied the Miguel T hectare was other than that of local Puuc Maya agriculturalists.

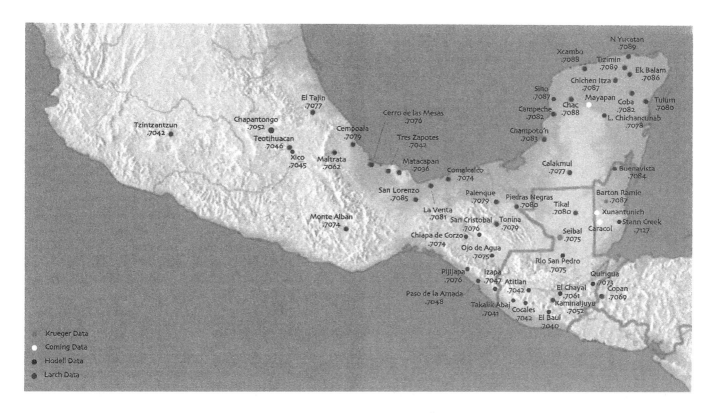

Figure 7.14. Distributional map of strontium values for sites across Mesoamerica. Strontium isotope analysis was completed on thirteen Chac burials to determine biological origin (after Smyth and Price 2006). The average values, however, show close correspondence with expectations for the region but are identical with Xcambó, an Early Classic period site along the north coast of Yucatan.

Chac, on the other hand, was founded in the Early Classic period and ceased to be a central place of political importance by the outset of the Terminal Classic period. Chac also appears to have experienced an intense relationship with foreign groups during the Middle Classic period, including Teotihuacan or its surrogates at Tikal, Kaminaljuyú, or elsewhere. The presence of central Mexican-style domestic architecture beneath more typical Maya residential buildings exhibits a sharp contrast in layout and organization. These large modular-style compounds are unique for the Puuc region, and no similar domestic habitation structures are currently known for northern Yucatan. The recovery of central Mexican iconography on artifacts and architecture in both domestic and monumental contexts, the production of local copies of Teotihuacan ceramics, specific lithic forms like dart points (for throwing sticks or atlatls?), and distinctive mortuary patterns that recall central Mexican rather than Maya traditions suggest complex ethnic interactions related to Teotihuacan. The production of decorative and technological "styles" as well as the domestic mortuary context in which they were found argue for a conscious attempt by transplants from another cultural tradition to maintain a separate social identity in death as well as life (Clayton 2005:433). This situation is especially relevant for those

who came from great distance, married into local populations, and sustained only sporadic or indirect ties to the home culture. Under these conditions, it is expected that foreign traditions would be maintained for no more than a few generations at best.

Although the nature of relations and interactions between Chac and central Mexico is a controversial subject, ethnic identity was clearly a factor in Chac's early settlement growth and site organization. If Chac was a northern Maya example of Santley's (1989) enclave settlement, a place containing resident Teotihuacanos or affiliated peoples from Kaminaljuyú, Tikal, or Matacapan, there ought to be other sites in the region with similar patterns of interaction. Unfortunately, tourist-based archaeology predominates in the region and rarely takes investigators away from the latest and largest monumental constructions.

Why is Teotihuacan at Chac when places like the trading gateway of Chunchucmil and the old center of Oxkintok on the western approaches to the Puuc are more easily reached? A potential answer is Chac's association with the Gruta de Chac. This immensely long cavern is the only permanent source of water for miles around and with associated settlement dated to the Early Classic period. Teotihuacanos may have been attracted to the Chac area for spiritual reasons because they saw it as a sacred place and analogous to the cave under the Pyramid of the Sun. The Early Classic water jars so abundant in the Chac cave with their bright orange slip, polychrome painting, and unique abstract designs may have been an attempt, in part, to render local copies of Thin Orange pottery and amphorae forms so characteristic of Teotihuacan. In fact, a number of Chac polychrome sherds have been recovered from the Platform and Sacta Group residential compounds and Great Pyramid Plaza, one of only a few places outside a cave context where this pottery has been found. In addition, thousands of sherds and numerous complete vessels of Chemax red-on-slate are found both in the cave and at the Chac site.

It has been shown that Chac predated Sayil and the chronological overlap and spatial proximity were linked to decline and florescence. There is good circumstantial evidence to suggest that Sayil benefited directly from its neighbor's misfortune and may have had a hand in Chac's demise. For example, the Great Pyramid Plaza was essentially destroyed and terminated ritually and/or violently around AD 750, as evidenced by the construction of various wall segments from stone taken from the plaza's vaulted buildings. The vacant eastern settlement zone and the hilltop Witz Temple (a lookout or garrison-like structure) located midway between the sites suggest that hostilities had been ongoing for some time before settlement abruptly shifted to Sayil. These factors suggest that this event occurred for political reasons and not due to a pattern of southeastward settlement expansion. It is even possible that ethnic animosities played a key role in the change of power from the old to the new center.

Conclusions

Teotihuacan's economic interest in northern Yucatan is difficult to discern. Perhaps Teotihuacan was politically and economically active at early Puuc sites like Chac and Oxkintok as well as centers on the coastal plain such as Chunchucmil, Dzibilchaltún, and Xcambó; in effect, they were working behind the scenes with their Maya surrogates at Kaminaljuyú, Tikal, and elsewhere, manipulating trade routes and perhaps demanding tribute. Was there a hierarchical relationship necessitating control of small but strategic centers, or was the relationship more asymmetrical, one in which Teotihuacan interacted cooperatively with a series of small lowland centers? Chac must have been symbolically important as the abode of the rain god(s) but also may have been located along a strategic overland trade route connecting the northern coastal plains to the central and southern Maya lowlands and perhaps back along the Gulf Coast, ultimately reaching the central highlands. This stopover along the "Teotihuacan Road" may have been so vital as to require the presence of resident Teotihuacanos acting as trade representatives, akin to the enclave hypothesized at Matacapan on the southern Gulf Coast (Santley 1989). Teotihuacan-inspired artifacts, remarkably similar apartment compound-like residences, and Middle Classic Maya and Tuxtla pottery are found at both archaeological sites.

Foreign interactions in the Puuc region were relatively short-lived, taking place over the course of a few generations or less sometime in the sixth century AD. This time is near the end of the centralized polity at Teotihuacan and during the so-called Classic Maya "hiatus" in southern Yucatan, a time when Teotihuacan is believed to have pulled out of the Petén region and major Maya centers like Tikal went into decline (Willey and Shimkin 1973). These two transitory events in Mesoamerica coincide with cultural development and foreign intrusions in northern Yucatan. The reduction and or even closure of important trade routes to the southern Maya lowlands caused by the regional violence of the "Star Wars" (Schele 1986; Schele and Freidel 1990), a time when Tikal, Calakmul, Caracol, and other Maya polities were engaged in protracted struggles, must have been catastrophic to the Teotihuacan elite. Such events would have sent shock waves through the political economy of central Mexico as the flow of valuable exotic goods in high demand, at least among the elite, became reduced to a trickle from the largest and richest tropical resource zone in Mesoamerica. Opening new routes of trade and/or expanding old ones by intensifying interactions and relationships with established centers of northern Yucatan appear to have been one response to political and economic instability.

The organizational and ethnic differences between two central places so closely spaced yet chronologically distinct, such as the Chac and Sayil settlements, suggest the development of political factions at hinterland centers that eventually surpass and absorb the parent population. Chac has the additional complication of an early foreign presence that has not been documented at other Puuc centers so far, except possibly at Oxkintok (Varela 1998; Varela and Braswell 2003). No archaeological zones in the Puuc have undergone such comprehensive settlement and surface survey combined with excavation at domestic and monumental architectural contexts as Chac and Sayil, suggesting that more work of this intensity and scope might produce comparable results. It is hoped that the ongoing investigations at Kiuic and vicinity and the new work beginning at the site of Xcoch will provide data that will help clarify some of the preliminary findings presented here.

There is now compelling evidence to support ethnic interactions organized around religious pilgrimage and specialized long-distance trade involving resident foreigners who impacted the domestic level of organization at Chac. This short-lived foreign interaction, however, had little lasting effect on domestic life at Sayil, but may have provided great political and economic opportunities for ambitious Maya lords of the hill region. Future research directed at revealing the process of Middle Classic interaction should help us better understand what role central Mexico played in the evolution of capital centers and state organized society in the Puuc region. Such work should have far-reaching implications providing new insights into highland-lowland interaction and the internationalization of Mesoamerica.

References

Andrews, E. Wyllys IV, and E. Wyllys Andrews V
1980 *Excavations at Dzibilchaltun, Yucatan, Mexico.* Middle American Research Institute, Publication 48. Tulane University, New Orleans.

Arnold, Philip J., III
1991 *Domestic Ceramic Production and Spatial Organization: Mexican Case Study in Ethnoarchaeology.* Cambridge University Press, New York.

Arnold, Philip J., III, Christopher A. Pool, Ronald Kneebone, and Robert S. Santley
1993 Intensive ceramic production and Classic-Period political economy in the Sierra de los Tuxtlas, Veracruz, Mexico. *Ancient Mesoamerica* 4:175–91.

Barth, Fredrik (editor)
1969 *Ethnic Groups and Boundaries: The Social Organization of Culture Difference.* Little, Brown and Company, Boston.

Braswell, Geoffrey E., John E. Clark, Kazuo Aoyama, Heather McKillop, and Michael Glascock
2000 Determining the geological provenance of obsidian artifacts from the Maya region: A test of the efficacy of visual sourcing. *Latin American Antiquity* 11:269–82.

Cabrera Castro, Rubén
1999a Los ritos funerarios en Teotihuacan y su diferenciación social. *Arqueología* VII(40):24–27.
1999b Las prácticas funerarias de los antiguos teotihucacanos. In *Prácticas funerarias en la Ciudad de los Dioses: Los enterramientos humanos de la antigua Teotihuacan*, edited by Linda Manzanilla and Carlos Serrano, pp. 503–39. UNAM, México, D.F.

Carmean, Kelli
1991 Architectural labor investment and social stratification at Sayil, Yucatan, Mexico. *Latin American Antiquity* 2:151–65.

Clayton, Sarah C.
2005 Interregional relationships in Mesoamerica: Interpreting Maya ceramics at Teotihuacan. *Latin American Antiquity* 16:427–48.

Cohen, Ronald, and John Middleton (editors)
1970 *From Tribe to Nation in Africa: Studies in Incorporation Processes.* Chandler Publishing Company, Scranton.

Cowgill, George L.
2003 Teotihuacan and Early Classic interaction: A perspective from outside the Maya region. In *The Maya and Teotihuacan: Reinterpreting Early Classic Interaction*, edited by G.E. Braswell, pp. 315–55. University of Texas Press, Austin.

Cucina, Andrea
2008 *Detecting Foreigners in Archaeological Human Dental Enamel in Yucatán, México.* Foundation for the Advancement of Mesoamerican Studies, Inc., Crystal River, Florida.

DeBoer, Warren R.
1990 Interaction, imitation, and communication as expressed in style: The Ucayali experience. In *The Uses of Style in Archaeology*, edited by M. Conkey and C. Hastorf, pp. 82–104. New Directions in Archaeology. Cambridge University Press, Cambridge.

Demarest, Arthur A., and A.E. Foias
1993 Mesoamerican horizons and the cultural transformations of Maya civilization. In *Latin American Horizons*, edited by Don S. Rice, pp. 146–91. Dumbarton Oaks Research Library and Collection, Washington, D.C.

Dietler, Michael, and Ingrid Herbich
1998 Habitus, techniques, style: An integrated approach to the social understanding of material culture and boundaries. In *The Archaeology of Social Boundaries*, edited by M. Stark, pp. 232–63. Smithsonian Institution Press, Washington, D.C.

Dunning, Nicholas P.
1989 *Archaeological Investigations at Sayil, Yucatan, Mexico: Intersite Reconnaissance and Soil Studies during the 1987 Field Season.* Publications in Anthropology No. 2. University of Pittsburgh, Pittsburgh.

Folan, Willian J., Ellen R. Kintz, and Laraine A. Fletcher
1983 *Coba: A Classic Maya Metropolis.* Academic Press, New York.

Holland, Dorothy, J. William Lachicotte, Debra Skinner, and Carole Cain
1998 *Identity and Agency in Cultural Worlds.* Harvard University Press, Cambridge, MA.

Killion, Thomas W., Jeremy A. Sabloff, Gair Tourtellot, and Nicholas P. Dunning
1989 Surface assemblages at Terminal Classic (A.D. 800–1000) Sayil, Puuc Region, Yucatan, Mexico. *Journal of Field Archaeology* 16:273–94.

Kurjack, Edward B.
1974 *Prehistoric Lowland Maya Community and Social Organization: A Case Study at Dzibilchaltun, Yucatan, Mexico.* Publication 38. Middle American Research Institute, Tulane University, New Orleans.

Linné, Sigvald
1934 *Archaeological Researches at Teotihuacan, Mexico.* Publication no. 1. Ethnographic Museum of Sweden, Stockholm.

López Vázquez, Miguel, and M. Yolanda Fernández Marquínez
1987 Excavaciones en el Grupo May. Estudio de la Arquitectura. In *Oxkintok 1*, edited by M. Rivera Dorado, pp. 31–43. Misión Arqueológica de España en México, Madrid.

Manzanilla, Linda
1993 Daily life in the Teotihuacan apartment compounds. In *Teotihuacan: Art from the City of the Gods*, edited by K. Berrin and E. Pasztory, pp. 91–99. Thames and Hudson, San Francisco.

Marcus, Joyce
2003 The Maya and Teotihuacan. In *The Maya and Teotihuacan: Reinterpreting Early Classic Interaction*, edited by G.E. Braswell, pp. 337–56. University of Texas Press, Austin.

Martin, Simon, and Nikolai Grube
2000   *Chronicle of the Maya Kings and Queens.* Thames and Hudson, London.

Millon, René (editor)
1973   *Urbanization at Teotihuacan, Mexico. Vol. 1. The Teotihuacan Map.* University of Texas Press, Austin.

Rattray, Evelyn C.
2001   *Teotihuacan: Ceramics, Chronology, and Cultural Trends.* INAH, Mexico City; University of Pittsburgh, Pittsburgh.

Reindel, Markus
1997   *Xkipché: Un Asentamiento Maya en el Norte de Yucatán, México.* Verlag Philipp von Zabern, Mainz am Rhein.

Rivera Dorado, Miguel, and Francisco Fernández Martín
1989   Excavaciones en el Satunsat. In *Oxkintok 2,* edited by M. Rivero Dorado, pp. 63–75. Misión Arqueológica de España en México, Madrid.

Rovner, Irwin, and Suzanne M. Lewenstein
1997   *Maya Stone Tools of Dzibilchaltun, Yucatan, and Becan and Chicanna, Campeche.* Publication 65. Middle American Research Institute, Tulane University, New Orleans.

Sabloff, Jeremy A., and Gair Tourtellot
1991   *The Ancient Maya City of Sayil: The Mapping of a Puuc Region Center.* Publication No. 60. Middle American Research Institute, Tulane University, New Orleans.

Sánchez Alaniz, José Ignacio, and Luis Alfonso González Miranda
1999   Entierros Infantiles en un Conjunto Habitacional Localizado al Sureste de la Ciudad de Teotihuacan. In *Prácticas Funerarias en la Ciudad de los Dioses: Los Enterramientos Humanos de la Antigua Teotihuacan,* edited by Linda Manzanilla and Carlos Serrano, pp. 399–414. UNAM, México, D.F.

Santley, Robert S.
1989   Obsidian working, long-distance exchange, and the Teotihuacan presence on the south Gulf Coast. In *Mesoamerica after the Decline of Teotihuacan A.D. 700–900,* edited by R.A. Diehl and J.C. Berlo, pp. 131–51. Dumbarton Oaks Research Library and Collection, Washington, D.C.

Santley, Robert, and Philip J. Arnold III
1996   Prehispanic settlement patterns in the Tuxtlas Mountains, southern Veracruz, Mexico. *Journal of Field Archaeology* 23:222–59.

Santley, Robert S., Philip J. Arnold III, and Christopher A. Pool
1989   Ceramic production systems at Matacapan, Veracruz, Mexico. *Journal of Field Archaeology* 13:155–75.

Santley, Robert S., Ponciano Ortiz C., Philip J. Arnold III, Michael P. Smyth et al.
1985   Final Field Report: The Matacapan Archaeological Project, 1984 Field Season. Submitted to the National Science Foundation and El Instituto Nacional de Antropología e Historia, México, D.F.

Santley, Robert S., Ponciano Ortiz C., and Christopher A. Pool
1987   Recent archaeological research at Matacapan, Veracruz: A summary of the results of the 1982 to 1986 field seasons. *Mexicon* 9:41–48.

Schele, Linda
1986   The Tlaloc Complex in the Classic Period: War and Interaction between the Lowland Maya and Teotihuacan. Paper presented at the Symposium on the New Dynamics, Kimbell Art Museum, Fort Worth.

Schele, Linda, and David Freidel
1990   *A Forest of Kings: The Untold Story of the Ancient Maya.* William Morrow, New York.

Schortman, Edward M.
1989   Interregional interaction in prehistory: The need for a new perspective. *American Antiquity* 54:52–65.

Serrano, Carlos, and Zaíd Lagunas
1975   Sistema de enterramiento y notas sobre el material osteológico de La Ventilla, Teotihuacan, México. *Anales del INAH* (1972–1973):105–44.

Shennan, Stephen
1989   Introduction: Archaeological approaches to cultural identity. In *Archaeological Approaches to Cultural Identity,* edited by S. Shennan, pp. 1–13. Unwin Hyman, London.

Sierra Sosa, Thelma N., and Ángel Martínez Lizarraga
2001   Los Entierros de Xcambó y sus Implicaciones Sociales. *I'INAJ Semilla de Maíz* 12:6–12.

Siverts, H.
1969   Ethnic stability and boundary dynamics in southern Mexico. In *Ethnic Groups and Boundaries: The Social Organization of Culture Difference,* edited by F. Barth, pp. 101–16. Little, Brown and Company, Boston.

Smyth, Michael P.
1998   Before the florescence: Chronological reconstructions at Chac II, Yucatan, Mexico. *Ancient Mesoamerica* 9:137–50.
1999   *A New Study of the Gruta de Chac, Yucatan, Mexico.* Foundation for the Advancement of Mesoamerican Studies, Inc., Crystal River, Florida.
2006   Architecture, caching, and foreign contacts at Chac (II), Yucatan, Mexico. *Latin American Antiquity* 17:123–49.
2008   Beyond economic imperialism: The Teotihuacan factor in northern Yucatan. *Journal of Anthropology Research* 64:395–409.

Smyth, Michael P., and Christopher D. Dore
1992   Large site archaeological methods at Sayil, Yucatán, México: Investigating community organization at a prehispanic Maya center. *Latin American Antiquity* 3:3–21.
1994   Maya urbanism at Sayil, Yucatán. *National Geographic Research and Exploration* 10:38–55.

Smyth, Michael P., Christopher D. Dore, and Nicholas P. Dunning
1995   Interpreting prehistoric settlement patterns: Lessons from the Maya center of Sayil, Yucatán. *Journal of Field Archaeology* 22(3):321–47.

Smyth, Michael P., José Ligorred P., David Ortegón Z., and Pat Farrell
1998   An Early Classic center in the Puuc region: New data from Chac II, Yucatan, Mexico. *Ancient Mesoamerica* 9:233–57.

Smyth, Michael P., and Daniel Rogart
2004   A Teotihuacan presence at Chac II, Yucatan, Mexico: Implications for early political economy of the Puuc region. *Ancient Mesoamerica* 15:17–47.

Smyth, Michael P., and T. Douglas Price
2006   Reporte del Análisis de los Restos Humanos por Análisis Isótopo de Estroncio, Recuperados como Parte de las Excavaciones en el Sitio de Chac II, Yucatán. Final Report to the Instituto Nacional de Antropología e Historia, México, D.F.

Spence, Michael W.
1992   Tlailotlacan, a Zapotec enclave in Teotihuacan. In *Art, Ideology, and the City of Teotihuacan*, edited by J.C. Berlo, pp. 59–88. Dumbarton Oaks, Washington, D.C.
1996   A comparative analysis of ethnic enclaves. In *Arqueología Mesoamericana: Homenaje a William T. Sanders*, Vol. I, edited by A.G. Mastache, J.R. Parsons, R.S. Santley, and M.C. Serra Puche, pp. 333–53. INAH, Mexico City.

Stone, Andrea
1989   Disconnection, foreign insignia, and political expansion: Teotihuacan and the warrior stelae of Piedras Negras. In *Mesoamerica after the Decline of Teotihuacan A.D. 700–900*, edited by R.A. Diehl and J.C. Berlo, pp. 153–72. Dumbarton Oaks Research Library and Collection, Washington, D.C.

Tiesler B., Vera
1999a   *Rasgos bioculturales entre los antiguos mayas: aspectos culturales y sociales*. Tesis de Doctorado en Antropología, UNAM, México, D.F.
1999b   Reporte del análisis de los restos humanos recuperados como parte de las excavaciones en el sitio de Chac, Yucatán: Temporada 1999. Submitted to INAH, México, D.F.
2000   Reporte del análisis de los restos humanos recuperados como parte de las excavaciones en el sitio de Chac, Yucatán: Temporada 2000. Submitted to INAH, México, D.F.
2001   Reporte del análisis de los restos humanos recuperados como parte de las excavaciones en el sitio de Chac, Yucatán: Temporada 2001. Submitted to INAH, México, D.F.

Tourtellot, Gair, and Jeremy A. Sabloff
1994   Community structure at Sayil: A case study of Puuc settlement. In *Hidden Among the Hills*, edited by H.J. Prem, pp. 71–90. Verlag von Flemming, Möckmühl.

Tourtellot, Gair, Jeremy A. Sabloff, and Michael P. Smyth
1990   Room counts and population estimation for Terminal Classic Sayil in the Puuc region, Yucatan, Mexico. In *Prehistoric Population History in the Maya Lowlands*, edited by T.P. Culbert and D.S. Rice, pp. 245–61. University of New Mexico Press, Albuquerque.

Tourtellot, Gair, Jeremy A. Sabloff, Patricia A. McAnany, Thomas W. Killion, Nicholas P. Dunning, Kelli Carmean, Rafael Cobos Palma, Christopher D. Dore, Bernd F. Fahmel Beyer, Sandra López Varela, C. Pérez Alvarez, and Susan J. Wurtzburg, with a contribution by Michael P. Smyth
1989   *Archaeological Investigations at Sayil, Yucatan, Mexico, Phase II: The 1987 Field Season*. Anthropological Papers. University of Pittsburgh, Pittsburgh.

Upham, Steadman
1990   *The Evolution of Political Systems: Socio-Politics in Small Scale Sedentary Societies*. Cambridge University Press, Cambridge.

Wiessner, Polly
1983   Style and social information in Kalahari San projectile points. *American Antiquity* 48:253–76.

Willey, Gordon R., and Demitri B. Shimkin
1973   The Maya collapse: A summary view. In *The Classic Maya Collapse*, edited by T. Patrick Culbert, pp. 457–501. University of New Mexico Press, Albuquerque.

Varela, Carmen T.
1998   *El Clásico Medio en el Noroccidente de Yucatán. La Fase Oxkintok Regional en Oxkintok (Yucatán) como paradigma*. BAR International Series, vol. 739. British Archaeological Reports, Oxford.

Varela, Carmen T., and Geoffrey E. Braswell
2003   Teotihuacan and Oxkintok: New perspectives from Yucatán. In *The Maya and Teotihuacan: Reinterpreting Early Classic Interaction*, edited by G.E. Braswell, pp. 249–71. University of Texas Press, Austin.

PART II
ANDEAN EXAMPLES

Introduction to Andean Examples

Claude Chapdelaine

The emergence of states in South America is a complex issue, since with the absence of writing, the domestic economy of Andean capitals must be reconstructed with archaeological data alone (Haas et al. 1987). The single exception is the recording device of the Inka (the *khipu*), with a few examples known from the earlier Wari period. One could argue that the *khipu*, a notation system made of knotted strings, could have acted as more than an account of different administrative aspects of Inka economy, but its decoding is still incomplete (Urton 2003; Urton and Brezine 2005).

Ceremonial centers of great size and composed of monumental buildings are a very old phenomenon in coastal Peru. Caral is now considered the most important of these religious centers, going back to the third millennium before Christ (Shady 2006). This burst of complexity is not an isolated phenomenon and the tradition of building impressive monuments for the performance of religious activities continued in several Peruvian coastal valleys, in particular the Casma Valley (Pozorski and Pozorski 1992) where an important concentration of ceremonial sites has allowed archaeologists to document an uninterrupted occupation sequence culminating first with Chavín and later with Moche. We lack complete agreement that Moche was the first true state. It would have been an incipient state, still lacking characteristics of more advanced polities such as the Chimú on the coast or the Inka in the Andean highlands. Although the nature of Moche

sociopolitical organization is debated, its geographic division into a Northern and Southern Moche state is gaining more support as is the awareness that stylistic phase IV is restricted to the Southern Moche state. Its temporal span is AD 450 to 800. The domestic economy of its capital, Huacas of Moche, is presented in Chapter 9.

Contemporaneous with Moche on the south coast of Peru was Nasca, which has never been considered a state (Silverman and Proulx 2002; Silverman 1993); the same conclusion was reached for Recuay and Cajamarca, two cultures occupying the eastern fringe of the Moche realm in the highlands.

Two expansionist states—Tiwanaku and Wari (see Chapter 8 by John Janusek and Chapter 10 by William Isbell)—share similarities and differences in state organization, economy, urbanism, and expansion. However, both state capitals, Tiwanaku and Huari, could be studied at the level of domestic economy.

A comment should be made about Wari as a territorial predatory state; the capacity of this strong polity to expand along the Andean Mountains is attested by the construction of massive regional centers such as Pikillacta and presumably Viracochapampa, but we do not see any direct influence on the north coast of Peru. After much fieldwork on the Moche during the last two decades, the lack of archaeological evidence for a Wari conquest is obvious, and scholars should abandon the idea that they conquered the north coast of Peru. It is now more appropriate to discuss their influence, which seems to be indirect, on the transformation of the north coast polities into two distinct but nevertheless comparable political authorities, Chimú to the south and Sicán (formerly known as Lambayeque) to the north.

One other north coast polity that presents data on the domestic economy of state capitals is the late Moche state, ranging from AD 700 to 800, associated with stylistic phase V, and centered in the Lambayeque region at Pampa Grande (Shimada 1994). The site was excavated long ago and well reported in a detailed study by Izumi Shimada, allowing the interested reader to compare this site to the capital of the Southern Moche state, which is presented in this volume. Of interest here about Pampa Grande is the beginning of storage facilities on a larger scale than those known from earlier Moche sites (Shimada 1994; Anders 1981), and evidence of multiple ethnic groups including Moche and Gallinazo (Shimada and Maguiña 1994). Storage is considered a key element in identifying state organization in the Andean world and it was part of the domestic economy at the Moche capital of Pampa Grande. Evidence for the coexistence of Moche and Gallinazo populations at the same site is really thought-provoking, especially at a Moche V center, since most scholars within an evolutionary perspective had believed that the Moche civilization had totally replaced the Gallinazo culture in the first three centuries of the first millennium AD. Unpublished data from the Jequetepeque, Virú, and Santa Valleys give more credibility to this idea of a Gallinazo culture keeping its identity for several centuries, and living alongside the dominant Moche.

The Sicán state and its two successive capitals, Batán Grande (AD 900–1100) and Túcume (AD 1100–1350), could also have been considered in this book (Shimada 1995; Heyerdahl et al. 1995). They both succeed the Moche V capital of Pampa Grande located in the same region. Of the two successive Sicán capitals, Túcume presents a more centralized picture of power with more than twenty *huacas* or mud-brick platforms arranged around a sacred mountain, Cerro El Purgatorio (Heyerdahl et al. 1995).

Batán Grande, more extensive, and the seat of a powerful dynasty, had royal burial chambers built at a depth of 12 m beside the monumental Huaca Loro (Shimada 1995). Craft production was a major component of the state economy and Sicán metallurgists were numerous and well skilled; their works were exported well beyond the limits of this polity. It could thus be concluded that the Sicán capital's domestic economy was oriented toward a state political economy supported by massive production of gilded copper objects with distinctive attributes of Sicán cultural identity. The Sicán state was conquered by the Chimú around AD 1350 and Chan Chan, the capital of the Chimor Kingdom, became the new home of many Sicán metallurgists. This integration of Sicán specialists into the Chimú domestic economy was to be repeated by the Inka after the conquest of Chan Chan around AD 1470.

Before the advent of the Inka, the best archaeological information for studying political economy probably comes from Chan Chan, the capital of the Chimú (Moseley and Day 1982; Moseley and Cordy-Collins 1990). John Topic has published several key articles on Chan Chan (Topic 2003, 1990), and the purpose of

his chapter in this volume (see Chapter 11) is to evaluate whether or not the domestic economy can be fully distinguished from the state political economy. Topic argues that the late Chimú kingdom developed into a true bureaucracy without any apparent record keeping. This position is based on the standardization of U-shaped structures associated with storage areas within palaces or *ciudadelas* and on evidence that craft production became more important than agricultural production during the late period. Topic is thus willing to link the storage capacity of luxury goods to an emergent bureaucracy developed from stewardship. Thus, storage space differentiates Chan Chan from Wari and Tiwanaku, which are less bureaucratic states given their lack (or scarcity) of storage units. Topic believes that the growing importance of Chan Chan as the center of an empire allowed craft production to become the driving force with a large number of craftsmen working in the barrios located near palaces and elite residences. He also develops the idea that the establishment of large communities of artisans within Chan Chan, defined as a variant of the Inka's *yanakuna*, was a Late Chimú innovation and a significant component of the political economy of the state.

The work of Janusek on Tiwanaku presents a new vision of this capital, with detailed insights on several aspects of the internal organization of the site, its functions, hierarchy, and activities, and his models provide new and provocative perspectives. Several stimulating comparisons could be made to help us understand other cases such as the Southern Moche or the Chimú.

Tiwanaku, at the beginning of the 1980s, was still considered an unpopulated ceremonial center, but now we believe it was a vibrant city with a population of 10,000 to 30,000. This is quite a change, brought about by long-term archaeological fieldwork. At the compound level in the inner city with distinct quarters, it is unfortunate that not a single compound has been excavated completely. No compound's shape and size are known with certainty. This will be a major achievement for the future, but the question will still be the following: is this compound unique or is it the standard type reproduced with minor changes throughout most of the planned city of Tiwanaku? Is it premature to consider the compound the salient unit of spatial segregation and social differentiation at Tiwanaku (as proposed by Janusek)? Although the residential and domestic spaces are more extensive and more fully investigated by new projects, their organization near the inner core resembles several domestic households that abut the walls of the *ciudadelas* in Chan Chan. The possibility that domestic architecture could be found within a Tiwanaku compound would also enable us to assess its resemblance to Wari urban patterns.

The presence of high-status residential areas near the impressive monuments of Tiwanaku was expected, and similar evidence, as well as evidence of specialized craft production, exists elsewhere in the Andes. A striking characteristic of Tiwanaku as an organic, dynamic web of social constituents is the integration of different ethnic groups into a Tiwanaku melting pot, as evidenced by the mix of traditions. The interesting part of the proposed scenario is that distinctive behavior seems to have encouraged each group to maintain the traditions of their place of origin. Compared to the Moche case presented in this volume, Tiwanaku's pattern of assimilation is different; although it might be classified as partial or incomplete, it is preferable to say the integration was less coercive and more flexible. All the residents of Tiwanaku had access to state symbols and products but at the same time were allowed to keep some elements of their original identity. From that perspective, Tiwanaku may have used religion to integrate these new members, while the Moche evidently used political and centralizing strategies, if we accept that they had to integrate new foreign members in their capital. Tiwanaku was definitely more ethnically diverse than Moche. At both sites, the habit of burying some of the deceased under living floors is shared by city dwellers, and at least two funerary chambers built above the plastered floor, visible to the living, were encountered in the urban sector of Huacas of Moche and behind the monumental Huaca de la Luna (Chapdelaine et al. 1998).

Another difference between Tiwanaku and the Moche capital is the scarcity of workshops near the monumental core at Tiwanaku, which would be consistent with the more religious functions of that site. The primacy of religious functions is supported by the extensive distribution of middens and ash pits reminiscent of feasts (which means that the capital had obtained, on a large scale, products such as maize to be consumed in these rituals). The absence of clear storage structures could mean that the state was not accumulating surpluses but was a major center for redistributing excess goods.

Tiwanaku can still be viewed as a state (even without large storage rooms) and in most ways comparable to Moche. At Tiwanaku, new data presented by Janusek confirm that feasting was carried out everywhere at this large urban center. This behavior could be considered evidence for a decentralized political economy, similar to the idea I presented—that is, the Moche leaders of the central urban zone were able to accumulate wealth within their own residential compounds, thereby preventing the Moche state from building storage units.

Janusek proposes two views of Tiwanaku: first, a densely populated center of a state power with a cosmopolitan flavor; and second, a center of social and ritual convergence or more simply, a major ceremonial center. After reviewing ethnographic data and regional settlement data, he concluded that Tiwanaku was both, with a distinct dual character: a "ceremonial city." Of some relevance, he argues that local resident groups played a key, but not exclusive, role in Tiwanaku's political economy. As an incentive for making broad comparisons about the domestic sphere of pristine states, Janusek concludes that "Tiwanaku demonstrates that ceremonial centers and populated urban centers are not mutually exclusive phenomena."

The Huari capital is huge and because of its size, its nature is not as well understood as other state capitals. William Isbell (Chapter 10) offers a retrospective view on the evolution of urbanism at Huari. Storage is not addressed. However, compelling evidence is given for considering selected compounds as palaces. Isbell uses the concept of "great houses" to stress the urban aspect of the orthogonal cellular compound and its socio-ritual integrated nature. The vision of Huari has become more religious, with numerous cemeteries and monumental funerary chambers made of cut stones, distinctive D-shaped structures with niches and offerings, and galleries with niches in restricted areas associated with feasting. Drinking corn beer (or *chicha*) from large decorated jars is an important ritual activity carried out in various sectors of the capital. The ethnic diversity has not been studied at the state capital but it is obvious that the ruling elite had to cope with numerous conquered groups in the Cusco region and the northern Andes (the latter area was where Recuay and Cajamarca cultures flourished before Wari intrusion). The impact of conquered lands on the evolution of Huari is not clear. The Ayacucho Basin was densely occupied by numerous Wari settlements and this population pressure may have been a strong factor in pushing Wari lords to wage war in many directions. The impact of this political change, from a state to an empire, should be analyzed at Huari to complement the wealth of data coming from Wari's provinces (McEwan 2005).

From a general perspective, but related to political economy, storage was a key argument in identifying the Wari state. The Huari site's orthogonal cellular compounds are identified as residences and some areas could have been used for storage. Where are the storage buildings managed by state officials? The construction of storage structures controlled by the state, if absent from the capital, are still being identified in provincial Wari centers. Unless formal storage buildings are identified within the limits of the capital of Huari, it may be the case that the leaders of elite residences were able to accumulate wealth within their compounds, which would be similar to the Moche case (see Chapter 9 by Chapdelaine).

Hierarchy is evident at Huari, based on data presented by Isbell, but craft production and specialization at Huari are assumed but not documented. Consumption was tremendous at Huari based on middens, and it is not impossible that most workshops providing goods to the urban dwellers were located on the periphery of the city.

It is unusual to end with the Inka, especially since "upstreaming" and ethnohistoric analogy are the most popular techniques for studying the history of an area. For once, the Inka are last in a volume, but they remain the basis for most analogies that can be made to understand the nature of prehispanic Andean groups. This last paper by Alan Covey (Chapter 12) on Cusco tackles major issues related to state domestic economy.

The basis of any reconstruction of Cusco is still being carried out with ethnohistorical accounts. Archaeology, however, promises to shed more light on specific areas of Greater Cusco that are described by Covey as consisting of three distinct sectors: (1) an urban core organized on the basis of moiety divisions of the royal Inka lineages and certain affiliated descent groups, (2) an area of suburban neighborhoods and satellite communities occupied by Inka and non-Inka populations, and (3) a region of rural farming settlements and elite estates surrounding the city itself. One question that could become a key issue related to Cusco's political economy is the location of specialized workshops. As pointed out by Covey: ". . . the Inka state seems to have focused high status craft production in Cusco itself," most probably for metalsmiths, but "at present, we cannot be certain whether craft producers lived in distinct neighborhoods and maintained workshops there, or whether they labored for the Inka elite in palace workshops designated for the purpose."

The development of Greater Cusco is reminiscent of Chan Chan with one exception: the craftsmen at Cusco may have worked outside the Inner City while they were horizontally integrated in workshops near palaces at Chan Chan. In both cities, craft production was at the center of the economy, fueled by the state and serving political purposes within the capital limits and also at regional centers of the more distant provinces.

The combination of Cusco being at the center of an empire and its rapid urban evolution as the most complex center of ambitious emperors is definitely the culmination of the embedded nature of Cusco's domestic economy into this unique imperial political economy. This vision or perspective, although based on ethnohistorical data with little archaeological verification, is the measure to which we can compare other Andean states' political economies.

Two key elements of Inka strategies were population resettlements, including specialists and diverse ethnic groups, and storage controlled with efficiency by state officials.

The domestic economy of Cusco is totally embedded in the state political economy, allowing the concentration of enormous amounts of material that will be transformed within Greater Cusco into wealth goods to promote the state in its four quarters. The Inka state was capable of coping with the growing demand of its millions of inhabitants. Centralization in the Greater Cusco was achieved prior to Spanish arrival and the question still left unanswered is the nature of the distribution system. There is no description in the early accounts of formal markets resembling those in Mesoamerica. The question has been posed often and no answer is available. The "markets" in Inka political economy are still well hidden. The distribution system for Cusco domestic economy may have followed at different scales the division of Greater Cusco into three distinct sectors. It was a patterned system of distribution involving the elite and segmented populations. The scale of exchange was probably smaller, less visible, with no currency, with trade and barter carried out at the village level and within different sectors of Greater Cusco through feasts and redistribution directly at or near state storage buildings. This lack of formal markets will remain a salient difference between the Mesoamerican cases and the Andean cases.

Cusco, viewed as the nexus of an empire on the move, expanding and consolidating its political and military position, was certainly as complex as any empire's capital, including Rome (MacCormack 2001) and, more appropriately, the Aztec capital of Tenochtitlan. Tradition was short, less than a century of imperial experience, but the power of the Inkas will continue to amaze us, and nobody can imagine in what direction their empire would have evolved if not for their rapid conquest by the Spaniards in the early sixteenth century.

References

Anders, Martha
1981   Investigation of state storage facilities in Pampa Grande, Peru. *Journal of Field Archaeology* 8:391–404.

Chapdelaine, Claude, María Isabel Paredes, Florencia Bracamonte, and Victor Pimentel
1998   Un tipo particular de entierro en la zona urbana del sitio Moche, costa norte del Perú. *Bulletin de l'Institut Français d'Études Andines* 27(2):241–64. Lima.

Haas, Jonathan S., Shelia Pozorski, and Thomas Pozorski (editors)
1987   *The Origins and Development of the Andean State*. Cambridge University Press, Cambridge.

Heyerdahl, Thor, Daniel Sandweiss, and Alfredo Narváez
1995   *The Pyramids of Túcume: The Quest for Peru's Forgotten City*. Thames & Hudson, London.

MacCormack, Sabine
2001   Cuzco, another Rome? In *Empires: Perspectives from Archaeology and History*, edited by Susan E. Alcock et al., pp. 419–35. Cambridge University Press, Cambridge.

McEwan, Gordon
2005   *Pikillacta: The Wari Empire in Cuzco*. University of Iowa Press, Iowa City.

Moseley, Michael E., and Kent Day (editors)
1982   *Chan Chan: Andean Desert City*. University of New Mexico Press, Albuquerque.

Moseley, Michael E., and Alana Cordy-Collins (editors)
1990   *The Northern Dynasties: Kingship and Statecraft in Chimor*. Dumbarton Oaks, Washington, D.C.

Pozorski, Shelia, and Thomas Pozorski
1992   Early civilization in the Casma Valley, Peru. *Antiquity* 66:845–70.

Shady Solís, Ruth
2006   America's first city? The case of Late Archaic Caral. In *Andean Archaeology III*, edited by William Isbell and Helaine Silverman, pp. 28–66. Springer, New York.

Shimada, Izumi
1994   *Pampa Grande and the Mochica Culture*. University of Texas Press, Austin.
1995   *Cultura Sicán*. Fundación del Banco Continental, Lima.

Shimada, Izumi, and Adriana Maguiña
1994   Nueva visión sobre la cultura Gallinazo y su relación con la cultura Moche. In *Moche: Propuestas y Perspectivas*, edited by S. Uceda and E. Mujica, pp. 31–58. Actas del Primer Coloquio sobre la Cultura Moche. Travaux de l'Institut Français d'Études Andines 79, Lima.

Silverman, Helaine
1993   *Cahuachi and the Ancient Nazca World*. University of Iowa Press, Iowa City.

Silverman, Helaine, and Donald Proulx
2002 *The Nasca.* Blackwell, Oxford, England.

Topic, John
1990 Craft production in the Kingdom of Chimor. In *The Northern Dynasties: Kingship and Statecraft in Chimor*, edited by Michael E. Moseley and Alana Cordy-Collins, pp. 145–76. Dumbarton Oaks, Washington, D.C.
2003 From stewards to bureaucrats: Architecture and information flow at Chan Chan, Peru. *Latin American Antiquity* 14(3):243–74.

Urton, Gary
2003 *Signs of the Inka Khipu.* University of Texas Press, Austin.

Urton, Gary, and Carrie J. Brezine
2005 Khipu accounting in ancient Peru. *Science* 309:1065–67.

8

Residence and Ritual in Tiwanaku

Hierarchy, Specialization, Ethnicity, and Ceremony

John W. Janusek

Introduction

This comparative volume provides a unique opportunity to investigate a specific category of urbanism. In current parlance, the term "capital" denotes an official seat of government, and in popular usage refers to the political center of a nation state. Applying the term to preindustrial states may be problematic, both because most were decidedly unlike contemporary nations and because using the term may inadvertently transfer the presumed structural and ideological homogeneity of modern nations to a whole range of variable spatial and sociopolitical phenomena. Throughout the past, specific cultural, geographical, and historical contexts gave rise to extraordinarily different expressions of urbanism. Nevertheless, by employing the term critically, and taking into account this situational variability, comparing past state centers from a global perspective yields fascinating insights into the origins and organization of early complex societies.

Consensus holds that most preindustrial states had urban centers that we can call "capitals." Ostensibly, these centers served several roles: they were symbolic centers, they provided residence for leaders and many elites, and they served as central places for an encompassing community's political, economic, and religious activity. For many archaeologists, each was a central place within a state's overarching political economy. Further, state capitals are thought to have included social groups that differed in status, occupation, and political-economic role. More recently, archaeologists have begun to study other domains of social difference (such as kinship, ethnicity, and gender) in past central cities.

In this chapter, I address these issues for the urban center of Tiwanaku, situated in the South American Andean highlands. I seek to:

(1) Investigate the social role and presence of local groups (such as households, compounds, and neighborhoods) in the urban landscape. Was Tiwanaku a densely populated city, and were resident households or other groups the foundation of Tiwanaku urbanism and political economy?

(2) Address the expression of social differentiation by focusing on status, specialization, group identity (and as a subcategory, ethnicity), and their combined roles in Tiwanaku urbanism and political economy. Was Tiwanaku socially diverse? How did social status, specialization, and other domains of social identity interrelate, and how did they play into Tiwanaku's emergent political economy?

(3) Address the idea that Tiwanaku principally served political administration and economic interaction. To be sure, many archaeologists have considered Tiwanaku a ceremonial center. What was this "state capital" after all: city or ritual center? What roles did households and other groups play in the city's landscape, its political economy, and its ritual cycles?

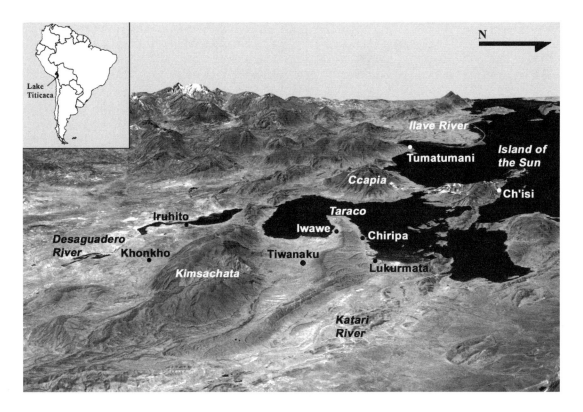

Figure 8.1. View of the southern Lake Titicaca Basin showing the location of Tiwanaku.

I argue here that Tiwanaku shared some characteristics with other past capitals, yet in many respects it was unique. I address the ways in which Tiwanaku urbanism both resonates and contrasts with conventional models of past state capitals. Tiwanaku was a political center and economic hub. It was also densely populated and was comprised of households and bounded compounds differentiated in status, specialization, and other domains of identity. Local social affiliations and even ethnic-like differences were fundamental elements of Tiwanaku urban culture.

Yet the Tiwanaku urban landscape was highly variable in social composition, urban role, and spatial organization. In contrast to Chapdelaine's findings at the Moche capital on the coast of Peru (see Chapter 9), Tiwanaku continues to surprise in regard to its social and spatial diversity. This makes sense when, by examining other persistent expressions of Tiwanaku urbanism, one comes to terms with Tiwanaku's ceremonial foundations (Janusek 2006, 2008). Rites of consumption and other ritual events historically gave rise to Tiwanaku, and they formed the critical contexts in which Tiwanaku became temporarily "hyper-urban" as a momentary, concrete place to anchor its far-reaching sociopolitical, economic, and religious community. Much of Tiwanaku's social diversity, and its inhabitants' relations with nearby settlements and distant societies, revolved around recurring feasts and rituals. These provided key contexts for political events, economic

interactions, and community formation. Tiwanaku offers a unique take on our understanding of past state centers.

Ceremonial Center, Autocratic City, or Other?

Located in the southern Lake Titicaca basin of contemporary Bolivia (Fig. 8.1), Tiwanaku was the center of a regionally influential and long-lived cultural and political phenomenon between AD 500 and 1000, roughly corresponding with the Andean Middle Horizon (Janusek 2008; Kolata 1993; Ponce 1981). It was located in the Andean high plateau, situated at approximately 3,800 m above sea level. This region presented certain challenges (but also opportunities) for urbanism, including restricted agropastoral productive potential. In addition, in the highland Andes, the periodic markets so common in other world regions were virtually absent (Murra 1972; Stanish 1992). Tiwanaku urbanism and cultural-political expansion after AD 500 followed a distinctive history grounded in unique environmental and socioeconomic conditions.

Archaeologists differ regarding the character of Tiwanaku's residential populations, as they do for many past capitals. A long-standing idea is that Tiwanaku was an unpopulated ceremonial center (Bennett 1934; Lumbreras 1974; Schaedel 1988). Struck by what he considered Tiwanaku's harsh environment and by an apparent absence of visible habitations, the nineteenth-century American explorer Ephraim Squier (1878:300) concluded that Tiwanaku must "have been a sacred spot or shrine, the position of which was determined by accident, an augury, or a dream." Early excavations at the site ostensibly confirmed this view. On separate occasions in the 1930s, Wendell Bennett and Stig Rydén excavated isolated units at Tiwanaku in part to locate these "invisible" habitations. Bennett was struck to find that, among isolated features and a couple of possible foundations, Tiwanaku cultural strata comprised enormous quantities of refuse and superimposed layers of midden. Having analyzed excavated pottery fragments, Rydén (1947) suggested that these middens were the product of recurring "ritual meals" at the site. Bennett (1934:480) arrived at the influential conclusion that Tiwanaku was a "vacant ceremonial center" composed of an "aggregation of temples."

Just as enduring has been the idea that Tiwanaku was an economically vibrant and densely inhabited settlement, and for some a pristine urban center—though until the 1980s, such a position arose largely bereft of direct evidence for Tiwanaku domestic life. An important realization was that Tiwanaku dwellings had likely consisted largely of adobe, an impermanent material that had long since eroded onto, and indeed had formed, the landscape surrounding the more prominent stone temples, portals, and monoliths. Reconnaissance around Tiwanaku's monuments revealed extensive distributions of artifacts and low mounded areas covering an area of 2.4 to 4.4 km^2 (Parsons 1968; Ponce 1991). The Bolivian archaeologist Carlos Ponce Sanginés considered Tiwanaku a densely populated urban center inhabited by elites, commoners, traders, and craft specialists. Yet state-run archaeology projects focused exclusively on excavating and reconstructing Tiwanaku's impressive monuments, leaving the extent, organization, and character of its residential sectors mere speculation. In a book summarizing Andean culture history, Edward Lanning (1967:116) cogently noted that Tiwanaku's "fame as a ceremonial center is probably due to the fact that all of the excavations . . . have been conducted in the nucleus of the city."

It was in the late 1980s, as part of the research program of the Proyecto Wila Jawira, that residential sectors became a primary focus of archaeological investigation at Tiwanaku. From 1988 to 1994, archaeologists excavated twelve areas of the site: four with visible monumental features or structures (Akapana, Putuni, Chunchukala, and Mollo Kontu Mound), and eight that yielded strong evidence for residential occupation (Fig. 8.2). Kolata's (1993, 2003) synthesis of some of this work offers a very distinctive portrait of Tiwanaku urbanism and residential life. He interprets Tiwanaku as an "intensely hierarchical" center of elite power and authority in which residence followed a spatially concentric gradient of social status that descended with distance from its primary monumental temples. He argues that a massive water-filled channel, or "moat," formed a symbolic boundary dividing elites (who symbolically linked themselves to those temples) from commoners residing in the urban periphery. Despite this profound urban social hierarchy, Kolata

(1993:173–74) argues that Tiwanaku was an elite-created, highly ordered "autocratic city" that "boasted little in the way of pluralism and heterogeneity."

The twentieth century has thus witnessed, along with increasing knowledge about Tiwanaku and its residential areas, a broad interpretive shift from Tiwanaku as a ceremonial center of a religious or theocratic phenomenon to Tiwanaku as the densely populated urban center of an archaic state. The presence of residential contexts at Tiwanaku raises many questions that I address below: How was residential life organized in Tiwanaku, spatially and socially? What social practices, whether marking status, specialization, or social identity, differentiated Tiwanaku residential populations? What social characteristics and practices linked these populations to one another, whether as broader neighborhoods or as a pan-urban "Tiwanaku" community? Finally, what drew people to Tiwanaku, and was it primarily a ceremonial center, a hierarchical and autocratic city, or something else?

The following section addresses the spatial organization of residential contexts in Tiwanaku, moving in scale from the household to the city. It draws on comparative household research at Tiwanaku, focusing on my research in residential areas east of the monumental core. It emphasizes the early phase of Tiwanaku state development and urbanism, a period termed Tiwanaku IV.

Residential Life in Tiwanaku

Tiwanaku has endured a long and dynamic history. Sectors of it were occupied as early as the Early-Middle Formative period (1500–100 BC), though these occupations have not been thoroughly investigated (Janusek 2004:100). Tiwanaku emerged as a major regional center during the subsequent Late Formative period (100 BC–AD 500), when the first known monumental buildings were constructed. The early center was bounded by a water-filled channel or "moat" (Kolata 1993; Posnansky 1945). Tiwanaku expanded precipitously in Tiwanaku IV (AD 500–800), when old monuments were embellished, new monuments were built, and areas far from these complexes were reclaimed for urban expansion. Tiwanaku V (AD 800–1100) witnessed Tiwanaku's political apogee and greatest residential density (Janusek 2004). The moat no longer bounded the early center, but marked a significant social and spatial boundary therein.

In proposing to do household archaeology at Tiwanaku, my primary objective was to define the spatial and material parameters of the household unit. I defined this as a minimal co-residential social group with corporate functions (Janusek 2003:268). Isolating this aspect of Tiwanaku domestic life was partially successful. Of all excavations conducted to date in Tiwanaku IV contexts, those in three areas of the site exposed structures that are clearly dwellings: that is, structures containing primary residues of the domestic activities of a household, such as sleeping, preparing and consuming food, raising children, and other daily and periodic tasks (Fig. 8.3).

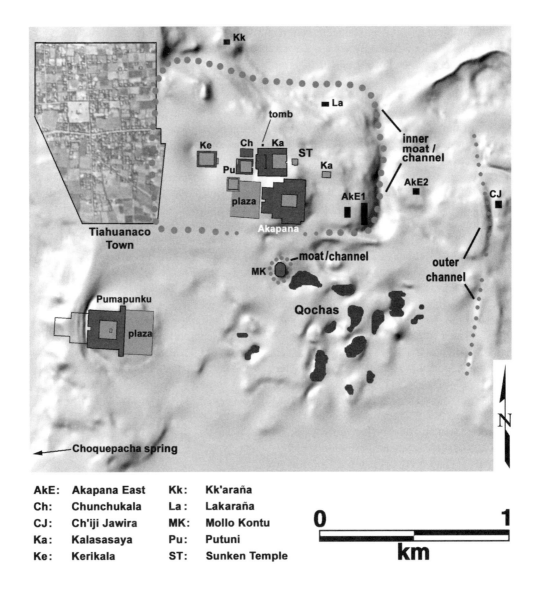

Figure 8.2. Map of Tiwanaku showing the location of sectors excavated by members of Proyecto Wila Jawira.

The two structures that most clearly represented dwellings were located in Akapana East 1M, near the east edge of the site core (that is, the west edge of the moat) (Janusek 2003, 2004:136–43). They abutted the west edge of the same compound wall. These were relatively small structures (about 5.5 by 2.5 m), each with a small kitchen containing one or more hearths and an adjacent sleeping chamber, and each associated with an outdoor patio, refuse middens, and domestic features. For lack of extensive excavations in the area, the overall spatial and social compositions of the compound are unclear. Artifacts from these contexts represented activities ranging from the acquisition, storage, and preparation of food, to the expedient production of bone and lithic tools, to domestic rituals. A single dwelling was located in Lakaraña, on the northeast edge of the site core (Escalante 1997:255–87, 2003), and another was in Akapana East

2, some 70 m east of the moat (Janusek 2003, 2004:140–43). Each of these was associated with hearths, patios, middens, storage bins, and artifacts representing a range of activities similar to those in Akapana East 1M. Further, each was located near compound wall foundations. To date, these structures and their associated areas are the clearest examples of the places where Tiwanaku households and their members lived and reproduced in Tiwanaku IV.

Evidence for dwellings is more equivocal in other areas of the site. In several areas, excavations revealed partial foundations that may or may not represent dwellings. Examples include rectilinear cobble and adobe foundations excavated in the sub-Putuni area west of the Kalasasaya (Couture and Sampeck 2003), Mollo Kontu South in the southern site periphery (Couture 2003), and Ch'iji Jawira at the east edge of the settlement (Fig. 8.4)

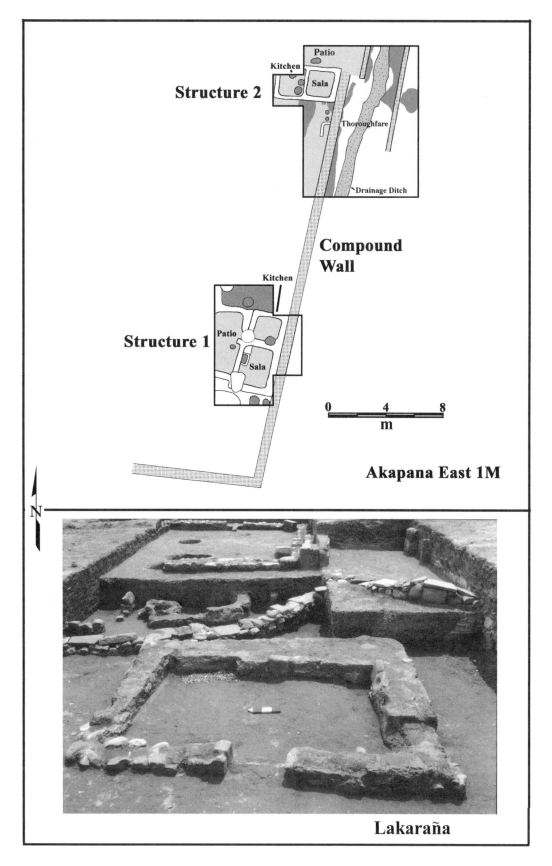

Figure 8.3. Map of dwellings and domestic areas in Akapana East and view of the Lakaraña sector of Tiwanaku.

Figure 8.4. Cobble and adobe structural foundations in Ch'iji Jawira, Tiwanaku (photo by Wolfgang Schüler).

(Rivera 2003). These structures are only partially known, due to a lack of more extensive excavation and to post-depositional destruction.

While none of these structures are unequivocal dwellings, each was associated with a range of features and artifacts comparable to those in Akapana East and Lakaraña. Further, each was located near a more substantial compound wall; in the case of Mollo Kontu South, the structure abutted it. Excavations in some areas of Tiwanaku revealed clusters of domestic features such as hearths, storage pits/bins, refuse pits, and deep wells with no apparent associated structures, as in Akapana East 1 (Janusek 2004:143–44), and in other areas, patios or ancillary spaces for outdoor activities, as in Lakaraña near the site's northern boundary. A conjunction of excavation strategy and prehispanic residential patterns leads me to characterize much of Tiwanaku's settlement space as residential, defined as the places where household members and others regularly conducted a broad range of domestic, specialized, and communal tasks, rather than domestic space in the strict sense of place where a particular household group dwelled and went about daily tasks.

Excavations commonly revealed foundations for walls that were more substantial (long and generally more than 80 cm

in width) than those of dwellings (less than 50 cm in width). These so-called compound walls were most frequently located in association with dwellings or other evidence for residential activity, and like all other structural foundations at the site, they uniformly followed an orientation slightly askew of (5–10 degrees east of) true north (Couture 2003; Janusek 2002, 2004). In the sub-Putuni, Akapana East 1 and 2, Mollo Kontu South, Lakaraña, and Ch'iji Jawira areas, compound walls enclosed one or more dwellings and their associated activity areas and middens. In Akapana East and Mollo Kontu South, these walls were directly associated with dwellings or other residential structures. This recurring pattern indicated that compounds were a (if not *the*) salient unit of spatial segregation and social differentiation at Tiwanaku, and that each enclosed the living and activity areas pertaining to several households and their affiliates.

Though it is likely that several compounds formed more encompassing neighborhoods or barrios in Tiwanaku, direct evidence for this idea hinges on future research. As I have suggested elsewhere, it is likely that extensive areas of the site that were ostensibly dedicated to broadly similar types of residential occupation and activities formed multi-compound neighborhoods in Tiwanaku (Janusek 2002, 2004). Such areas may include

Figure 8.5. Architectural complex on top of the Akapana, Tiwanaku, that was likely dedicated to residential activities of some of Tiwanaku's ritual specialists.

Akapana East and Ch'iji Jawira. Akapana East comprised several multi-dwelling compounds dedicated to domestic and most likely other activities on the near east side of the monumental core. Excavations in Akapana East revealed a street with an ad hoc drainage ditch running between, and spatially dividing, two of these compounds. Settled on a low knoll at the east edge of the settlement, Ch'iji Jawira was doubly separated from the rest of Tiwanaku by a water-filled channel and a compound wall. This was an extensive residential area in Tiwanaku that, as noted below, was dedicated at least in part to ceramic production.

The site of Tiwanaku covers an area of 4 to 6 km² in the Tiwanaku Valley (Kolata 1993; Lemuz 2005), yet the excavated residential areas discussed thus far form a relatively small percentage of the site's total spatial extent. Monumental temples and their associated plazas and courtyards cover at least another 1 km², focused around the two complexes of the Akapana-Kalasasaya and the Pumapunku. Much of the Mollo Kontu sector of the site was given over to artificial or modified *qochas*, prehispanic sunken basins that provided horticulture and herding in areas of high phreatic levels. Water channels such as the proposed moat crisscrossed other areas, and their edges may have served similar purposes. Other areas of the site, such as the area between Marca Pata and Ch'iji Jawira, revealed minimal evidence for human occupation. In short, Tiwanaku was not entirely dedicated to domestic life. It was diversified in role and significance.

Social Diversity in Tiwanaku: Hierarchy, Specialization, and Social Identity

Residential areas differed significantly in spatial organization, architectural construction, and artifactual representation, and excavations to date indicate that bounded compounds and possibly neighborhoods formed the most salient units of spatial and social differentiation. Material correlates for social differences among Tiwanaku's residential areas can be characterized as those distinguishing social status, those related to craft specialization, and those marking other aspects of group identity (Blom 2005; Janusek 2002, 2003, 2004; Janusek and Blom 2006; Kolata 1993; Rivera 2003). Material culture at Tiwanaku that marked these complementary and interwoven social differences are represented both in different types of materials and in stylistic or other differences in the same categories of materials.

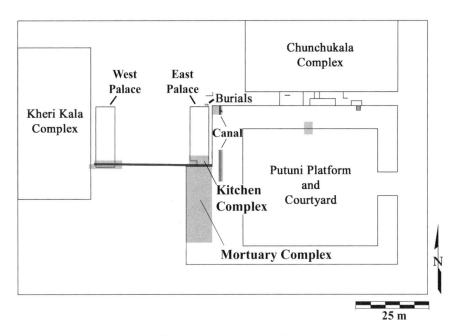

Figure 8.6. The Putuni Complex in Tiwanaku.

Hierarchy

Some Tiwanaku residents enjoyed high social status, and the spatial organization of status here formed a roughly concentric order. I define status with respect to the notion of distinction (Bourdieu 1993), which emphasizes the importance of social practices that are reproduced and evaluated in a social-spatial field (such as Tiwanaku) characterized by differential distributions of economic, social, and symbolic capital. Social distinction is most clearly manifested in structural complexes in and around the monumental core that, while they do not look like dwellings, formed architectural segments of larger residential spaces. The two excavated residential complexes associated with elite activity include one atop the Akapana and one on the west side of the Putuni. Both were likely constructed in Tiwanaku IV but were most intensively used and, in the case of Putuni, elaborated in Tiwanaku V.

The architectural complex atop the Akapana consisted of a series of connected rooms on ashlar foundations surrounding an extensive, stone-paved patio (Fig. 8.5) (Manzanilla 1992:54–70). Ceramic assemblages included significant frequencies of cooking and liquid fermentation/storage jars compared to other contexts of the Akapana (4–8% and 10–26%, respectively), indicating that food and beverage production were key activities here (Alconini 1995). A reasonable interpretation is that the complex housed or provided space for high-status ritual specialists (Kolata 1993:118; Manzanilla and Woodard 1990) and/or their associated attendants who prepared food and drink for the Akapana rituals they orchestrated.

The Putuni area also was a place for elite-focused activity. If material transformations in the early ninth century are an indica-

tion, the groups associated with this place emerged as a distinct social class in Tiwanaku V (Couture 2002; Janusek 2004). The Tiwanaku IV occupation was divided by a compound wall, north of which were multi-room structures surrounding a large, specialized kitchen dedicated to preparing food and drink. South of the wall was a mortuary cluster that contained fine sumptuary offerings, including elaborate vessels, rare minerals, bone beads, and precious metal adornments. Construction in the area during the ninth century—part of a broader event of urban renewal—buried these occupations under an entirely new architectural complex. The product was the extensive Putuni platform-and-courtyard complex and, associated with it on its northwest side, two large structures or "palaces" facing a stone-paved plaza (Fig. 8.6). The completely excavated east structure measured 22 by 6 m (132 m^2) and consisted of five rooms around a private patio, its walls plastered and painted in multiple colors (Couture 2002; Couture and Sampeck 2003; Kolata 1993:153–54). Floors yielded rare mineral objects and metal adornments. Both occupations were distinctive in that their structures incorporated well-wrought ashlar masonry and in that they enjoyed access to a monumental, subterranean stone-lined drainage network that effectively directed waste and runoff northward toward the Tiwanaku River.

High-status residential areas concentrated near the monumental complexes of Tiwanaku's settlement core. The material culture and characteristic practices marking distinction included locality in the center, architectural elaboration, use of elaborate ceramic wares and exotic bodily adornments, and access to effective sanitation (Couture 2002; Couture and Sampeck 2003). The moat appears to have played a significant and highly visible boundary in this regard. If it was built to demarcate the settle-

Figure 8.7. A "slumped" *tazón*, for consuming food and drink, crafted in the Ch'iji Jawira sector of Tiwanaku.

ment during the Late Formative, during the Tiwanaku period it came to distinguish the settlement core and its inhabitants from the growing urban periphery (Janusek 2004:157). This gradient, which centripetally focused social power and ideological legitimacy toward the center (though not exclusively), defined a differential distribution of social, economic, and symbolic capital in the emergent city. As noted below, the social hierarchy that crystallized at Tiwanaku was also linked to social and spatial aspects of ethnicity, specialization, and urban history.

Specialization

Some Tiwanaku residents performed specialized occupations. Archaeologists have encountered evidence for specialized production at several Tiwanaku settlements in the nearby region, including obsidian flake production at the site of Obsidiana in the lower Tiwanaku Valley (Albarracín-Jordan 1996). They have also documented residentially-based specialized production at major nearby centers, including the production of bone flutes at Lukurmata in the Katari Valley north of Tiwanaku (Janusek 1999, 2004) and of a plaster-like substance at Khonkho Wankane in the Upper Desaguadero basin to the south.

Excavations at Tiwanaku revealed one area dedicated to specialized craft production—the Ch'iji Jawira district at the east edge of Tiwanaku. The inhabitants of this district produced certain types of ceramic vessels: large jars for fermenting and storing alcoholic and perhaps other beverages, and a specific type of serving bowl, the flaring-sided *tazón* (Fig. 8.7) (Rivera 2003). Situated adjacent to a nearby stream that separated the area from Tiwanaku, and downwind of prevailing northwest winds, inhabit-

ants were ideally located to engage in such an industry. Firing practices in the area were expedient, and consisted of temporary large enclosures and small, semi-subterranean pit kilns. Excavations in associated contexts yielded by-products and implements of ceramic manufacture including misfired wasters, "slumped vessels," partially baked clay lumps and coils, plaster molds, burnishing tools, and ground pigments. Archaeobotanical analyses indicated that the plant fuels preferred in Andean communities today were far denser in Ch'iji Jawira than elsewhere in Tiwanaku (Wright et al. 2003). In Ch'iji Jawira, specialized production, which contributed to the overarching political economy, was conducted and managed as the socially and spatially embedded activity of a local social group at the far edge of the center.

The social organization of economic specialization appears to have been largely locally managed and situated. For example, based on regional-scale lithic analysis, Martin Giesso (2003) argues that only certain skilled households crafted projectile points to fulfill a labor tax, as a form of production "attached" to Tiwanaku elite management and desires. The lack of direct evidence for such production indicates that it occurred in discrete social contexts and places. Tiwanaku political economy was socially embedded and locally organized, whether it was or not largely guided by and geared toward its emergent elites (Janusek 1999). Regarding storage, the only complexes known from the Tiwanaku core were small and located in bounded compounds at Lukurmata and Tiwanaku (Escalante 1997, 2003; Janusek 2004). This pattern differs significantly from that of the Wari and later Inca states, in which storage complexes were strategically located outside local residential sectors and settlements (Levine 1985:145; McEwan 2005; Morris and Thompson 1985). If

Tiwanaku storage served urban and state interests in earmarking certain goods to state authorities for consumption and redistribution, they were community storage systems located within local bounded compounds and neighborhoods (see Smyth 1989).

Other manifestations of economic specialization are quite possibly invisible to us, at least for the moment. Some residential areas that yielded no clear evidence for craft production may have housed attendants in Tiwanaku's temples, officials in Tiwanaku's emergent political bureaucracy, or those practicing other careers that left little or no material trace. Though it is clear that not everyone in Tiwanaku enjoyed elite status, the data for specialized production leave it unclear whether all of those who resided in Tiwanaku were linked directly or indirectly to the elite groups who resided near its main temples. Nevertheless, data relating to complementary domains of social differentiation indicate that Tiwanaku was socially diverse.

Social Identity and Ethnicity

Marking status and doing specific things were practices that defined a group's identity in Tiwanaku, and bounded compounds and more encompassing neighborhoods were salient spatial and social contexts for their performance. Social identity can be defined as subjective affiliation with specific people, things, symbols, or practices. It is possible that extended households or craft production groups formed differentiated identities *within* encompassing compounds or neighborhoods. However, determining this will require the excavation of much or all of an entire compound, something that remains to be done.

What is clear at Tiwanaku, as in all societies, is that residential groups maintained multiple nested and overlapping identities, of which a position in Tiwanaku's emergent social hierarchy and a role in its political economy played but parts. Other palpable aspects of group identity at Tiwanaku were grounded in recurring local traditions and histories, place of residence in the urban landscape, daily and periodic interaction networks, and enduring ties to homelands and other areas beyond Tiwanaku. Some can be characterized as ethnicity, which I consider a specific manifestation of identity that is relatively broad in scope and most salient in an interregional interaction network or hierarchical political community (sensu Comaroff and Comaroff 1991).

Archaeological evidence for the expression of group identity in Tiwanaku residential sectors (aside from those manifested in local spatial arrangements, occupations, and status markers) was found in local stylistic assemblages, dietary habits, mortuary practices, and styles of body modification. Deborah Blom and I argue elsewhere that the archaeological detection of social identity requires an analysis conjoining multiple dimensions of cultural practice (Janusek and Blom 2006). Since these patterns have been discussed at length elsewhere (Blom 2005; Janusek 2002, 2003, 2004; Rivera 2003), I summarize them here.

First, the stylistic aspects of ceramic assemblages, including characteristics of technical production, vessel form, and iconographic depiction, differed significantly among many bounded residential sectors (Janusek 2002; Rivera 2003). Of significance, ceramic assemblages in Ch'iji Jawira, at the east edge of Tiwanaku, were most unusual. Among other things, the latter included high frequencies (about 18% of analyzed assemblages) of non-Tiwanaku and "hybrid" vessel sherds associated with the Cochabamba region of relatively warm valleys approximately 200 km east of Tiwanaku.

Second, Tiwanaku inhabitants maintained diverse diets. Melanie Wright and colleagues (2003) determined through archaeobotanical analysis that proportions of crop remains varied significantly among bounded residential sectors. High-altitude *Chenopodium* (quinoa) grains were most frequently represented and best distributed at Tiwanaku, followed by tubers and maize. In particular, the distribution of maize was anomalous. As a grain that grows well only in valley regions below the altiplano, maize was an exotic crop that we expected to find only in high-status residential areas such as Putuni. It was used in great quantities to produce fermented *chicha* beer for ritual events. Yet maize was most frequent in Akapana East 2 and best distributed in Ch'iji Jawira, which also yielded relatively high proportions of nonlocal wares from the valleys in which maize grows. Thus, identities that transcended social status in Tiwanaku's local universe fostered the acquisition of valued consumable goods in Tiwanaku. These identities may have thrived on recurring long-distance interactions conducted via llama caravans and enduring links to distant homelands.

It is significant that some deceased were buried under living spaces in Tiwanaku, and that not all were relegated to discrete cemeteries as in many societies, including modern Western nation states. Evidence for this was found in Akapana, Putuni, Akapana East, Ch'iji Jawira, and other Tiwanaku-affiliated sites (Couture and Sampeck 2003; Janusek 2004; Kolata 1993; Manzanilla 1992; Rivera 2003). This recurring mortuary pattern indicates that keeping certain deceased individuals close to home was an important element of life, identity, and local memory for at least some of Tiwanaku's residential groups. Human burial beneath or near inhabited dwellings was a practice that was vibrant during the pre-Tiwanaku Late Formative in the region, and most likely originated during the preceding Early-Middle Formative periods and perhaps sooner (Hastorf 2003). The desire to keep the corpses of the deceased and their mortuary contexts near living spaces indicates that memorialization and periodic commemoration of ancestors and deceased relatives were important to social groups in Tiwanaku. In Putuni and Akapana East 2, mortuary contexts were constructed so as to remain visible for the living. In Putuni, several consisted of above-ground niches surrounding its ceremonial courtyard, and in Akapana East 2, a sub-patio multiple burial was marked on the living surface by a stone (Couture 2002; Janusek 2004). These patterns suggest that local groups periodically remembered and bestowed offerings on deceased members, some of whom were likely considered progenitor ancestors. Mortuary patterns indicate that local social memory, however fabricated and enacted, was critical in fostering identity in Tiwanaku.

Body modification was a potent and highly personal way of marking identity in Tiwanaku society (Blom 2005; Blom et al. 1998; Janusek and Blom 2006). If woven clothing was the most potent manner of "wearing" social identity in Tiwanaku, its lack of preservation in the Andean highlands leaves us to consider other aspects of bodily adornment, of which cranial modification appears to have been most critical. Bioarchaeologists have identified three broad head shapes for Tiwanaku populations: modified "annular" skulls produced by turbanlike headbands, "tabular" skulls produced by wooden contraptions, and unmodified skulls (Fig. 8.8). Head-shape styles crosscut age, sex, and social status. All of these styles were common in Tiwanaku, in some cases within the same compound. Cranial modification appears to have expressed ethnicity. Humans with annular skulls were most frequently located at Tiwanaku-affiliated sites in the Katari Valley north of Tiwanaku and nearby regions, while humans with tabular skulls represented one hundred percent of human burials excavated in the Tiwanaku-affiliated cemeteries of Chen Chen in Moquegua, some 200 km to the west.

Deborah Blom and I (2006) hypothesize that Tiwanaku was a focal place of convergence for people of multiple bodily styles, as well as differing statuses, specializations, mortuary traditions, and social networks. These bodily forms indexed linkages to broader regional identities with discrete affiliations to nonlocal places and societies. The fact that people "wearing" all styles were buried in Tiwanaku, even within the same compound or neighborhood, indicates that people of diverse ethnicities lived and worked together (if in different capacities or statuses) and most likely intermarried.

The best local evidence for the expression of ethnicity in Tiwanaku comes from Ch'iji Jawira (Rivera 2003). Among its distinctive serving-ceremonial assemblages were high frequencies of so-called "Cochabamba Tiwanaku" wares associated with the Cochabamba Valley region some 200 km southwest. Also notable was the absence here of ceramic incense burners, ritual vessels ubiquitous in other Tiwanaku residential compounds. The area's peripheral location and specialized activities, in addition to such differences, may indicate that resident specialists maintained close affiliations elsewhere, and specially to the temperate Cochabamba region. Pending chemical analysis of human remains at Tiwanaku, it is hypothesized that inhabitants of Ch'iji Jawira, like those with shared styles of body modification in Tiwanaku, may have originally emigrated from Cochabamba or its environs (Janusek 2002, 2004:164). In that case, the roughly concentric gradient of urban space and status in Tiwanaku was simultaneously a gradient of cultural affiliation that separated relatively "pure" Tiwanaku groups (such as those in Akapana, Putuni, and Akapana East 1M) from groups in the settlement periphery, and outside the moat, with strong "foreign" ties. This same gradient also defined the history of the settlement by distinguishing the new neighborhoods of the periphery from the long-established compounds and monuments of the core, thereby focusing social legitimacy and power centripetally on the latter and defining an urban historical consciousness not unlike other past cities, such as Tenochtitlan and Rome.

Residence and Tiwanaku Urbanism: A Summary

A more or less conventional model of preindustrial urbanism arises out of a view that focuses on the material evidence for residential occupation and domestic life in Tiwanaku. Based on this evidence, we can clearly argue that Tiwanaku was not a "vacant" ceremonial center. We can argue that Tiwanaku was a densely populated urban center with a resident population on the order of perhaps 10,000 to 30,000 by AD 800 (considering its maximum extent in relation to non-residential areas and local residential cycles of abandonment and occupation). Comparative evidence indicates that differential status and access to valued goods and resources differentiated Tiwanaku residents, as Kolata hypothesized, and that status differentiation was configured along a spatial gradient centered on Tiwanaku's bounded monumental complexes and urban core. Yet Tiwanaku was socially heterogeneous in ways that transcend Kolata's patrimonial urban model, one that shuns vibrant local economies, ideologies, and identities from the center. Tiwanaku was not only densely occupied, but was far more plural than archaeologists had imagined. Its overall gridlike compound organization, social hierarchy, occupational differentiation, and incorporation of groups that forged local memories, customs, and far-ranging interaction networks are reminiscent of Mesoamerica's Teotihuacan, if on a much smaller scale.

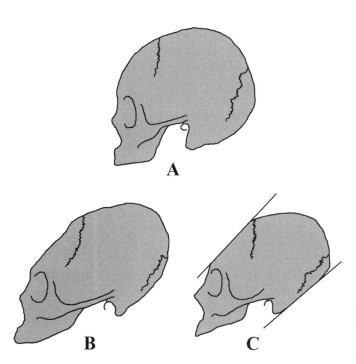

Figure 8.8. Common head-shape styles in Tiwanaku. *A*, unmodified; *B*, annular or elongated; *C*, front-occipital or flattened.

Like past residents of Teotihuacan, moreover, Tiwanaku residents unanimously employed Tiwanaku-style material culture in their daily practices. Differences among these groups were manifested in varieties of Tiwanaku practices, objects, and material and bodily styles. The shared material characteristics of these assemblages—in burial rites, drinking vessels, and ceramic iconography—manifested a common "Tiwanaku identity" that interwove with other, more localized domains of identity. Considering that "becoming" or "being" Tiwanaku was enacted in relation to the many societies and states that interacted in the Andes during the Middle Horizon, this domain of identification was also "ethnic" and to some extent consciously deployed (Janusek 2008). Thus, identifying with and living and working in Tiwanaku entailed active political, economic, and ritual roles. Furthermore, despite significant local heterogeneity, it is possible that most or all of those who resided in Tiwanaku performed some role related to elite or ritual concerns, whether as servants, bureaucrats, specialists, or ritual attendants.

Beyond Residential Life: Limits to the Conventional Urban Model

Despite solid evidence that Tiwanaku was an urban state capital, an emerging corpus of material evidence presents some limitations to the idea that Tiwanaku was like other preindustrial cities. Conjoined evidence points to the importance of religion and ritualism in Tiwanaku's emergence and political economy. They help explain the profound local influence and relatively geographically limited influence (unlike the Central Andean Wari and Inca states) of Tiwanaku cultural practices among its constituent communities (see Goldstein 2005; Janusek 2008; Schreiber 2001). In this section I discuss recent and well-published research that outlines a slightly different view of Tiwanaku urbanism.

Tiwanaku Ceremonialism

Ongoing research on the Late Formative foundations of Tiwanaku cultural development indicates that its center emerged amidst a regional peer-polity network of "multi-community polities" (Bandy 2001; Janusek 2004; Stanish 1999). While these polities remain to be precisely defined, it appears they were diverse in character, shifting in regional influence, and grounded in periodic communal rituals. Khonkho Wankane, a Late Formative (100 BC–AD 500) center 25 km directly south of Tiwanaku, is a key case in point. Ongoing excavations reveal a lightly occupied ceremonial center that was built in Late Formative 1, restructured in Late Formative 2, and decreased in size just before Tiwanaku's rise to prominence (Janusek 2006). With a small permanent occupation, Khonkho most likely became populous during periodic ritual events when people from far regions came to participate in ritual celebrations and construction activities. These were auspicious and socially dense moments when inclusive regional identities were breathed life, regional

power structures temporarily crystallized, and pan-community histories created, reproduced, and refabricated.

Ritual activity was pivotal at Tiwanaku in Late Formative and Tiwanaku periods. Tiwanaku's Late Formative components, if less intensively investigated, demonstrate a parallel trajectory of expansion, construction, and transformation. Early occupations centered on temple complexes for periodic ritual activities, including feasting, and monuments dedicated to the creation of Tiwanaku ritual persons (Couture 2002; Janusek 2006). Built complexes for local ritual activity, most likely tended by local residents, were located near the edges of settlement (Janusek 2004:110–12). Throughout the Middle Horizon, calendrical and other periodic rituals remained critical for Tiwanaku (Benítez 2009), and may have provided moments for the ongoing construction and maintenance of its monuments (Vranich 1999). Large courtyards occupy the Kalasasaya, Pumapunku, Putuni, and other monumental complexes; recent excavation has exposed massive plazas adjacent to Tiwanaku's two principal Middle Horizon temples: the Pumapunku and Akapana. These data point to the importance of periodic rituals and, increasingly through time, rituals of consumption as recurring events that shaped shifting sociopolitical dynamics in the south-central Andes. From its formative foundations forward, Tiwanaku was a profound religious-ritual phenomenon.

Non-Domestic Residences in Tiwanaku

Current research on Tiwanaku's residential components highlights the complexity of their patterns. Two ongoing projects at the site address the character of Tiwanaku residential occupations in the urban periphery. The Mollo Kontu project, directed by Nicole Couture and Deborah Blom, investigates residential organization in the southeast quadrant of the city, which harbored several interconnected *qochas* (Couture and Blom 2004). Excavations in Mollo Kontu South indicated that residential occupation organized into supra-household compounds characterized parts of this sector during the Middle Horizon. Nevertheless, recent investigation questions the ubiquity of this model. New excavations in Mollo Kontu Mound reveal very complex strata of lenses and midden, in some cases associated with human burials and other features. Project investigators have located no clear dwellings or other types of structures. Artifactual data point to the likelihood that the area was used from the Late Formative through the Tiwanaku periods, and the strata comprise long-term palimpsests of ephemeral or temporary occupation.

A second archaeological investigation is directed by Katherine Davis at the site of Muru Ut Pata on the northeast edge of Tiwanaku (Davis 2006). Davis set out to investigate domestic life in a local community at the edge of the Tiwanaku urban district. Supporting Bennett's and Rydén's findings, Davis found abundant evidence for refuse disposal in sheet middens and refuse/ash pits. Local activities included domestic, craft-related, and ritual practices. Further, her excavations yielded rectilinear structures similar to those found at Tiwanaku. Yet as she argues, it is not clear that these were residential dwellings. Nor is it clear that they were organized into a compound or bounded neighborhood group, as were other residential areas of the site. This evidence does not negate what we know about residential life in Tiwanaku, but like recent evidence from Mollo Kontu, it offers an important caveat regarding the ubiquitous applicability of the compound-based residential model across Tiwanaku.

Tiwanaku residential organization was complex, and the site was not simply a grid-organized urban center focused on a monumental core. As mentioned above, many structures at Tiwanaku cannot be securely categorized as dwellings. Furthermore, many structures, in particular those occupied late in the Middle Horizon, appear to have been temporarily or periodically occupied. A prime example was the Tiwanaku V occupation of Akapana East (Janusek 2003, 2004). In this area, compounds once dedicated to primary or secondary residential activity were entirely transformed in a major project of urban renewal. Renewal here produced relatively extensive open spaces associated with a variety of structures, few of which can be unequivocally considered dwellings. Several small rectangular structures encountered in Akapana East 1 revealed only the slightest of compacted surfaces and few of the domestic features associated with typical dwellings. I have argued that these structures were only periodically occupied or used in some manner for important ritual occasions. Drawing an analogy with similar contemporary structures in Bolivian towns, I argue that they served as storage (for costumes, jars of native *chicha* beer, and so on), as workspace (for example, to prepare feasts), or to house visitors during important Tiwanaku ritual events. The fact that most such structures were located in Tiwanaku V contexts postdating AD 800, in relation to an increasing frequency of liquid fermentation and serving wares (Janusek 2003; Mathews 2003), suggests that such structures were closely tied to the increasing importance of rituals of consumption in Tiwanaku.

Rydén Redux and the Ubiquitous Tiwanaku Ash Pit

If compound-bounded dwelling areas were not ubiquitous throughout Tiwanaku, the refuse middens and ash pits that Bennett and Rydén first noted are ubiquitous in the excavations that archaeologists have conducted at the site. As Tiwanaku transformed from AD 500 to 800 into an urban settlement, material refuse became an ever-present element of its expanding settlement landscape. It is not surprising that dealing with refuse became an increasingly important part of life as Tiwanaku changed from one among many ritual-political centers in a multi-community political field to the primary urban center in the south-central Andes. This pattern characterizes emergent urbanism worldwide; population nucleation and intensified production tend to produce great quantities of material "stuff" per hectare. Excavations that seek to investigate Tiwanaku household life—from Bennett and Rydén through Rivera and Janusek to Couture and Davis—inevitably yield far more than anything that can be construed as primary residential deposition, including extensive refuse lenses, sheet

middens, and "ash pits" (Couture and Blom 2004; Davis 2006; Janusek 2004; Rivera 2003). Combining the total "residential" area excavated to date at Tiwanaku, I estimate that approximately 40–50% consisted of secondary deposition.

So-called "ash pits" stand out in Tiwanaku (Fig. 8.9). Excavation at the site is inevitably hampered to some degree by encountering Tiwanaku refuse pits that had destroyed huge sections of prior occupations. They and abundant refuse deposits in general are rare in Late Formative contexts and are less common at other Tiwanaku sites. Ash pits were particularly common in Akapana East (including Akapana East 1M, 1, and 2), Kk'araña, Ch'iji Jawira, and Mollo Kontu. Many ash pits are amorphous, consisting of huge excavated depressions with abundant exhausted artifacts, broken or eroded adobe bricks, and camelid dung. I interpret these as borrow pits that yielded adobe construction material and then served as handy deposits for refuse. Other ash pits consisted of old subterranean wells, storage bins, and other pits that had been converted into ash pits upon their obsolescence. In all cases in which such features were recovered in Tiwanaku, they had been ultimately filled with ash and refuse: in wells, up to six meters deep.

The nature and quantity of refuse found in Tiwanaku sheet middens (common in Ch'iji Jawira) and ash pits are diagnostic of some of the activity that took place in its settlement peripheries. Pellets of camelid dung were frequent components of most secondary contexts. Camelid dung for centuries has been a critical source of fuel in this part of the Andes, and its high temperature combustion makes it ideal as much for domestic hearths as for ceramic and other material production (Winterhalder 1974). The ash itself tends to be colored a blue to green hue of gray. This color was uncommon in Late Formative contexts in the southern basin; at Khonkho, it was located only in one area of the site, an area that other material patterns suggest was for communal food and drink production for rituals of consumption in nearby temple complexes (Zovar, in press). Pending chemical analysis, I suggest that it derives from the high-temperature combustion of llama dung (also Katherine Davis, pers. comm., 2005). This parallels other evidence from Tiwanaku ash pits. They also yielded immense quantities of cooking, storage/fermentation, and serving-ceremonial ware sherds; splintered and butchered camelid, guinea pig, and bird bones; exhausted bone and stone implements; and preserved food remains (including maize kernels and cobs and quinoa seeds; Wright et al. 2003). Some contained "perfectly good" items, such as adobe bricks, reconstructable vessels, and cut stone blocks. Most such pits revealed less than four depositional strata, indicating that they were filled relatively quickly in a few dumping events. In a few pits, pieces of the same vessel were located in multiple strata.

The amount and variety of refuse located in Tiwanaku's sheet middens and ash pits were enormous. I believe they are the product, in part, of recurring feasts and other rituals that occurred at multiple social scales and in multiple spatial contexts at Tiwanaku. In relation to the relatively sparse density of primary dwelling areas in the settlement, it is clear that the refuse rep-

Figure 8.9. Examples of Tiwanaku "ash pits."

resents more than domestic garbage. It is difficult to prove this point definitively because many of these contexts are located in or near residential spaces, in some cases contemporaneous with primary residential occupations and in other cases preceding or postdating them. They are not limited to spatially segmented or artifactually differentiated feasting spaces or contexts; rather, they are everywhere. Evidence suggests that Tiwanaku middens and ash pits, which involved significant labor input, were the

product of periodic ritual events, including local residential and more inclusive center-wide feasts for which people of diverse compounds, neighborhoods, and perhaps Andean regions would have gathered. Thus, Rydén was precocious: "ritual meals" apparently were a central element of Tiwanaku culture from its Late Formative beginnings through its Middle Horizon hegemony. Further, they were not limited to monumental complexes. They were an important part of life across emergent centers.

Social and Ceremonial Convergence in Tiwanaku

The argument presented above casts Tiwanaku in two distinct but not mutually exclusive lights. For the moment, let us consider them models. In one model, Tiwanaku emerged as an urban center sometime after AD 500, and for five or six centuries remained a center of state power in the south-central Andes. Tiwanaku's constituent populations shared similar livelihoods, practices, values, and identities, but were differentiated in status, activities, local affiliations, and historical consciousness. A place in the hierarchy, a role in the economic system, and a place in Tiwanaku's diversified social/urban landscape formed overlapping domains of identity and activity in the broader political economy. Some social differences were likely ethnic. While Tiwanaku was densely populated, as Ponce and Kolata hypothesized, it was also diversified and cosmopolitan.

In the other model, Tiwanaku was a center of social and ritual convergence. In this view, Tiwanaku emerged as one of many ritual-political centers in the region, in which periodic ceremony and feasting became increasingly important, in part for building a broad Tiwanaku cultural identity over the generations of its hegemony. If Tiwanaku was not "vacant," it was a major ceremonial center. So what was it, populated city or ceremonial center?

Two discussions shed light on this question and the nature of Tiwanaku: one outlines the more recent patterns of settlement nucleation in the region, and the other outlines the regional settlement around Tiwanaku during the Middle Horizon.

Recent Social Organization in the South-Central Andes

Tiwanaku's dual character is best contextualized by first examining later, historically-documented sociopolitical organization in the region. Tiwanaku's sociopolitical disintegration in AD 1000–1200 was a process of cultural regeneration that ultimately produced a regional landscape of non-nucleated, relatively dispersed, locally hierarchical and pastorally-focused communities (Albarracín-Jordan 1996; Graffam 1992; Janusek 2005). Important changes, including successive phases of Inca and Spanish hegemony, altered local social-spatial organization and economic-ethnic relations over the next few centuries.

Nevertheless, Tiwanaku cultural and political disintegration initiated a trajectory of regional social-spatial change that remains vital today. The ultimate phase of this trajectory, which occurred under Spanish Colonial rule, was the creation of nucleated settlements or *reducciones* to facilitate state control and economic appropriation. Prior to this, centers of social convergence that had emerged after Tiwanaku's collapse ranged from major settlements to non-settled ceremonial spaces such as mountaintops, cemeteries, and local chapels (see Stanish 2003). The fundamental basis of social status, economy, and identification was the *ayllu*, an Andean permutation of "community" that referred (variably across space and society) to a corporate group (of "kin"), that to varying degrees shared economic resources, political interests, ritual places (and rites), and deceased ancestors. *Ayllu* members

tended to live in local hamlets and villages distributed across highly variable landscapes. They were organized according to scalar "hierarchies of encompassment" (Abercrombie 1998) and sociopolitical hierarchies of distinction. An *ayllu* and its leadership claimed a particular social place, status, and in some cases productive activity through membership in extensive regional interaction networks and encompassing sociopolitical systems.

This post-Tiwanaku social world gave rise to a novel expression of "urbanism" that remains vibrant today, and that may well partake of Tiwanaku's more ancient form of ceremonial urbanism. Major towns in the south-central Andes, each termed *pueblo* or *marka*, were centers of social-ritual convergence and symbolic places of social unity for the dispersed communities that identified with them. Each maintained a relatively small permanent occupation, but formed symbolic and ceremonial "anchors" for *ayllu* identities. Yet each *ayllu* maintained representative residential spaces in the local town (in some cases spatially mirroring their location in the regional landscape), and houses pertaining to a particular *ayllu* or hamlet tended to cluster in specific neighborhoods. These towns were densely populated only during key ceremonial occasions. Nonlocal people, usually either members of the various rural communities surrounding the town or stake-claiming community members now living in nearby cities, came to reside temporarily in the town while helping to prepare meals, orchestrate dances, or ferment or provide drinks—or simply to have a good, raucous time.

Structures providing residence, workspace, and storage (such as for costumes and alcohol) for such events were extremely important in these centers, and may be analogous to those archaeologically encountered in Tiwanaku's Akapana East sector. Permanent populations in these recent towns were relatively small overall, but they pulsated periodically and exploded momentarily during important calendrical and other ceremonies. At these times, plazas, streets, and the residential compounds of feast hosts were jammed with people from outlying places and communities, and routine life was abandoned to music, dancing, and drinking. But many such rituals are also important contexts for exchanging or selling goods, social "networking," and most explicitly, forming and transforming power relations. During such events, social status and other forms of identity (ethnic or otherwise) were affirmed, contested, and transformed. Feast-hosting itself remains critical to becoming a respected adult member who "is heard" in a community, and is the key way for more ambitious persons to build political careers. The current solstice ritual at Khonkho Wankane is a "total" social event (sensu Mauss 1990) that involves feasting, economic interaction, social networking, and the annual election of regional native leaders (Fig. 8.10).

Settlement Organization in the Tiwanaku Region

Tiwanaku's regional setting facilitated a similar pulsating ceremonial urbanism, if in a different cultural field that was more regionally integrated and centrally coordinated. Tiwanaku was fundamentally unlike Teotihuacan in that its growth throughout

Figure 8.10. The election of indigenous leaders at the June solstice Aymara "New Year" ceremony, Q'unq'u Liqiliqi, Bolivia, 2006. The ritual takes place atop the site of Khonkho Wankane.

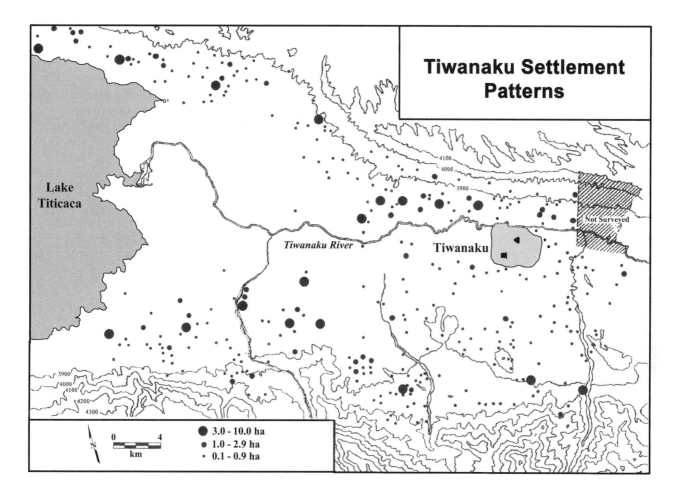

Figure 8.11. Regional settlement in the Tiwanaku Valley during Tiwanaku IV (adapted from Albarracín-Jordan 1996).

the Middle Horizon was characterized not by demographic implosion (Sanders et al. 1979), but by regional population growth and settlement increase in the Tiwanaku and adjacent valleys. Survey to date in the Tiwanaku Valley (the Upper Valley is currently being investigated) has revealed nearly three hundred sites dating to the Tiwanaku period, a dramatic increase in number from the Late Formative (Fig. 8.11) (Albarracín-Jordan 1996; Albarracín-Jordan and Mathews 1990; Mathews 1992). Human settlement was well distributed across valley resource zones, and comprised multiple size-based tiers. Pedestrian survey and multiple statistical analyses (McAndrews et al. 1997) indicate that Tiwanaku Valley settlements formed clusters centered on small towns, all of which clustered around Tiwanaku, which served as both primary local center and state capital (Janusek and Blom 2006). These patterns indicate that the prehispanic Tiwanaku Valley comprised several multi-settlement, semiautonomous communities. This pattern is reminiscent of that of later *ayllus*, which in turn centered on one or more central places for periodic religious ceremonies and rituals of consumption.

Urban and rural domains of Tiwanaku social organization were inextricably intertwined, as they have been in recent Andean communities. There is convincing evidence that some groups immigrated to Tiwanaku, and that local activities, affiliations, and memories helped forge the increasingly hierarchical and hegemonic state system. There is further evidence that local urban ties to distant places played a major role in Tiwanaku's rise to power, its vitality, and its political-religious longevity. Much like contemporary pueblos, Tiwanaku was indebted to the local, non-urban, and "foreign" populations that identified with it. It anchored the social coherence of its vast political community in great part through periodic feasts and ceremonies. Tiwanaku was a ceremonial center, an urban phenomenon, and a concrete symbol. Like later pueblos, Tiwanaku was an "incomplete" settlement with which local communities identified, to which they periodically paid homage, and to which they occasionally came for key religious ceremonies and feasts. This was Tiwanaku's strength and ultimately its liability.

It is important to note that Tiwanaku ritual was not ephemeral in relation to political and economic activities. In fact, as they do in the recent and contemporary Andes, past feasts and rituals formed the situational matrix for social networking, economic interchange, and political events. One can imagine that periodic ceremonies in Tiwanaku were times when llama caravans laden with goods from disparate regions descended on the center. Extensive herds may have been put up in the Mollo Kontu sector or outside the center near one of several marshy springs in the surrounding valley. One can also imagine that some periodic ceremonies were times when representatives of multiple communities comprising a vast regional community united, and when political decisions were made. Further archaeological evidence promises to shed more light on these potential aspects of prehispanic Tiwanaku.

Conclusions

As the capital of a pre-Inca Andean state, Tiwanaku was a ceremonial city. Formative occupations point to its origins as a lightly inhabited ceremonial center similar to contemporaneous Khonkho Wankane. During the early Andean Middle Horizon, it grew exponentially in size and population, and populations occupied increasingly distant places around the massive monumental complexes, courtyards, and plazas that accommodated a diverse array of ritual activities. In broad terms, Tiwanaku was transformed from one of several ceremonial centers of interacting multi-community polities into an extensive urban center.

To address the first of the three points discussed in this paper, local residential groups played key, but by no means exclusive, roles in Tiwanaku's political economy. Although the dwelling areas of co-residential households were located in parts of Tiwanaku, most structures excavated to date are equivocal on this point. The most salient co-residential group was the bounded compound, and possibly the multi-compound neighborhood. In most excavated cases, compounds bounded several residential structures and their associated residential areas. Yet residential compounds both contained and were surrounded by vast sheet middens and ash pits, which I argue were in great part new disposal practices associated with local ceremonies. Some compounds were located near ritual mounds or complexes; many other areas were dedicated to productive and other activities that were not strictly residential. Thus, domestic life was one of many other activities that characterized Tiwanaku's urban landscape. Addressing the overall political economy of the center demands a scale of research that addresses the place of urban domestic life in the settlement and the region, and considers Tiwanaku's overarching significance at regional and pan-regional scales. In particular, it demands attention to the ritual prestige and events that drew people to Tiwanaku, whether permanently or temporarily.

To address the second point, Tiwanaku's resident populations were diversified in status, occupation, and other domains of social identity. Tiwanaku's urban landscape formed a roughly concentric gradient of social hierarchy. Status appears to have been correlated with residential proximity to monumental complexes, distinctive social practices, sanitation, access to and use of exotic and prestige objects, distinctive body adornments, and

a sense of "ethnic purity" relative to others. Some groups practiced distinctive crafts, and in cases known to date, these were locally managed and socially embedded trades that took place alongside domestic activities. Kolata may be correct in noting that all who lived in Tiwanaku played roles directed toward elite desires and activities. Yet if so, residential groups forged or maintained distinctive social relations, economic networks, ritual practices, and in some cases ethnic identities. These other domains of social identity both grounded and transcended those of status and occupation. Tiwanaku's resident population was cosmopolitan, and this is the evidential tip of the iceberg regarding evidence for recurring feasts and other rituals in Tiwanaku's urban peripheries; Tiwanaku's religious prestige outside the center (Albarracín-Jordan 1996; Seddon 1998); and the diverse practices and identities of the people who affiliated with and most likely periodically came to Tiwanaku, whether for overtly religious, economic, or political reasons (e.g., Anderson 1999; Blom 2005; Goldstein 2005).

As an emergent state capital, Tiwanaku's significance as a ceremonial center, like its resident populations, increased exponentially and continued to do so until the tenth century. More than ever, by Tiwanaku IV, Tiwanaku was a place of ceremonial convergence and of recurring rites of consumption. The spatiality of primary and secondary residues of such activities indicates that they were not restricted to the urban core. Rather, they occurred at multiple social scales in local residential compounds and neighborhoods. I hypothesize that Tiwanaku population expanded and contracted in cyclical rhythms according to such events, and that local areas such as Ch'iji Jawira and Mollo Kontu may have temporarily housed pilgrims, ritual participants, traders, and relatives from distant sites and regions. These occasions were not simply about feasting and religious ceremonies. Rather, feasts and ceremonies provided periodic contexts for intense social and economic interaction, when extensive llama caravans descended on Tiwanaku laden with exotic goods and highly desired products from distant regions. Much of Tiwanaku's economy was inextricably tied to its ritual prestige. In this sense, Tiwanaku also became a mega-hub for circuits of caravan trade in the south-central Andes (Browman 1981; Núñez and Dillehay 1995).

This pattern of urbanism is not altogether unique in past state phenomena of the Andes or elsewhere. Teotihuacan in central Mexico thrived for centuries as a massive ceremonial city, as did Classic Maya lowland centers (if with highly distinctive residential patterns). Centuries earlier in Mesopotamia, Uruk was famed for its recurring rituals and festive occasions. A contemporaneous phenomenon that is perhaps analogous to Tiwanaku was the Andean coastal center of Pachacamac. By the Late Horizon, Pachacamac was neither an empty oracle center nor simply a sprawling city, but an urban center that thrived on its profound religious prestige and recurring ceremonial events (at overlapping social scales and in diverse spatial contexts at the center) in which participants of diverse origins participated (Eeckhout 2004; Shimada 1991; Shimada et al. 2004; Uhle 1991).

Tiwanaku demonstrates that ceremonial centers and populated urban centers are not mutually exclusive phenomena, as some past models of the site stress. This point resonates with other political capitals, and adds an often-downplayed dimension to conventional views of past urbanism. I believe it also emphasizes the point recently made by Yoffee (2005:16) that in many early states economic and administrative linkages were tenuous, and "that centrality is mainly concerned with the creation of new symbols of social identity, ideologies of power, and representations of history." Tiwanaku was the key place to which diverse populations identified, and its transformation into a state capital involved intensified social hierarchy, more centralized political power, and new representations of history. Ceremonialism was as critical for the creation of a common Tiwanaku community and new ideologies of power as it was for the historical processes of state development and urbanism.

References

Abercrombie, T.A.
1998　*Pathways of Memory and Power: Ethnography and History among an Andean People.* University of Wisconsin Press, Madison.

Albarracín-Jordan, J.V.
1996　*Tiwanaku: Arqueología Regional y Dinámica Segmentaria.* Plural Editores, La Paz, Bolivia.

Albarracín-Jordan, J.V., and J.E. Mathews
1990　*Asentamientos Prehispánicos del Valle de Tiwanaku,* Vol. 1. CIMA, La Paz, Bolivia.

Alconini Mujica, S.
1995　*Rito, Símbolo e Historia en la Pirámide de Akapana, Tiwanaku: Un Análisis de Cerámica Ceremonial Prehispánica.* Editorial Acción, La Paz, Bolivia.

Anderson, K.
1999　Tiwanaku Political Economy: The View from Cochabamba. Paper presented at the 64th Annual Meeting of the Society for American Archaeology, Chicago.

Bandy, M.S.
2001　*Population and History in the Ancient Titicaca Basin.* PhD dissertation, University of California, Berkeley.

Benítez, L.
2009　Descendants of the sun: Calendars, myth, and the Tiwanaku state. In *Tiwanaku: Papers from the 2005 Mayer Center Symposium at the Denver Art Museum,* edited by M. Young-Sanchez. Denver Art Museum, Denver.

Bennett, W.C.
1934　Excavations at Tiahuanaco. *Anthropological Papers of the American Museum of Natural History* XXXIV:359–494.

Blom, D.E.
2005　Embodying borders: Human body modification and diversity in Tiwanaku society. *Journal of Anthropological Archaeology* 24:1–34.

Blom, D.E., B. Hallgrímsson, L. Keng, M.C. Lozada C., and J.E. Buikstra
1998　Tiwanaku 'colonization': Bioarchaeological implications for migration in the Moquegua Valley, Peru. *World Archaeology* 30(2):238–61.

Bourdieu, P.
1993　*Distinction: A Social Critique of the Judgement of Taste.* Harvard University Press, Cambridge.

Browman, D.L.
1981　New light on Andean Tiwanaku. *American Scientist* 69(4):408–19.

Comaroff, J., and J. Comaroff
1991　*Of Revelation and Revolution: Christianity, Colonialism, and Consciousness in South Africa.* University of Chicago Press, Chicago.

Couture, N.C.
2002　*The Construction of Power: Monumental Space and an Elite Residence at Tiwanaku, Bolivia.* PhD dissertation, Department of Anthropology, University of Chicago, Chicago.
2003　Ritual, monumentalism, and residence at Mollo Kontu, Tiwanaku. In *Tiwanaku and Its Hinterland: Archaeology and Paleoecology of an Andean Civilization,* Vol. 2, edited by A.L. Kolata, pp. 202–25. Smithsonian Institution Press, Washington, D.C.

Couture, N.C., and D.E. Blom
2004　*Informe sobre los trabajos realizados por el Proyecto Jacha Marka en los años de 2001 y 2002.* Research report submitted to the Viceministry of Culture, La Paz, Bolivia.

Couture, N.C., and K. Sampeck
2003　Putuni: A history of palace architecture in Tiwanaku. In *Tiwanaku and Its Hinterland: Archaeology and Paleoecology of an Andean Civilization,* Vol. 2, edited by A.L. Kolata, pp. 226–63. Smithsonian Institution Press, Washington, D.C.

Davis, Katherine M.
2006　Interpreting Spaces Outside of the Core: Muru Ut Pata, Tiwanaku. Paper presented at the 25th Northeast Conference on Andean Archaeology and Ethnohistory, Philadelphia.

Eeckhout, P.
2004　Pachacamac y el Proyecto Ychsma. *Bulletin de L'Institut Français d'Etudes Andines* 33(3):425–88.

Escalante Moscoso, J.F.
1997　*Arquitectura Prehispánica en los Andes Bolivianos.* CIMA, La Paz, Bolivia.
2003　Residential architecture in La K'arana, Tiwanaku. In *Tiwanaku and Its Hinterland: Archaeology and Paleoecology of an Andean Civilization,* Vol. 2, edited by A.L. Kolata, pp. 316–26. Smithsonian Institution Press, Washington, D.C.

Giesso, M.
2003   Stone tool production in the Tiwanaku heartland. In *Tiwanaku and Its Hinterland: Archaeology and Paleoecology of an Andean Civilization*, Vol. 2, edited by A.L. Kolata, pp. 363–83. Smithsonian Institution Press, Washington, D.C.

Goldstein, P.S.
2005   *Andean Diaspora: The Tiwanaku Colonies and the Origins of South American Empire*. University Press of Florida, Gainesville.

Graffam, G.C.
1992   Beyond state collapse: Rural history, raised fields and pastoralism in the south Andes. *American Anthropologist* 94(4):882–904.

Hastorf, C.A.
2003   Community with the ancestors: Ceremonies and social memory in the Middle Formative at Chiripa, Bolivia. *Journal of Anthropological Archaeology* 22:305–32.

Janusek, J.W.
1999   Craft and local power: Embedded specialization in Tiwanaku cities. *Latin American Antiquity* 10(2):107–31.
2002   Out of many, one: Style and social boundaries in Tiwanaku. *Latin American Antiquity* 13(1):35–61.
2003   The changing face of Tiwanaku residential life: State and social identity in an Andean city. In *Tiwanaku and Its Hinterland: Archaeology and Paleoecology of an Andean Civilization*, Vol. 2, edited by A.L. Kolata, pp. 264–95. Smithsonian Institution Press, Washington, D.C.
2004   *Identity and Power in the Ancient Andes: Tiwanaku Cities through Time*. Routledge, London.
2005   Collapse as cultural revolution: Power and identity in the Tiwanaku to Pacajes transition. In *Foundations of Power in the Prehispanic Andes*, edited by K. Vaughn, D. Ogburn, and C.A. Conlee, pp. 175–210. American Anthropological Association, Arlington, VA.
2006   The changing 'nature' of Tiwanaku religion and the rise of an Andean state. *World Archaeology* 38(3):469–92.
2008   *Ancient Tiwanaku*. Cambridge University Press, Cambridge.

Janusek, J.W., and D.E. Blom
2006   Identifying Tiwanaku urban populations: Style, identity, and ceremony in Andean cities. In *Urbanization in the Preindustrial World: A Cross-Cultural Perspective*, edited by G. Storey, pp. 233–51. University of Alabama Press, Tuscaloosa.

Kolata, A.L.
1993   *Tiwanaku: Portrait of an Andean Civilization*. Blackwell, Cambridge.
2003   The social production of Tiwanaku: Political economy and authority in a native Andean state. In *Tiwanaku and Its Hinterland: Archaeology and Paleoecology of an Andean Civilization*, Vol. 2, edited by A.L. Kolata, pp. 449–72. Smithsonian Institution Press, Washington, D.C.

Lanning, E.P.
1967   *Peru Before the Incas*. Prentice-Hall, Englewood Cliffs, NJ.

Lemuz, C.
2005   *Normalización de Datos de Asentamiento en la Cuenca Sur de Lago Titicaca*. Report submitted to the Dirección Nacional de Arqueología de Bolivia (DINAR), La Paz.

Levine, T.
1985   Inca state storage in three highland regions: A comparative study. In *Inca Storage Systems*, edited by T. Levine, pp. 107–50. University of Oklahoma Press, Norman.

Lumbreras, L.G.
1974   *The Peoples and Cultures of Ancient Peru*, translated by B.J. Meggers. Smithsonian Institution Press, Washington, D.C.

Manzanilla, L.
1992   *Akapana: Una Pirámide en el Centro del Mundo*. Instituto de Investigaciones Antropológicas, Universidad Nacional Autónoma de México, Mexico City.

Manzanilla, L., and E.K. Woodard
1990   Restos humanos asociados a la Pirámide de Akapana (Tiwanaku, Bolivia). *Latin American Antiquity* 1(2):133–49.

Mathews, J.E.
1992   *Prehispanic Settlement and Agriculture in the Middle Tiwanaku Valley, Bolivia*. PhD dissertation, Department of Anthropology, University of Chicago, Chicago.
2003   Prehistoric settlement patterns and in the middle Tiwanaku Valley. In *Tiwanaku and Its Hinterland: Archaeology and Paleoecology of an Andean Civilization*, Vol. 2, edited by A.L. Kolata, pp. 112–28. Smithsonian Institution Press, Washington, D.C.

Mauss, M.
1990   *The Gift: Forms and Functions of Exchange in Archaic Societies*. Routledge, London.

McAndrews, T., J. Albarracín-Jordan, and M. Bermann
1997   Regional settlement patterns in the Tiwanaku Valley of Bolivia. *Journal of Field Archaeology* 24(1):67–84.

McEwan, G.F. (editor)
2005   *Pikillacta: The Wari Empire in Cuzco*. University of Iowa Press, Iowa City.

Morris, C., and D.E. Thompson
1985   *Huánuco Pampa: An Inca City and Its Hinterland*. Thames and Hudson, London.

Murra, J.V.
1972   El "control vertical" de un máximo de pisos ecológicos en la economía de las sociedades andinas. In *Visita de la Provincia de León de Huánuco en 1562*, Vol. 2, edited by J.V. Murra, pp. 429–76. Universidad Nacional Hermilio Valdizán, Huánuco.

Núñez Atencio, L., and T.C. Dillehay
1995[1979]   *Movilidad Giratoria, Armonía Social y Desarrollo en los Andes Meridionales: Patrones de Tráfico e Interacción Económica*. Universidad Católica del Norte, Antofagasta.

Orta, A.
2004   *Catechizing Culture: Missionaries, Aymara, and the "New Evangelization."* Columbia University Press, New York.

Parsons, J.R.
1968   An estimate of size and population for Middle Horizon Tiahuanaco, Bolivia. *American Antiquity* 33:243–45.

Ponce Sanginés, C.
1981   *Tiwanaku: Espacio, Tiempo, Cultura. Ensayo de síntesis arqueológica.* Los Amigos del Libro, La Paz, Bolivia.
1991   El urbanismo de Tiwanaku. *Pumapunku: Nueva Época* 1:7–27.

Posnansky, A.
1945   *Tihuanacu: The Cradle of American Man*, Vols. I and II. J.J. Augustin, New York.

Rivera Casanovas, C.S.
2003   Ch'iji Jawira: A case of ceramic specialization in the Tiwanaku urban periphery. In *Tiwanaku and Its Hinterland: Archaeology and Paleoecology of an Andean Civilization*, Vol. 2, edited by A.L. Kolata, pp. 296–315. Smithsonian Institution Press, Washington, D.C.

Rodas, D., A.T. Ohnstad, and J.W. Janusek
2005   *Residencia y producción especializada en Khonkho Wankane (Sector 4). Khonkho Wankane: Primer Informe Preliminar del Proyecto Arqueológico Jach'a Machaca*, edited by J.W. Janusek, pp. 154–71. Research report submitted to the Viceministry of Culture, La Paz, Bolivia.

Rydén, S.
1947   *Archaeological Researches in the Highlands of Bolivia.* Elanders Boktryckeri Aktiebolag, Göteborg.

Sanders, W.T., J.R. Parsons, and R.S. Santley
1979   *The Basin of Mexico: Ecological Processes in the Evolution of a Civilization.* Academic Press, New York.

Service, E.R.
1975   *Origins of the State and Civilization: The Process of Political Evolution.* Norton, New York.

Schaedel, R.P.
1988   Andean world view: Hierarchy or reciprocity, regulation or control? *Current Anthropology* 29(5):768–75.

Schreiber, K.
2001   The Wari empire of Middle Horizon Peru: The epistemological challenge of documenting an empire without documentary evidence. In *Empires: Perspectives from Archaeology and Ethnohistory*, edited by S.E. Alcock, pp. 70–92. Cambridge University Press, New York.

Seddon, M.T.
1998   *Ritual, Power, and the Development of a Complex Society.* PhD thesis, University of Chicago, Chicago.

Shimada, I.
1991[1913]   Pachacamac archaeology: Retrospect and prospect. In *Pachacamac*, edited by M. Uhle, pp. xv–xvi. University of Pennsylvania, Philadelphia.

Shimada, I., R. Segura L., M. Rostworowski de Diez Canseco, and H. Watanabe
2004   Una nueva evaluación de la Plaza de los Peregrinos d Pachacamac: Aportes de la Primera Campaña 2003 del Proyecto Arqueológico Pachacamac. *Bulletin de L'Institut Français d'Etudes Andines* 33(3):507–38.

Smyth, M.P.
1989   Domestic storage behavior in Mesoamerica: An ethnoarchaeological approach. In *Archaeological Method and Theory*, Vol. 2, edited by M.B. Schiffer, pp. 89–138. University of Arizona Press, Tucson.

Squier, E.G.
1878   *Peru: Incidents of Travel and Exploration in the Land of the Incas.* Harper Brothers, New York.

Stanish, C.
1992   *Ancient Andean Political Economy.* University of Texas Press, Austin.
1999   Settlement pattern shifts and political ranking in the Lake Titicaca Basin, Peru. In *Settlement Pattern Studies in the Americas*, edited by B.R. Billman and G.M. Feinman, pp. 116–28. Smithsonian Institution Press, Washington, D.C.
2003   *Ancient Titicaca: The Evolution of Complex Society in Southern Peru and Northern Bolivia.* University of California Press, Berkeley.

Uhle, M.
1991[1903]   Pachacamac: Report of the William Pepper, M.D., LL.D., Peruvian expedition of 1896. In *Pachacamac: A Reprint of the 1903 Edition by Max Uhle.* University Museum of Archaeology and Anthropology, University of Pennsylvania, Philadelphia.

Vranich, A.
1999   *Interpreting the Meaning of Ritual Spaces: The Temple Complex of Pumapunku, Tiwanaku, Bolivia.* PhD dissertation, Department of Anthropology, University of Pennsylvania, Philadelphia.

Weber, M.
1958   The city. In *The City*, edited by D. Martingale and G. Neuwirth, pp. 65–230. The Free Press, New York.

Winterhalder, B., R. Larson, and R. Thomas
1974   Dung as an essential resource in a highland Peruvian community. *Human Ecology* 2:89–104.

Wright, M.F., C.A. Hastorf, and H. Lennstrom
2003   Pre-Hispanic agriculture and plant use at Tiwanaku: Social and political implications. In *Tiwanaku and Its Hinterland: Archaeology and Paleoecology of an Andean Civilization*, Vol. 2, edited by A.L. Kolata, pp. 384–403. Smithsonian Institution Press, Washington, D.C.

Yoffee, N.
2005   *Myths of the Archaic State: Evolution of the Earliest Cities, States, and Civilizations.* Cambridge University Press, Cambridge.

Zovar, Jennifer
in press   El hogar cambiando: Arquitectura doméstica en Khonkho Wankane, Bolivia. In *Proceedings of the Arequipa Conference*, edited by Justin Jennings.

9

Domestic Life in and around the Urban Sector of the Huacas of Moche Site, Northern Peru

Claude Chapdelaine

The Huacas of Moche is a unique urban center that developed during the first centuries AD. We argue that it was the first capital of the expansionist Southern Moche state. Several residential compounds have been excavated between the two monumental buildings. Architectural features and household activities carried out at the site or close by will be addressed in the context of exploring specialization within the organization of domestic life. Social hierarchy at the Huacas of Moche site will be examined by defining the roles played by urban residents in the conduct of daily state affairs. We conclude with the homogeneous ethnic population at this Moche capital and its strategies for integrating conquered ethnic groups into this polity.

Introduction

The urban sector between two immense buildings, Huaca del Sol and Huaca de la Luna, is a key area for understanding the functioning of a pristine state capital, especially its domestic sphere. Since 1995, this site has been the subject of intensive research under the direction of Dr. Santiago Uceda (Universidad Nacional de Trujillo), who has shed new light every year on the urban sector and on the Huaca de la Luna's monumental complex (Uceda and Morales 2005, 2004; Uceda and Mujica 2003). Given that the work is ongoing, we should expect our views to change on a regular basis; it is with this perspective that we present some of our tentative interpretations based on our own six years of

excavation at the site, carried out between 1995 and 2000. The growing body of data will take time to analyze fully to confirm or refute the prevailing ideas developed over the last decade as to the nature of the Huacas of Moche site and its role as the capital of the expansionist Southern Moche state. This territorial state expanded toward southern valleys where archaeological evidence of Moche domination is very convincing, as expressed by the massive regional centers such as Guadalupito (formerly known as Pampa de los Incas) in the Santa Valley and Pañamarca in the Nepeña Valley. We now regard the Southern Moche state as having a core comprising the Moche and Chicama Valleys and a periphery that included both conquered southern valleys and southern valleys added without having been subjugated by force. The Santa Valley is a good example of a conquered valley, while the Virú Valley was politically integrated without force (Bourget 2004, 2003; Millaire 2004). The Paiján desert acted as the northern limit during the time period equivalent to Moche Phase IV (AD 450–750), while the southern limit was the Nepeña Valley (Fig. 9.1). Given the lack of true Moche urban centers in the Culebras and Huarmey Valleys, they are both excluded, although Moche influence might have had some affect on the local populations there (see Bonavia 1982 and Prümers 2000 for the Huarmey Valley, and Przadka and Giersz 2003 for the Culebras Valley). The sociopolitical organization of the Moche state north of the Paiján desert is still open to debate and discussion (e.g., Castillo and Donnan 1994).

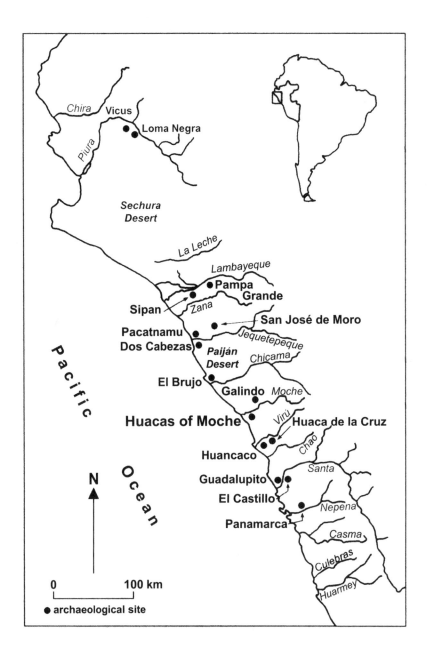

Figure 9.1. Location of important Moche archaeological sites mentioned in the text.

The Site of Huacas of Moche: Its Limits and Urban Structure

In order to discuss the political economy of the Moche state, it is necessary to present its chronology and cultural sequence, followed by a description of the capital's limits and urban structure. After fifteen years of continuous work at the site, and ten years within the limits of the Urban Sector, our horizontal and vertical excavations have revealed a long history. The generally accepted Moche timespan is between AD 100 and 800 with a

climax between AD 350 and 750 for the combined Phases III and IV. It is unclear whether or not the Huacas of Moche site was a small Gallinazo settlement prior to the emergence of the Moche cultural identity (see Bawden 1996 for a different view).

The relative chronology based on ceramic morphological and stylistic attributes (cf. stirrup spout bottles and other ceramic types) established by Rafael Larco Hoyle (2001, 1948) is still relevant for the Moche Valley cultural sequence, and we can extend this relative chronology to the Santa Valley based on our results from five years of excavation and data analysis (Chapdelaine et al. 2005, 2004, 2003; Chapdelaine and Pimentel 2003, 2002, 2001). A series of radiocarbon dates, more than 50 for the two valleys, confirms the consistency of the dates, the artifact style, and their position within the archaeological context (Chapdelaine 2003, 2002, 2001, 2000; Uceda et al. 2001). Internal coherence is rather strong. The Huacas of Moche site is definitely a city built during several phases; its 500-year archaeological record is compressed within refuse 7 m thick.

Few data, however, are available to discuss the site's nature and size during the initial Phases I and II. The cultural layers that may pertain to this time interval lie more than 6 m below the present surface (Chapdelaine et al. 2004; Chapdelaine et al. 2001). Their depth is a very important limiting factor that is also true for the Moche III occupation, which lies at least 2 m beneath the most recent Moche Phase IV occupation. Nevertheless, limited data gathered in several areas of the Urban Sector (consisting of stratigraphic cuts, burials, and diagnostic artifacts) indicate a large Moche Phase III habitation site with smaller, but still impressive, monumental buildings (Uceda and Canziani 1998). A large Moche settlement seems to emerge during Phase III, and its growth was impressive. It is thus possible to argue that the urban nature of the Huacas of Moche was already developed during Phase III. It is difficult to gain a representative sample of the Huacas of Moche site during Phase III because that material lies under refuse 2 m thick. Nevertheless, the rapid growth of the site, associated with the construction of the two monumental buildings, is a clear case of power centralization. How fast that labor effort was accomplished is difficult to quantify but Phase III seemed to have lasted 150 years (AD 300–450). It is obvious that the new city was not built overnight, but more probably at a steady rate. This centralization probably led to the consolidation of the site as the most important residential center of the whole Moche Valley. During this process, it is assumed that an incipient state at the valley level emerged and its expansionist needs also grew, as suggested by the extensive distribution of Moche ceramics of Phase III style in most north coast valleys.

In the following section, I will use the available data to discuss the domestic sphere within the state political economy from the latest occupations of the Huacas of Moche site dating to Phase IV (AD 400/450 to 700/800). During that time interval, a well-developed settlement hierarchy existed, with the Huacas of Moche site being the largest Moche site of the Moche Valley, and with very few sites considered to be secondary centers (Billman 2002, 1997, 1996). The point I want to make here is that Huacas of Moche had no rival or opposition within the Moche Valley; its challengers or competitors existed elsewhere (that is, in adjacent valleys).

Within the Moche Valley, the distinction between rural and urban spheres was clear by the beginning of Moche Phase IV. City dwellers probably were dependent on the mobile rural people to bring in raw materials such as cotton, and on trade for finished products, especially identity markers such as painted and sculptured/modeled ceramics, figurines, metal objects, and decorated textiles. The Huacas of Moche site was definitely the core of an economic system, and the periphery (defined as the Lower Moche Valley) had a symbiotic relation with an informal but controlled market exchange. The Moche elite was in charge of several aspects of the economy, such as ensuring the arrival of key raw materials for its craftsmen and supervising, through officers, the orderly conduct of daily affairs within and around the city.

The abandonment of the site was a slow process and at odds with the leading paradigm of the 1980s and 1990s (see Moseley 1992; Shimada 1994; Bawden 1996). Indeed, the Huacas of Moche site was never an important site during Phase V; very few artifacts belonging to this phase have been recovered from either the surface or late burials. The surprising evidence is that radiocarbon dates indicate a longer Phase IV occupation at the site (Chapdelaine 2000). These radiocarbon dates from Phase IV contexts are reinforced by several burials found close to the surface and containing typical Moche IV ceramics. These new data allow us to reject the old paradigm favoring a rapid abandonment of the site around AD 600 and the end of the Phase IV style. It is now evident that Phase IV ceramics and the occupation of Huacas of Moche site continued for at least a century or two. The inhabitants were thus making Moche Phase IV ceramics around AD 700 and possibly some time during the eighth century. Our new hypothesis is that Moche Phases IV and V were probably contemporaneous in the Moche Valley. A very conservative population occupied the Huacas of Moche site while Galindo, the new Moche Phase V regional center, developed at the valley neck far from the sea and from the former capital. This scenario is now accepted (Bawden 2004:127–28), as is the contemporaneity between Gallinazo and Moche cultures.

The **limits** of the Huacas of Moche site are well known; the site lies between two hills, Cerro Blanco at the eastern limit and Cerro Negro at the northern limit (Fig. 9.2). The Huaca del Sol is often considered the western limit, especially with the existence of a modern canal west of it that follows the main Moche River channel. The exact western limit could have been the Moche River, giving a more fluid western limit to the site. West of the Moche River, the valley floor is flat, and was probably used for agriculture, as it is today.

The southern limit of the site was unknown until 1999 when we decided to do some digging in the area very close to the protected limit of the site (that is, about 450 m south of Huaca de la Luna). We were looking for the city's lower class, who probably lived at the margins of the urban center. Instead, we found a long wall, running east to west, wide enough to walk on top of, and tall enough to provide a clear view of the city to the north and the surrounding desert to the south. North of that wall and inside the city limit, a late compound close to the surface was uncovered. It was badly eroded and judging from its poor quality of construction, the inhabitants of this late Moche IV occupation may have been members of a lower class. Outside that wall, we located two cemeteries: an extensive one that was badly looted, and another one on an upper slope in the desert not too far from the wall.

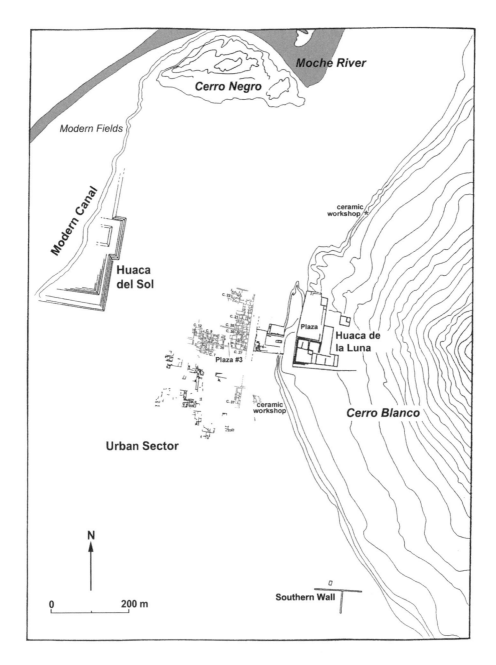

Figure 9.2. General plan of the Huacas of Moche site.

Associated with the wall, we found some large ceramic emblems representing a symbol frequently found in Moche iconography (Fig. 9.3). This representation of a "life" or "catfish" is found on several painted and sculptured walls of Huaca de la Luna (Uceda 2001:55). It has also been reported at Huaca Cao Viejo in the Chicama Valley (Franco et al. 2003:147) and depicted on an impressive necklace associated with Sipán royalty (Alva 1994:143; Alva and Donnan 1993:208). The wall was probably part of the symbolism that the city wished to display to visitors, along with the already dominant Moche marine iconography.

Along the outside of that massive east-west wall is a series of stairs, suggesting that the wall was not a defensive wall, but instead served as a clear architectural indication that visitors were entering the inner city from the southern limits of the city. The discovery of this wall confirms the one-kilometer-long north-south axis; combined with the 600 m between the two huacas, it provides a figure of approximately 60 ha for the inner city, or what could be considered a downtown with a dense and urban population.

The **periphery** of the site has been a neglected subject, mainly because of destruction caused by mega-Niño events, recent

0 　　　　 10 cm

Figure 9.3. A ceramic decorative plaque found in association with the southern wall.

residential compounds as well as the diversity of luxury goods, the demographic density, although very difficult to assess, could have been as low as 6,000 individuals. This number could be obtained with an average of 100 inhabitants per hectare, which is considered low for the Santa Valley (Wilson 1988:78), while streets and public spaces within the urban sector occupy an unknown portion of the 60 ha. Using a density figure of 100 to 150 inhabitants per hectare, an estimate ranging between 6,000 and 9,000 individuals would be a conservative estimate. But if we included in this estimate the commuting population coming into the city to do business and living within a periphery of about 10 km, the population could have reached at least 10,000 and most probably 15,000 souls, providing a total of 16,000 to 24,000 individuals during the Southern Moche state's climax. This is my guess. Considering the intensification and capacities of the irrigation canals and the energy input visible in the construction of massive buildings, it is safe, in my mind, to favor a large, concentrated Moche population in the lower Moche Valley interacting on a regular basis at the major site, Huacas of Moche.

The **structure** of the urban sector is more complex and organized than we thought at the beginning of our project (Uceda and Chapdelaine 1998). The dominant axis is of course the placement of the two huacas in front of each other, Huaca del Sol having its back to the Moche River, and Huaca de la Luna at the foot of Cerro Blanco. The small Cerro Negro offers protection from the flood of the Moche River during a mega-Niño event. The modern canal that passes northwest of this rock formation is probably in the same general location as the prehistoric Moche canal. The inner core of the site is thus delimited by natural landmarks, two hills and a river with an open side facing the desert to the south. This quadrangular arrangement has an open area that was the only potential zone for residential occupation and for workshops, as proposed very early by Max Uhle.

This urban sector has revealed some secrets over the last ten years. The major findings worth mentioning are: (1) the recognition of streets dividing the urban sector into sectors and delimiting architectural complexes; (2) the delimitation of huge compounds that might not represent individual or family households; (3) small-scale plazas located at street intersections with possibly different functions; and (4) specialized and unspecialized workshops located within major compounds (Fig. 9.4). This urban network of streets, plazas, and compounds (Uceda 2005; Chapdelaine 2003, 2002) suggests that several functions were carried out within the excavated compounds, giving us a complex image of what was going on in this truly unique city (see Marcus 1983 for a Mesoamerican perspective). Although it is tempting to see sections of the inner city as being organized by the kind of work undertaken there, it is not clear-cut, as yet, and the internal organization of the compounds linked by narrow streets is not similar to some modern cities that have distinctive industrial and residential quarters. The interpretation of Moche households is clearly at a crossroads and this growing body of data will be synthesized in the near future to characterize organization inside the compounds and between compounds using a synchronic approach.

agricultural development, and the growth and encroachment of the modern city of Trujillo. I think the periphery was probably more linear, along the Moche River toward the Pacific Ocean, north along the irrigation networks, and possibly west within the valley floor in a somewhat dispersed and widely scattered settlement pattern to avoid the occupation of the best agricultural lands. The radius of this periphery is not clear but a substantial number of small communities were directly linked to the Huacas of Moche site. Fishermen were very close to the city and they could bring their catch of the day into the city. The same symbiotic pattern existed between city dwellers and agriculturists. We should add that llamas were becoming more important and should be taken into account, and herders were probably new leading actors in the daily economic sphere at the site (Vásquez et al. 2003; Roselló et al. 2001).

The emerging image of this unique urban center is an inner core densely occupied, surrounded by an irregular network of smaller sites stretching from the sea to at least 10 km inland that provided a large and rich hinterland or periphery to this bustling capital city. If we assumed that only privileged people had access to the inner core, based on the construction quality and size of

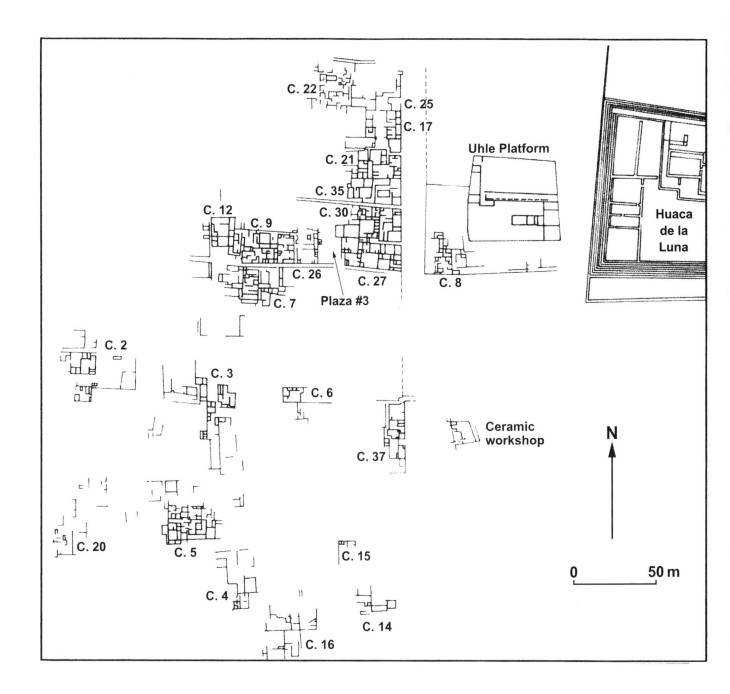

Figure 9.4. Plan of the excavated area of the urban sector of Huacas of Moche site with the location of major compounds and ceramic workshops.

Domestic Life at the Huacas of Moche: Craft Production, Storage, and Redistribution of Goods

Specialization is often assumed to be present by archaeologists who work on state-level societies. Such specialization also implies the existence of specialists working full-time and developing skills of the highest order. The problem is to understand how specialization functions, and how it affects the domestic sphere of city dwellers. Specialization is regularly studied by assessing the degree of standardization within the material culture (Eerkens and Bettinger 2001; Longacre 1999). In state-level society, production is often controlled by the ruling body. Standardization could reduce the options and costs to consumers, trying to satisfy most of them with fewer products or with the most efficiently produced product, produced at a minimal cost. Specialization is thus often linked to mass production of a standardized product, efficiency being more important than quality or stylistic expression. Specialization and standardization can reduce variability in the archaeological record, and the assumption is that the ruling elite is controlling most of the production, including domestic goods. This perception or inference should not be used as a rigid model because some key elements are very difficult to evaluate. Indeed, specialization and standardization are part of a process and a comparative approach is necessary to determine at what point in the process specialization and standardization occur (Costin and Hagstrum 1996). In the case of Moche ceramic production, standardization of several types of products, especially domestic vessels, was attained and a standardized quality for decorated or modeled vessels was reached, both technological and morphological; nevertheless, at the same time there was a strong florescence of stylistic diversity (see Bernier 2005 for a detailed presentation of Moche craft specialists at the Huacas of Moche site).

The inferred specialists living and/or working at the Huacas of Moche site are people engaged in:

1. the production of adobes nearby and laborers who worked within the city,
2. ceramic production at various workshops within the city,
3. metallurgy workshops within the city and possibly nearby,
4. weaving in city compounds and nearby,
5. lapidary workshops within the city and nearby,
6. beer brewing for ritual feasts in several large compounds, and
7. herding llamas (and possibly alpacas).

Before examining data that support the existence of these specialists, it is worth mentioning that agricultural tools (more precisely, hoes) are missing from the site's database while this type of tool is found regularly in habitation sites of the Moche Valley. Grinding stones (metates and manos), with typical use-wear characteristics, are found in most compounds and are interpreted as tools to transform agricultural products brought to the city by members of nearby farming villages. In other words, we do not have clear evidence of agriculturalists living within the city, and food supply was part of a distribution system that is not well understood. In several compounds, copper fishhooks and stone weights for fishing nets have been found, indicating that some members of the population were engaged in fishing, possibly in the Moche River or in the Pacific Ocean.

The Production of Adobes

The principal construction element is the sun-dried mud brick or adobe used in all buildings at the site. Hundreds of millions of adobes were made to construct the monumental buildings of the city over several centuries. It is assumed that the construction itself could have been done by some of the inhabitants, but that specialists made the adobes themselves. Several morphological analyses of Moche adobes have been performed and most studies comment on their regular shape and size (32 × 20 × 15 cm), as well as standardized quality that is difficult to quantify. The Moche adobe could thus be classified as a product having most of the characteristics of a standardized product, and fulfilling the needs of a large population. We do not know where the adobe making took place, but it is safe to assume that major workshops were located nearby to reduce the transportation costs. This proposition does not deny the possibility of a larger network involving several distant communities, which might have organized a longer journey to come and sell or deliver adobes in tribute to state leaders. In both scenarios, the use of llamas to transport large numbers of adobes was probably important.

Ceramic Production

Two ceramic workshops have been identified, but only one was excavated in the 1990s. This first ceramic workshop, partially excavated, is located about 100 m south of Huaca de la Luna, on the valley floor. Production of elite goods is attested and the workshop was maintained over several reconstructions of plastered clay floors. The second workshop, associated with the production of large domestic wares, has been identified on the basis of surface remains (Bernier 2005:189–90; Jara 1999). Its location on a slope of Cerro Blanco about 300 m north of Huaca de la Luna seems odd when considering the distance to both water and clay sources. No excavations have been conducted in this ceramic workshop.

The large quantity of both domestic and decorated ceramics used and discarded at the site is the best indicator of massive ceramic production and the existence of several other workshops within the city limits or nearby. The high quality and stylistic diversity of Moche decorated ceramics are always considered to be indicative of the presence of specialists. These skilled pottery specialists probably devoted most of their time to their trade, making them the kind of full-time artisans usually expected to exist in most state societies. The other topic to investigate is the specific working conditions of these ceramicists, to see if they were autonomous or attached to the elite. That topic has been investigated recently and there are data to support both autonomous and attached workers in the surprisingly small- to medium-sized workshops for the expected massive production (Bernier 2005).

The city's inhabitants were big consumers of ceramics and part of a dynamic regional exchange network that ensured access to this type of good, especially if we accept its usefulness as an identity marker with its distinctive Moche symbols. The massive production of high quality ceramics, supported by the development and intensive use of moldmade technology (Fig. 9.5), allowed the ruling body to promote the production and distribution of ceramics as a tool of state promotion and propaganda.

Metallurgy Workshops

One metallurgy kiln has been excavated within an undetermined workshop in Compound 7 (Chapdelaine 2002:70–71, 1998:92–93, 1997:50–52), while a small but extensively excavated workshop was documented within the limits of Compound 27 (Uceda and Rengifo 2006; Rengifo and Rojas 2005). The location of these two metallurgy workshops within the center of the urban sector is certainly peculiar if we assume that the use of fire, constant heat, and the smell of burning fuel would have been an annoyance to neighbors.

The two workshops probably had distinct functions: gold melting and possibly smelting in Compound 7, and the manufacture of various objects in Compound 27. They seem to be small-scale workshops and it could be interpreted as an indication that metal production was also of less importance within the limits of the city. New findings might change this impression, although it is difficult to explain their location downtown.

It is a well-known fact that the availability of copper is limited, if present at all, in the lower portions of the northern valleys. Most of the known sources are in the mountains outside the reach of Moche miners. This scarcity makes copper, as well as gold and silver, precious metals that are used mainly in the production of non-utilitarian goods reserved for the upper classes of this stratified society. A large number of copper artifacts were identified as gilded copper or *tumbaga*, based on neutron activation analysis. The gold contamination of the clay coating in the interior of a furnace located in Compound 7 points to its use to make copper gilded with gold objects (Chapdelaine et al. 2001:388–89).

Weaving in City Compounds

It is well known from several Mesoamerican and Andean ethnographic cases that textiles, usually decorated, were among the most important goods for the ruling elite. Textiles could be woven in a specialized workshop, although weaving could take place in every household. Based on the distribution of spindle whorls in almost all compounds, we can suggest that spinning and making thread was a widespread activity. Members of each family could participate in spinning, the first step before the production of clothes and other textiles.

Textile production was clearly a major economic activity at the Huacas of Moche site. However, poor preservation prevents us from dealing with this issue in a more detailed fashion. Hundreds of Moche III and IV textiles were recovered in the Santa Valley

excavations, where preservation was very good. We can only imagine what we are missing from the capital city of Huacas de Moche, which has such poor preservation.

Spindle whorls are small, decorated ceramic artifacts, and are found in great numbers in various compounds of the capital (Chapdelaine et al. 2001). In the Santa Valley, this artifact is also found, but the emerging impression is that its frequency is much higher in the urban context of the two regional centers of El Castillo and Guadalupito. In other words, spindle whorls are not found on a regular basis on small habitation sites of the Santa Valley, and my educated guess is that they are linked to the state production of good quality textiles, which is similar to the argument that the capital of the Moche had massive production of high-quality ceramics. So textiles, or perhaps some distinctive textiles, can be viewed as urban end products executed with threads obtained from many households.

Lapidary Workshops

Personal adornments are often made of stone, a material that could last a long time, even more than a lifetime. Two small-scale stone workshops have been located and partially excavated in Compounds 12 and 37 (Bernier 2005; Chapdelaine et al. 2004:163–73). Low prestige stone material is dominant at these workshops but it should be stressed that small quantities of turquoise have been identified. This prestigious stone, often found in exquisite mosaic configuration with gold and silver, is a strong status marker in Moche society. It is a rare raw material of unknown origin, but its social importance is obvious. It is worth mentioning the absence at Huacas de Moche of the prestigious *Spondylus* shell, which is used to make small ornaments for the ruling class.

Beer Making

This activity may not be associated with specialists but the presence of several large storage jars (*tinajas*) in one room could be associated with beer brewing. Such concentrations of storage jars have been discovered in Compounds 7, 9, 20, and 37. It is thus possible that the ruler of each large compound was responsible for providing his guests with this ritual maize beer during feasts conducted inside the home.

Herding Camelids

The growing importance of llamas in the middens of each household indicates that these animals, although converted into food, were also very important for their wool and maybe even more valuable for transporting goods inside the valley and beyond (Vásquez et al. 2003). No known corral exists inside the city limits, but it is easy to believe corrals were present on the periphery of the site. Herding is thus a new occupation that might have been carried out by specialists, especially if caravans were established to make long trips on a regular basis.

Figure 9.5. Distinctive Moche ceramic items. *a*, small bowl; *b*, clay mold; *c*, moldmade figurines; *d*, flaring bowl; *e*, *canchero*; *f*, bottle with lateral handle; *g*, neck jar (*cántaro*); *h*, stirrup spout bottle.

Additional Thoughts on Specialization, Domestic Life, and Distribution of Goods

The accumulating data strongly suggest three basic conclusions about specialization and the domestic life at Huacas of Moche: (1) *consumption* of large quantities of manufactured goods are usually the products of specialists; (2) *craft production* existed as a major activity within the inner city; and (3) most goods were *available* for the urban class through an effective distribution system.

The excavation of completely exposed Moche compounds is giving us a new perspective on urbanism and the storage and redistribution of goods. The domestic life of the urban dwellers seems to have been centered within a large multipurpose room (with benches) that acted as the core of the household. This room was probably the place occupied by the leading members of the household. From this large central room with controlled access, one enters small rooms, often with bins or niches, presumably functioning as storage areas.

The size and number of these small rooms indicate without doubt that the household leaders had the right to accumulate wealth in large quantities and this type of storage was not directly controlled by the state. We must add that these leaders were high-rank state officials and that their compounds are also considered to be elite residences (Chapdelaine 2006). It is possible that these urban leaders, living downtown, were strong enough to prevent the construction of state buildings specifically for storing surplus. This type of decentralized storage within the limits of the inner city might be a transitional stage in the development of a more controlling state political economy.

For the redistribution of goods, the informal exchange between urban dwellers and the nearby producers may have taken place near the outskirts of the site or in different sectors of the urban center. Our guess is that the small plazas could have been used for selected types of exchange. This hypothesis gained some strength with the complete excavation of Plaza 3, located east of Compound 26. Evidence for product distribution was encountered in this complex plaza with its niches, storage rooms, and high number of camelids and sea lions (Uceda 2005:299–302; Chiguala 2004). Plaza 3 is thus classified as an open public space with no hearths, with several storage rooms, and with a central area that may have served as a special place to facilitate the distribution of goods.

The exchange system linking segments of the Moche society is still largely unknown, but we do know that finished objects produced in workshops of the urban dwellers were exchanged for staple foods and raw materials with the fishing and farming villages located nearby, and possibly with far-away communities of the Moche Valley and neighboring valleys.

The domestic sphere at Huacas of Moche is characterized by the presence of several types of specialists engaged in mass production. With this large-scale craft production, comprising different specialists and thousands of consumers, Huacas of Moche is indeed a city and the capital of a state.

Social Hierarchy at Huacas of Moche Site

Social hierarchy within Moche society was first illustrated by the Huaca de la Cruz tomb, considered a high-rank official based on several high quality ceramic vessels and other luxurious offerings (Strong and Evans 1952). The Sipán discovery gave the scientific community a vivid picture of what a royal tomb looked like in the Moche world (Alva and Donnan 1993). Social classes became very clear with the identification of the upper class.

Investigations of the social hierarchy at Huacas of Moche site is handicapped by the extensive looting that the Spaniards carried out at the site during the Colonial period, and by the fact that we have not yet discovered an equivalent royal tomb like that seen at Sipán. Although I am convinced that tombs of the royal class existed at the Huacas of Moche site, several social classes could be identified from the enormous database (Bourget 2005; Tello et al. 2003; Millaire 2002; Donnan 1995; Donnan and Mackey 1978).

Social stratification is strongly suggested by funerary patterns. Energy investment in the burial chamber, in body treatment, in offerings, and burial location all indicate the existence of socioeconomic classes but their precise definitions are still debated (Millaire 2002; Chapdelaine 2001; Donnan 2003, 1995; Donnan and Mackey 1978). Portrait vessels could also be used to infer social stratification (Donnan 2004).

Stratification is also visible through internal architectural organization of large compounds. Size varies as well as construction quality (van Gijseghem 2001). Overall, most of the compounds are identified as elite residences and their leaders should belong to an urban class with some economic and sociopolitical differences between its members. These differences are certainly linked to differential access to resources and wealth, which varied among household leaders. The urban class, used here as a concept to group all the inhabitants of the city, was not engaged in the production of staple goods but rather more finished products resulting from the transformation of raw materials (Chapdelaine 2001). Social and economic movements within this urban class are evident and most of its members could be classified as a kind of economic middle class. The urban class played a major role in the conduct of daily state affairs and they may have been political rulers as well.

Distinct economic activities for the excavated compounds at Huacas of Moche are becoming a strong argument for understanding the hierarchy of this urban population. A multifunctional range of activities has been proposed for most of the large and complex compounds. These functions could be domestic, ritual (including feasts), craft production, and administration. Textile production has been proposed for Compound 9, while other specific functions have been identified for Compounds 7 and 27 (metallurgy), Compounds 12 and 37 (lapidary workshops), Compounds 5 and 35 (administration), and Compound 8 (religious elite). The inventories of material culture encountered in these compounds indicate an impressive diversity of artifacts, stressing the strong dichotomy between utilitarian and non-utilitarian artifacts (Chapdelaine 2006; Uceda 2005).

The study of different ceramic categories, especially vessel types, and their proposed functions, is pointing clearly toward the multifunctional nature of most of the compounds. In all the compounds, evidence of domestic activities and storage facilities are the most striking. Most compounds were also used for burials and different types of goods, such as musical instruments and figurines, associated with ritual activities. As noted by Uceda, ceremonies may have been conducted by families and carried on inside these compounds, judging from the high frequencies of figurines. Figurines are not common in most of the excavated burials of the urban zone and from the Huaca de la Luna sector (Uceda 2005:292).

Status differentiation could also be studied through an analysis of faunal data. The differential access to wealth is usually a good indicator. Unfortunately, maize is not well preserved at Huacas of Moche and this key staple food (probably along with a wide array of other plants such as *yuca, camote,* squash, avocado, chili pepper, lima bean, and peanut [see Chapdelaine and Pimentel 2003 for the importance of *yuca* in the Santa Valley]) might indicate the status of a compound's occupants. Also indicative of wealth could be the amount of llama bones and the quantity and diversity of seafoods, taking into account that they must be acquired through an exchange system. In all the excavated compounds, diet is based more on camelids and guinea pigs than on mollusks, birds, and fish (Vásquez et al. 2003). The main staple was probably cultivated plants but given their absence in the archaeological record at the Huacas of Moche, we have to rely on other categories of data. For example, clear differentiation between compounds is provided by the quantity of camelid bones. Thus, we have an incomplete picture and it is very difficult to conclude anything when using only faunal data.

The architecture, burial patterns, material culture, ceramics, and diet all suggest the elite character of these urban dwellers. I agree with Santiago Uceda who, after reviewing the archaeological data of sixteen compounds, states that they are not only residential in nature but are multifunctional and pertaining to a upper-class architecture (Uceda 2005:291). All the evidence gathered over the last fifteen years of excavation argues that the city of Huacas of Moche represented a stratified urban center and the capital of the Southern Moche state.

Ethnicity at the Huacas of Moche Site

In complex societies, social construction is a long process with a continuous mixing of people of various origins who adopt an ethnicity, but within just a few generations, could have been assimilated (Barth 1969; Emberling 1997). On the north coast of Peru, culture change has been constant since the Early Horizon. In a sequential, linear fashion, the Cupisnique culture was replaced by Salinar, followed by Gallinazo and Moche. It is often mentioned that the Moche conquered the Gallinazo,

replacing their elite and assimilating most of the administered population composed of laborers. What can we say of the fate of Cupisnique and Salinar populations? If cultural change was gradual, over several generations, mixed assemblages should have been encountered. This is not the case, and this impression could be a result of too few archaeological projects dedicated to these cultures. Rapid change is often consistent with the intrusion of a new population with a distinctive culture. Although difficult to explain, population movements from an unknown origin are inferred in order to understand the rapid spread of new cultural markers.

In archaeology, we traditionally pursue the identification of the cultural identity of a site's inhabitants by studying the associated material culture, knowing that the non-material side of a culture or an ethnic group could tell much more. If the assemblages composed of ceramic, stone, ivory, bone, and shell objects are homogeneous and most stylistic features could be used as cultural markers, we can identify a specific culture. Shared material culture could thus become ethnic markers along with burial practices and public and domestic architecture (see Janusek 2005). Several scholars have proposed different approaches for looking at ethnic groups within complex societies (Goldstein 2005; Reycraft 2005; Burmeister 2000; Jones 1997; Aldenderfer and Stanish 1993; Stanish 1989).

An innovative approach designed by Burmeister (2000) to study migration and shed light on the emergence of the Anglo-Saxon elite in Great Britain in the middle of the first millennium AD can be used to discuss ethnicity at the Huacas of Moche site. Burmeister proposed a way to look for ethnic groups within a new environment—the private domain—inside houses and burials, arguing that some personal belongings of ethnic significance could be kept for several generations.

Domestic life at Huacas of Moche is now being studied at the household level, and it is worth evaluating Burmeister's assumption that an ethnic group will keep some ethnic markers as long as possible when they are within the boundaries of their house, their most private domain. Most of the data accumulated so far belong to the last centuries of occupation, AD 500–800, and the people under study were living under a *Pax Mochica,* during which time the site entered its final cultural climax, engaged in economic surplus and enjoying the surplus brought from their southern valleys. The presence of exotic goods should have been at its peak with several diplomatic alliances and agreements with neighboring ethnic and polity groups. Unfortunately, that is not what we see in the archaeological record. Instead, although some foreign raw materials could have been brought to the site in large quantities, they were not preserved (for example, raw materials such as camelid wool and colorful feathers). In general, raw materials brought to the site were mostly transformed into Moche style objects. This situation is true for the material culture found in urban compounds as well as for the offerings in burials. As a cautionary tale, the Santa Valley data give a complementary view of Moche contexts where typical highland ceramics are found in very small numbers in refuse while textiles are now frequently found. It seems that foreign ceramics were not attractive to the Moche, but textiles were. Since preservation is not good at Huacas of Moche, textiles are rarely present in our assemblages; it is thus difficult to assess the importance of this category of evidence and more difficult to propose ethnic mixing or frequent interaction and exchange between highland people and coastal Moche (see Lau 2004:191–95 for a Recuay point of view). These highland peoples could be identified as part of the Cajamarca or Recuay cultures.

The other possible ethnic group present at the Huacas of Moche site is the Gallinazo. They were assimilated; their decorated vessels were not produced at grand scale and thus were less visible in the archaeological record, and possibly replaced rapidly by the new and dynamic Moche style. Following Burmeister, it is interesting that some minor Gallinazo types of ceramics were maintained by artisans, not as a private domain, but by making distinctive decorated domestic pottery, the production of which may have been less controlled by Moche state officials. These pots became one way to keep alive their cultural identity or to remember their former cultural identity and group membership.

Knowing that the inhabitants of the urban sector of Huacas of Moche had a very homogeneous material culture, indicating a strong Moche identity, it is our conviction that it was a consequence of a long and successful process of cultural assimilation. Other ethnic markers such as hairstyle, language, religious cult, and other traits that do not become transformed into artifacts could lead to the recognition of a multi-ethnic Moche urban population. For the moment we have to work with available data and it is obvious that the urban occupants of the Huacas of Moche site are a very homogeneous ethnic group. This shared ethnicity might well have allowed a rapid integration of people of different ethnic origin in the making of a strong, centralized, and possibly coercive state.

For the moment, we can suggest that the assimilation of ethnic groups was completed by the beginning of Moche Phase IV and that either Gallinazo or other coastal groups and highland groups were living as Moche in the capital city. Even within their private domain, inside a household room or a burial chamber, these ethnic groups did not use an ethnic marker to indicate they were originally of non-Moche origin. We lack this type of evidence in the five completely exposed large residential compounds we excavated and in more than a hundred carefully excavated individual burials at the Huacas of Moche site.

However, keeping in mind that ethnic groups could have been living within the limits of the Huacas of Moche site, it is also strongly possible that they were established away from the downtown where most of the excavated compounds are located. Even if we believe that the capital city of the Southern Moche state was occupied by multi-ethnic groups dominated by Moche material culture, the power of assimilation was strong enough to eliminate most of the visible ethnic markers of these coastal and highland populations. But they all share for several generations a

phenomenal success with the *Pax Mochica* and the development of a Moche identity.

The material culture approach could be complemented by other approaches, in particular the biological approach with mtDNA analysis. Recent studies shed some light on the biological relations between different Moche centers and are relevant for us since there is a relationship between sacrificial victims and normally interred individuals in several locations at the Huacas of Moche site (Shimada et al. 2005; Sutter and Cortez 2005).

The sacrificial site excavated in front of Platform II in the Huaca de la Luna complex contained close to 70 individuals, all males between 15 and 40 years old (Bourget 2005, 2001, 1998). The origins of these sacrificial victims have been the center of a debate, which is linked to the nature of Moche sociopolitical organization (see Quilter 2002). Warfare is often viewed as a consequence of a state's expansionist character. From the perspective of the predatory Southern Moche state, three options were likely: (1) the victims were from different valleys controlled by the Moche, including the possibility that they were members of the Moche ethnic group; (2) the victims were taken from the Huacas of Moche site or from communities of the Moche Valley, making it an intra-valley affair; and (3) the victims are non-Moche, enemies captured during expansionist wars. The mtDNA results are quite surprising when we compare the mtDNA of victims in the Huaca de la Luna burials to those from the Urban Sector. Shimada and his collaborators favor the second option: "Given that even small samples of Mochica burials at Sipan and El Brujo show much more haplotype variability than the Huaca de la Luna sample, we must also consider the possibility that the sacrificed individuals at Huaca de la Luna all pertained to the same select local population (e.g. an exclusive elite male society) as the sacrificers and other relatively high-status residents at the site of Moche. In other words, we suggest that, at least for the sacrifices documented by Bourget in Plaza 3A, victims may have been selected through Moche Valley-wide intragroup ritual combats" (Shimada et al. 2005:80).

The mtDNA results support the material culture; that is, both suggest a surprising genetic homogeneity of the urban occupants. However, analysis of bio-distances of dental traits on 545 individuals from different sites, including the victims from Huaca de la Luna Plaza 3A, provides a different conclusion. The results indicate that the sacrificial victims differ significantly from the other selected samples and that they were drawn from a number of competing Moche polities (Sutter and Cortez 2005:530). These data complement the mtDNA and support the first option, which saw the victims as coming from outside the Moche Valley but pertaining to the Moche ethnic group. However, the nature of these bioarchaeological approaches is complex and new studies must be performed as well as other new techniques such as strontium and oxygen isotopic analysis (which have been used successfully at Teotihuacan [Price et al. 2000]). The Moche case is ripe for their application.

Conclusion

Given that Huacas of Moche is a city with a clear urban layout—with streets, plazas, public buildings, mixed residential and workshop compounds—the domestic life of these city dwellers can be understood only by constructing a strong link between them and the rural groups they depended upon, people who brought food and raw materials to the city where they could be transformed into finished products. Marine resources of the Pacific Ocean are only 5 km away, an easy walk on flat terrain.

Our view of Huacas of Moche is that its inner city was occupied by privileged people engaged in specific tasks that complemented the needs of people living outside the city, but within a 10 km radius. The outer city is much bigger and transportation was facilitated by flat topography, existing foot trails maintained by the state, and the growing importance of llamas linking those living downtown to their neighbors living in the periphery. Any discussion of domestic life at the capital city of the Southern Moche state must take into account the complementary relationship between the visible urban center and the less visible smaller communities nearby; they acted in tandem for the success of this great civilization, which featured the monumental Huacas del Sol and de la Luna.

The site was definitely the core of most activities related to the domestic sphere. The urban occupants, who also played a major role in political and religious domains, were engaged in various economic activities. Numerous workshops have been identified, most of them assumed to be small to medium in size, which is not what we were expecting given the mass production of finished objects within most states' political economy. The area between the two huacas, the urban sector, has revealed several compounds and large tracts yet to be excavated. It may take another twenty years to uncover the full diversity of activities that took place in these compounds, but we already have enough data to argue that this was a unique city with streets, plazas, public buildings, cemeteries, and complex multifunctional compounds. We have been excavating what was probably the first real city on the north coast of Peru.

The material culture showing that a homogeneous ethnic group occupied the Moche capital is supported by recent mtDNA analysis. Other evidence, however, seems to alter this view of great ethnic homogeneity, but future work should help resolve this complex issue. Since the Moche were not alone and the Southern Moche state was expansionist, it is obvious that members of other ethnic groups such as the coastal Gallinazo and highlanders of the Cajamarca and Recuay cultures were involved directly with this predatory polity. We can only assume that the assimilation and integration of these other ethnic groups into Moche culture was rapid because these outsiders left very few traces in the archaeological record. It is worth mentioning that the last layers of occupation (or Moche Phase IV) should be more homogeneous because that era witnessed the consolidation of the territorial state as the state reached its climax. We are tempted to suggest that the Moche Phase III layers could eventually reveal more cultural heterogeneity but lack of data from those layers prevents our being able to support this suggestion at present.

The urban class residing at Huacas of Moche, dwelling in the core but with strong links to the periphery or hinterland, worked hard for the development and maintenance of the Southern Moche state. This state was able to maintain itself for about 500 years, quite an accomplishment among civilizations.

References

Aldenderfer, Mark, and Charles Stanish
1993 Domestic architecture, household archaeology, and the past in the south-central Andes. In *Domestic Architecture, Ethnicity, and Complementarity in the South-Central Andes*, edited by Mark Aldenderfer, pp. 1–12. University of Iowa Press, Iowa City.

Alva, Walter
1994 *Sipán, Descubrimiento e Investigación*. Colección Cultura y Artes del Antiguo Perú, Lima.

Alva, Walter, and Christopher B. Donnan
1993 *Royal Tombs of Sipan*. Fowler Museum of Cultural History, UCLA.

Barth, Fredrik
1969 *Ethnic Groups and Boundaries: The Social Organization of Culture Difference*. Little, Brown and Company, Boston.

Bawden, Garth
1996 *The Moche*. Blackwell Publishers, London.
2004 The art of Moche politics. In *Andean Archaeology*, edited by Helaine Silverman, pp. 116–29. Blackwell Publishers, London.

Bernier, H.
2005 *Étude archéologique de la production artisanale spécialisée au site Huacas de Moche, côte nord du Pérou*. PhD dissertation, Department of Anthropology, Université de Montréal.

Billman, Brian
1996 *Prehistoric Political Organization in the Moche Valley, Peru*. PhD dissertation, Department of Anthropology, University of California, Santa Barbara.
1997 Population pressure and the origins of warfare in the Moche Valley, Peru. In *Integrating Archaeological Demography: Multidisciplinary Approaches to Prehistoric Populations*, edited by R.R. Paine, pp. 285–310. Occasional Paper 24. Center for Archaeological Investigations, Carbondale.
2002 Irrigation and the origins of the Southern Moche state on the north coast of Peru. *Latin American Antiquity* 13(4):371–400.

Bonavia, Duccio
1982 *Precerámico Peruano: Los Gavilanes, Mar, Desierto y Oasis en la Historia del Hombre*. Corporación de Financiera de Desarrollo S.A, COFIDE and Instituto Arqueológico Alemán, Lima, Perú.

Bourget, Steve
1998   Pratiques sacrificielles et funéraires au site Moche de la Huaca de la Luna, côte nord du Pérou. *Bulletin de l'Institut français d'études andines* 27(1):41–74.
2001   Children and ancestors: Ritual practices at the Moche site of Huaca de la Luna, north coast of Peru. In *Ritual Sacrifice in Ancient Peru*, edited by Elizabeth Benson and Anita Cook, pp. 93–118. University of Texas Press, Austin.
2003   Somos diferentes: dinámica ocupacional del sitio Castillo de Huancaco, valle de Virú. In *Moche: Hacia el final del milenio*, Tomo I, edited by S. Uceda and E. Mujica, pp. 245–67. Actas del Segundo Coloquio sobre la Cultura Moche. Universidad Nacional de Trujillo and Pontificia Universidad Católica del Perú, Lima.
2004   A Case of Mistaken Identity? The Moche Presence in the Viru Valley. Paper presented at the 69th Annual SAA Meeting, Montreal (e-paper at www.anthro.umontreal.ca).
2005   Who were the priests, the warriors, and the prisoners? A peculiar problem of identity in Moche culture and iconography, north coast of Peru. In *Us and Them: Archaeology and Ethnicity in the Andes*, edited by Richard M. Reycraft, pp. 73–85. Monograph 53. Cotsen Institute of Archaeology, UCLA.

Burmeister, Stefan
2000   Archaeology and migration. *Current Anthropology* 41(4):539–67.

Castillo, Luis Jaime, and Christopher B. Donnan
1994   Los Mochica del Norte y los Mochica del Sur. In *Vicús*, edited by Krzystof Makowski et al., pp. 143–76. Banco de Crédito del Perú, Lima.

Chapdelaine, Claude
1997   Le tissu urbain du site Moche, une cité péruvienne précolombienne. In *À l'ombre du Cerro Blanco. Nouvelles découvertes sur le site Moche, Côte nord du Pérou*, edited by Claude Chapdelaine, pp. 11–81. Les Cahiers d'anthropologie no. 1. Université de Montréal, Montréal.
1998   Excavaciones en la zona urbana Moche durante 1996. In *Investigaciones Huaca de la Luna 1996*, edited by S. Uceda, E. Mujica, and R. Morales, pp. 85–115. Facultad de Ciencias Sociales, Universidad Nacional de Trujillo, Perú.
2000   Struggling for survival: The urban class of the Moche site, north coast of Peru. In *Environmental Disaster and the Archaeology of Human Response*, edited by Garth Bawden and Richard M. Reycraft, pp. 121–42. Anthropological Papers no. 7. Maxwell Museum of Anthropology, Albuquerque, New Mexico.
2001   The growing power of a Moche urban class. In *Moche: Art and Political Representation in Ancient Peru*, edited by Joanne Pillsbury, pp. 69–87. National Gallery of Art, Washington, D.C.
2002   Out in the streets of Moche: Urbanism and socio-political organization at a Moche IV urban center. In *Advances in Andean Archaeology and Ethnohistory*, edited by William Isbell and Helaine Silverman, pp. 53–88. Plenum Press, New York.
2003   La Ciudad de Moche: Urbanismo y Estado. In *Moche: Hacia el final del milenio*, Tomo II, edited by S. Uceda and E. Mujica, pp. 247–85. Actas del Segundo Coloquio sobre la Cultura Moche. Universidad Nacional de Trujillo and Pontificia Universidad Católica del Perú, Lima.
2006   Looking for Moche palaces in the elite residences of the Huacas of Moche site. In *Palaces and Power in the Americas: From Peru to the Northwest Coast*, edited by J. Christie and P. Sharro, pp. 23–43. University of Texas Press, Austin.

Chapdelaine, C., H. Bernier, and V. Pimentel
2004   Investigaciones en la Zona Urbana Moche, temporadas 1998 y 1999. In *Investigaciones en la Huaca de la Luna 1998–1999*, edited by S. Uceda, E. Mujica, and R. Morales, pp. 123–201. Facultad de Ciencias Sociales, Universidad Nacional de Trujillo, Perú.

Chapdelaine, C., G. Kennedy, and S. Uceda
2001   Neutron activation analysis of metal artifacts from the Moche site, north coast of Peru. *Archaeometry* 43(3):373–91.

Chapdelaine, C., J.-F. Millaire, and G. Kennedy
2001   Compositional analysis and provenance study of spindle whorls from the Moche site, north coast of Peru. *Journal of Archaeological Science* 28:795–806.

Chapdelaine, C., and V. Pimentel
2001   Informe del Proyecto Arqueológico PSUM (Proyecto Santa de la Universidad de Montreal) 2000: *La presencia Moche en el valle del Santa, Costa Norte del Perú*. Informe sometido al Instituto Nacional de la Cultura, Lima, Perú. http://www.mapageweb.umontreal.ca/chapdelc.
2002   Informe del Proyecto Arqueológico PSUM (Proyecto Santa de la Universidad de Montreal) 2001: *La presencia Moche en el valle del Santa, Costa Norte del Perú*. Informe sometido al Instituto Nacional de la Cultura, Lima, Perú. http://www.mapageweb.umontreal.ca/chapdelc.
2003   Un tejido único Moche III del sitio Castillo de Santa: Una escena de cosecha de yuca. *Bulletin de l'Institut français d'études andines* 32(1):23–50.

Chapdelaine, C., V. Pimentel, and Hélène Bernier
2001   A glimpse at Moche Phase III occupation at the Huacas of Moche site, northern Peru. *Antiquity* 75:361–72.
2003   Informe del Proyecto Arqueológico PSUM (Proyecto Santa de la Universidad de Montreal) 2002: *La presencia Moche en el valle del Santa, Costa Norte del Perú*. Informe sometido al Instituto Nacional de la Cultura, Lima, Perú. http://www.mapageweb.umontreal.ca/chapdelc.

Chapdelaine, C., V. Pimentel, and J. Gamboa
2005   Contextos funerarios Moche del sitio El Castillo de Santa: una primera aproximación. In *Corriente Arqueológica. Muerte y evidencias funerarias en los Andes Centrales: Avances y perspectivas*, no. 1, edited by C. Olaya and M. Romero, pp. 13–41. Universidad Nacional Federico Villarreal, Lima, Perú.

Chapdelaine, C., V. Pimentel, G. Gagné, J. Gamboa, D. Regalado, and D. Chicoine
2004   Nuevos datos sobre Huaca China, Valle de Santa, Perú. *Bulletin de l'Institut français d'études andines* 33(1):55–80.

Chiguala, J.
2004   La Plaza 3. In *Proyecto Arqueológico Huaca de la Luna, Informe técnico 2004*, edited by Santiago Uceda and Ricardo Morales, pp. 153–74. Facultad de Ciencias Sociales, Universidad Nacional de Trujillo, Perú.

Costin, Cathy L., and Melissa B. Hagstrum
1996   Standardization, labor investment, skill, and the organization of ceramic production in late prehispanic highland Peru. *American Antiquity* 60(4):619–39.

Donnan, Christopher B.
1995 Moche mortuary practice. In *Tombs for the Living: Andean Mortuary Practices*, edited by Tom Dillehay, pp. 111–59. Dumbarton Oaks Research Library and Collection, Washington, D.C.
2003 Tumbas con entierros en miniaturas: un nuevo tipo funerario Moche. In *Moche: Hacia el final del milenio*, Tomo I, edited by S. Uceda and E. Mujica, pp. 43–78. Actas del Segundo Coloquio sobre la Cultura Moche. Universidad Nacional de Trujillo and Pontificia Universidad Católica del Perú, Lima.
2004 *Moche Portraits from Ancient Peru*. University of Texas Press, Austin.

Donnan, Christopher B., and Carol J. Mackey
1978 *Ancient Burial Patterns of the Moche Valley, Peru*. University of Texas Press, Austin.

Eerkens, Jelmer W., and Robert L. Bettinger
2001 Techniques for assessing standardization in artifact assemblages: Can we scale material variability? *American Antiquity* 66(3):493–504.

Emberling, Geoff
1997 Ethnicity in complex societies: Archaeological perspectives. *Journal of Archaeological Research* 5(4):295–344.

Franco, R., C. Gálvez, and S. Vásquez
2003 Modelos, función y cronología de la Huaca Cao Viejo, complejo El Brujo. In *Moche: Hacia el final del milenio*, Tomo II, edited by S. Uceda and E. Mujica, pp. 125–78. Actas del Segundo Coloquio sobre la Cultura Moche. Universidad Nacional de Trujillo and Pontificia Universidad Católica del Perú, Lima.

Goldstein, Paul S.
2005 *Andean Diaspora, The Tiwanaku Colonies and the Origins of South American Empire*. University Press of Florida, Gainesville.

Janusek, John W.
2005 Of pots and people: Ceramic style and social identity in the Tiwanaku state. In *Us and Them: Archaeology and Ethnicity in the Andes*, edited by Richard M. Reycraft, pp. 34–53. Monograph 53. Cotsen Institute of Archaeology, UCLA.

Jara, G.
1999 *Producción de vasijas domésticas en un taller alfarero Moche en la falda noreste de Cerro Blanco, valle de Moche*. Proyecto de Licenciatura, Facultad de Ciencias Sociales, Universidad Nacional de Trujillo, Perú.

Jones, Sian
1997 *The Archaeology of Ethnicity, Constructing Identities in the Past and Present*. Routledge Press, London.

Larco Hoyle, Rafael
1948 *Cronología Arqueológica del Norte del Perú*. Sociedad Geográfica Americana, Buenos Aires.
2001 *Los Mochicas*. 2 tomos. Museo Arqueológico Rafael Larco Herrera, Lima, Perú.

Lau, George F.
2004 The Recuay culture of Peru's north-central highlands: A reappraisal of chronology and its implications. *Journal of Field Archaeology* 29(1–2):177–202.

Longacre, William A.
1999 Standardization and specialization: What's the link? In *Pottery and People, A Dynamic Interaction*, edited by James M. Skibo and Gary M. Feinman, pp. 44–58. University of Utah Press, Salt Lake City.

Marcus, Joyce
1983 On the nature of the Mesoamerican city. In *Prehistoric Settlement Patterns, Essays in Honor of Gordon R. Willey*, edited by Evon Z. Vogt and Richard M. Leventhal, pp. 195–242. University of New Mexico Press and Peabody Museum of Archaeology and Ethnology, Harvard University, Cambridge.

Millaire, Jean-François
2002 *Moche Burial Patterns. An Investigation into Prehispanic Social Structure*. BAR International Series 1066. BAR, Oxford.
2004 Gallinazo-Moche Interactions at Huaca Santa Clara, Viru Valley, North Coast of Peru. Paper presented at the 69th Annual SAA Meeting, Montreal (e-paper at www.anthro.umontreal.ca).

Moseley, Michael E.
1992 *The Incas and their Ancestors*. Thames and Hudson, New York.

Price, T. Douglas, Linda Manzanilla, and William D. Middleton
2000 Immigration and the ancient city of Teotihuacan in Mexico: A study of strontium isotope ratios in human bone and teeth. *Journal of Archaeological Science* 27:903–13.

Prümers, Heiko
2000 "El Castillo" de Huarmey: Una plataforma funeraria del Horizonte Medio. *Boletín de Arqueología PUCP* 4:289–312.

Przadka, Patrycja, and Milosz Giresz
2003 *Sitios Arqueológicos de la zona del Valle de Culebras*, Vol. 1. Valle Bajo. Sociedad Polaca de Estudios Latinoamericanos, Varsovia.

Quilter, Jeffrey
2002 Moche politics, religion, and warfare. *Journal of World Prehistory* 16(2):145–95.

Rengifo, Carlos, and Carol Rojas
2005 Especialistas y centros de producción en el complejo arqueológico Huacas de Moche: evidencias de un taller orfebre. In *Proyecto Arqueológico Huaca de la Luna, Informe técnico 2004*, edited by S. Uceda and R. Morales, pp. 377–90. Facultad de Ciencias Sociales, Universidad Nacional de Trujillo, Perú.

Reycraft, Richard M. (editor)
2005 *Us and Them: Archaeology and Ethnicity in the Andes*. Monograph 53. Cotsen Institute of Archaeology, UCLA.

Roselló, E., V. Vásquez, A. Morales, and T. Rosales
2001 Marine resources from an urban Moche (470–600 AD) area in the Huacas del Sol y de la Luna archaeological complex, Trujillo, Peru. *International Journal of Osteoarchaeology* 11:72–87.

Shimada, Izumi
1994 *Pampa Grande and the Mochica Culture*. University of Texas Press, Austin.

Shimada, I., S. Ken-ichi, S. Bourget, W. Alva, and S. Uceda
2005   mtDNA analysis of Mochica and Sican populations of pre-Hispanic Peru. In *Biomolecular Archaeology Genetic Approaches to the Past*, edited by David Reed, pp. 61–92. Occasional Paper no. 32. Center for Archaeological Investigations, Southern Illinois University, Carbondale.

Stanish, Charles
1989   Household archeology: Testing models of zonal complementarity in the south central Andes. *American Anthropologist* 91(1):7–24.
2005   Discussion: Migration, colonies, and ethnicity in the south-central Andes. In *Us and Them: Archaeology and Ethnicity in the Andes*, edited by Richard M. Reycraft, pp. 226–32. Monograph 53. Cotsen Institute of Archaeology, UCLA.

Strong, William D., and Clifford Evans
1952   *Cultural Stratigraphy in the Viru Valley, Northern Peru: The Formative and Florescent Epoch*. Columbia Studies in Archaeology and Ethnology 4. Columbia University Press, New York.

Sutter, Richard C., and R.J. Cortez
2005   The nature of Moche human sacrifice, a bio-archaeological perspective. *Current Anthropology* 46(4):521–49.

Tello, R., J. Armas, and C. Chapdelaine
2003   Prácticas funerarias Moche en el complejo arqueológico Huacas del Sol y de la Luna. In *Moche: Hacia el final del milenio*, Tomo I, edited by S. Uceda and E. Mujica, pp. 151–87. Actas del Segundo Coloquio sobre la Cultura Moche, Universidad Nacional de Trujillo and Pontificia Universidad Católica del Perú, Lima.

Uceda, Santiago
2001   Investigations at Huaca de la Luna, Moche Valley: An example of Moche religious architecture. In *Moche: Art and Political Representation in Ancient Peru*, edited by Joanne Pillsbury, pp. 47–68. National Gallery of Art, Washington, D.C.
2005   Los de arriba y los de abajo: relaciones sociales, políticas y económicas entre el templo y los habitantes en el núcleo urbano de las Huacas de Moche. In *Proyecto Arqueológico Huaca de la Luna, Informe técnico 2004*, edited by S. Uceda and R. Morales, pp. 283–318. Facultad de Ciencias Sociales, Universidad Nacional de Trujillo, Perú.

Uceda, S., and J. Canziani
1998   Análisis de la secuencia arquitectónica y nuevas perspectivas de investigación en la Huaca de la Luna. In *Investigaciones en la Huaca de la Luna 1996*, edited by S. Uceda, E. Mujica, and R. Morales, pp. 139–58. Facultad de Ciencias Sociales, Universidad Nacional de Trujillo, Perú.

Uceda, S., and C. Chapdelaine
1998   El Centro Urbano de las Huacas del Sol y la Luna. *Arkinka* 33:94–103.

Uceda, S., C. Chapdelaine, C. Chauchat, and J. Verano
2001   Fechas Radiocarbónicas para el Complejo Arqueológico Huacas del Sol y La Luna: Una primera cronología del sitio. In *Investigaciones en la Huaca de la Luna*, edited by S. Uceda, E. Mujica, and R. Morales, pp. 215–25. Facultad de Ciencias Sociales, Universidad Nacional de Trujillo, Perú.

Uceda, S., and R. Morales
2004   *Proyecto Arqueológico Huaca de la Luna, Informe técnico 2003*. Facultad de Ciencias Sociales, Universidad Nacional de Trujillo, Perú.
2005   *Proyecto Arqueológico Huaca de la Luna, Informe técnico 2004*. Facultad de Ciencias Sociales, Universidad Nacional de Trujillo, Perú.

Uceda, S., and E. Mujica (editors)
2003   *Moche: Hacia el final del milenio*. 2 vols. Actas del Segundo Coloquio sobre la Cultura Moche. Universidad Nacional de Trujillo and Pontificia Universidad Católica del Perú, Lima.

Uceda, Santiago, and Carlos Rengifo
2006   La especialización del trabajo: teoría y arqueología. El caso de los orfebres Mochicas. *Bulletin de l'Institut Français d'Études Andines* 35(2):149–85.

Van Gijseghem, Hendrik
2001   Household and family at Moche, Peru: An analysis of building and residence patterns in a prehispanic urban center. *Latin American Antiquity* 12(3):257–73.

Vásquez, V., T. Rosales, A. Morales, and E. Roselló
2003   Zooarqueología de la zona urbana Moche, complejo Huacas del Sol y de la Luna, valle de Moche. In *Moche: Hacia el final del milenio*, Tomo II, edited by S. Uceda and E. Mujica, pp. 33–64. Actas del Segundo Coloquio sobre la Cultura Moche. Universidad Nacional de Trujillo and Pontificia Universidad Católica del Perú, Lima.

Wilson, David J.
1988   *Prehispanic Settlement Patterns in the Lower Santa Valley, Peru: A Regional Perspective on the Origins and Development of Complex North Coast Society*, Smithsonian Institution Press, Washington, D.C.

10

Huari: A New Direction in Central Andean Urban Evolution

William H. Isbell

Introduction

The ruins of Huari[1] sprawl across several square kilometers of highland Peru's Ayacucho Valley (Fig. 10.1). Deep middens with millions of sherds testify to dense habitation in the ancient city. Great walls, complex architectural outlines, and dressed stones hint at its magnitude. Huari's distinctive art spread over a vast territory, demonstrating its prestige and power. Clearly, Huari is among the principal participants in the Central Andean urban process, although it remains one of the least investigated of the ancient world's great capital cities.

This discussion is pieced together from the archaeology of several sites in the Ayacucho Valley, necessary because the early stages of development at Huari itself are so poorly known. The evolutionary account is complex, composed of a sequence of changes that profoundly modified the trajectory of city and state development in the central Andes, a change whose principal features probably endured until the Spanish conquest. First, the location of Ayacucho's central settlements shifted from hilltops with walled ceremonial centers like Ñawinpukyo, and Huari's antecedent, Cerro Churucana, to intermediate, flatter elevation ridges along a steep-sided canyon with lush valley-bottom below. This was probably due in large part to new irrigation technology, particularly the ability to engineer long and difficult canals, combined with the political skills required for organizing vast labor contingents to dig and manage them. With this change, cities became large population centers with permanent residents.

More or less as central settlements shifted from hilltops to lower-elevation ridges, the built environment also changed. Walled centers with ceremonial and administrative buildings clustered around a nuclear plaza were replaced by rambling settlements composed of walled compounds with interior courtyards and room complexes. The central plaza (and indeed, any apparent settlement focus) disappeared, replaced by communities composed of one or more—and in the Ayacucho Valley heartland, usually many—large building enclosures so strictly organized within that they were named "orthogonal cellular" architecture (Isbell 1991). This spatial change seems to be the materialization of a new kind of social organization dominated by "great houses" (Joyce and Gillespie 2000) that promoted a hierarchical social system of classes.

The built environment was not the only domain involved in the evolutionary transformation. Material culture, and especially ceramics used in the preparation and serving of food and drink, experienced change, developing broadly distributed new forms that surely imply the emergence of a new, international identity associated with Huari as a capital city.

Archaeological investigations at Huari were paralyzed from 1980 through the mid-1990s by Peru's *Sendero Luminoso* war, but breakthrough insights occurred as a result of a 1985 symposium.

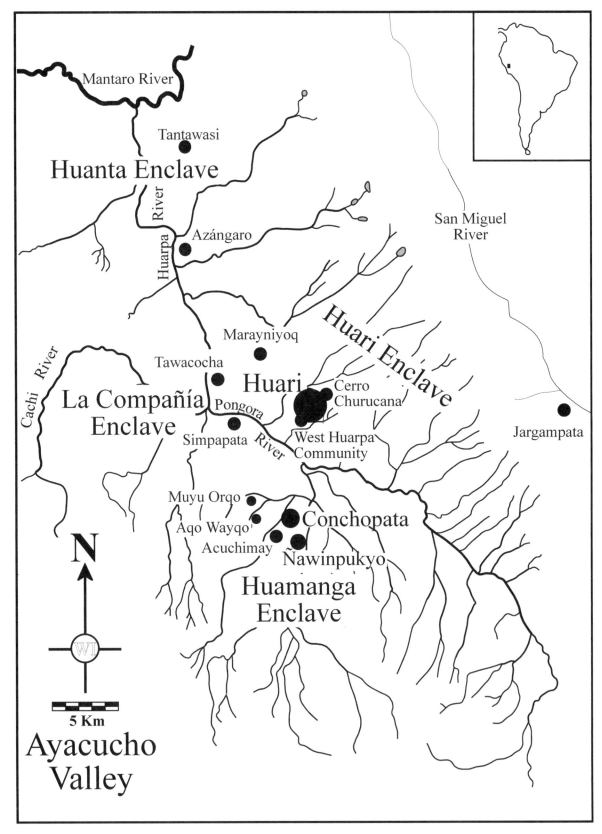

Figure 10.1. Ayacucho Valley, Peru, locating principal archaeological sites.

Great rectangular compounds, and their "orthogonal cellular" style, were recognized as the material culture most diagnostic of Huari and the "Middle Horizon" created by its expansionism (Isbell and McEwan 1991; see also Isbell 1997, 2001a). More recent conferences have led to the examination of rectangular Wari compounds as palaces (Isbell 2004b; see also Isbell 2006).

Excavations at Huari have provided important information about the Vegachayoq Moqo sector (Bragayrac 1991; González and Bragayrac 1986; González et al. 1996; Pérez 2002) and neighboring Monjachayoq (Solano and Guerrero 1981), further investigated by Ismael Pérez (1998b, 1999, 2001, 2002). Mario Benavides (1991) studied Cheqo Wasi, and Isbell dug Moraduchayuq and sampled several other areas (Isbell 1997; Isbell et al. 1991). A 2005–2006 contract project[2] explored the road cut of the highway bulldozed through Huari in 1973–1974. Research has also been conducted at the sites of Conchopata (Cook and Benco 2001; Isbell 2001b, 2004a; Isbell and Cook 2002; Lumbreras 1974, 1981; Pérez 1998a; Pérez and Ochatoma 1998; Ochatoma 2005; Ochatoma and Cabrera 1999, 2000, 2001a, 2001b, 2001c, 2001d, 2002; Pozzi Escot 1985, 1991; Tung and Cook 2006), Ñawinpukyo (Cabrera 1998; Leoni 2004, 2005, 2006; Machaca 1997), and Aqo Wayqo (Cabrera 1996; Ochatoma 1988; Ochatoma and Cabrera 2001d), as they have been threatened, and then destroyed, by expansion of the modern city of Ayacucho. Conchopata was the second city in the Ayacucho Valley during Huari's ascendancy, while Ñawinpukyo was one of the principal ceremonial centers during its early rise. Aqo Wayqo may have been a farming community, but more probably it was something like a villa of elites.

As field work furnished new information about Huari's urban landscape, a theoretical breakthrough established new understandings of its great architectural enclosures. Lévi-Strauss (1982, 1987, 1991) demonstrated the importance of the "house" for the evolution of kinship organization into class structure. "House societies," composed of "great houses," were explored cross-culturally (see Carsten and Hugh-Jones 1995) and theorized by anthropologists and archaeologists (Gillespie 2000a, 2000b, 2000c; Joyce 2000; Kirch 2000; Marshall 2000; McKinnon 2000; Sandstrom 2000; Tringham 2000; Waterson 2000).

Prehistorians now understand great houses as corporate social units that are often materialized in impressive buildings (Marshall 2000; Waterson 2000), sometimes a palace. Cross-culturally, house societies tend to employ a kinship idiom, but recruitment to houses is much more permissive, often including any cognatic link, affinal ties, and even fictional kinship when prospective members behave like kin and are viewed as valuable additions to the group. The flexibility of recruitment and the emphasis on successful social strategies make great houses extremely durable. They compete with other houses, accumulating estates, titles, privileges, and property. In a context of increasing wealth, house-societies promote social inequality, creating gradations in wealth and power that lead to class structure and formal hierarchy.

Gillespie (2000a, 2000b) and Joyce (2000) show that great houses emphasize ancestors, burying the most important dead in, or near, the residence (Kirch 2000). Houses host feasts and present ritual performances, competing among themselves for relative status (Marshall 2000). Social memory is created in ways that integrate the building with its residents (Tringham 2000), often employing innovative symbols as well as heirlooms and ornaments with complex social biographies to confirm privilege and promote differences in rank (Joyce 2000).

As cross-cultural studies identified features of house societies, Andean archaeologists determined the nature of Wari orthogonal compounds (Isbell 1991, 1997, 2001b, 2001c; Jennings and Craig 2001[3]; Schreiber 1992). They revealed feasting and competitive drinking bouts as key activities in Wari architectural spaces (Cook and Glowacki 2003; Isbell 1985). Elite mortuary rooms were discovered within orthogonal compounds (Isbell 2001b, 2004c), and Wari scholars demonstrated the appropriation of hierarchical SAIS[4] iconography for communicating new status distinctions (Cook 1994; Isbell and Cook 1987; Isbell and Knobloch 2006; Knobloch 1989; Makowski 2000). Ornaments and heirlooms that were deployed in Wari rituals (Cook 1992, 2001a, 2001b) and new offering practices that mark architectural spaces have been described (Groleau 2005; Isbell and Groleau, in press). "House society" provides a valuable tool for understanding Huari, and "great houses" will help explain its urban processes.

Chronological Framework for Huari Urbanization

Peruvian archaeology employs a chronology of time periods (Rowe 1962). The most important for tracing the development of Huari are the Early Horizon (1000–200 BC), the Early Intermediate period (200 BC–AD 650), and the Middle Horizon (AD 650–1000). In earlier discussions of Huari cultural evolution, five phases were employed, based primarily on architectural changes within the capital that are more or less synchronized with the general Peruvian chronology (Isbell 1997, 2001a; Isbell et al. 1991) as follows.

Churucana	1200–200 BC
Vista Alegre	200 BC–AD 500
Quebrada de Ocros	AD 500–650
Moraduchayuq	AD 650–800
Royac Perja	AD 800–1000

Radiocarbon dates have not been calibrated. In Peruvian archaeology, the general chronology continues using uncalibrated dates, although this is changing quickly. A reevaluation of Huari (and Wari) dates for a calibrated re-dating of the Middle Horizon is much needed but it will require a lengthy work, greatly beyond the scope of this summary paper.

Emergence of House Society Organization:
The Churucana and Vista Alegre Phases

Located in Peru's central highlands (Fig. 10.1), the Ayacucho Valley ranges in elevation from about 2,000 to 4,000 m above sea level. During Churucana times, the valley boasted several modest ceremonial centers composed of a terraced mound, level plaza, and little residential debris. At this time, the only occupation known within the Huari archaeological zone was on the high and rounded hill of Cerro Churucana (Fig. 10.1). Wichqana-style pottery of the first millennium BC (Ochatoma and Cabrera 1998: Fig. 3) appears under 1.4 m of refuse with Huarpa-style pottery, and 10 cm of mixed Huarpa and Huari ceramics at the surface. Little can be said about the size of this oldest settlement, although Vista Alegre phase pottery of Huarpa style, as well as scattered stone from prehistoric constructions, is distributed over at least 5 ha, implying a substantial settlement during at least the second phase. By that time, the community may have reached a population of 1,000–2,000 persons, probably making it the central settlement of an early Huari enclave.

With no Vista Alegre phase architecture at Cerro Churucana, we can examine contemporary Ñawinpukyo, located on a similar hilltop about 15 km to the south, in the Huamanga enclave, for a sense of the form and development of early Ayacucho central settlements. In all probability, the two were competitors.

During Vista Alegre times, Ñawinpukyo's summit was encircled by a stone wall (about one m thick) that enclosed an area of about a half hectare (Figs. 10.1, 10.2A; Leoni 2004, 2005, 2006). Traces of walls lower on the slope suggest the summit may have been surrounded by several concentric circles. A broad opening is located in the southwest corner of the top enclosure, probably an entrance into a more or less vacant "plaza" area. Test excavations in rubble concentrations along the inside edge of the wall show that numerous buildings, circular and rectangular, were constructed against it. A considerable amount of broken pottery implies intensive use of the space, probably ceremonial and residential.

One well-preserved and almost entirely excavated building was prominently placed near the center of the plaza (Fig. 10.2B). It was round, with three concentric walls. Its narrow doorway faces the important snow-capped mountain peak of Rasuwillka; under its floor were concentrations of llama bones, suggesting animal sacrifice followed by feasting.

About 100 m west of the plaza, Juan Leoni (2004:195–97, Figs. 6.1, 6.11) excavated traces of a residential compound (Fig. 10.2C), rectangular in form, that was both larger and more complex than anything formerly known in Ayacucho. Although incomplete, it appears to have been orthogonal, stone-walled, and planned in advance. Apparently some Vista Alegre residents were not content with modest nuclear family homes, and this new building type probably represents an important early step in the evolution of great houses.

Additional research is needed to detail the autochthonous developmental trajectory of orthogonal compounds in Ayacucho,

beginning in late Vista Alegre times. Unfortunately, Ñawinpukyo has been invaded by modern residents. At Huari, low-elevation Vista Alegre settlements complement the large community on Cerro Churucana. Most were probably hamlets lacking substantial architecture, but a large and permanent village had appeared in the southwest portion of Huari's archaeological zone. Named the "West Huarpa Community," a dense midden with Huarpa ceramics was exposed in the 1973 highway cut, and destroyed before construction was completed (Fig. 10.3). Today, for some 50 m east, along the road cut, there are 3 to 4 m of stratified architectural remains that appear to have begun in Vista Alegre or very early Quebrada de Ocros times. A test excavation on the north side of the highway revealed small residential rooms constructed in a series of additions, of the kind I call "cumulative architecture," as opposed to planned orthogonal architecture (Isbell et al. 1991). However, deeply buried chambers on the south side of the highway are probably sub-floor tombs for elites of some status. Excavations in 2005–2006 revealed architecture above that includes domestic rooms and a little D-shaped building, but contract goals did not allow archaeologists to define larger patterns, such as compound enclosures. Nevertheless, it seems likely that excavations east of the West Huarpa Community will reveal deeply buried building remains of Late Vista Alegre date that participated in the emergence of great houses and orthogonal cellular compounds.

Quebrada de Ocros Phase Huari (AD 500–650)

Quebrada de Ocros phase Huari is poorly known, but its Vista Alegre phase West Huarpa Community was located on a relatively flat ridge, at the edge of a deep canyon, where it could probably be reached by irrigation waters (Figs. 10.3, 10.1). Wari planners had learned to engineer long canals and Wari leaders were commanding large contingents of workers. New central settlements had running water.

In Quebrada de Ocros times, the West Huarpa Community expanded eastward almost a kilometer, becoming an area of 500 to 1,000 ha, so a population of 10,000 to 20,000 residents seems likely. Rulers emerged, as demonstrated by a palace and a royal tomb, but almost nothing is known about great houses, quotidian life, and changing urban landscape. For these data we must turn to secondary Conchopata.

About 250 m east of the old West Huarpa Community, on the north side of the highway, is Vegachayoq Moqo, one of the new city's first great walled compounds—that was apparently quite irregular (Figs. 10.4, 10.3; Bragayrac 1991; González and Bragayrac 1986; González et al. 1996; Pérez 1999). Early excavators called this building complex a temple, but I believe this inference to be too simple (Isbell 2001b, 2004b). A better interpretation of Vegachayoq Moqo is a building whose function changed every few generations, from a palace, to an elite mortuary monument, to a popular cemetery. If many of Huari's buildings underwent similarly complex "life cycles," understanding the Huari city certainly poses a challenge for archaeologists.

A deep floor in the bottom of one excavation at Vegachayoq Moqo (Fig. 10.5, lowest profile; Bragayrac 1991) may document terminal Vista Alegre phase construction, and if so, growth of the West Huarpa Community into Huari began earlier than realized. Formally, Vegachayoq Moqo consists of a courtyard or plaza and a platform pyramid rising about 8 m high in two terraces that included three mounds of slightly different elevations, forming a U-shaped enclosure around the east end of the courtyard (Figs. 10.4, 10.5). The main body delimiting the courtyard on its east was the largest, about 70 to 80 m long and 40 m wide. Mounds at the south and north completed the three-lobed, U-shaped volume.

I believe that Vegachayoq Moqo's terraced mound bordered an open assembly area to create a roofed and raised stage where rulership could be displayed (Fig. 10.5, bottom). About 3 m behind the terraces, on top of the mound, is an ashlar wall that probably separated ceremonial-administrative space from residential buildings (González et al. 1996:35–37).

Royal or elite tombs are not known at Vegachayoq Moqo, but across the street (although formal streets are probably later features at Huari) is a sector known as Monjachayoq. Its ruins include a huge mortuary complex that was almost certainly a royal tomb (Fig. 10.4; Isbell 2004c). Freestanding buildings have been reduced to little more than foundations by looting, but the subterranean architecture is better preserved, including a long gallery and a lower level of megalithic chambers (Pérez 1999, 2001, 2002; see also Isbell 2004b). A third subterranean level is also of megalithic construction—a narrow gallery complex shaped more or less like a llama in profile. In the floor of the llama gallery is a circular pit lined with rough stones and sealed with a lithic cap, constituting a fourth underground level. There seems little doubt that the deep gallery complex is a tomb of royal magnitude, with lesser chambers above for associated burials. All was looted, becoming a stone quarry in Spanish Colonial times.

Half a kilometer east of Vegachayoq Moqo and Monjachayoq is Moraduchayuq (Figs. 10.3, 10.6A). In Vista Alegre times, there must have been a natural sink hole at the location, at least 25 m across and 10 m deep, where the bedrock had collapsed. As the Quebrada de Ocros phase began, several circular buildings of rough stone stood a few meters north of this hole, perhaps a row of them running east-west. Trash in the buildings probably dates later in time, but large quantities of blue stone suggest manufacturing of luxury goods.

By mid-Quebrada de Ocros times, a spectacular sunken court with walls of carefully dressed and fitted stones had been built inside the sink hole. It was perfectly square, 24 m on each side (Fig. 10.6A). Charcoal from fill behind its outer wall yielded an uncalibrated radiocarbon date of AD 580 ± 60. The form as well as the stonework are reminiscent of Tiwanaku architecture (see Isbell et al. 1991 for description, and Isbell 1991 for relations with Tiwanaku). Perhaps Huari and Tiwanaku had already confronted one another on the far south coast, and Huari generals had brought captured Tiwanaku soldiers back to the capital to construct monuments in a foreign, prestigious style.

The earliest floor of the Moraduchayuq temple was of white plaster, laid only a few centimeters above the base of its polygonal block wall. Several subsequent cut-stone floors were added over fills, so the sunken court became gradually shallower. An uncalibrated radiocarbon date of AD 720 ± 60 belongs to the next to last floor, suggesting that the temple continued in use at least into the early Moraduchayuq phase.

Neither of the excavated Quebrada de Ocros precincts reveals much about quotidian life, but very recent excavations have exposed continuous, dense construction between Vegachayoq Moqo/Monjachayoq, and Moraduchayuq (Figs. 10.3, 10.7). Ismael Pérez (1999) was allowed to excavate next to the site museum, exposing narrow halls suggestive of lateral rooms characteristic of patio group enclosures. They contained dense concentrations of ceramics, especially Quebrada de Ocros pottery, implying habitation in organized building complexes more suggestive of great houses than of simple domestic dwellings.

In 2005–2006, a large area in front of Huari's site museum was opened (Fig. 10.7A; see note 2), along the north edge of the highway, exposing a monumental orthogonal compound, or compounds. Several tombs similar to those of Conchopata's supreme lords, but third-order elites in the Wari scale, were discovered among them (Fig. 10.7B, C), supporting the inference that great houses were reforming Huari's landscape. Elsewhere along the road cut, residential architecture is also plentiful, but less complete, and all undated.

Conchopata (Fig. 10.8) reveals much more about community layout when the Quebrada de Ocros phase began than does the larger, more complex, and deeply buried Huari. Like Huari's West Huarpa Community, Conchopata's major architectural remains concentrate along the edge of a flattish ridge top. The stream in the adjacent canyon and high-elevation springs provided irrigation and drinking water to the settlement (Fig. 10.1).

During Vista Alegre times, what was to become Conchopata's central plaza was a cemetery containing several modest graves of the Huarpa culture. During the Quebrada de Ocros phase, buildings were constructed along a kilometer of the ridge edge, totaling 200 to 400 ha. Excavations over six decades, from Julio Tello (1942) to the present (Benavides 1965; Cook and Benco 2001; Isbell 2001b, 2004a, 2007; Isbell and Cook 2002; Isbell and Groleau, in press; Lumbreras 1974, 1981; Pérez 1998a; Pérez and Ochatoma 1998; Ochatoma 2005; Ochatoma and Cabrera 1999, 2000, 2001a, 2001b, 2001c, 2001d, 2002; Pozzi Escot 1985, 1991; Tung and Cook 2006), have revealed the largest continuous archaeological exposure of a Wari city in the Andean highlands, although today Conchopata is almost completely destroyed by the growth of the modern city of Ayacucho.

Early Conchopata had elements of Ayacucho's old hilltop capitals (organization around a central plaza) as well as characteristics of later Wari cities (walled, orthogonal cellular compounds). Two rectangular building compounds faced one another across a central plaza of pinkish sand, inspiring the name Pink Plaza (Fig. 10.8). Building Complex BC-A is best interpreted as an elite

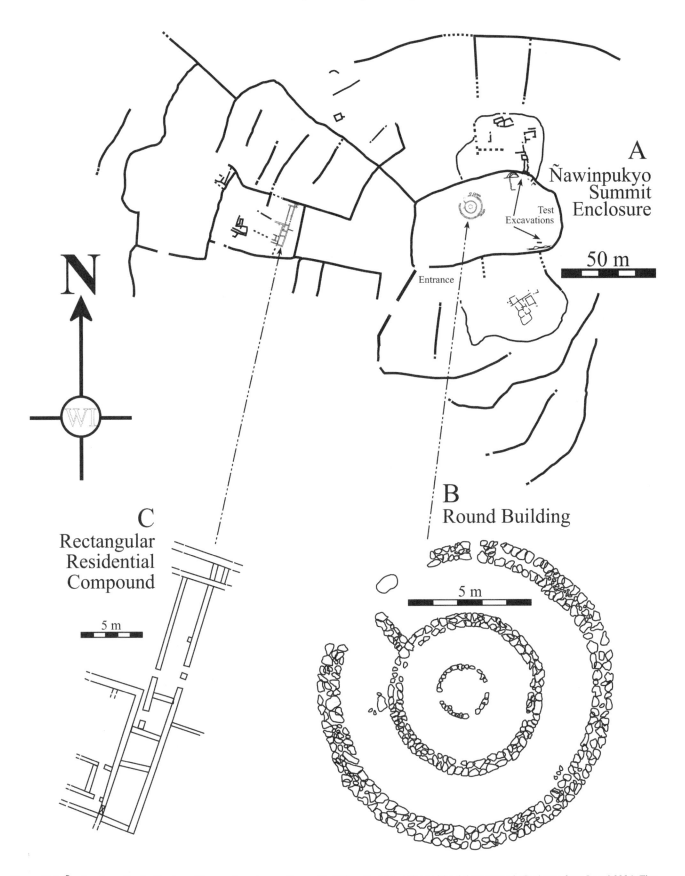

Figure 10.2. Ñawinpukyo site. *A*, site plan with summit enclosure; *B*, round building; *C*, rectangular residential compound. (Redrawn from Leoni 2004: Figs. 3.4, 5.1, 5.7, 6.11)

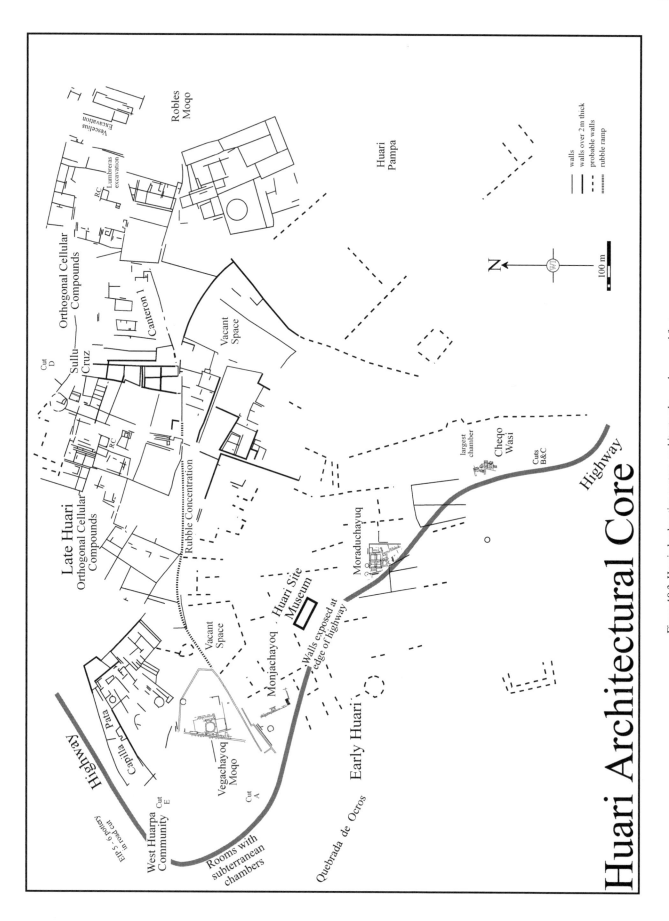

Huari Architectural Core

Figure 10.3. Huari plan locating sectors, architectural complexes, and features.

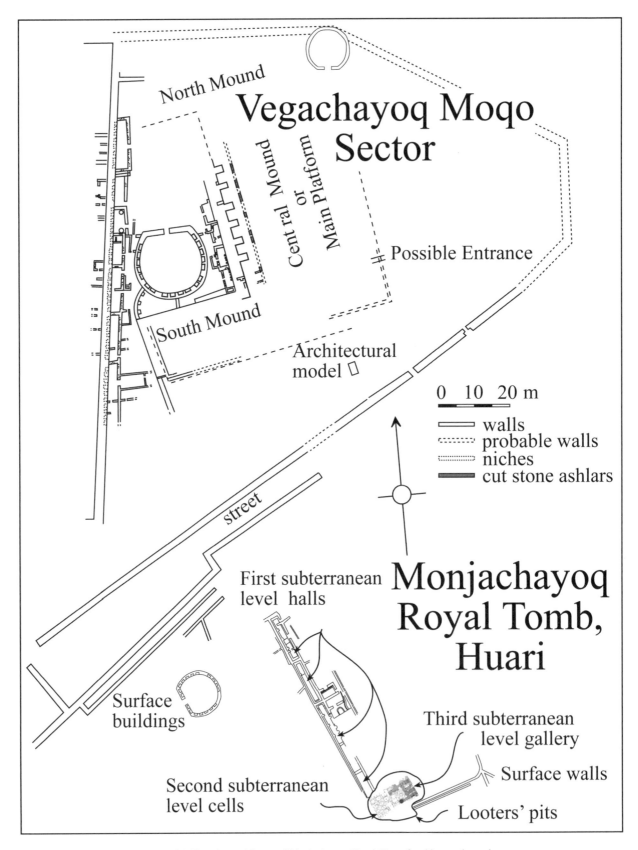

Figure 10.4. Vegachayoq Moqo and Monjachayoq, Huari. Plan of architectural remains.

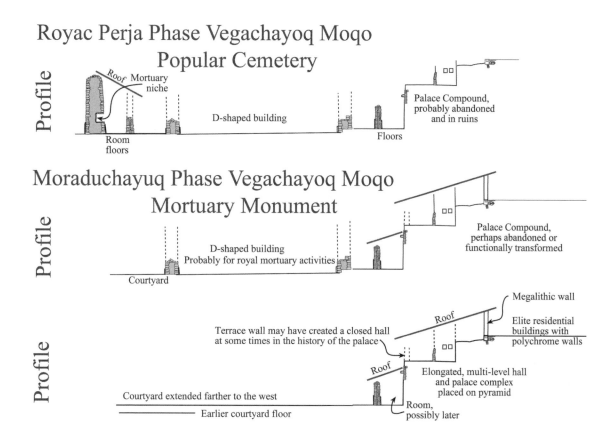

Royac Perja Phase Vegachayoq Moqo
Popular Cemetery

Profile

Roof Mortuary niche

Mortuary niche

D-shaped building

Room floors

Floors

Palace Compound, probably abandoned and in ruins

Moraduchayuq Phase Vegachayoq Moqo
Mortuary Monument

Profile

D-shaped building
Probably for royal mortuary activities

Courtyard

Palace Compound, perhaps abandoned or functionally transformed

Profile

Megalithic wall

Terrace wall may have created a closed hall at some times in the history of the palace

Roof

Elite residential buildings with polychrome walls

Roof

Elongated, multi-level hall and palace complex placed on pyramid

Courtyard extended farther to the west

Earlier courtyard floor

Room, possibly later

Quebrada de Ocros Phase Vegachayoq Moqo
Royal Palace

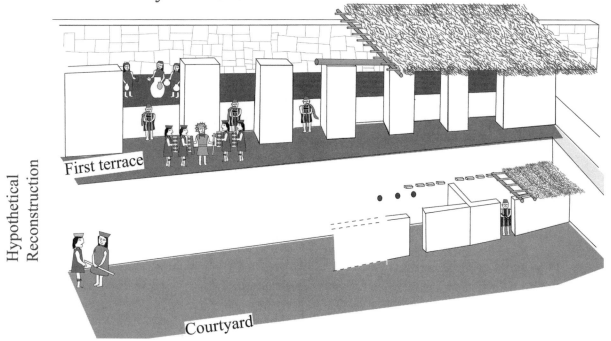

Hypothetical Reconstruction

First terrace

Courtyard

Figure 10.5. Huari's Vegachayoq Moqo showing architectural profile (*above*), located on Figure 10.4, as it developed from the Quebrada de Ocros phase to the Moraduchayuq phase and the Royac Perja phase. *below*, hypothetical reconstruction of the courtyard and terraces of the Vegachayoq Moqo palace during Quebrada de Ocros times.

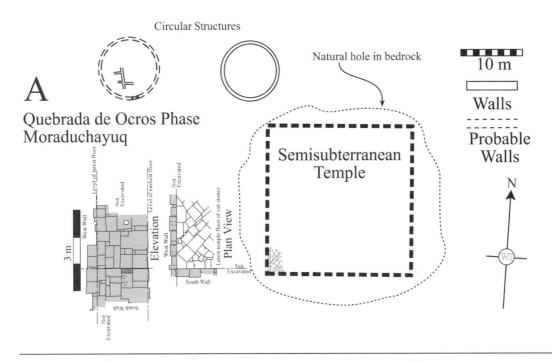

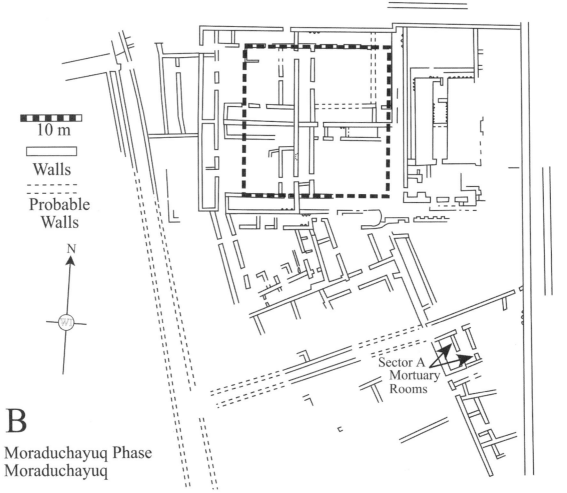

Figure 10.6. Plan of Huari's Moraduchayuq sector. *above*, in the Quebrada de Ocros phase; *below*, in the Moraduchayuq phase.

Figure 10.7. Huari, excavations of 2005–2006, between highway and site museum, located on Figure 10.3. *A*, walls of a great compound or compounds; *B*, tombs in the compound; *C*, two-part megalithic lid with central hole, held in place over tomb by walls of a mortuary room, built on the edge of the lid.

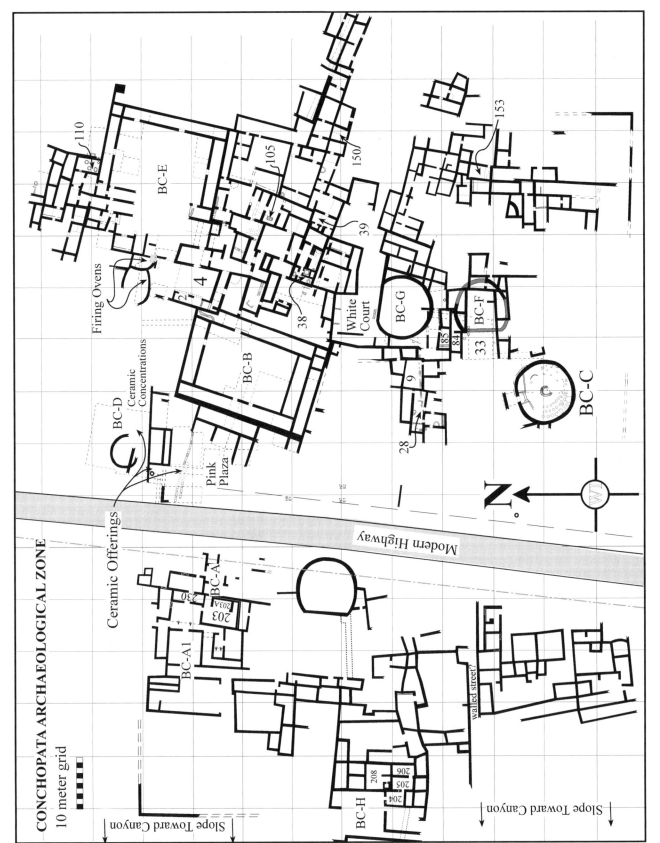

Figure 10.8. Conchopata plan locating architectural complexes, rooms, and features.

residential compound (Lumbreras 1974, 1981; Pozzi Escot 1985, 1991) that was modified and enlarged several times. Room 203 (Fig. 10.9) contains an impressive complex of tombs, including a mortuary house (Room 203A) (see Isbell 2004c) that surely contained the remains of ancestors.

Building Complex BC-B (Fig. 10.8) is a rectangular compound with long, narrow rooms enclosing a central patio, located across the Pink Plaza from BC-A. It was a primitive version of the Wari patio group (Isbell 1991), constructed of unbonded walls, but maintaining a symmetrical plan around a patio. Set into its patio floor next to a doorway opening toward the Pink Plaza was a giant urn. The discovery of numerous fine serving vessels supports the inference that this urn, and others like it, were employed to serve beverages to individuals entering the patio. Large numbers of butchered llama bones were found in one of the compound's lateral rooms (Rosenfeld 2004, 2006), implying that the primary function of BC-B was hosting social events, especially feasts—suggesting the interpretation as a feasting hall.

Building Complexes BC-A and BC-B faced one another across the Pink Plaza, fulfilling complementary functions. I believe that, combined, they can be recognized as an early example in the development of a new kind of building in which residential, hosting, mortuary, and administrative functions were fulfilled—a palace, and a great house.

During early Quebrada de Ocros times, a round or D-shaped building labeled BC-D lay north of the central plaza. South of the building, and buried below the floor of the plaza, were many offerings (Isbell 2001b, 2007; Isbell and Cook 1987, 2002) of oversize ceramics, some decorated with a "staff god" and "profile attendants," SAIS figures that occur on Tiwanaku's Gate of the Sun (Isbell and Knobloch 2006). These elaborate symbols surely were part of a new system of social difference, and practices involving festive drinking that contributed to constructing a new international Huari identity. Tools for manufacturing ceramics (from polishers to molds) were found close by, and about 30 m to the east, ceramic firing ovens were excavated (Fig. 10.8; Leoni 2001).

Another Quebrada de Ocros phase circular building probably fronted the south edge of Conchopata's early plaza. Labeled BC-C (Fig. 10.8), it was involved in brewing as well as other ceremonial activities (Tung 2003; Tung and Cook 2006).

Behind the buildings facing Conchopata's early plaza was housing for urban residents. Foundations were found in several places, underlying later buildings. At least some of these buildings were interconnected and agglutinated rooms, probably constructed in sequential additions rather than as subdivisions of large, planned compounds—what I call "cumulative architecture" (Isbell 1991). However, little of this early construction is preserved, so the evolution of large compounds and great houses remains poorly known, even at Conchopata.

Moraduchayuq Phase Huari (AD 650–800)

Moraduchayuq phase Huari formalized a new urban landscape and social organization. Orthogonal cellular compounds divided into repetitive, apartment-like cells (see Isbell 1991) characterized Huari, and class structure became the norm of urban life, at least in burial. A central plaza as focus of city organization seems to have disappeared in favor of a collection of great houses, each with its own courtyards and patios (Figs. 10.3, 10.7A). No royal tombs can be assigned to this phase, probably because of the scarcity of research and, of course, the intensity of looting. On the other hand, second-order and third-order elite tombs are documented, as well as non-elite and commoner graves. Temple/palace architecture surely continued, but apartment-house residence for mid-status inhabitants appears, so social hierarchy is well documented at Huari.

Moraduchayuq phase urban modification included continued remodeling at the Vegachayoq Moqo complex, adding a large D-shaped building (with 18 great niches) in the old courtyard (Figs. 10.4, 10.5). Sometime later, much of the courtyard was cut off by a great wall built a short distance west of the D-shaped building. This may have taken place late in Moraduchayuq or early in Royac Perja times but most importantly, the immense wall contains modest and poor graves. These remains were placed in cavities within the wall; at least a few secondary burials were sealed in wall niches. Some modest burials were apparently individual and primary, but looting has severely confused the original patterns.

Excavations in Huari's Cheqo Wasi sector (Figs. 10.10, 10.3) reveal the tombs of second-order nobles, spectacular megalithic chambers (Benavides 1984, 1991; Isbell 2004c; Pérez 1999, 2002). Although very difficult to date because of intensive looting, Cheqo Wasi was probably constructed in early Moraduchayuq times, as the city continued its growth eastward. These sepulchers are less grand than the royal tomb at Monjachayoq but are more impressive than mortuary rooms in Sector A, attached to the Moraduchayuq compound. Significantly, Cheqo Wasi includes residential buildings, apparent even in their extremely looted condition. This was not a dedicated elite cemetery, but a combination of elite graves and living quarters, as might be expected in the compounds of great houses.

During this phase, orthogonal cellular architecture became prominent and was frequently employed in urban renewal, significantly increasing living space. The Moraduchayuq compound (Fig. 10.6B) is a good example. Sometime after a final remodeling of Moraduchayuq's early subterranean temple, its floor was covered with clean fill. New walls of rough stone were built, resting on these fills and the old temple walls. As the foundations were completed, a system of drains was constructed. A perimeter wall was built that, in the east, abuts a parallel-walled street, although this street may have been constructed later than the compound.

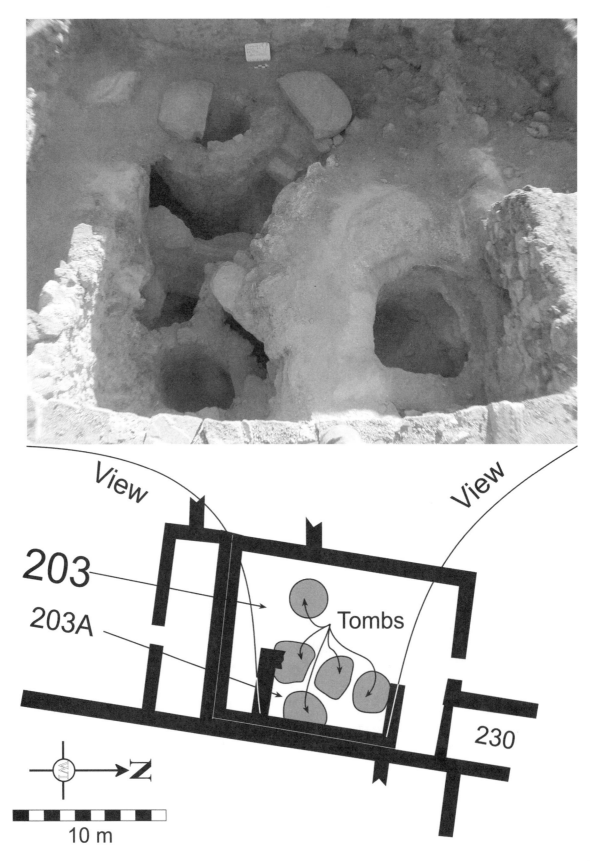

Figure 10.9. Conchopata mortuary Room 203 with mortuary house and tombs. Note notched, two-part megalithic lid of westernmost tomb. Only half of the lid is in place. Similar lids for the other tombs have disappeared.

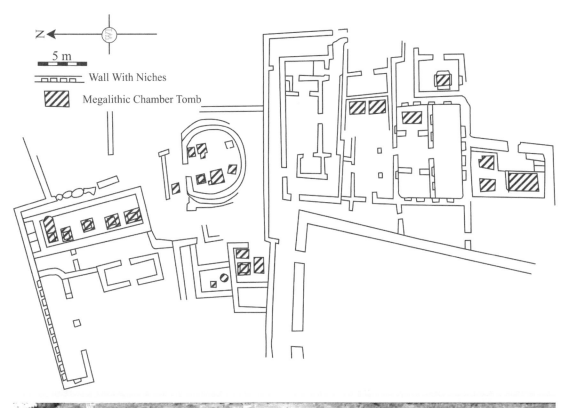

Figure 10.10. Huari, Cheqo Wasi sector. *above*, plan; *below*, one of the megalithic chamber tombs.

Next, Moraduchayuq's north and west walls were added, with doorways in precisely anticipated places. The south boundary of the construction, a narrow hall (perhaps an early street), is 25° out of alignment with the orthogonal compound, suggesting that it was part of an earlier construction. Consequently, the space available for renewal seems to have been irregular in shape.

Continuing the construction sequence, the portion of the Moraduchayuq compound overlying the old temple was divided into four courts, first by a north-south wall and then an east-west wall, with doorways in appropriate places. Next, elongated lateral rooms were constructed around the edges of each of the four spaces, and a white plaster paving was placed on all the walls and floors. Between the filled temple and Sector A, additional space was available, albeit of irregular plan. Moraduchayuq's architects solved this by adding 4 or 5 patio groups that were slightly trapezoidal (Fig. 10.6*B*). In its final form, the Moraduchayuq compound contained 8 or 9 patio groups of 250 to 350 m² each, and an eastern platform area that contained more than 600 m². The entire complex occupied about 2,700 m² or slightly more than a quarter hectare (Brewster-Wray 1990). Although not a large building, the planning and construction of Moraduchayuq required leadership, especially apparent in the predetermined forms and sequence of construction. It also probably involved conscripted workers, and supervision by an architect/builder. Virtually identical building forms and sequences characterize Wari orthogonal cellular construction wherever it occurs (Isbell 1991; Schreiber 1992).

Moraduchayuq's patio group courtyards had plaster floors, with drains connected to canals beneath them. Each floor was raised along its edges, about 15 to 25 cm, forming a stone-faced bench usually a little more than a meter wide. This kept rainwater out of the lateral rooms, and I suspect that the elevated benches were covered by long eaves projecting from roofs over lateral rooms. Consequently, these benches were securely sheltered, but well lighted, making them excellent work and living space.

Generally entered through doorways from the courtyard, some ground-level lateral rooms had distinctive furnishings built into their floors. A few have remains of hearths, while others have stone and plaster benches or counters intended for particular activities. Some, but not all, of the lateral rooms have plaster-lined cists under their floors that once contained caches of luxury goods. These, most likely, were sleeping spaces, where owners could protect their valuables during the nighttime. Obviously the rooms were intended for domestic, residential activities, although they were surely dark and cold.

Stone corbels in several well preserved walls show that Moraduchayuq's lateral rooms were two- and possibly three-stories tall. Unfortunately, all have collapsed, and disturbance from looting makes it impossible to determine what activities went on in which levels of patio-group apartments. Although probably residential, upper levels could have been specialized storage.

Formal repetition in the patio groups in the Moraduchayuq compound suggests that all served similar functions. This inference is supported by similar trash from one patio group to another, including similar relative frequencies of ceramic vessel shapes. However, within patio groups, some lateral halls lack distinguishing floor features, while others contained built-in furnishings of stone and clay, a hearth area, and/or clay-lined pits below the plaster floor. More research will be required, but I suspect that each patio group contained several types of lateral halls and that the types recur throughout the patio groups. Trash discovered in Moraduchayuq's patio groups contains products of daily life, including food preparation and consumption. Consequently, the compound appears to have been residential quarters, occupied by repetitive domestic units—probably families. The patio group was the standard module for orthogonal cellular architecture, but courtyard space was converted into rooms when needed by abutting walls onto the outside of lateral rooms, a technique characteristic of Wari's cumulative architecture.

No burials were found in the Moraduchayuq compound, but two mortuary rooms occur in attached Sector A (Fig. 10.6*B*). It is not clear that these burials represent dead from the compound, but the buildings were interconnected, so it seems likely. Sector A tombs, although severely looted, are very similar to some examples from better-known Conchopata, especially elites interred in mortuary rooms within residential compounds. The major difference is that at Conchopata, less impressive burials appear as well, placed in cavity graves in simple residential rooms, and poor burials appear below the floors of common spaces, in plain pits. Absence of comparable low-status burials at Moraduchayuq may be due to sample error. Alternatively, popular cemeteries, such as the great wall added late in the history of Vegachayoq Moqo, located outside residential compounds may have become the resting place for low-status individuals. Another alternative, though less likely, is that there were no low-status residents at Moradyachayuq to be buried there. Be that as it may, mortuary-room burials in Sector A are consistent with a third level in Wari society, below the occupants of royal tombs, and below those buried in megalithic chambers. On the other hand, Sector A burials were more wealthy and influential than plain burials or modestly furnished graves intruded into the great wall at Vegachayoq Moqo and found throughout the Conchopata ruins.

Within Moraduchayuq's patio groups, no diagnostic refuse was found implying explicit occupational activities—such as farm implements, weaving tools, pottery manufacturing implements, or other artifacts. Luxury goods were common enough to imply that the occupants were moderately wealthy. Animal bones show that only choice cuts of meat were brought into the compound, the animals having apparently been butchered elsewhere. Waste flakes from stone tools are consistent with resharpening, not manufacture. Neither agricultural implements nor weapons are common. Few weaving tools were identified. On the other hand, pottery is densely represented, with bowls and cups unusually common in comparison with vessels for food preparation and storage. This implies a lot of serving of food and drink—communal dining or feasting. While a restaurant or inn would produce large numbers of serving vessels, one would also expect many large vessels for preparing food, not adequately represented at Moraduchayuq. Consequently, much of the food and drink served at Moraduchayuq seems to have been prepared elsewhere.

Some pottery found at Moraduchayuq belongs to a style characteristic of the distant Cajamarca Valley; it was probably imported. The amount is not sufficient to imply a community of Cajamarca immigrants at Moraduchayuq, or elsewhere at Huari, for that matter. Furthermore, ceramics influenced by Tiwanaku pottery shapes—but not imported objects—are even more frequent at Moraduchayuq and elsewhere throughout Huari, especially a tall drinking flagon called a *kero*. The appearance of these exotic new objects does not seem to imply communities of foreigners, but significant interaction and exchange throughout the Andean culture area. More importantly, the innovative material culture probably testifies to the emergence of a new, international Huari identity, associated with new practices involving this material culture, especially the consumption of corn beer in *keros*. I am reminded of the martini, martini glass, and practice of "happy hour" in modern international business culture. A process of ethnogenesis was at work at Huari.

On the basis of all these indicators, Moraduchayuq's residents can be said to have been moderately well off. Apparently they were not engaged in farming, fighting, or craft production, at least not primarily. They lived in buildings constructed with corporate labor where a great deal of food and drink (that had apparently been prepared elsewhere) was served. Perhaps they were visitors being feasted by urban hosts. However, specially lined pits containing caches of luxury goods under the floors of some lateral rooms imply storage of jewelry by the residents, to be brought out on special occasions. If so, residents must have been long term. This array of material remains seems best explained if the principal residents were middle-level administrators who periodically hosted subordinates in their patios, using the resources of a larger institution—perhaps a great house, but possibly the bureaucracy of state.

Let us suppose that residence at Moraduchayuq was permanent, by families, and that each floor of each patio group housed 2 nuclear families, with an average of 5 members. If this were the case, each family had access to two lateral rooms and the communal courtyard. If patio groups had two floors, 4 families (or about 20 individuals) shared each courtyard. Consequently, in 8 or 9 patio groups occupying a quarter of a hectare, 160 to 180 persons were housed, at full capacity. If this density is generalized to the whole, it suggests about 600 persons per hectare of orthogonal cellular architecture, at full occupancy.

Surface remains at Huari reveal at least 6 to 8 orthogonal cellular compounds occupying a minimum of 25 ha along Huari's northern margin (Fig. 10.3). All are probably Moraduchayuq phase constructions. Using assumptions and figures suggested above—600 residents per hectare, and 25 ha of new buildings—the Moraduchayuq phase witnessed at least 15,000 new residents in the Huari capital. Adding the Quebrada de Ocros total, Huari's residential population reached about 25,000 to 40,000. Intuitively, this seems a reasonable estimate.

I have argued that Moraduchayuq's residents used their patios to host festivities for people they supervised. Indeed, the wealth, burials, space, and architectural planning all suggest they were low-level nobility. If the subordinates hosted were employed by the state and received homes as part of their remuneration, they probably lived in other parts of the city, or in the country. Perhaps they were agricultural field workers. Presumably they came to Moraduchayuq for instructions, and for periodic festivities. Perhaps they did service there, so some floor space was occupied by them, not by permanent residents. Perhaps my demographic estimate is high.

But Moraduchayuq's residents could have been members of a great house. If so, were the subordinates feasted lower status members of the same house? And if so, did they live in the same buildings, or occupy more humble abodes somewhere within a greater Moraduchayuq house?

At the Conchopata site, burials within architectural complexes of interconnected spaces include elite mortuary rooms, modest cist burials, and poor pit interments. This suggests a house shared by residents who varied significantly in status. Similar co-residence including primary offspring, more distant kin, adoptive members, and servants characterized Inca "households" in Sonqo (Murra 1991), which can probably be considered modest examples of great houses. But at Moraduchayuq and its Sector A, no burials were discovered belonging to modest and poor individuals. Until more research can be conducted, I favor the inference that wealthy and poor members of great houses shared space, as seems to have been the case at Conchopata, but new research is needed to reveal more about life at Moraduchayuq and, hopefully, the nature of Huari's residence in orthogonal cellular compounds. Perhaps at Conchopata the orthogonal cellular compounds were great houses, while at Huari at least some were state facilities. Much remains to be learned.

Planned streets probably became a new feature of Moraduchayuq Huari as underdeveloped space filled up and efficient transit was threatened. Of course, streets at Huari have not been studied, but if the avenue between Vegachayoq Moqo and Monjachayoq is correctly mapped (Figs. 10.4, 10.3), streets at least sometimes included annexes where pedestrians of diverse backgrounds could pause, perhaps meeting and conversing. By Moraduchayuq times, Huari had become a city in the sense emphasized by Monica Smith (2000), a place where residents encountered and interacted with different kinds of people—in religions, kin, status, age, gender, ethnicity, and great-house affiliation—who, in a world of hamlets and villages, would never encounter one another.

Huari city planning was formalized in Moraduchayuq times, but little is known about the organization of urban landscape. More is known about Conchopata, although orthogonal cellular architecture at this secondary city remained small and simple in comparison with Huari, and always combined with less organized cumulative architecture.

At Conchopata, social and spatial changes followed those at Huari, although the city did not grow in size, and may have declined somewhat in Moraduchayuq times. The central Pink Plaza of Quebrada de Ocros times was abandoned and a white plaster surface was laid across much of our excavated area, but no central plaza can be identified. Instead, another orthogonal patio group with interior courtyard was built, labeled BC-E. It was probably a new palace (Fig. 10.8).

Attached to BC-E were rectangular room groups that must have been residences for elites, for several include impressive mortuary rooms (numbers 110, 38, and 105). Perhaps these tombs, of third-order elites on the Wari mortuary scale (Isbell 2004), represent a succession of lords who ruled from the little palace, or a lord and his primary descendants. Be that as it may, this compound seems to have been a great house.

Many of the buildings on the map of Conchopata (Fig. 10.8) probably belong to Moraduchayuq and subsequent Royac Perja times. Palace BC-E with its additions occupied a great deal of the center of the site. But planned streets never became a feature of Conchopata. One walled passage in the southwestern part of the city was surely used for transit, but it looks more like space remaining between two compounds, not planned public space to which buildings were oriented. Others of Conchopata's lanes of communication seem to be underdeveloped space as well, not walled avenues like those at Huari by this time.

D-shaped temple buildings continued to be built at Conchopata. After BC-C was burned and buried, BC-F was constructed (Fig. 10.8). Soon, it too was abandoned and filled with trash. But by that time BC-G had been built, with its foundation cutting through the white plaster pavement of this phase. BC-F was also filled with fragments of deliberately smashed, oversize ceramics (many decorated with images from the SAIS religious repertoire) along with trophy skulls and an upright stone (see Ochatoma 2005; Ochatoma and Cabrera 2001a, 2001b, 2001c, 2001d, 2002).

I suspect that during the Moraduchayuq phase, Conchopata was run more or less like a palace economy, with royal women—especially secondary wives and concubines—contributing much of the labor required for the festivities that framed daily life in the little city. Female burials significantly outnumber male burials, a fact that implies polygynous families, at least among the elite. One of the few elite mortuary contexts discovered intact is Room 105, where a deep tomb contained 15 individuals. A male between 23 and 27 years of age was placed near the bottom of the tomb. In addition to infants and children, he was accompanied by six adult females of various ages, and a seventh probable adult female (Tung 2003; Tung and Cook 2006). I believe the grave represents the family of a lower-status nobleman (Isbell 2007). The women attached to palace households were probably the potters who painted Conchopata's spectacular ceramics, as well as brewers, cooks, and servers of feasts. This seems supported by the distribution of ceramic manufacturing tools that do not identify workshops, or occur only with low-status household refuse. The tools appear in elite and ceremonial areas as well as in simple homes—almost everywhere.

Conchopata's women successfully promoted their social situations. They represented themselves on pottery, both utilitarian and ceremonial, apparently in mythical as well as quotidian contexts. They produced spectacular pots, sometimes working in temporary but important and highly visible places (Isbell 2007). One woman was apparently a humble brewer, for a complete set of huge jars and other equipment, including serving cups, was smashed on the floor above the modest cist tomb in her abandoned three-room home. Indeed, someone continued to visit her grave, opening a hole through a wall above the tomb cap, reminiscent of carefully cut holes in much more elite tomb lids (Isbell and Groleau, in press).

Royac Perja Phase Huari (AD 800–1000)

Royac Perja ended with the abandonment of Huari, but it is the least known of the city's temporal phases. Indeed, until recently, Huari was thought to have been abandoned earlier, about AD 800. In the Moraduchayuq compound, patio groups were deserted sequentially. Dense concentrations of trash on patio floors show that there were still people in the city, but significant areas were vacant. The last patio groups to be forsaken were located next to perimeter wall doorways. But eventually, even these apartments were vacated. We can infer this because the people took their possessions with them, except for a few objects they forgot, or smashed as they were leaving. And most obviously, since no trash was dumped on these floors, we can infer that there were no longer enough inhabitants in the city to generate significant refuse.

At Vegachayoq Moqo, sometime after the D-shaped building was added to the compound's patio, a great wall was constructed across the west end of the courtyard, out of alignment with other constructions (Figs. 10.4, 10.5, 10.3). On its east face, this wall has large niches, about a meter square, at least one containing a secondary burial sealed inside. Further, many more interments were inserted into the wall, which must have been a popular cemetery throughout the final occupation of Huari.

Other changes seem to be Royac Perja in date (Fig. 10.3). Downtown Huari has areas that lack evidence of architectural remains. Given Huari's propensity for leveling old buildings to construct new ones, I inferred that vacant lots were in renewal when the city was abandoned, so the new buildings intended for these spaces were never begun (Isbell et al. 1991; Isbell 1997, 2001a). Support for this argument is a long concentration of stone and rubble, or perhaps a provisional wall, that crosses much of Huari from southwest to northeast. I suspect this feature functioned as a causeway for transporting workers and building materials across walled sectors of Huari's architectural core.

Huari's surface remains include several buildings that are obviously trapezoidal (Fig. 10.3: Capilla Pata, Sullu Cruz). They are immense constructions that depart from the cannons of orthogonal cellular architecture. Their interiors consist of very large spaces, apparently without significant division.

There are no patio groups, narrow halls, or lines of corbels for upper floors. Perhaps these buildings were never finished. Or perhaps the final form intended was so different from Huari's more traditional orthogonal cellular or cumulative vernacular architecture that archaeologists do not yet recognize them. Be that as it may, these buildings are provisionally relegated to the Royac Perja phase.

At Conchopata, there was no late building phase, and the city had probably shrunk to half its population by Royac Perja times. No palaces or great houses seem to have been occupied, and potters were no longer manufacturing giant brewing and feasting vessels decorated with SAIS religious icons. In fact, people seem to have resided in single-room houses, making finely crafted effigy whistles that were small enough to be carried with ease.

By about AD 1000, Huari, Conchopata, and the other cities of Ayacucho's Middle Horizon were empty. Gradually the great buildings collapsed and Huari reverted to cultivated fields. Ayacucho's inhabitants accepted simpler life ways, with no evidence of cities, great houses, orthogonal architectural compounds, complex art, or state government.

Conclusions

Huari became a great city inhabited for more than a century by 25,000 to 40,000 residents. Its development involved a sequence of important changes, not a single revolution. Between late Vista Alegre and mid-Quebrada de Ocros times, central settlement site location changed. Furthermore, great houses appeared as a new social and architectural building block of the city and state. By the Moraduchayuq phase, highly formalized and repetitive orthogonal cellular architecture was commonplace. These changes were primarily local in origin.

Temples and ceremonial activities occupied much of the time and space in early Huari and Conchopata. Royal and elite burials appear. At Conchopata, an immense amount of effort went into hosting feasts and drinking bouts, from producing brewing jars to constructing feasting halls. Urban economics were palace-based, focused on feasting, with women of polygynous lords doing much of the work preparing elaborate displays punctuating quotidian life. Great-house palaces were occupied by persons of ranks that ranged from the highest elites to humble commoners, all probably organized by kinship idiom in relation to focal ancestors buried in the mortuary rooms within the group's compound. Heirlooms and ornaments of green stone, *Spondylus* shell, bronze, gold, and silver were increasingly important. But social class was becoming increasingly prominent, as documented by mortuary remains.

In Moraduchayuq times, orthogonal cellular architecture was perfected, a building style adapted to extremely dense occupation. At least six or eight additional compounds were constructed across northern Huari—probably all great houses, not barrios as many assume. The city's population nearly doubled, and life became more secular. At least one of the temples of older southern Huari was interred, and its space rehabilitated into an orthogonal cellular apartment house. Other palaces and temples were modified. Walled streets restructured the city, creating spaces where pedestrians interacted, probably altering the experience of the city.

Huari's Moraduchayuq compound does not seem to have been a manufacturing center, but more administrative—as concluded above, based on the lack of agricultural or other specialized tools, ample but repetitive spaces constructed by corvée labor, high frequency of serving vessels, third-rank burials, and so on. To judge by the residents of the Moraduchayuq compound, life was not arduous (good-quality food, wealth items in caches and burials), but it was very constrained—the compound was impressively walled and internally focused on its own patios and courts. These people were neither wealthy nor poor; they did not toil in subsistence or craft production, but managed personnel, at least partially through feasts. Patio-group architecture allowed some flexibility for changing conditions, but the repetitive nature of cellular compounds suggests that individuality was unavailable to this social class, and conformity was expected of almost everyone. Living quarters were extremely private, with high walls separating every space. The residential unit was probably the family, with its place located within a larger complex that was probably a great house of real and fictive relatives. Interior rooms were dark and cold. Sanitation must have been dreadful. On the brighter side, patios were sunny and sheltered, so daily life probably took place in confined, but relatively comfortable, space. Second and even third floors, little understood by archaeologists, may have been more spacious than we think. Perhaps there were even flat roofs where a much more open life style went on. Women achieved significant recognition and freedom.

In the final Royac Perja phase, Conchopata's palaces disappeared, and potters ceased to produce ceramics for feasts and drinking bouts. Instead, they manufactured highly portable items that seem to reflect new kinds of practices, identities, and ceremonies. At Huari, an urban renewal program was initiated that involved clearing spaces and constructing new buildings whose form was not consistent with earlier great houses or orthogonal cellular compounds. But the renewal failed, and by about AD 1000, Huari and its secondary cities were empty, the result of processes that remain obscure.

Much research is needed but it is clear that Huari's evolution was autochthonous, representing the development of a distinct form of city associated with a kind of house society that may have had many uniquely Andean qualities. The complex sequence of changes demonstrates that Peruvian urbanism was not the result of a single great revolution, and certainly not a revolution that took place in one precocious location and spread across the central Andes. Changes were local, and multiple, following one upon the other. One key transformation for Huari was the great house, with orderly, rectangular architectural compounds that created a new "cityscape."

Endnotes

1. Huari is also spelled Wari. To avoid confusion, I use "Huari" for the capital city, its people, and their material remains. "Wari" is employed for the more broadly diffused culture, its sites, and artifacts.

2. This research was directed by archaeologist Alejandra Figueroa. Unfortunately, I have not been able to gain access to the recent report, so my presentation is based on a two-day visit to the excavations toward their end in January 2006, as well as discussion with Lic. Figueroa and several of the crew chiefs.

3. I am skeptical about the results of this study for, in my opinion, the definition of Huari architecture was not sufficiently rigorous to exclude sites of other cultures from the sample analyzed.

4. SAIS stands for the "Southern Andean Iconographic Series" and includes art and iconography formerly called Tiahuanaco, Tiahuanacoid, etc., distributed from San Pedro de Atacama to northern Peru. Isbell and Knobloch (2009) argue that objective evaluation of the origin and development of this iconography is impossible as long as the name implies ultimate association with the Tiwanaku site.

References

Benavides C., Mario
1965 *Estudio de la Ceramica Decorada de Qonchopata*. Tesis para optar el grado de Bachiller en Ciencias Sociales, Universidad Nacional San Cristóbal de Huamanga.
1984 *Carácter del Estado Warí*. Universidad Nacional Mayor San Cristóbal de Huamanga, Ayacucho.
1991 Cheqo Wasi, Huari. In *Huari Administrative Structure: Prehistoric Monumental Architecture and State Government*, edited by William H. Isbell and Gordon F. McEwan, pp. 55–69. Dumbarton Oaks, Washington, D.C.

Bragayrac Dávila, Enrique
1991 Archaeological excavations in the Vegachayoq Moqo sector of Huari. In *Huari Administrative Structure: Prehistoric Monumental Architecture and State Government*, edited by William H. Isbell and Gordon F. McEwan, pp. 71–80. Dumbarton Oaks, Washington, D.C.

Brewster-Wray, Christine C.
1990 *Moraduchayuq: An Administrative Compound at the Site of Huari, Peru*. PhD dissertation, Department of Anthropology, State University of New York, Binghamton.

Cabrera Romero, Martha
1996 *Unidades habitacionales, iconografía y rituales en un poblado rural de la época Huari*. Tesis para optar el grado de Licenciado en Arqueología, Universidad Nacional San Cristóbal de Huamanga, Ayacucho.
1998 Evaluación arqueológica en el complejo turístico de Ñawimpuquio. Informe del proyecto presentado al Instituto Nacional de Cultura del Perú.

Carsten, Janet, and Stephen Hugh-Jones
1995 *About the House: Lévi-Strauss and Beyond*. Cambridge University Press, Cambridge.

Cook, Anita
1992 The stone ancestors: Idioms of imperial attire and rank among Huari figurines. *Latin American Antiquity* 3:341–64.
1994 *Wari y Tiwanaku: Entre el Estilo y la Imagen*. Pontificia Universidad Católica del Perú, Lima.
2001a Huari D-shaped structures, sacrificial offerings, and divine rulership. In *Ritual Sacrifice in Ancient America*, edited by Elizabeth P. Benson and Anita G. Cook, pp. 137–63. University of Texas Press, Austin.
2001b Los nobles ancestros de piedra: el lenguaje de la vestimenta y rango imperial entre las figurillas Huari. In *Wari: Arte Precolumbino Peruano*, edited by Luis Millones, Martha Cabrera Romero, Anita Cook, Enrique González Carré, William H. Isbell, Frank Meddens, Christian Mesía Montenegro, José Ochatoma Paravicino, Denise Pozzi Escot, and Carlos Williams León, pp. 229–71. Fundación El Monte, Sevilla.

Cook, Anita G., and Nancy Benco
2001 Vasijas para la fiesta y la fama: producción artesanal en un centro urbano Huari. In *Boletín de Arqueología PUCP, No. 4, 2000: Huari y Tiwanaku: Modelos vs. Evidencias, Primera Parte*, edited by Peter Kaulicke and William H. Isbell, pp. 489–504. Departamento de Humanidades, Especialidad de Arqueología, Pontificia Universidad Católica del Perú, Lima.

Cook, Anita G., and Mary Glowacki
2003 Pots, politics, and power: Huari ceramic assemblages and imperial administration. In *The Archaeology and Politics of Food and Feasting in Early States and Empires*, edited by Tamara L. Bray, pp. 173–202. Kluwer Academic/Plenum Publishing, New York.

Gillespie, Susan D.
2000a Beyond kinship: An introduction. In *Beyond Kinship: Social and Material Reproduction in House Societies*, edited by Rosemary A. Joyce and Susan D. Gillespie, pp. 1–21. University of Pennsylvania Press, Philadelphia.
2000b Lévi-Strauss: Maison and Société à Maisons. In *Beyond Kinship: Social and Material Reproduction in House Societies*, edited by Rosemary A. Joyce and Susan D. Gillespie, pp. 22–52. University of Pennsylvania Press, Philadelphia.
2000c Maya "Nested Houses": The ritual construction of place. In *Beyond Kinship: Social and Material Reproduction in House Societies*, edited by Rosemary A. Joyce and Susan D. Gillespie, pp. 135–60. University of Pennsylvania Press, Philadelphia.

González Carré, Enrique, and Enrique Bragayrac D.
1986 El Templo Mayor de Wari, Ayacucho. *Boletín de Lima* 8(47):9–20.

González Carré, Enrique, Enrique Bragayrac Dávila, Cirilo Vivanco Pomacanchari, Vera Tiesler-Blos, and Máximo López-Quispe
1996 *El Templo Mayor en la ciudad de Wari*. Laboratorio de Arqueología, Facultad de Ciencias Sociales, Universidad Nacional de San Cristóbal de Huamanga, Ayacucho.

Groleau, Amy
2005 *House-Keeping and House-Leaving: A Case Study of Oversize Ceramic Offering and Modes of Abandonment from Middle Horizon, Peru*. Master's thesis, Department of Anthropology, State University of New York, Binghamton.

Isbell, William H.
1985 El Origen del Estado en el Valle de Ayacucho. *Revista Andina* 3(1):57–106.

1991 Huari administration and the orthogonal cellular architecture horizon. In *Huari Administrative Structure: Prehistoric Monumental Architecture and State Government*, edited by William H. Isbell and Gordon F. McEwan, pp. 293–315. Dumbarton Oaks, Washington, D.C.

1997 Reconstructing Huari: A cultural chronology from the capital city. In *Emergence and Change in Early Urban Societies*, edited by Linda Manzanilla, pp. 181–227. Plenum Press, New York and London.

2001a Huari: Crecimiento y desarrollo de la capital imperial. In *Wari: Arte Precolombino Peruano*, edited by Luis Millones, Martha Cabrera Romero, Anita Cook, Enrique González Carré, William H. Isbell, Frank Meddens, Christian Mesía-Montenegro, José Ochatoma Paravicino, Denise Pozzi Escot, and Carlos Williams-León, pp. 99–172. Fundación El Monte, Sevilla.

2001b Repensando el Horizonte Medio: el caso de Conchopata, Ayacucho, Perú. In *Boletín de Arqueología PUCP, No. 4, 2000: Huari y Tiwanaku: Modelos vs. Evidencias, Primera Parte*, edited by Peter Kaulicke and William H. Isbell, pp. 9–68. Departamento de Humanidades, Especialidad de Arqueología, Pontificia Universidad Católica del Perú, Lima.

2001c Huari y Tiahuanaco, Arquitectura, Identidad y Religión. In *Los Dioses del Antiguo Perú*, Vol. II, edited by Krzysztof Makowski, pp. 1–37. Colección Arte y Tesoros del Perú. Banco de Crédito del Perú, Lima, Perú.

2004a Beer of kings: Great pots of potent brew marked royal rituals in Peru. *Archaeology Magazine* 57:32–33.

2004b Palaces and politics in the Andean Middle Horizon. In *Palaces of the Ancient New World*, edited by Susan Toby Evans and Joanne Pillsbury, pp. 191–246. Dumbarton Oaks, Washington, D.C.

2004c Mortuary preferences: A Huari case study from Middle Horizon Peru. *Latin American Antiquity* 15:3–32.

2006 Landscape of power: A network of palaces in Middle Horizon Peru. In *Palaces and Power in the Americas: From Peru to the Northwest Coast*, edited by Jessica Joyce Christie and Patricia Joan Sarro, pp. 44–98. University of Texas Press, Austin.

2007 A community of potters or multicrafting wives of polygynous lords? In *Craft Production in Complex Societies*, edited by Izumi Shimada, pp. 68–97. University of Utah Press, Salt Lake City.

Isbell, William H., Christine Brewster-Wray, and Lynda Spickard
1991 Architecture and spatial organization at Huari. In *Huari Administrative Structure: Prehistoric Monumental Architecture and State Government*, edited by William H. Isbell and Gordon F. McEwan, pp. 19–53. Dumbarton Oaks, Washington, D.C.

Isbell, William H., and Anita G. Cook
1987 Ideological origins of an Andean conquest state. *Archaeology* 40:27–33.

2002 A new perspective on Conchopata and the Andean Middle Horizon. In *Andean Archaeology Vol. II: Art, Landscape and Society*, edited by Helaine Silverman and William H. Isbell, pp. 249–305. Kluwer Academic/Plenum Publishers, New York.

Isbell, William H., and Amy Groleau
in press The venerated woman of Conchopata: Inferences from mortuary behavior. In *From Subsistence to Social Strategies: New Directions in the Study of Daily Meals and Feasting Events*, edited by Elizabeth Klarich. Colorado Press, Denver.

Isbell, William H., and Patricia J. Knobloch
2006 Missing links, imaginary links: Staff god imagery in the south Andean past. In *Andean Archaeology Vol. III: North and South*, edited by William H. Isbell and Helaine Silverman, pp. 307–51. Springer, New York.

2009 SAIS—The origin, development and dating of Tiahuanaco-Huari iconography. In *Tiwanaku: Papers from the 2005 Mayer Center Symposium at the Denver Art Museum*, edited by Margaret Young-Sanchez, pp. 163–210. Frederick and Jan Mayer Center for pre-Columbian and Spanish Colonial Art at the Denver Art Museum, Denver.

Isbell, William H., and Gordon F. McEwan (editors)
1991 *Huari Administrative Structure: Prehistoric Monumental Architecture and State Government*. Dumbarton Oaks, Washington, D.C.

Jennings, Justin, and Nathan Craig
2001 Polity wide analysis and imperial political economy: The relationship between valley political complexity and administrative centers in the Wari Empire of the central Andes. *Journal of Anthropological Archaeology* 20:479–502.

Joyce, Rosemary A.
2000 Heirlooms and houses: Materiality and social memory. In *Beyond Kinship: Social and Material Reproduction in House Societies*, edited by Rosemary A. Joyce and Susan D. Gillespie, pp. 189–212. University of Pennsylvania Press, Philadelphia.

Joyce, Rosemary A., and Susan D. Gillespie
2000 *Beyond Kinship: Social and Material Reproduction in House Societies*. University of Pennsylvania Press, Philadelphia.

Kirch, Patrick V.
2000 Temples as "holy houses": The transformation of ritual architecture in traditional Polynesian societies. In *Beyond Kinship: Social and Material Reproduction in House Societies*, edited by Rosemary A. Joyce and Susan D. Gillespie, pp. 103–14. University of Pennsylvania Press, Philadelphia.

Knobloch, Patricia
1976 *A Study of the Huarpa Ceramic Style of the Andean Early Intermediate Period*. Master's thesis, Department of Anthropology, State University of New York, Binghamton.

1983 *The Study of Andean Huari Ceramics from the Early Intermediate Period to the Middle Horizon Epoch 1*. PhD dissertation, Department of Anthropology, State University of New York, Binghamton.

1989 Artisans of the realm. In *Ancient Art of the Andean World*, edited by Shozo Masuda and Izumi Shimada, pp. 107–23. Iwanami Shoten Publishers, Toyko (English translation: http://www-rohan.sdsu.edu/~bharley/ArtisansoftheRealm.html).

1991 Stylistic date of ceramics from the Huari centers. In *Huari Administrative Structure: Prehistoric Monumental Architecture and State Government*, edited by William H. Isbell and Gordon F. McEwan, pp. 247–58. Dumbarton Oaks, Washington, D.C.

2000 Wari ritual power at Conchopata: An interpretation of *Anadananthera colubrina* iconography. *Latin America Antiquity* 11:387–402.

Leoni, Juan Bautista
2001   Kilns and Houses: Ceramic Production and its Social Contexts
        at the Site of Conchopata, Ayacucho, Peru. Paper presented at
        the 66th Annual Meeting of the Society for American Archae-
        ology, New Orleans, April 18–22.
2004   *Ritual, Place and Memory in the Construction of Community
        Identity: A Diachronic View from Ñawinpukyo, Ayacucho,
        Peru.* PhD dissertation, Department of Anthropology, State
        University of New York, Binghamton.
2005   Cambio y continuidad en la arquitectura ceremonial Ayacuch-
        ana de los Períodos Intermedio Temprano y Horizonte Medio.
        Revista Andina 41:155–76.
2006   Ritual and society in Early Intermediate period Ayacucho: A
        view from the site of Ñawinpukyo. In *Andean Archaeology
        III: North and South*, edited by William H. Isbell and Helaine
        Silverman, pp. 279–306. Springer, New York and London.

Lévi-Strauss, Claude
1982   *The Way of the Masks*, translated by S. Modelski. University
        of Washington Press, Seattle.
1987   *Anthropology and Myth: Lectures 1951–1982*, translated by R.
        Willis. Blackwell, Oxford.
1991   Maison. In *Dictionnaire de l'ethnologie et de l'anthropologie*,
        edited by P. Bonte and M. Izard, pp. 434–36. Presses Univer-
        sitaires de France, Paris.

Lumbreras, Luis G.
1974   *Las fundaciones de Huamanga.* Editorial Nueva Educación, Lima.
1981   The stratigraphy of the open sites. In *Prehistory of the
        Ayacucho Basin, Peru*, edited by Richard S. MacNeish, Angel
        García-Cook, Luis G. Lumbreras, Robert K. Vierra, and An-
        toinette Nelken-Terner, pp. 167–98. University of Michigan
        Press, Ann Arbor.

Machaca Calle, Gudelia
1997   *Secuencia cultural y nuevas evidencias de formación urbana
        en Ñawinpuquio.* Tesis para optar el título de Licenciada en
        Arqueología, Universidad Nacional de San Cristóbal de Hua-
        manga, Ayacucho.

Makowski Hanula, Krzysztof
2000   ¿Convención figurativa o personalidad?: Las deidades
        frontales de báculos en las iconografías Wari y Tiwanaku.
        Paper presented at III Simposio Internacional de Arqueología
        PUCP, Lima.

Marshall, Yvonne
2000   Transformation of Nuu-chah-nulth houses. In *Beyond Kinship:
        Social and Material Reproduction in House Societies*, edited
        by Rosemary A. Joyce and Susan D. Gillespie, pp. 73–102.
        University of Pennsylvania Press, Philadelphia.

McKinnon, Susan
2000   The Tanimbarese Tavu: The ideology of growth and the mate-
        rial configurations of houses and hierarchy in an Indonesian
        society. In *Beyond Kinship: Social and Material Reproduction
        in House Societies*, edited by Rosemary A. Joyce and Susan
        D. Gillespie, pp. 161–76. University of Pennsylvania Press,
        Philadelphia.

Murra, John V.
1991   *Visita de los Valles de Sonqo [Bolivia] (1568–1570).* Instituto
        de Estudios Fiscales, Madrid.

Ochatoma Paravicino, José
1988   *Aqo Wayqo: Poblado rural de la época Wari.* Consejo Nacio-
        nal de Ciencia y Tecnología, Lima.
1992   Acerca del Formativo en Ayacucho. In *Estudios de Arque-
        ología Peruana*, edited by Duccio Bonavia, pp. 193–214.
        Fomciencias, Lima.
2005   *Vida cotidiana y áreas de actividad: Los alfareros de Con-
        chopata-Huari.* Tesis doctoral en Antropología, Universidad
        Nacional Autónoma de México, México.

Ochatoma Paravicino, José, and Martha Cabrera Romero
1997   *El modo de vida en un poblado rural Huari.* Escuela de
        Formacion Profesional de Arqueología e Historia, Universidad
        Nacional de San Cristóbal de Huamanga, Ayacucho, Perú.
1998   El Periodo Formativo en Ayacucho: balances y perspectivas.
        In *Boletín de Arqueología PUCP, No. 2, 1998: Perspectivas
        regionales del Periodo Formativo en el Perú*, edited by Peter
        Kaulicke, pp. 289–302. Departamento de Humanidades, Espe-
        cialidad de Arqueología, Pontificia Universidad Católica del
        Perú, Lima.
1999   Recientes descubrimientos en el sitio Huari de Conchopata-
        Ayacucho. Paper presented at 64th Annual Meeting of the
        Society for American Archaeology (Publicado por la Facultad
        de Ciencias Sociales, Universidad Nacional de San Cristóbal
        de Huamanga), Chicago.
2000   *Excavaciones en un poblado alfarero de la Epoca Huari.* In-
        forme del Proyecto. Facultad de Ciencias Sociales, Universi-
        dad Nacional de San Cristóbal de Huamanga, Ayacucho, Perú.
2001a   Arquitectura y áreas de actividad en Conchopata. In *Boletín de
        Arqueología PUCP, No. 4, 2000: Huari y Tiwanaku: Modelos
        vs. Evidencias, Primera Parte*, edited by Peter Kaulicke and
        William H. Isbell, pp. 449–88. Departamento de Humani-
        dades, Especialidad de Arqueología, Pontificia Universidad
        Católica del Perú, Lima.
2001b   Descubrimiento del área ceremonial en Conchopata, Huari.
        In *XII Congreso Peruano del Hombre y la Cultura Andina*,
        Tomo II, edited by Ismael Pérez, Walter Aguilar, and Medardo
        Purizaga, pp. 212–44. Universidad Nacional de San Cristóbal
        de Huamanga, Ayacucho, Perú.
2001c   Ideología religiosa y organizacion militar en la iconografía del
        área ceremonial de Conchopata. In *Wari: Arte Precolombino
        Peruano*, edited by Luis Millones, Martha Cabrera Romero,
        Anita Cook, Enrique González Carré, William H. Isbell, Frank
        Meddens, Christian Mesía-Montenegro, José Ochatoma Para-
        vicino, Denise Pozzi Escot, and Carlos Williams-León, pp.
        173–211. Fundación El Monte, Sevilla.
2001d   *Poblados rurales Huari: Una visión desde Aqo Wayqo.* CANO
        asociados SAC, Lima.
2002   Religious ideology and military organization in the iconog-
        raphy of a D-shaped ceremonial precinct at Conchopata. In
        Andean Archaeology Vol. II: Art, Landscape and Society,
        edited by Helaine Silverman and William H. Isbell, pp.
        225–47. Kluwer Academic/Plenum Publishing, New York and
        London.

Pérez Calderón, Ismael
1998a   Excavación y definición de un taller de alfareros Huari en
        Conchopata. *Conchopata: Revista de Arqueología (Univer-
        sidad Nacional de San Cristóbal de Huamanga, Oficina de
        Investigación)* 1:93–137.
1998b   *Informe de los trabajos de arqueología y conservación en el
        sector de Monqachayoc, Huari.* Informe al Instituto Nacional
        de Cultura de Perú, Filial Ayacucho.

1999   *Huari: Misteriosa ciudad de piedra.* Facultad de Ciencias Sociales, Universidad Nacional San Cristóbal de Huamanga, Ayacucho, Perú.

2001   Investigaciones en la periferia del complejo Huari. In *XII Congreso Peruano del Hombre y la Cultura Andina*, Tomo II, edited by Ismael Pérez, Walter Aguilar, and Medardo Purizaga, pp. 246–70. Universidad Nacional de San Cristóbal de Huamanga, Ayacucho, Perú.

2002   Estructuras megalíticas funerarias en el complejo Wari. In *Boletín de Arqueología PUCP, No. 4, 2000: Wari y Tiwanaku: Modelos vs. Evidencia, Primera Parte*, edited by Peter Kaulicke and William H. Isbell. Departamento de Humanidades, Especialidad de Arqueología, Pontificia Universidad Católica del Perú, Lima.

Pérez Calderón, Ismael, and José A. Ochatoma Paravicino
1998   Viviendas, talleres y hornos de produccion alfarera Huari en Conchopata. *Conchopata: Revista de Arqueologia (Universidad Nacional de San Cristóbal de Huamanga, Oficina de Investigación)* 1:72–92.

Pozzi Escot B., Denise
1985   Conchopata: Un poblado de especialistas durante el Horizonte Medio. *Boletín del Instituto Francés de Estudios Andinos* 14(3/4):115–29.

1991   Conchopata: A community of potters. In *Huari Administrative Structure: Prehistoric Monumental Architecture and State Government*, edited by William H. Isbell and Gordon F. McEwan, pp. 81–92. Dumbarton Oaks Research Library and Collection, Washington, D.C.

Rosenfeld, Silvana
2004   Zooarchaeology at Conchopata, a Huari Urban Center. Paper presented at the 2004 Annual Meeting of the Society for American Archaeology, Montreal.

2006   Feasting and Animal Offerings in the Andes: The Case of Conchopata (Ayacucho, Peru). Paper presented at the 71st Annual Meeting of the Society for American Archaeology, Puerto Rico.

Rowe, John H.
1962   Stages and periods in archaeological interpretation. *Southwestern Journal of Anthropology* 18:40–54.

Sandstrom, Alan R.
2000   Toponymic groups and house organization: The Nahuas of northern Veracruz, Mexico. In *Beyond Kinship: Social and Material Reproduction in House Societies*, edited by Rosemary A. Joyce and Susan D. Gillespie, pp. 53–72. University of Pennsylvania Press, Philadelphia.

Schreiber, Katharina J.
1992   *Wari Imperialism in Middle Horizon Peru.* Anthropological Papers, no. 87. Museum of Anthropology, University of Michigan, Ann Arbor.

Smith, Monica L.
2003   Introduction: The social construction of ancient cities. In *The Social Construction of Ancient Cities*, edited by Monica L. Smith, pp. 1–36. Smithsonian Institution, Washington, D.C.

Solano Ramos, Francisco F., and Venturo P. Guerrero Anaya
1981   *Estudio arqueológico en el sector de Monqachayoq, Wari.* Tesis para optar el grado de Bachiller en Ciencias Sociales: Antropología, Universidad Nacional San Cristóbal de Huamanga, Universidad Nacional de San Cristóbal de Huamanga, Ayacucho, Perú.

Tello, Julio C.
1942   Disertación del Dr. Julio C. Tello, por Mibe. *Huamanga*, Año VIII(48):62–63.

Tringham, Ruth
2000   The continuous house: A view from the deep past. In *Beyond Kinship: Social and Material Reproduction in House Societies*, edited by Rosemary A. Joyce and Susan D. Gillespie, pp. 115–34. University of Pennsylvania Press, Philadelphia.

Tung, Tiffiny A.
2003   *A Bioarchaeological Perspective on Wari Imperialism in the Andes of Peru: A View from Heartland and Hinterland Skeletal Populations.* PhD dissertation, Department of Anthropology, University of North Carolina, Chapel Hill, NC.

Tung, Tiffiny A., and Anita Cook
2006   Intermediate-elite agency in the Wari Empire: The bioarchaeological and mortuary evidence. In *Intermediate Elites in Pre-Columbian States and Empires*, edited by Christina M. Elson and Alan Covey, pp. 68–93. University of Arizona Press, Tucson.

Waterson, Roxana
2000   House, place and memory in Tana Toraja (Indonesia). In *Beyond Kinship: Social and Material Reproduction in House Societies*, edited by Rosemary A. Joyce and Susan D. Gillespie, pp. 177–88. University of Pennsylvania Press, Philadelphia.

11

Domestic Economy as Political Economy at Chan Chan, Perú

John R. Topic

Introduction

In dealing with capital cities, the analytical emphasis is often on the political economy rather than on the domestic economy. Here I equate domestic economy with the production and distribution of goods by the group of people comprising the household, or residential unit; as we will see, substantial variation can be documented in the size and organization of residential units at Chan Chan. Political economy is equated here with the system of taxation, production, and distribution controlled by the political elite of Chan Chan. As I thought about this chapter, I wondered about the extent to which we could separate the political economy from the domestic economy in a city like Chan Chan, or, indeed, in general. In the modern Canadian context, for example, we pay taxes on what we earn and on what we purchase; we also consume such government services as police and fire protection, regulated food and drug production and distribution, and access to public highways. Where can we draw the line—either on a day-to-day basis or on a structural basis—between the operation of political and domestic economies? Or, to paraphrase former Prime Minister Pierre Elliott Trudeau, "What place does the state have in the bedrooms (or in the case of Chan Chan, the kitchens) of its citizens?"

As Hastorf and D'Altroy (2001:4) note: "In the Inca state, as elsewhere, people participated in both the domestic and political economies simultaneously, often in their home communities and own households. Evidence for the political economy, consequently, may be found in domestic contexts, just as evidence for domestic activities may sometimes be recovered from situations that existed on a larger political scale."

Moreover, as Netherly (1977, 1990, 1993) has documented, polities on the north coast of Peru, as elsewhere in the Andes, were structured into a hierarchy of local lords. Each lord exercised primary control over a group of subjects (a *parcialidad*). The lords were organized in ranked pairs. Within each pair, a primary lord ruled his own *parcialidad* as well as exercising some control (along with the secondary lord, or *segunda persona*) over the other *parcialidad*. Each pair of lords was further grouped with another pair of lords into a nested dual hierarchy. In one well documented example from the Chicama Valley, a local level polity was composed of eight lords in four hierarchical levels (Netherly 1993: Fig. 1.1) so that members of some *parcialidades* could be called upon to contribute to political economies managed by several different lords at increasingly higher levels of the hierarchy. Polities such as this Chicama Valley example were, in turn, integrated into the Chimú kingdom with its capital at Chan Chan, resulting in at least a five-tiered political (and taxation) hierarchy.

Occupational specialization was a defining characteristic of coastal polities (Rostworowski 1975, 1977a, 1977b). Polities had separate *parcialidades* of fishermen and farmers, and there are also references to *parcialidades* of artisans such as potters, metalsmiths, cloth painters, and so on, with their own lords (Netherly 1977: Chap. VI).

What members of the *parcialidades* contributed to the political economy was labor (Murra 1980; Netherly 1977: Chap. V). As the size of the polity expanded, the amount of labor contributed by domestic units undoubtedly increased since taxpayers were contributing to multiple levels of the hierarchy. The labor was invested in the construction and maintenance of irrigation systems, roads, and palaces; tilling the lords' fields; various types of service, such as serving in the army or bearing litters; or weaving and other types of craft production.

Lords maintained large households, and Netherly (1977: Chap. 5, 6) provides a summary of the available information. The households included large numbers of women and servants, some of whom may have been craft specialists. There were also doorkeepers, guards, and entertainers. Because of the prevalence of polygyny at the elite level of society, there were also lots of children in the households. Thus, while some of the members of a lordly household were related by affinal or consanguinial ties, others were unrelated retainers. Yet these households were integrated social and economic units: some of the members of the household accompanied the lord in death and all were supported by the resources of the household economy.

The lords needed these large households to provide access to personal labor (*servicio personal*, in the Colonial phrase) that helped them fulfill their ritual roles as well as the obligation to reciprocate generously the labor provided by their subjects. A key component of this reciprocity was the provision of *chicha* (maize beer) to people performing their labor service. There are a number of early Colonial petitions to Spanish authorities on the part of north coast lords for licenses to provide *chicha* to workers and even to maintain permanent "taverns." This requirement that the lord feast his subjects blends the lordly domestic economy with the political economy.

This information on local lords is largely drawn from the ethnohistoric literature. This literature dates to a time after the Chimú had been under Inca domination for two to three generations and then suffered from the disruption and demographic collapse associated with the Spanish invasion. Moreover, by the time these documents were composed, Chan Chan was abandoned, so we do not have a description that applies directly to the capital. Instead, the documents describe the lower ranking lords in what had been the Chimú kingdom. While they provide some insight into both domestic and political economy, Chan Chan, as a capital city, was much more dominated by the political economy.

In our examination of the economies at Chan Chan, we will look at different segments of the population, both elite and non-elite. We will define, as much as possible, household organization, the kinds of economic activities that took place within households, and the degree to which households appear to have been able to act autonomously in making decisions about their economic activities. Because corvée (in Quechua, *mit'a*) labor

was the main mechanism of taxation, it will be interesting to see the extent to which corvée was used to construct residential architecture. The flow of food, raw materials, and artifacts is another source of information on economic activity.

In the conclusion, we will examine how certain domestic economies, particularly those of specialized artisans, were strategically drawn into the courtly political economy on a massive scale to resolve developing contradictions between the ideal of reciprocity between ruler and ruled, on the one hand, and the increasing demand for labor on the part of the rulers, on the other hand. The result was the formation of a class of full-time servants of the state and the nobility who were designated as *yanakuna* in the Inca language (Quechua).

Chan Chan

Chan Chan was the capital of the Chimú kingdom (also referred to as the Kingdom of Chimor). Although the site itself was founded about AD 850 (Topic and Moseley 1985) and was probably the most important site in the Moche Valley at (or soon after) its founding, its status as a capital city evolved gradually. Theresa Topic (1990) has discussed the evidence for the expansion of Chan Chan's influence through military means. She notes that the Chimú first consolidated power in the Moche Valley and probably annexed the adjacent Virú and Chicama Valleys between about AD 900 and AD 1000 or 1050. There was a more aggressive expansion between about AD 1130 and AD 1200, resulting in control of the valleys from Jequetepeque in the north to Santa in the south; control was also extended some 10 km further inland in the Moche Valley than in the previous phase. The Casma Valley, to the south of Chan Chan, was probably incorporated into the kingdom in the early part of the fourteenth century while the Lambayeque region, to the north, was probably incorporated in the later part of the fourteenth century (Donnan 1990; Kolata 1990; Mackey and Klymyshyn 1990; Shimada 1990; J. Topic 1990:149; Topic and Moseley 1985: Table 1; T. Topic 1990:189). Beyond this core area, Mackey and Klymyshyn (1990:219–20; see also Richardson et al. 1990) see less evidence for administrative consolidation in the historically described frontier areas, stretching from Túmbez to Motupe in the north and from Casma to Carabayllo in the south.

Chan Chan was at the height of its power, and with the largest population in its history, when it was conquered by the Inca (ca. 1470). Architecture at Chan Chan includes monumental enclosures, called *ciudadelas*; less impressive enclosures, referred to as elite compounds; and small, irregularly agglutinated rooms (e.g., Day 1982b). There are also artificial platform mounds, sunken gardens, wells, open spaces, and cemeteries. What is preserved on the surface of the site is a mixture of structures and features dating to quite different time periods.

Our evidence for the early phases of occupation at the site is very limited (Topic and Moseley 1985), while we have quite a bit of information about the latest phase of occupation. Because of this bias in the information available, I will focus on the site as it might have been functioning about AD 1450.

Ciudadelas

The monumental enclosures, or *ciudadelas*, are interpreted as the palaces of the rulers and center of a redistributive economy (Day 1982a:63–65). The *ciudadelas* preserved on the surface of the site were built at different times throughout the history of Chan Chan (Kolata 1982, 1990; Topic and Moseley 1985). The *ciudadelas* that were functioning at about the time of our AD 1450 "snapshot" were Rivero and Tschudi, located toward the southern end of the site (Topic and Moseley 1985) (Fig. 11.1). The later *ciudadelas* are more standardized than the earlier *ciudadelas* and are divided into two, somewhat similar sectors: the North Sector and the Central Sector (Fig. 11.2). Each of these sectors has an entry court, storage courts, and courts with U-shaped administrative structures called *audiencias*. The later *ciudadelas* also have more variable eastern sectors with storage and *audiencia* courts (Topic 2003:266). Toward the southern end of the *ciudadelas*, there is a burial platform and an area called a *canchón*, with domestic debris and small, informal rooms, which are interpreted as housing for service and maintenance personnel (Day 1982a:61; McGrath 1973). As the palaces of the Chimú kings, the *ciudadelas* would have been similar to the households described for the local lords, but larger in scale.

The governmental functions of the *ciudadelas* are well represented by the storage areas and *audiencias*. I have interpreted the *audiencias* as information recording devices used by a bureaucracy to track the flow of goods into and out of the storage areas (Topic 2003). While some of those goods may have been the private wealth of the king, most were undoubtedly related to the functioning of the political economy (Topic and Moseley 1985; J. Topic 1990, 2003).[1] There is less evidence for the residential function of the *ciudadelas*, although some scholars suggest that the Central Sector served as the king's residence (e.g., Kolata 1990:140), while the burial platform in the south served as his tomb (Conrad 1982). I have already mentioned the evidence in the *canchón* for a service population.

In the best described *ciudadela*, Rivero, there were apparently also two kitchen areas, located just east of the Entry Courts in the North and Central Sectors (Fig. 11.2). The excavator (Day 1973:272–73) originally considered these kitchens to be facilities dedicated to providing food for the occupants of each sector. Because of the close proximity of the kitchens to the Entry Courts, however, I interpret their function as providing food and *chicha* for feasts held in the Entry Courts. A wooden architectural model was discovered in a Chimú tomb at the Huaca de la Luna in 1995 that depicts a feast, apparently in honor of three mummy bundles, taking place in a space very similar to the Entry Courts (Uceda 1997). In addition to the mummy bundles, small carved figures (including drummers, a person playing a rattle, *chicha* brewers, large pots for the *chicha*, and a cup bearer) are posed around the court. Thus, the kitchens may have been associated

with political feasting of the type described in the early Colonial documents cited above. Of course, they may also have provided food for the *ciudadela* household.

There is at least indirect evidence that the *ciudadelas* were constructed by corvée labor (see also Flannery 1998:21). Although Rivero and Tschudi are not the largest *ciudadelas*, they are impressive compounds with exterior walls preserved to a height of more than 9 m. Rivero encloses 87,900 m² (Day 1982), while Tschudi is almost twice that size. Day (1982:56–57) notes that the enclosing walls were built in horizontal and vertical segments that probably represent units of corvée labor (see also Moseley 1975). Some of the vertical joints are marked by large canes that may have been used to lay out task units. Kolata (1982:68) points out that although the adobes used to construct the *ciudadelas* varied in size from the bottom to the tops of the walls, the height to width ratio was maintained within each *ciudadela*. Some internal features (for example, architecture in the *canchón*) may have been added or modified by members of the household itself, but the construction of wells, the burial platform, the areas of artificial fill beneath *audiencia* courts, and primary walls was probably accomplished with corvée labor.

In short, while the *ciudadelas* provide information related to the political economy, it is difficult to coax out any information specifically about the elite domestic economy. If the *ciudadelas* housed the royal family, one would expect sizable apartments with a bustling domestic economy focused around the provisioning of the members of the household. However, we have not been able to clearly identify the apartments of the king, his wives, and children. Moore (2005:193–204) has an interesting commentary on this problem; although there is no clear evidence for "royal apartments," he does accept the view that the *ciudadelas* were, in fact, royal palaces. In any case, based on ethnohistoric evidence, much of the provisioning of the royal family would have been a part of political economy, drafting corvée labor to cultivate fields for the king and perform other services.

Retainer Areas Associated with the Ciudadelas

Outside the *ciudadelas*, there are artificially constructed platforms with rooms built on top of them. These areas have been interpreted as housing retainers associated with the elite residing within the *ciudadelas* (J. Topic 1982, 1990). Included within these "rooms-on-platforms" complexes are Units BK, BL, BM, VI, VII, VIII, the eastern part of Unit S, and the southeastern part of Unit BJ (see Fig. 11.1). The rooms are primarily of the small, irregularly agglutinated type, but Unit VI (associated with Ciudadela Tschudi) and the southeastern part of Unit BJ (associated with Ciudadela Rivero) also have architecture of the elite compound type.

There is considerable variation in the rooms-on-platforms complexes. Part of this variation may be due to their construction at different times, as indeed the *ciudadelas* were also constructed at widely different times (Topic and Moseley 1985:161–62). Only five examples were tested, and none of these can be considered

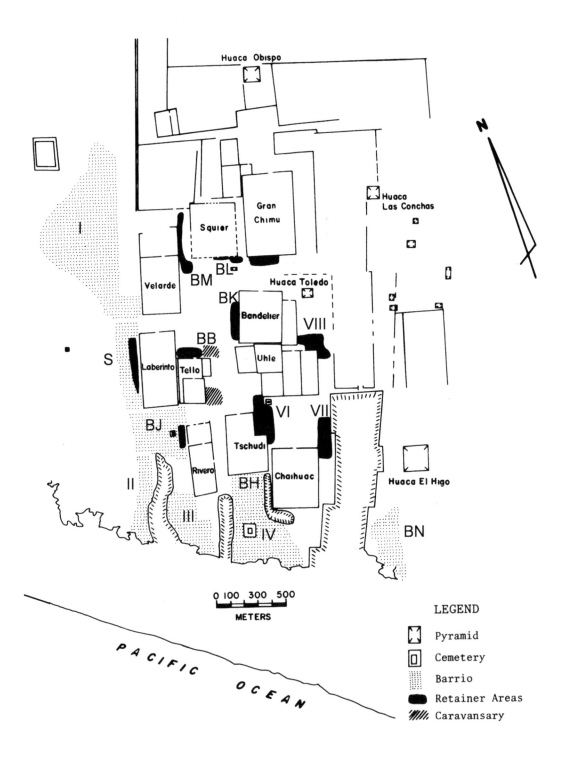

Figure 11.1. Central Chan Chan with the locations of the *ciudadelas*, barrios, caravansaries, retainer areas, pyramidal mounds, and sunken field systems.

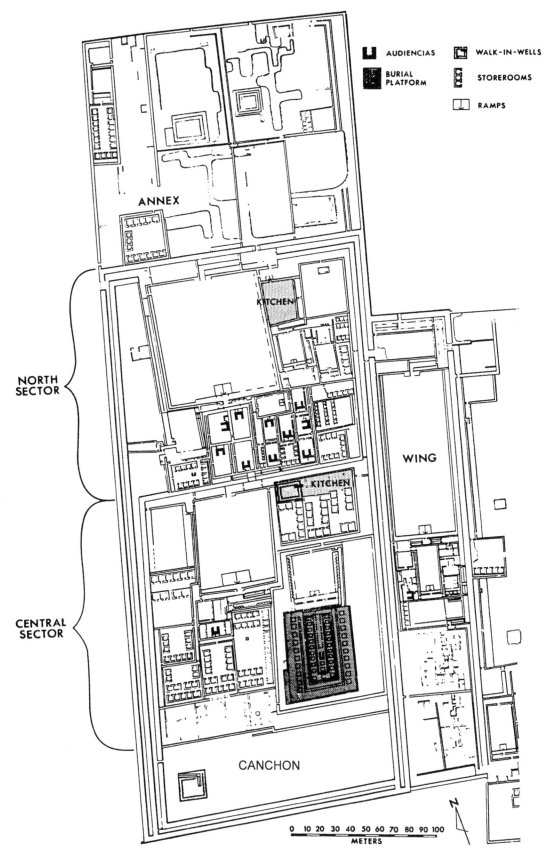

Figure 11.2. Ciudadela Rivero (after Day 1973).

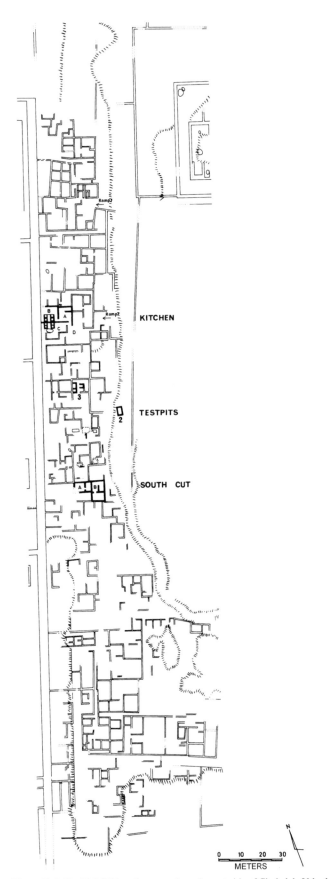

KITCHEN

TESTPITS

SOUTH CUT

0   10   20   30
METERS

N

Figure 11.3. The Unit BM retainer area along the east side of Ciudadela Velarde.

typical of the group as a whole. Extensive excavations were carried out in only two of the units.

The best evidence for economic activities comes from Unit BM, associated with Ciudadela Velarde (Fig. 11.3). Although one of the later *ciudadelas*, Velarde was constructed earlier than the date I am using for this snapshot, but the retainer area was still in use in 1450 (Topic 1977: Table 7). The primary economic activity of these retainers seems to have been weaving and metalworking (J. Topic 1990). The weavers used both cotton yarn and wool yarn. The cotton may have been procured from satellite communities such as Cerro la Virgen (Pozorski 1982:189), located about 5 km to the northwest of Chan Chan. The wool yarn was probably imported from the highlands in pre-spun and pre-dyed skeins (Rowe 1984:25; J. Topic 1982, 1990). The metalworkers relied on copper or copper-arsenic bronze, also imported from the highlands (J. Topic 1990). The imported raw materials were probably brought into Chan Chan through the caravansaries described below.

The major excavation in Unit BM investigated the kitchen area (Fig. 11.4). This was a large, communal kitchen, which may have supplied food to most or even all the residents of the unit (J. Topic 1990). There were pens for raising guinea pigs and traces of probable llama dung on the floor of one room. Two *arcones*, administrative structures that are variants of the *audiencias* used in the *ciudadelas*, served to store food. The bins in the *arcones* held gourds and gourd seeds, *cherimoya* seeds, maize cobs, llama bones, the bones from two deer's feet, and a single dog bone. There were also the skeletal remains of mice and rats that had gotten into the food. In an adjacent room there were two large hearths. There was a third hearth and a bench that had held three large grinding stones (these had been looted before we excavated the area) in another room. The residents of the units probably raised only the guinea pigs as part of an independent domestic economy, while most of the food was supplied to them through the state's redistributive system.

A test pit into the platform itself revealed more than 4 m of fill. An original platform was built by constructing a thick adobe retaining wall and dumping about 3 m of gravel fill between the retaining wall and the wall of the north annex of Ciudadela Velarde. The platform was later raised and widened by adding more gravel, sand and dirt fill. This construction was probably carried out by corvée labor sponsored by the state and suggests that the residents enjoyed higher status than most commoners. Another indication of their status was an offering of six large *Spondylus* shells and some small pieces of slag under the floor of the kitchen.

While none of the architecture excavated in Unit BM was clearly residential in nature, we did excavate what seemed to be a residential complex in Unit BK, associated with Ciudadela Bandelier (J. Topic 1990) (Figs. 11.5, 11.6). Ciudadela Bandelier is again one of the later *ciudadelas*, but it too was constructed before AD 1450; the architecture in Unit BK was still occupied at that date, however. The Unit BK platform is much less massive than the Unit BM platform, with only 30 to 50 cm of sterile

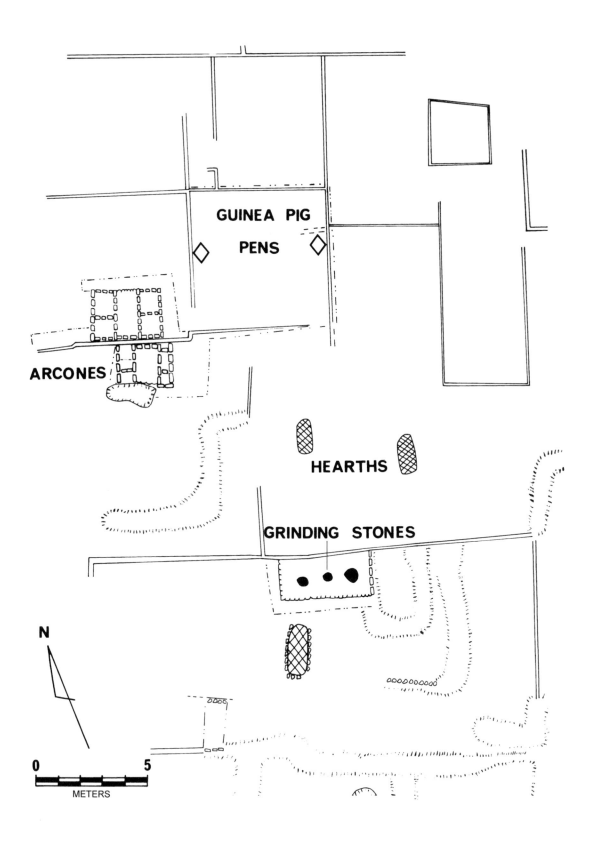

Figure 11.4. The kitchen facilities in Unit BM.

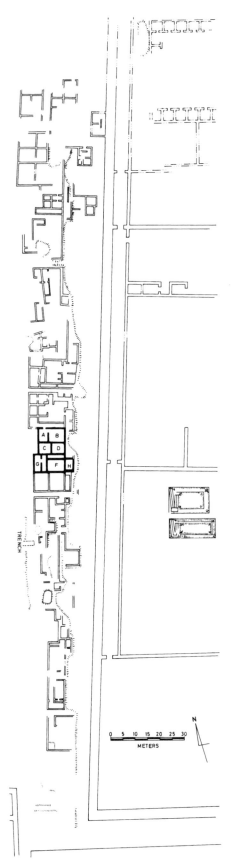

Figure 11.5. The Unit BK retainer area along the west side of Ciudadela Bandelier.

sand fill. The architecture was very nicely constructed, usually employing cobble stones for the foundation and adobes for the superstructure (Fig. 11.6). Many of the floors and walls were plastered with clay. Several rooms had benches and ramps reminiscent of the pattern of benches and ramps found in the more elite architecture at Chan Chan and the architectural model mentioned above. However, the rooms were not as large as those found in elite areas.

There is much less evidence for the economic activities that took place in Unit BK. There was a ball of yarn, but no other weaving tools. There were also pieces of polished mother-of-pearl and small bronze artifacts, like tweezers, beads, and a needle, but there was no evidence that these artifacts were being produced in the complex. Finally, we were unable to identify any kitchen facilities anywhere in the unit.

These examples of rooms-on-platforms illustrate some of the variation present in the group. They also suggest that the residents were of somewhat higher status than most commoners, that they had access to food and raw materials through the state redistributive system, and that corvée labor was used for at least part of the construction of these units. Again, we have more evidence for how the political economy supported these groups of people than we do for an autonomous domestic economy.

The Caravansaries

Evidence for the articulation of the urban economy with distant resources comes from two caravansaries (Topic 1982). These were located near the center of the site along the east and northeast sides of Ciudadela Tello (Fig. 11.1). My excavations focused on the northern caravansary, located just off the northeast corner of Tello (Fig. 11.7). This caravansary had a well enclosed in a small elite compound. An *audiencia* and an *arcón* were inside the compound, and another *arcón* was located outside the well enclosure. These administrative structures imply a bureaucratic presence in the caravansary, but exactly what the bureaucracy was doing here is not clear.

Outside the well enclosure, the excavated small, irregularly agglutinated rooms had a number of benches that may have been used as sleeping platforms (Fig. 11.8). Kitchen facilities were not incorporated into these living areas, however. Instead, two large hearths were found in one room along the south side of the well enclosure and another hearth was found in a room east of the well enclosure (Fig. 11.7: TP2 and TP8). As in the case of the retainers associated with Ciudadela Velarde, these hearths suggest communal food preparation for the occupants of the area. Ulana Klymyshyn's (1976) excavations in an elite compound in the southern caravansary also uncovered a communal kitchen and another *arcón*.

There was no evidence for craft production in the caravansary that I excavated, but there was a small artificial platform on the east side of the unit that provides the best evidence for the function of the area (Fig. 11.7: F5). This platform was apparently a

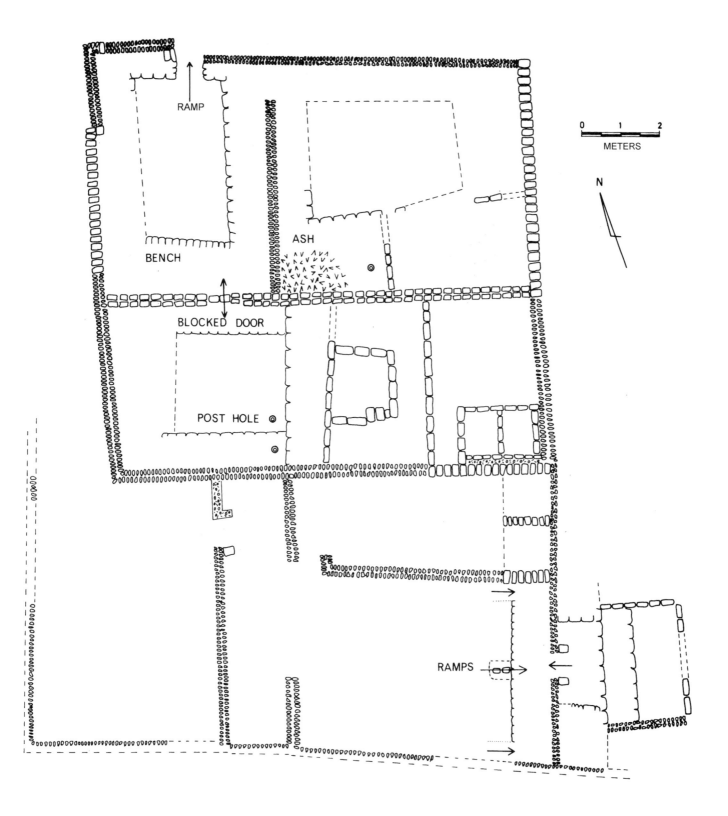

Figure 11.6. A probable residential complex within Unit BK.

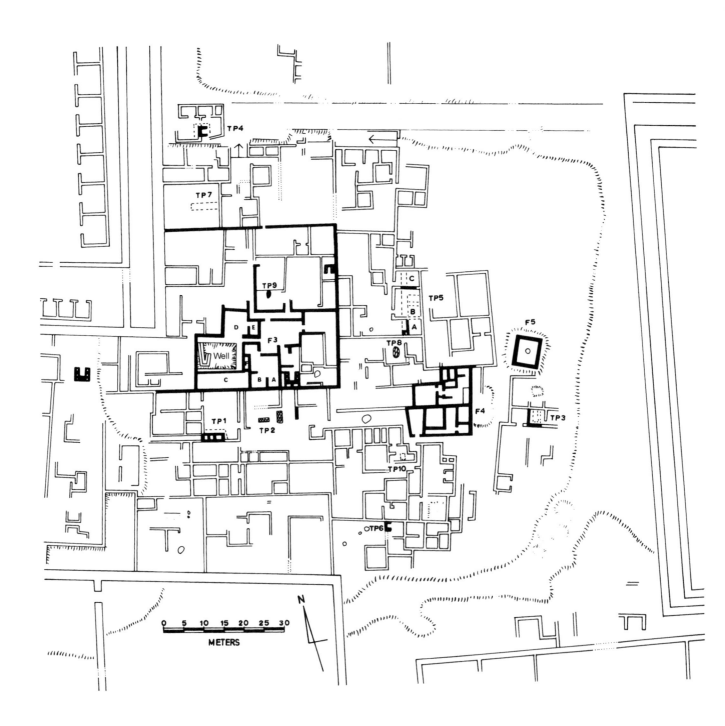

Figure 11.7. Unit BB: the northern caravansary.

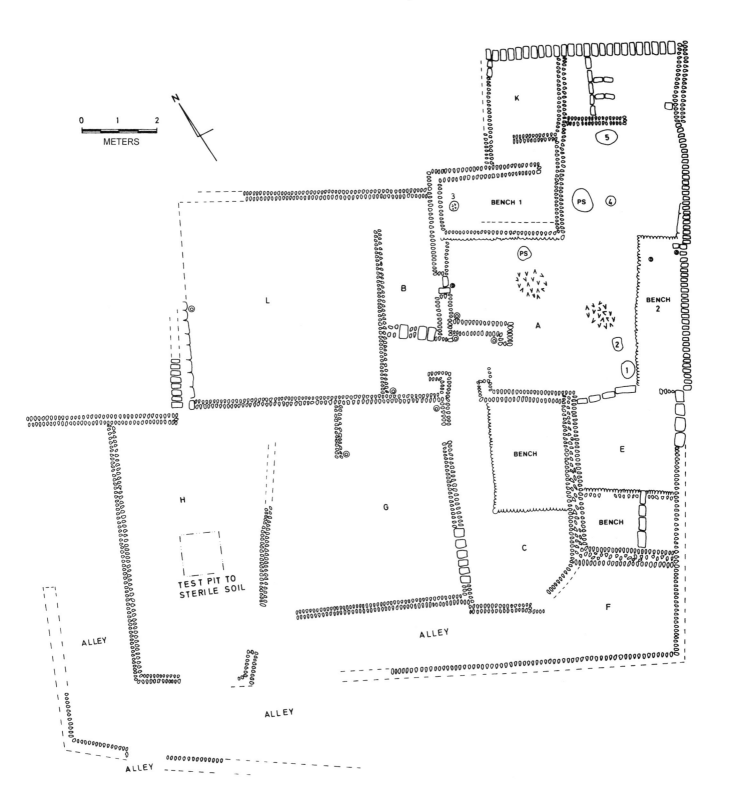

Figure 11.8. An area of probable transient housing for caravan drivers within Unit BB.

shrine: it was filled with sacrificed llama carcasses and other offerings. The llamas were interred articulated and with their skins intact; they were certainly not the remains of meals. In addition to the llamas, we found a military macaw (*Ara militaris*), *mishpingo* beads (*Nectandra* sp.), a textile made completely out of wool, and two *ollas* that had probably contained food offerings. The woolen textile is interesting because all textiles produced at Chan Chan seem to have been made of cotton or had cotton warps with woolen weft. The textile from the platform is unique both in composition and in style, and was probably woven in the highlands. The *mishpingo* beads and macaw suggest contacts with the eastern slopes of the Andes or Amazon basin. The food offerings were suggested by two *ollas* that contained mouse dung, but the food itself was not preserved.

Although not excavated, there is another, similar platform at the south end of the twin caravansaries. The fact that there were two kitchens and two shrines suggests the moiety structure so typical of Andean societies.

There is again little evidence of a developed domestic economy. The caravan drivers were housed in communal sleeping rooms and fed from communal kitchens. One large room had substantial quantities of llama dung on the floor and may have been used to corral the llamas forming the caravans. The impression is that the people housed in the caravansaries were transients rather than permanent residents of Chan Chan. They were provided for by the administration of the site while they were in temporary residence.

Barrios

The bulk of the population at Chan Chan lived in four barrios located along the western and southern edges of the site (Fig. 11.1). The term "barrio" is used in the sense of "ward" or neighborhood, and connotes a relatively self-contained residential community. Each of the barrios is composed of a mixture of small, irregularly agglutinated rooms, elite compounds, wells, and a cemetery in a double-walled enclosure. The small, irregularly agglutinated rooms served as houses and workshops (Fig. 11.9). The size and distribution of the excavated houses suggest that the residential units were nuclear families. Usually the largest room in a house was a kitchen that had a long hearth excavated into the floor (J. Topic 1982, 1990). There might be other associated features in the kitchen such as grinding stones, guinea pig pens, an area for corralling llamas, and some storage and cooking vessels (Fig. 11.9: Complexes 1 and 2). The elite compounds sometimes enclosed wells or served as administrative complexes and may have housed a more elite component of the barrio population. The cemetery enclosures are particularly important structures since they suggest that each barrio had a sense of community identity: the people who lived together were also buried together in their barrio. The barrios, then, may represent *parcialidades*, which would have had their own lords who were probably ranked in a system composed of two pairs of moieties.

A small cemetery enclosure is located within Unit I and a larger enclosure is located just north of Unit I (Fig. 11.1). Unit S formed a second barrio, with its cemetery enclosure located to the west of the concentration of architecture along the length of Ciudadela Laberinto. Units BJ, II, and III formed another barrio, with a cemetery in the eastern part of Unit BJ. The fourth barrio was south of Tschudi and was composed of Units BH and IV.

There are also extensive looted cemeteries located along the south end of Units II, III, and IV, but these are earlier than the enclosed cemeteries (Topic 1977: Chap. II; Topic and Moseley 1985:161); later architecture has been damaged by the looting of these cemeteries and they are also cut through by the sunken field systems constructed between the units. The enclosed cemeteries, in fact, are the result of an urban renewal program that was underway at about the time of our "snapshot." This renewal program correlates with the construction and occupation of Ciudadelas Rivero and Tschudi and it is interesting to note that a cemetery enclosure was provided for the rooms-on-platform complex associated with Tschudi (Unit VI). Two lines of evidence suggest that the renewal project was carried out by corvée labor rather than by the residents of the barrios themselves.

The first line of evidence relates to the ongoing expansion of the barrios. In the area to the west of Units II, BJ, and S, there are a number of piles of river rolled cobbles and a few long walls that delineate large spaces (Moseley and Mackey 1974: General Plan of Central Chan Chan). A somewhat similar distribution of walls and cobble piles was observed on the east side of the site in Unit BN (Topic 1977:492–523). There, workers had been expanding the sunken field system by excavating numerous, closely spaced rectangular pits. As they excavated the pits, they sorted the backdirt, removing gravel and sand from the area but stockpiling cobbles. The cobbles were distributed in piles in an area where architecture was under construction (Fig. 11.10). The first stage of construction was to lay out long cobblestone walls, often only a course or two high, which delineated large quadrangles separated by alleys. Since the work of expanding the sunken field systems would be a typical task for corvée labor, the similar stockpiling of cobbles and laying out of large quadrangles on the western edge of the site might also have been done by corvée labor.

The second line of evidence follows on the first (Topic 1982: 151–54). In Unit BJ, where the cemetery enclosure is located within an area of completed and occupied architecture, blocks have a structure that is similar to the process observed in Unit BN. Blocks are first delineated by long walls and then subdivided into smaller complexes (Fig. 11.11). A rectilinear pattern of alleyways results from the delineation of the blocks. In Unit S, on the other hand, the cemetery enclosure is located in an area of incomplete architecture. The completed architecture in Unit S is organized in blocks, too, but these blocks grew by the addition of walls to the margins of an existing room block as more space was needed. Alleys are not well defined, being simply the areas where rooms had not been built (Fig. 11.12).

Figure 11.9. Part of a block in Unit BJ. Complexes 1 and 2 are clearly domestic in nature and probably represent single-family houses. Complex 3 is a workshop area that had been converted from a residential function. The function of Complex 4 is not clear, but it was related to craft production activities.

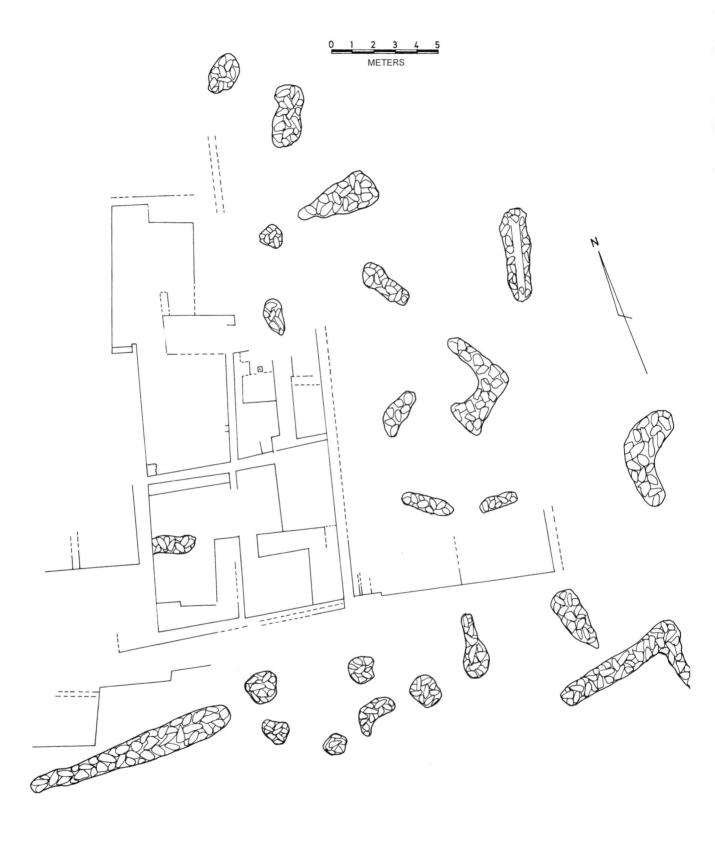

Figure 11.10. An area of architecture under construction in Unit BN. The piles of cobblestones were intended to be used in the construction of more walls.

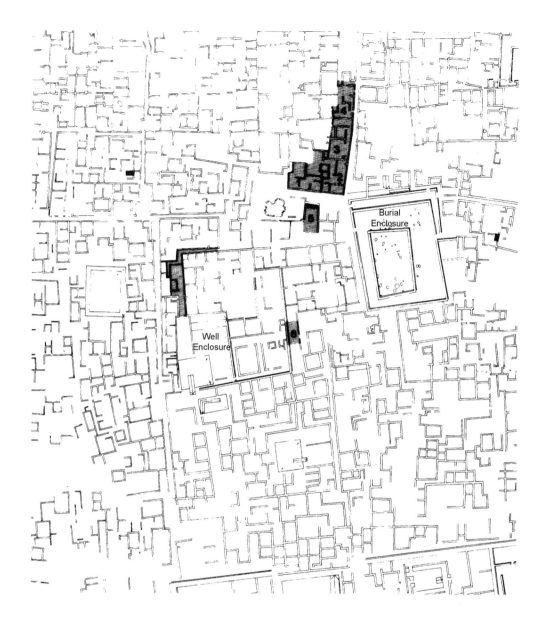

Figure 11.11. The central part of Unit BJ showing the structure of the blocks of rooms and the locations of some excavations.

The block structure in Unit S seems to be an earlier type of block than that found in Unit BJ; the implication is that the policy of investing corvée labor in barrio construction was a very late innovation. Similarly, the fact that earlier burials were placed in a large, undifferentiated cemetery at the south end of the site while the later cemetery enclosures were associated with particular areas of residential barrio architecture implies that the barrios, as four discreet communities or *parcialidades*, were also a late innovation.

Even where the structure of the blocks may have resulted from the use of corvée labor (such as in Unit BJ), internal house features (such as benches, hearths and bins) were probably added by the residents. Also, there is clear evidence, in the form of blocked doors, for the transfer of space from one domestic unit to another (Fig. 11.9). Complex 3 in Unit BJ, for example, seems to represent a house that was later converted into shop space. Thus, residents were able to make decisions about the detailed use of space within household contexts.

In addition to data from my own excavations, we have an excellent study of the barrio diet by Shelia Pozorski (1976, 1982). She excavated two quantified samples from Unit S and two from Unit BJ. She also compared the diet at Chan Chan to three other Chimú sites. Her main conclusion is that the barrio diet was essentially furnished by the state (Pozorski 1982:192). Llamas provided the bulk of the animal protein, and were probably supplied by the state. However, since llama dung was found trampled

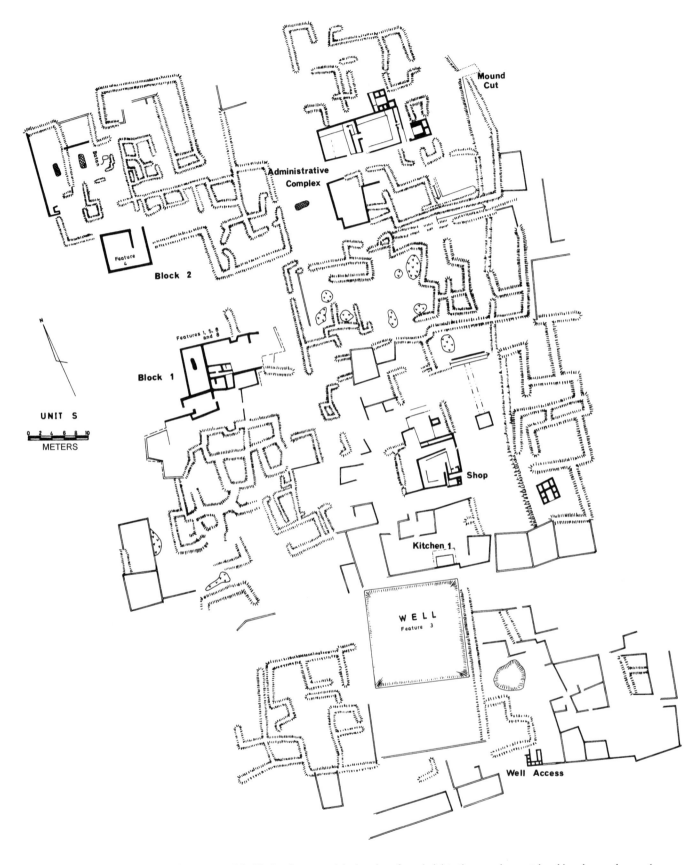

Figure 11.12. Part of Unit S showing the structure of the blocks of rooms and the location of an administrative complex, metalworking shop, and an *arcón* associated with the control of access to the well. The bins in the *arcón* contained materials related to craft production.

in thick layers in many of the kitchens, they were probably kept for some amount of time in the barrios and butchered there. Dogs and guinea pigs may represent the domestic economy's contribution to the diet, but neither was an important protein source. There were also a few bird bones and sea lion bones that may have been provided through the domestic economy. Pozorski (1976:162) points out that both the fish and shellfish inventories are dominated by single species (*Paralonchurus peruanus* and *Donax peruvianus*, respectively), suggesting that these resources were also supplied through the redistributive system, while other fish and shellfish species that occurred much less frequently might have been part of the domestic economy. Fruits constituted a surprising amount of the plant diet, especially *lúcuma* and *guanábana*, but also avocado and *cansaboca*. Plants of less importance included maize, beans, squash, *Capsicum*, peanuts, and gourds. Since the barrio residents did not have access to agricultural lands, the plant portions of the diet were probably also provided through the state redistribution system (Pozorski 1982:182).

I have pointed out previously that storage facilities in the barrios were used primarily for craft supplies, tools, and partially finished artifacts (Topic 1982:170–71). There were no bulk storage facilities for agricultural products in the barrios as there were at a rural site like Cerro de la Virgen. This implies that distributions of food were made periodically from the storerooms in the *ciudadelas*, probably channeled through some of the elite compounds located within the barrios.

One of the wild plants that occurred frequently in the barrios was *Tillandsia* sp., a bromeliad that is common along the desert coast, especially on hill slopes that capture the mists rolling off the ocean. *Tillandsia*, along with the pits of fruit, maize cobs, and peanut shells, was used as a fuel for cooking. It would be interesting to know if this plant was foraged as part of the domestic economy from the surrounding area or whether it, too, was part of a centralized redistributive system.

Large quantities of burned *Tillandsia* were found in two scoriated areas excavated and analyzed by Lechtman and Moseley (1975). One of these scoriated areas is a large building in Unit VI (the Tschudi Scoria) while the other is located in the area between Units BB, BK, and BM (the Central Scoria). Lechtman and Moseley (1975:161) estimate that the amount of *Tillandsia* that burned to produce the Tschudi Scoria was originally a bed of dry plants 1.2 to 3 m thick. The bed of *Tillandsia* that produced the Central Scoria would have been almost that thick. In a pre-publication review of the article, Cyril Stanley Smith (Lechtman and Moseley 1975: Note 8, pp. 163–65) suggested that the *Tillandsia* might represent stored fuel. While Lechtman and Moseley felt that Smith had made an interesting suggestion, they thought that it did not resolve all the problems of interpreting the scoria.

I agree that the scorias are still problematic, but I think that the *Tillandsia* found in the Central Scoria, in particular, might be a candidate for fuel storage. The Central Scoria is located near the end of the ca. AD 1450 access routes (Topic 1977: Fig. 5) and near the caravansaries. This location (cf. Lechtman and Moseley 1975:165) might actually be a reasonable location for the managing elite of Chan Chan to accumulate and dry such an essential resource as cooking fuel. We need to remember that until the twentieth century, European and North American cities were surrounded by managed woodlots; woodlots were essential to the functioning of urban centers. Fuel is an important resource; *Tillandsia*, a bromeliad that draws its nutrients from the air, might well require processing before it would be dry enough to burn.

The primary economic activity in the barrios was, of course, craft production. I have previously discussed Chimú craft production in some detail (J. Topic 1977, 1990) and will raise only a few points here. Craft production was an essential component of the political economy of Chan Chan. Virtually all raw materials were procured by the state and provided to the artisans through the redistributive system. This certainly includes the cotton and wool for the textile industry and the bronze ingots for the metal industry, which were the most important industries. It probably also includes materials such as wood and mother-of-pearl that were used in less prominent industries. In passing, I might also note that pottery was not produced in the barrios and was probably also provided through the state redistributive system.

On the other hand, the artisans probably produced some of their own tools: gouges from llama metatarsals, loom parts from wood, chisels from bronze, and, possibly, metalworking hammers and anvils from beach cobbles. In a house in Unit S, there was clear evidence for the manufacture of spindle whorls from soft stone (Topic 1970). A fragment of a ceramic *tuyere* (blowtube for creating the draft in metallurgical furnaces) was found in an administrative complex in Unit S; it had copper particles embedded in the paste, indicating that it had been made in an area where copper was commonly available, possibly in a nearby workshop where scrap metal was remelted into ingots (J. Topic 1990:158) (see also Fig. 11.12).

The textiles and metal artifacts produced in the barrios, in turn, fueled the Chimú political economy (J. Topic 1990:165–66, 170–71). These products were undoubtedly collected by the Chimú elite and redistributed as gifts in order to complete their obligations to reciprocate the labor of their subjects (see also Rowe 1946:268). To facilitate the movement of raw materials and finished products into and out of the barrios, administrative facilities were built. The architectural feature most closely associated with administration in the barrios is the *arcón*, a variant of the *audiencias* that were the administrative structures used in the *ciudadelas* (Topic 2003). While *audiencias* are three-sided structures with niches in the walls, *arcones* are three-sided structures with bins. In the barrios, they are found in workshops, in administrative complexes, and on the access routes to wells (J. Topic 1990: Figs. 7–9) (Figs. 11.12, 11.13). The artifacts found associated with the *arcones* link them securely to craft production. Indeed, in many instances, administrators using *arcones* were probably artisans themselves.

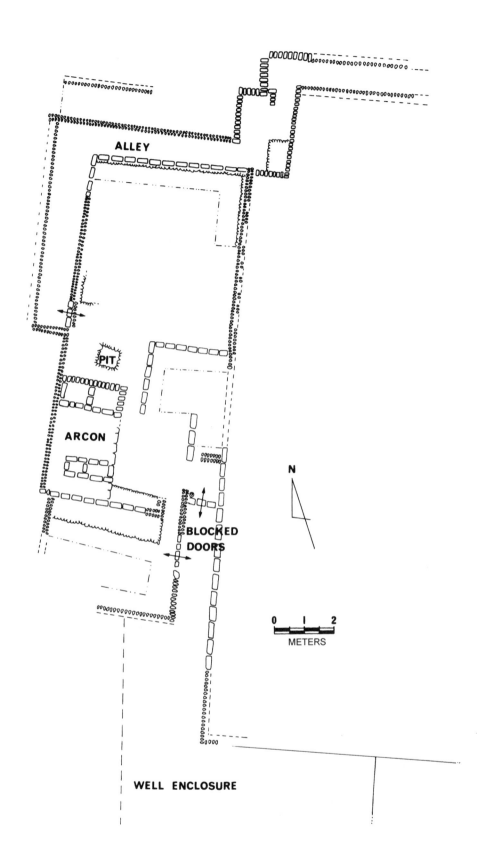

Figure 11.13. An *arcón* associated with the control of well access in Unit BJ. The bins in the *arcón* contained materials related to craft production.

Summary and Conclusion

The most important economic activities at Chan Chan were related to the political economy, although some aspects of a more independent domestic economy can be recognized at the margins of the political economy.

The *ciudadelas*, households of the principal lords of the realm, were at the center of this political economy. The storage capacity of the *ciudadelas* allowed the lords to supply the artisans in the barrios and retainer areas as well as to redistribute their products. Officials in the *audiencias* kept the accounts of the inflow and outflow of goods from the storerooms (Topic 2003). The lords feasted subjects in the entry courts. Thus, much of the architecture within the *ciudadela* can be directly related to the political economy. Undoubtedly there were some more strictly domestic activities that also took place within the *ciudadelas* but they are harder to identify.

The political economy extended outside the *ciudadelas* into the rooms-on-platforms. The people living in these areas may, in fact, have been considered to be additional members of the royal household with separate apartments. They seem to have had a somewhat higher status than the occupants of the caravansaries or barrios. Again, we have little evidence for an independent domestic economy, since their food and raw materials seem to have come through the state redistributive system. Like the occupants of the barrios, they probably manufactured their own tools and modified the details of their domestic architecture. At least in Unit BM, however, kitchen facilities were more centralized than in the barrios. There is some indication that the metal industry in these areas might have focused more on the finishing stages of production, while much of the preparation of sheet metal took place in the barrios (J. Topic 1990). Hence, these products may have entered more directly into the royal domestic economy; we have less qualitative evidence for the textile industry.

The caravansaries seem to have been occupied by the caravan drivers, some administrative personnel, and probably service personnel. There is no evidence for permanent households. Instead, the drivers were probably transients based outside the city. The administrative and service personnel probably resided in other sectors of the city. Administrative activities are not well documented, but may have involved both the provisioning of the drivers and the preliminary processing of the imported commodities. Service personnel provided meals, at least.

The barrios are where we see what most closely approximates individual family domestic units. Yet again, they are closely tied to the political economy. They were largely provisioned through the goods stored in the *ciudadelas* and some of the elite compounds. The production of the barrio artisans, some of which took place right in their residences, was a crucial component of the political economy. The same administrative system that provisioned the barrios channelled their products through the elite compounds and into the *ciudadelas*.

The *ciudadelas*, then, were the heart of the Chan Chan economy, pumping supplies to the urban population and craft products to lower level lords and their subjects. To this extent I agree with Kolata's (1983) interpretation of Chimú political economy as an extension of the royal household. However, I am not comfortable with stopping at that interpretation if Chan Chan is then considered to be simply a larger example of the large households described for the local lords in the introduction to this essay.

The *ciudadelas* themselves and the associated rooms on platforms could be considered larger versions of the households of lower ranking lords (again, Moore [2005] has an interesting discussion of lordly households that is often divergent from what I am presenting here). However, the barrios represent another level of centralization of power. At the time of our "snapshot," the barrios may have housed some 12,000 adult male and female artisans in four separate communities or *parcialidades*. I have argued before (Topic 1982, 1990, 2003) that this concentration of artisans is truly unique within the Chimú kingdom, and that these people occupied a status somewhat similar to the Inca status of *yanakuna*.

The *yanakuna* were people, sometimes but not always artisans, who worked full-time for the state or for elite households, and therefore were exempt from the corvée labor tax (Rowe 1946:189). The artisans in Chan Chan's barrios certainly seem to have worked full-time for the state; hence, they were supported from the state's resources. The Inca situation was slightly different: artisans worked full-time for the state and their products were distributed as gifts to satisfy the reciprocal obligations of the emperors, yet they were usually provided with agricultural lands in order to support themselves. The provision (or lack of provision) of agricultural lands to craft specialists is one of the major differences between coastal and highland societies: coastal societies did not provide agricultural land, while highland societies did (Netherly 1977; Rostworowski 1975, 1977a, 1977b; Spurling 1992). Still, in both situations, these were entire (sometimes reconstituted) communities that were brought into the political economy as *yanakuna*.

The Colonial documentation in Spanish often glosses the term "*yanakuna*" as "*criado*" (in English, the term "*criado*" can be glossed as someone brought up within a household, a retainer, or a household servant). Certainly in the Colonial period this was an accurate description, as indigenous people attached themselves to Spanish households to avoid taxation. This may also have been the pre-Late Chimú model of *yanakuna*, where a limited number of families were drafted into the service of lordly households; the residents of the *canchones* in the *ciudadelas* at Chan Chan may represent *yanakuna* of the household servant or retainer variety.

However, the *yanakuna* included other categories of people also. As discussed at the beginning of this essay, Chimú local lords controlled small groups of artisans attached to their households, apparently subject also to their own craft specialist lords. The residents of the artisan's quarter at Huaca Gloria (Donnan 1990; J. Topic 1990) may be examples of this type of *yanakuna*. At Chan Chan, these retainers may be represented by the residents of the rooms-on-platforms. As discussed above, the close association with the *ciudadelas* as well as the evidence from Unit BM that these artisans focused more on finishing processes may indicate that they were producing more directly for the royal households than for the broader state economy. In this sense, these retainers would also be somewhat comparable to the Inca *yanakuna* associated with the Inca royal estates who were often agricultural workers rather than artisans and whose production also directly supported the royal households (e.g., Niles 1987).

In both the Late Chimú and the Inca contexts, it seems that substantial communities were converted into *yanakuna*. In the Inca case, there were both agricultural workers, as just mentioned, and artisans. The Inca moved communities of artisans into many provinces, where they produced for the state (e.g., Spurling 1992). For the Chimú, we can only document the artisans of the barrios of Chan Chan.[2] In both cases, however, this type of *yanakuna* was less closely associated with the support of the royal household itself and more associated with the economy of the state in the broader sense. The Inca use of *yanakuna* is certainly more extensive, and probably more complex, than the Chimú situation, which underlines the fact that the expansion of the *yanakuna* class was one of the principal politico-economic processes underway in late prehispanic times.

Rowe (1948) pointed out that the word "*yaná*" existed in the north coast *Muchic* language; *yanakuna* is the plural in Quechua of *yana* (with the accent on the penultimate). He speculated that if the institution of *yanakunaje* had begun with the Chimú, the expanding Inca empire may well have adopted it as an administrative solution to organizational problems. He also pointed out that this was a big "if." I think there is some reason to accept his speculation because it resolves some problems faced by expanding polities in the Andes.

The major organizational problem faced by expanding states, I submit, is related to the contradiction between the nested hierarchical nature of Andean polities and a political philosophy that emphasized consensual community organization.

At a local level, economic decisions were ideally communal, cooperative, and consensual; at this level, labor, directed by local authorities, benefited the community as a whole more directly. As polities expanded, however, people started to owe labor to strangers and labor demands also increased. People were being consulted less and commanded more. Still, even in hierarchical state situations, Andean political philosophy emphasized the need for lords to "request" service from their subjects and the obligation for the lords to reciprocate that service with generosity (Guamán Poma de Ayala 1980; Netherly 1977). The need to request service and reciprocate with generosity was not an abstract philosophical principle, but rather, one that was taken very seriously by both the rulers and the ruled, as indicated by the petitions of north coast lords to maintain taverns (mentioned above) and to travel by horse or litter to request the service from their people (Netherly 1977). Still, as the physical, social, and genealogical distance increased between the highest level rulers and their subjects, this system of asymmetrical reciprocity was surely stressed.

The solution was to redefine the political and social relationships of crucial segments of the population. Large communities could be declared to be *yanakuna*, exempt from the tribute owed to their former local lords and even exempt from the state-level *mit'a*. In turn, their production greatly increased the resources available to the highest levels of the hierarchy. The process essentially drafts the domestic economies of communities converted to *yanakuna* status into a significant component of the political economy of the state.

While *yanakuna* of the household or "servant" variety existed prior to the late phase at Chan Chan, the establishment of large communities of artisans more loosely tied to the royal households and more directly tied to the state economy was a Late Chimú innovation. In the Chimú case, the state supported barrio artisans from state revenues, and used their production to support state policies. While the Inca later expanded upon this idea, the threshold reached during the late phase at Chan Chan was a significant contribution to the development of Andean statecraft.

Acknowledgments

I thank Dr. Michael E. Moseley for inviting me to participate in the Moche Valley–Chan Chan Project. Dr. Moseley and Dr. Carol J. Mackey, co-directors of the project, have been generous with advice and support. The project was funded by the National Geographic Society, and my participation was partially supported also by grants from the Ford Foundation, the Committee on Latin American Studies of Harvard University, and an NSF Dissertation Improvement Grant. This paper draws heavily on the work of my colleagues on the project, whose work is only partially cited here. I would also like to acknowledge the influence that an article, currently in press, had on my thinking while writing this chapter (Ana María Lorandi: El control del estado en las fronteras del imperio: *mitimaes* y alteración de las estructuras étnicas originarias. In *La arqueología y la etnohistoria: un encuentro andino*, edited by John R. Topic. Instituto de Estudios Peruanos and Institute of Andean Research, Lima). My wife, Theresa Lange Topic, has always been the perfect sounding board.

Endnotes

1. There is no direct evidence for the contents of the storerooms in the *ciudadelas* (Day 1973:185, 1982a:60). As discussed later in this paper and in the articles cited above (especially Topic 2003), the presence of a large non-food-producing artisan population at the site predicts a redistributive system to provide for the flow of food, fuel, raw materials, and finished craft products.

2. The Chimú may also have moved artisans from the conquered provinces into Chan Chan (J. Topic 1977, 1990; Topic and Moseley 1985). Because of the apparently rapid expansion of craft production at Chan Chan during my Phase 4, I hypothesized that artisans had been relocated from conquered provinces to the capital, starting about AD 1350. This hypothesis still needs further confirmation.

References

Conrad, Geoffrey W.
1982 The burial platforms of Chan Chan: Some social and political implications. In *Chan Chan: Andean Desert City*, edited by M.E. Moseley and K.C. Day, pp. 87–117. University of New Mexico Press, Albuquerque.

Day, Kent C.
1973 *Architecture of Ciudadela Rivero, Chan Chan, Peru*. PhD dissertation, Harvard University.
1982a Ciudadelas: Their form and function. In *Chan Chan: Andean Desert City*, edited by M.E. Moseley and K.C. Day, pp. 55–66. School of American Research and University of New Mexico Press, Albuquerque.
1982b Preface. In *Chan Chan: Andean Desert City*, edited by M.E. Moseley and K.C. Day, pp. xiii–xx. University of New Mexico Press, Albuquerque.

Donnan, Christopher B.
1990 An assessment of the validity of the Naymlap Dynasty. In *The Northern Dynasties: Kingship and Statecraft in Chimor*, edited by M.E. Moseley and A. Cordy-Collins, pp. 243–74. Dumbarton Oaks, Washington, D.C.

Flannery, Kent V.
1998 The ground plans of archaic states. In *Archaic States*, edited by G.M. Feinman and J. Marcus, pp. 15–57. School of American Research Press, Santa Fe.

Guamán Poma de Ayala, Felipe
1980[1615] *El primer nueva crónica i buen gobierno*. Siglo Veintiuno editores, México, D.F.

Hastorf, Christine A., and Terence N. D'Altroy
2001 The domestic economy, households, and imperial transformation. In *Empire and Domestic Economy*, edited by T.N. D'Altroy and C.A. Hastorf, pp. 3–25. Kluwer Academic/Plenum Publishers, New York.

Klymyshyn, Alexandra M.U.
1976 *Intermediate Architecture, Chan Chan, Peru*. PhD dissertation, Department of Anthropology, Harvard University, Cambridge, MA.

Kolata, Alan L.
1982 Chronology and settlement growth at Chan Chan. In *Chan Chan: Andean Desert City*, edited by M.E. Moseley and K.C. Day, pp. 67–85. School of American Research and University of New Mexico Press, Albuquerque.
1983 Chan Chan and Cuzco: On the nature of the ancient Andean city. In *Civilization in the Ancient Americas: Essays in Honor of Gordon R. Willey*, edited by R.M. Leventhal and A.L. Kolata, pp. 345–71. University of New Mexico Press, Albuquerque; Peabody Museum of Archaeology and Ethnology, Cambridge.
1990 The urban concept of Chan Chan. In *The Northern Dynasties: Kingship and Statecraft in Chimor*, edited by M.E. Moseley and A. Cordy-Collins, pp. 107–44. Dumbarton Oaks Research Library and Collection, Washington, D.C.

Lechtman, Heather, and Michael Edward Moseley
1975 The scoria at Chan Chan: Non-metallurgical deposits. *Ñawpa Pacha* 10–12(1972–1974):135–70.

Mackey, Carol J., and A.M. Ulana Klymyshyn
1990 The southern frontier of the Chimu Empire. In *The Northern Dynasties: Kingship and Statecraft in Chimor*, edited by M.E. Moseley and A. Cordy-Collins, pp. 195–226. Dumbarton Oaks Research Library and Collection, Washington, D.C.

McGrath, James E.
1973 *The Canchones of Chan Chan, Peru: Evidence for a Retainer Class in a Preindustrial Urban Center*. Bachelor's thesis, Harvard University.

Moore, Jerry D.
2005 *Cultural Landscapes in the Ancient Andes: Archaeologies of Place*. University Press of Florida, Gainesville.

Moseley, Michael E.
1975 Prehistoric principles of labor organization in the Moche Valley, Peru. *American Antiquity* 40(2):191–96.

Moseley, Michael Edward, and Carol J. Mackey
1974 *Twenty-Four Architectural Plans of Chan Chan, Peru*. Peabody Museum Press, Cambridge.

Murra, John V.
1980 *The Economic Organization of the Inca State*. JAI Press, Greenwich.

Netherly, Patricia J.
1977 *Local Level Lords on the North Coast of Peru*. PhD dissertation, Cornell University, Ithaca, NY.
1990 Out of many, one: The organization of rule in the north coast polities. In *The Northern Dynasties: Kingship and Statecraft in Chimor*, edited by M.E. Moseley and A. Cordy-Collins, pp. 461–87. Dumbarton Oaks, Washington, D.C.
1993 The nature of the Andean state. In *Configurations of Power: Holistic Anthropology in Theory and Practice*, edited by J.S. Henderson and P.J. Netherly, pp. 11–35. Cornell University Press, Ithaca, NY.

Niles, Susan A.
1987 *Callachaca: Style and Status in an Inca Community*. University of Iowa Press, Iowa City.

Pozorski, Shelia G.
1976 *Prehistoric Subsistence Patterns and Site Economics in the Moche Valley, Peru*. PhD dissertation, University of Texas, Austin.
1982 Subsistence systems in the Chimú state. In *Chan Chan: Andean Desert City*, edited by M.E. Moseley and K.C. Day, pp. 177–96. University of New Mexico Press, Albuquerque.

Richardson III, James B., et al.
1990 The northern frontier of the kingdom of Chimor: The Piura, Chira, and Tumbez Valleys. In *The Northern Dynasties: Kingship and Statecraft in Chimor*, edited by M.E. Moseley and A. Cordy-Collins, pp. 419–45. Dumbarton Oaks, Washington, D.C.

Rostworowski, María
1975   Pescadores, artesanos, y mercaderes costeños en el Perú
        prehispánico. *Revista del Museo Nacional* 41:311–49. Lima.
1977a   Coastal fishermen, merchants, and artisans in pre-Hispanic
        Perú. In *The Sea in the Pre-Columbian World*, edited by E.P.
        Benson, pp. 167–86. Dumbarton Oaks, Washington, D.C.
1977b   *Etnía y sociedad: Costa peruana prehispánica*, Vol. 4. Insti-
        tuto de Estudios Peruanos, Lima.

Rowe, Ann Pollard
1984   *Costumes and Featherwork of the Lords of Chimor: Textiles
        from Peru's North Coast*. Textile Museum, Washington, D.C.

Rowe, John H.
1946   Inca culture at the time of the Spanish Conquest. In *Handbook
        of South American Indians, Vol. 2: The Andean Civilizations*,
        edited by J.H. Steward, pp. 183–330. Bureau of American
        Ethnology, Smithsonian Institution, Washington, D.C.
1948   The Kingdom of Chimor. *Acta Americana* VI(1–2):26–59.

Shimada, Izumi
1990   Cultural continuities and discontinuities on the northern north
        coast of Peru, Middle-Late Horizons. In *The Northern Dynas-
        ties: Kingship and Statecraft in Chimor*, edited by M.E. Mo-
        seley and A. Cordy-Collins, pp. 297–392. Dumbarton Oaks,
        Washington, D.C.

Spurling, Geoffrey Eugene
1992   *The Organization of Craft Production in the Inka State: The
        Potters and Weavers of Milliraya*. PhD dissertation, Cornell
        University, Ithaca, NY.

Topic, John R.
1970   *A Lower Class Residential Area of Chan Chan, Peru: Initial
        Excavations*. Bachelor's thesis, Harvard University.
1977   *The Lower Class at Chan Chan: A Qualitative Approach*. PhD
        dissertation, Harvard University.
1982   Lower class social and economic organization at Chan Chan.
        In *Chan Chan: Andean Desert City*, edited by M.E. Moseley
        and K.C. Day, pp. 145–76. University of New Mexico Press,
        Albuquerque.
1990   Craft production and the Kingdom of Chimor. In *The North-
        ern Dynasties: Kingship and Statecraft in Chimor*, edited by
        M.E. Moseley and A. Cordy-Collins, pp. 145–76. Dumbarton
        Oaks Research Library and Collection, Washington, D.C.
2003   From stewards to bureaucrats: Architecture and information flow
        at Chan Chan, Peru. *Latin American Antiquity* 14(3):243–74.

Topic, John R., and Michael E. Moseley
1985   Chan Chan: A case study of urban change in Peru. *Ñawpa
        Pacha* 21(1983):153–82.

Topic, Theresa Lange
1990   Territorial expansion and the Kingdom of Chimor. In *The
        Northern Dynasties: Kingship and Statecraft in Chimor*,
        edited by M.E. Moseley and A. Cordy-Collins, pp. 177–94.
        Dumbarton Oaks, Washington, D.C.

Uceda, Santiago
1997   Esculturas en miniatura y una maqueta en madera. In *Inves-
        tigaciones en la Huaca de la Luna 1995*, edited by S. Uceda,
        E. Mujica, and R. Morales, pp. 151–76. Facultad de Ciencias
        Sociales, Universidad Nacional de la Libertad, Trujillo.

12

Domestic Life and Craft Specialization in Inka Cusco and Its Rural Hinterland

R. Alan Covey

Introduction

Cusco was the capital of the largest native state to develop in the prehispanic Americas, a city with a population of several tens of thousands (Fig. 12.1). Eyewitness accounts of the Inka capital describe it as a wealthy city surrounded by a densely occupied rural hinterland. Imperial elites and their retainers lived in Cusco, as did some craft specialists and civic and religious officials. As an imperial capital, Cusco was the location where important political, economic, and ritual activities transpired, but it was also a place where an ethnically diverse and hierarchically complex population lived and labored to sustain imperial administration.

Historians and archaeologists have written numerous overviews of Inka Cusco, focusing particular attention on ethnohistoric descriptions of elite life, important activities occurring at urban monuments, and the archaeological (particularly the architectonic) remains of the imperial capital (among more recent overviews are Agurto Calvo 1980; Bauer 2004:91–157; D'Altroy 2002:109–40; Hyslop 1990:29–68). This chapter summarizes the available evidence and gleans new perspectives on residential patterns in Inka Cusco, with attention given to the ways that the urban plan and its municipal administration accommodated ethnic diversity and the staple and wealth demands of an imperial capital (Fig. 12.2).

Documentary and Archaeological Sources

Inka Cusco was largely destroyed during the native uprising of 1535, and the Colonial Spanish city experienced substantial changes in its layout and population—both in its size and constituency—in the century that followed (Rowe 1967:59). The observations of early Spanish eyewitnesses provide invaluable perspectives on the imperial city, but they tend to focus on the wealth of the city rather than on its inhabitants. Later writers provide more detail on the residential aspects of the city, but they describe a community already reconfigured as a Spanish Colonial city. Administrative documents provide important information on status and ethnicity in the early Colonial period, although projecting this information back to pre-contact times is problematic. Archaeology could add important details to flesh out the documentary record, but few horizontal excavations under the modern city of Cusco have been well published.

Eyewitness Descriptions of Inka Cusco

A limited number of eyewitness descriptions of Inka Cusco exist, and many of these were not written immediately after the European invasion. These sources focus on the civic-ceremonial core of the city and the palaces and temples surrounding it. Three Spaniards sent to Cusco in 1533 to bring gold and silver back

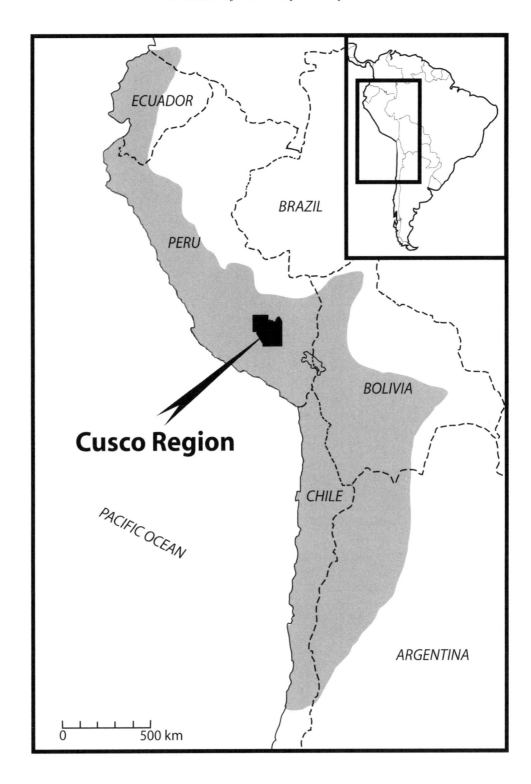

Figure 12.1. Approximate limits of Inka imperial territory.

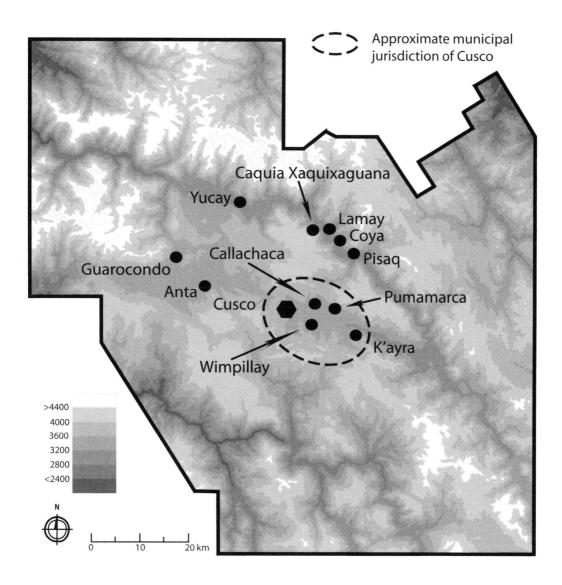

Figure 12.2. The Cusco region, with approximate municipal boundaries and the locations of selected rural sites.

to Cajamarca reported that in eight days there they were unable to see the entire city, not simply because of its size, but also because the natives kept them from doing so (Xérez 1985:149; cf. Anonymous Conqueror 1930:254–58). With the arrival of the main Spanish force at the end of that year, the European focus on the Inka capital remained on its monuments and the locations where wealth was kept or displayed. Several authors offer detailed accounts of wealth storage in the city (see below), as well as descriptions of noteworthy temples, palaces, and the fortress of Saqsaywaman.

These sources provide some general descriptions of the city itself, noting a hierarchy of residence types that included palaces and wealthy houses, as well as houses made of stone and adobe with thatched roofs (Pizarro 1986: Chap. 15; Noticia del Perú 1968; Sancho de la Hoz 1962: Chap. 17; Ruiz de Arce 1933:368). Residential parts of the city were densely settled and laid out on a grid, with narrow, paved streets that had channeled water in the middle of them. The eyewitness accounts indicate that royal palaces were found in or near the civic-ceremonial core, while dwellings of provincial lords and lesser nobility were distributed throughout the surrounding districts. It is not clear whether barrios of more modest housing were found clustered in certain parts of the city, but at least one author states that the poor were not permitted to reside in Cusco.

Chronicle Accounts of Residence in Inka Cusco

Chroniclers viewing Cusco as a Spanish Colonial settlement had only an indirect sense of the layout of the Inka city, but they tend to have a more nuanced sense of its inhabitants and how they lived. These sources identify spatial divisions within the city, including areas affiliated with the royal Inka moieties (e.g., Cieza de León 1985: Chap. 92; cf. Betanzos 1999: Part 1, Chap. 16), districts surrounding the urban core (e.g., Garcilaso de la Vega 1966: Book 7, Chap. 8), and locations where non-Inka groups from the provinces resided. Chroniclers frequently credit a specific Inka ruler with the establishment of the urban form, merging personal observations of the Colonial city with oral histories of Inka origins in a way that is not completely reliable. The identification of residential divisions varies between authors, evidence that these descriptions of Inka Cusco are not entirely reliable.

Administrative Documents

Administrative records from the early Colonial period—particularly from the 1570s onward—help to identify the residential locations of different parts of Cusco's Colonial population in the Colonial city. Legal documents provide information on the residence location of witnesses (e.g., Levillier 1940), while tribute records identify the populations of the parishes comprising the city at that time (e.g., Cook 1975). Many parishes can be identified as being in the same location as certain districts or satellite communities of the Inka city, and there is invaluable information regarding the settlement of the Inka nobility, a Colonial retainer population, and members of ethnic groups with origins in Inka provincial regions. Extrapolating such information back to the pre-contact period is problematic, although some general inferences may be made.

Architecture and Archaeological Evidence

Architecture is the most readily identifiable physical remain of the Inka city, although it is one that presents interpretive problems (Rowe 1967). By registering wall remains thought to pertain to the Inka imperial period, it has been possible to identify Cusco as having been a settlement of several square kilometers, although it has been impossible to identify differential status through household artifact assemblages, or to recognize craft workshops said to have existed in the city (see below). Peruvian archaeologists and some foreign researchers have conducted excavation projects within this area, generally as opportunistic test units or as salvage projects. The results of excavation work are not well published at present, making it difficult to test most of the assertions of the ethnohistoric record independently.

Despite the limitations inherent to the available ethnohistoric and archaeological record, it is possible to work synthetically to make some cursory observations on residential patterns, ethnicity, and craft production in the Inka capital.

Ethnicity, Status, and Residence Location in Inka Cusco

The Inka realm incorporated a wide range of ethnic groups and a considerable variation in local ecology and political organization. The Inkas were the most successful Andean state in linking the Pacific coast, central Andean highlands, and the Amazonian slope, and one of the many strategies for binding the imperial heartland with provincial regions was the transfer of population. Local Inka populations were sent from the Cusco region to colonize provincial areas (especially those in the highlands), while peripheral populations were required to resettle in the area surrounding the capital, either as temporary labor colonists representing provincial ethnic groups (*mitmaqkuna*), or as individuals removed permanently from those groups to provide service to the Inka elite (*yanakuna*). Provincial elites were expected to maintain homes in Cusco and reside there for part of the year (Ruiz de Arce 1933:368). Population transfers changed the ethnic composition of the Inka capital, concentrating a cosmopolitan colonist/retainer population among the imperial nobility.

The ethnic and social transformation of Inka Cusco took place over a century or so (ca. AD 1400–1535); during that time, the city was rebuilt to be an appropriate capital for a wealthy and expanding empire. Imperial Cusco should be thought of as a dynamic city in an ongoing process of being reshaped by ambitious emperors, as well as by commoner populations settling in and around the city and swelling its population. Cusco should also be conceived of as comprising more than just the civic-ceremonial core and its associated noble residences—the city's urban, suburban, and rural population was distributed over a much larger area. If Cusco's municipal boundaries are approximated based on ritual activities of the Inka nobility (e.g., Bauer 1998; Covey 2006), they were roughly equivalent to the natural boundaries of the Cusco Basin, a 400 km^2 region surrounding the capital (Fig. 12.3). This region can be subdivided into three main residence areas: (1) an urban core organized on the basis of moiety divisions of the royal Inka lineages and certain affiliated descent groups, (2) an area of suburban neighborhoods and satellite communities occupied by Inka and non-Inka populations, and (3) a region of rural farming settlements and elite estates surrounding the city itself.

The Urban Core: Inka Moiety Residential Patterns

The central parts of Cusco were constructed of masonry, and the urban palaces of the later emperors were found here, particularly in the area surrounding the central plaza (Fig. 12.4). Young men from noble families in the provinces were housed in the ruler's palace (Cieza de León 1985: Chap. 92), where they were instructed in Inka culture and administrative practices, while the most beautiful and noble young women from across the empire were cloistered in the *aqllawasi* complex, where they learned to produce fine cloth and ritual food and drink. In addition to Inka and provincial nobility, a large retainer population (called *yanakuna*) lived in the north and east sectors of the city and provided the elite with service—individuals identified as *yanakuna*

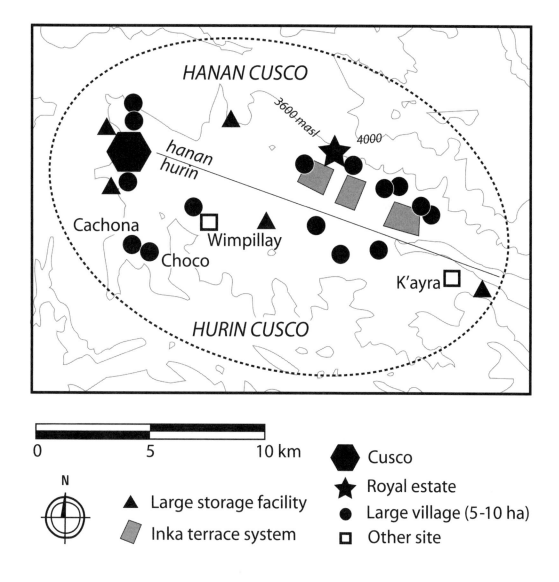

Figure 12.3. The Cusco Basin, with important Inka settlements, terraces, and storage facilities. Based on Bauer 2004.

continued to live in these parts of the city in early Colonial times (Table 12.1).[1] The servant population was drawn from throughout the Inka realm, making this part of the city ethnically diverse.

The residential sectors of the urban core were divided between the upper (*Hanan Cusco*) and lower (*Hurin Cusco*) moieties, each of which comprised the descendants of a number of Inka rulers (Ondegardo 1916:10–11) (Table 12.2). There is some evidence that boundaries between *Hanan* and *Hurin* were defined in part by access to irrigation resources and ritual activities associated with maintaining them (Bauer 1998; Sherbondy 1987). According to certain chroniclers, the *Hanan Cusco* moiety was established by the sixth Inka ruler (Inka Roq'a) and his wife, who invested labor tribute to construct the Chacan canal system in lands located above the city (e.g., Cieza de León 1988: Chap. 35). *Hanan Cusco* comprised six or seven generations of the descendants of this

ruler, and its members resided in the neighborhoods and satellite communities in the higher ground of the north part of the city.

Hurin Cusco lineages represent a broader social group that traced common descent from the founding Inka ancestor (Manqo Qhapaq), and Inkas of this group who lived in Cusco proper resided in the lower neighborhoods of the east part of the city. The exact boundary between *Hanan* and *Hurin* neighborhoods— and exactly how discrete the two residential areas were—is not completely clear, and contemporary researchers have used the Colonial documents to prepare maps with differing divisions (e.g., Bauer 2004:111; D'Altroy 2002:112; Hyslop 1990:33). The urban core and principal settlement areas of *Hanan* and *Hurin Cusco* seem to have been defined by the area bounded by the two main rivers of the city (the Tullumayo and Saphy), an area covering a square kilometer or less.

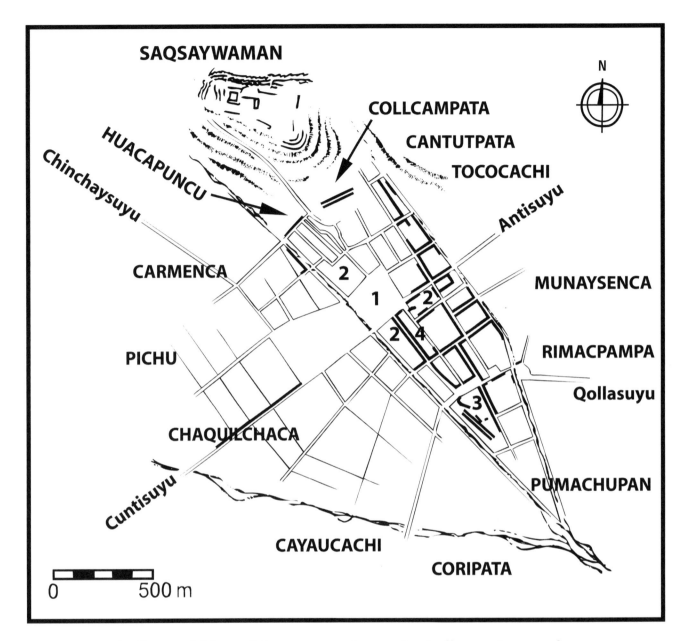

1. Central Plaza (Haucaypata) 3. Aqllawasi complex
2. Royal Palaces 4. Qorikancha

Figure 12.4. The urban core of Cusco, showing important monuments and surrounding neighborhoods.

Table 12.1. Early Colonial records of Inka (*Cuzqueño*) and retainer (*yanakuna*) populations, by barrio.

Parish	Cuzqueños	Yanakuna
Nuestra Señora de Belén	255	170
Santiago	244	75
Hospital	180	305
Santa Ana	200*	58
San Cristóbal	225	216
San Blas	304	260
San Sebastián	46	116
San Gerónimo	40	204

(Source: Cook 1975:211–12)
*Two hundred Chachapoyas and Cañaris were designated as *Cuzqueños* and taxed accordingly. There were another 275 individuals from these groups who were exempted from tribute for services given to the Crown.

Table 12.2. Moiety divisions of royal Inka descent groups of Cusco.

Royal Descent Group [Ruler]	Moiety
Chima panaka [Manqo Qhapaq]	Hurin Cusco*
Raurau panaka [Zinchi Roq'a]	Hurin Cusco
Hawaynin panaka [Lloq'e Yupanki]	Hurin Cusco
Uskamayta panaka [Mayta Qhapaq]	Hurin Cusco
Apumayta panaka [Qhapaq Yupanki]	Hurin Cusco
Wikak'iraw panaka [Inka Roq'a]	Hanan Cusco
Awqaylli panaka [Yawar Waq'aq]	Hanan Cusco
Zukzu panaka [Wiraqocha Inka]	Hanan Cusco
Hatun ayllu/Iñaqa panaka [Pachakutiq Inka Yupanki]	Hanan Cusco
Qhapaq ayllu [Thupa Inka Yupanki]	Hanan Cusco
[Wayna Qhapaq]	Hanan Cusco

(Source: Bauer 1998:40–46; D'Altroy 2002:100)
*Some sources list the founding ancestor apart from either moiety.

The Outer City: Non-Royal Neighborhoods and Provincial Communities

While the Inka nobles and their servants occupied most of the residential areas to the north and east of the central plaza, areas to the south and west were occupied not only by Inkas, but also by local non-noble descent groups, provincial officials, and some craft specialists (Table 12.3). Areas lying outside the urban core described above may have been conceived of as separate wards or districts of the city whose streets and domestic structures were laid out in state-organized programs of urban development. Writing in 1602, Garcilaso de la Vega (1966: Book 7, Chap. 8) recalled the layout of Colonial Cusco during his youth (around 1560), naming thirteen wards or districts that surrounded the urban core of Cusco: Collcampata, Cantutpata, Pumacurcu, Tococachi, Munaicenca, Rimacpampa, Pumapchupan, Cayaucachi, Chaquillchaca, Pichu, Quillipata, Carmenca, and Huacapuncu. These neighborhoods were very much a part of the Inka capital, but little is known about their constituent residents. As Table 12.2 shows, there is evidence that provincial officials resided in some of these areas, and there is written evidence suggesting that provincial groups were placed together in certain parts of the city by the Inka elite. Pedro de Cieza de León, writing in 1553, noted that

though the city was full of numbers of strange and remote tribes, such as Indians from Chile and Pasto, Cañaris, Chachapoyas, Huancas, Collas, and other peoples of these provinces, each race dwelt together in the place allotted to it by the governors of the city. The latter preserved the customs of their fathers, followed the usages of their provinces, and would easily have been recognized from the insignia they wore on their heads even though there were a hundred-thousand men gathered together. [1985: Chap. 93; quoted in Garcilaso de la Vega 1966: Book 7, Chap. 9]

Some craft specialists (for example, goldsmiths and silversmiths) are known to have lived in this part of the city (Cieza de León 1985: Chap. 92), but whether there were particular occupation-related neighborhoods remains to be explored in detail (see below).

Cusco's Rural Hinterland

Like many cities, Cusco consisted of a civic-ceremonial core and urban residential space that gradually gave way to a network of rural communities that produced food for the capital. Suburban communities at the margin of the city were occupied by local farming populations whose traditional lands were encroached on by urban growth, as well as by provincial groups drawn to the capital by opportunity or compelled to settle there by the

Table 12.3. Parishes of early Colonial Cusco and ethnic residence patterns.

Parish [Inka name]	Ethnic Group	Occupations
San Francisco [Pichu]	Chupaychu	unknown
San Blas [Tococachi]	Inka	administrator
San Cristóbal [Collcampata]	Inka	administrator
Santa Cruz	Wanka	provincial administration
Santa Ana [Huacapuncu]	Wanka, Chachapoya, Cañari	provincial administration
Belén [Cayaucachi]	Inka, unspecified*	supervisor of bird-keepers
[Carmenca]	Atavillo, Cañari, Chachapoya	administrators, retainers, supervisor of herders
unspecified	Chupaychu, Huamachuco, Inka	administrators, retainers

(Source: Levillier 1940)
*Tributary records listing new tax requirements from 1572 distinguish between *Cuzqueños* and *yanakuna* for the different parishes of Cusco (Table 12.1).

Inka elite. Beyond these settlements lay farming communities occupied by local groups, members of Inka royal lineages, and provincial populations.

Some rural communities, such as the towns of Choco and Cachona, appear to have retained a considerable degree of local autonomy and control over their productive resources. Based on regional survey data, it is evident that many rural villages were settled several centuries before the Inka imperial period and grew to modest sizes (5–10 ha) during long periods of occupation (Bauer 2004). While Inka elites invested labor tribute in expanding agricultural infrastructure in the region surrounding Cusco, many rural communities were relatively unaffected by these works and remained distinct entities until the *reducciones* of the 1570s.

The documentary record identifies members of royal Inka lineages living in the rural parts of the Cusco Basin (Table 12.4). Members of *Hurin Cusco* descent groups lived in and around the towns of the southern part of the basin, where some villages had been settled for a millennium or longer. Numerous chronicles and archival documents refer to the communities of Cayaucache (contemporary Belén, a residential ward of Cusco), Wimpillay, and K'ayra as places occupied by descendants of *Hurin Cusco* rulers (e.g., Levillier 1940). Members of *Hanan Cusco* descent groups—especially descendants of pre-imperial rulers—are identifiable in communities on the north side of the basin, particularly in areas where new irrigation canals and terraces were built as the Inka state formed (Bauer and Covey 2002). Later rulers developed impressive estates outside the Cusco Basin, which were closely tied to their families.

Some provincial settlers may have joined the local population in the Cusco Basin, but it appears that areas beyond Cusco's mu-

nicipal boundaries were much more strongly affected by imperial population transfer projects. Instead, state intensification projects within the Cusco Basin appear to have eased land pressures for existing Inka populations and their neighbors.

Domestic architecture has been identified at a very limited number of rural sites in the Cusco Basin (e.g., Niles 1987), where there is a clear variation in the degree of central planning and site size. Some sites (for example, Qotakalli) were laid out on a grid, while others (for example, Raqay-Raqayniyoq) appear to have grown opportunistically (Niles 1987:31–40). While some rural domestic structures were built of fieldstones set in mud mortar, many were probably made of unfired mud brick. Planned patio groups, which may have been a typical residential unit in urban areas (the *kancha* group, a compound of rectangular structures laid out around an open patio, is a typical Inka domestic form), are not common in the remaining rural architecture of the Cusco Basin (Fig. 12.5). Instead, single-room rectangular structures without associated patio spaces seem to typify such areas. These structures are of a modest size (usually not much larger than 50 m²), lack discernible internal spatial divisions, and are not laid out in groups or walled compounds that would suggest extended family residence.

Production Specialists in Cusco's Political Economy

Colonial period documents from Inka provincial regions show that exotic materials and wealth goods were transported from certain provinces to the capital, and Cusco contained storage facilities for precious metals, fine textiles, and non-staple materials used to produce craft goods, ritual objects, and weaponry. Pedro

Table 12.4. Distribution of members of royal Inka lineages in the Cusco Basin.

Lineage	Communities
Manqo Qhapaq	Wimpillay, K'ayra
Zinchi Roq'a	Belén, Wimpillay
Lloq'e Yupanki	
Mayta Qhapaq	Hariaymina
Qhapaq Yupanki	
Inka Roq'a	Uro, Pumamarca
Yawar Waq'aq	Lamay
Wiraqocha Inka	Caruamba, Anta, San Blas, Guarocondo, Callachaca
Pachakutiq Inka Yupanki	Calgua, Pisaq, Coya, Pomapata, San Blas
Thupa Inka Yupanki	Caquia Xaquixaguana, San Cristóbal
Wayna Qhapaq	Yucay

(Source: Levillier 1940)

Pizarro recalled that upon entering Cusco for the first time in 1533, the Spaniards found stores of fine and coarse cloth; a wide array of colorful bird feathers and worked feathers; vestments made of *Spondylus* shell, precious metals, and fine beadwork; finely made sandals; copper bars; vessels of silver and gold; and considerable stores of lances, arrows, darts, maces, and other weapons (Pizarro 1986: Chap. 15; cf. Noticia del Perú 1968:393; Trujillo 1985:206; Sancho de la Hoz 1962: Chap. 17). Specialists were critical for acquiring and processing raw materials (for example, metal ores, marine shell, dyes and pigments, wool, colored feathers) and for working these materials into wealth goods that supported the imperial political economy and added pomp to the ritual and political pageantry of the capital.

The Inka empire designated production specialists with titles with the suffix -*kamayuq*, which in Quechua may be translated as "possessing the essence of [activity]." Thus, a gold miner was a *qorikamayuq*, while a saltmaker was a *kachikamayuq* and a farmer specializing in producing early varieties of maize was a *michkakamayuq*. The 1567 chronicle of Francisco Falcón lists nearly fifty *kamayuq* titles, which can be divided into a few basic categories, including: (1) subsistence, (2) construction or maintenance of imperial infrastructure, (3) acquisition of raw materials, (4) production of craft goods and products for elite or ceremonial use, and (5) administrative and religious activities. The first three of these categories presume a presence of specialists in both the imperial heartland and provincial contexts as the empire intensified local economies and extracted exotic raw materials to be fashioned into wealth goods. Craft production and religious and administrative activities also took place in specific provincial contexts, and early Colonial documents identify communities of potters, woodworkers, and cloth producers that were

placed by the Inka among some provincial populations (e.g., Diez de San Miguel 1964; Levillier 1940; Ortiz de Zúñiga 1967, 1972). These communities were generally small, consisting of no more than about twenty households. Specialist enclaves and communities are known for the rural hinterland surrounding Cusco, where groups of construction workers, textile producers, and saltmakers were still living several decades after the Conquest (Covey 2006).

While a considerable amount of craft production occurred in provincial contexts, the Inka state seems to have focused high-status craft production in Cusco itself. Pedro Sancho's description of storage in Cusco indicates that the city held large quantities of raw materials for fashioning high-status wealth goods, and provincial tributary records suggest that while staple goods were taken to provincial centers for storage, raw materials for wealth production were collected at these centers and sent to Cusco (Diez de San Miguel 1964; Levillier 1940; Ortiz de Zúñiga 1967, 1972; Sancho de la Hoz 1962: Chap. 17). Falcón's chronicle distinguishes between artisans working on common (*hawa*) and high-status (*llañu*) textiles, sandals, and featherwork, and he also mentions a class of specialists (*llaqsakamayuq*) engaged in fine craft production that included lapidary and shell work, as well as possibly smelting metal ores and fashioning metal into adornments (cf. González Holguín 1989:207; Santo Tomás 1951:307). Such specialists do not appear to have been present in local provincial settings, and may have been restricted to the capital and a limited number of other important centers. For example, an archival document from 1585 identifies a group of lowland silversmiths reduced in the parish of Santiago in Cusco. They had been brought to Cusco by the emperor Wayna Qhapaq to serve him, and were supposedly provided with agricultural lands to the west of the city for their sustenance (AGN, Títulos de Propiedad 1585: L. 23, C. 431). Descriptions of storage and market spaces in Cusco suggest that the Inka elite controlled production tightly, but that artisans resided outside palace compounds and were at least partly responsible for their own subsistence.

The documentary evidence provides some tantalizing clues about craft production patterns at the Inka capital, but the archaeological record presents problems for anthropological interpretation. Theoretical approaches to Inka staple and wealth finance (e.g., D'Altroy and Earle 1985) emphasize the concentration of wealth goods at the capital, but the Spanish focus on wealth goods in elite contexts (palaces, temples, and especially elite tombs) led to the systematic plundering of Inka wealth and destruction of the contexts in which it was found in and around the imperial capital. The continuing occupation of the city of Cusco makes large-scale horizontal excavation projects impractical under most circumstances, so archaeologists are constrained in their ability to study the contexts for craft production at the Inka capital.

Complicating this situation is the excellent preservation found on the Pacific coast, where thousands of Inka burials have been excavated (and many thousands more have been looted for the illicit antiquities market). Most of our knowledge of Inka textiles,

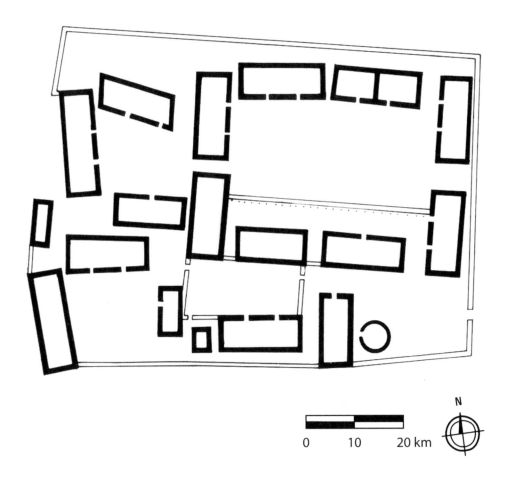

Figure 12.5. An elite residential compound from Zone IIIC-4 at the Inka provincial city of Huánuco Pampa. Early eyewitnesses describe Inka Cusco as dotted with elite compounds and palaces, although published excavations do not permit the archaeological evaluation of these descriptions at present. Reproduced with permission of the American Museum of Natural History.

intact ceramic vessels, metal adornments, and other craft goods comes from mortuary contexts, the vast majority of which are from poorly provenienced burials in provincial areas dominated by local states that were wealthy and fairly autonomous under Inka hegemony. Archaeologists have had more success identifying craft production at the capitals of semiautonomous coastal states such as Chan Chan (Topic 1990) and La Centinela (Kroeber and Strong 1924), while well-identified workshops remain to be excavated in the Cusco region. This presents some serious interpretive problems for archaeologists who wish to consider Inka wealth goods in their reconstruction of the imperial political economy.

Excavation evidence from rural sites in the Cusco region (especially in the Vilcanota-Urubamba Valley to the north of Cusco) indicates that some ceramic production and textile production occurred in local contexts; it is presumed based on the ethnohistoric record that such production focused on lower-status products, while the work of artisans—especially metalworking, and the production of featherwork and fine textiles—occurred within the municipal boundaries of Cusco and in a few restricted (elite-dominated) locations in the imperial heartland. These

wealth goods were not produced for sale or barter in marketplace exchanges, but were redistributed as gifts from the Inka ruler to loyal subjects. Marketplace activities appear to have taken place periodically in the Cusipata plaza adjoining the Haucaypata in the city center. The early Colonial vocabulary for markets and exchange suggests that these were not dedicated commercial locations, but instead were open spaces where commerce took place on designated market days. Thus, there *were* designated places for exchange activities in Cusco, but we know very little about how food distribution actually functioned.

Conclusion

The picture of Inka Cusco that emerges from the available documentary and archaeological evidence is a city steeped in the history of its own development, but one that reflected the wealth and diversity of the empire that it governed. The streets and plazas of Cusco would have been filled with people and goods from throughout the empire, and the arrival and departure of royal officials, military expeditions, and provincial nobles would have punctuated the energy of daily life in the cosmopolitan city. The diversity of costumes, customs, and languages encountered in the Inka capital bespoke the ethnic heterogeneity of the empire, while the juxtaposition of a wealthy and powerful elite with local farmers, artisans, labor colonists, and servants underscored the social hierarchy that attempted to hold such diversity under a single government.

The archaeological record for suburban and hinterland Cusco areas alone is not sufficient to unravel ethnic diversity through differences in consumption patterns, house layouts, and ritual behavior. A few general observations and avenues for future research may be identified. First, differences in house layout are apparent throughout the Cusco region, but not enough work has been done to distinguish what part of the diversity has to do with the existing local populace, what part has to do with the influx of large numbers of provincial workers, and how much is state-sponsored form. Second, a substantial investment needs to be made in household archaeology to assess different consumption patterns—Ann Kendall's excavations in the Cusichaca Valley (70 km from Cusco) represent virtually the only published household data (e.g., Kendall 1994). Finally, the discussion of ethnic settlement patterns in and around the Inka capital requires a larger regional perspective. We know of ritual variation in the region surrounding the Cusco Basin, and can identify local groups whose identity ties them to the local landscape at or before the time of Inka state formation—this falls beyond the urban scope for ethnic variation, however, and its discussion would require addressing the complex patterns of resettlement and retainership in the royal estates surrounding the Cusco Valley.

Wealth goods were a key feature of the imperial political economy, and the storage of large quantities of raw materials (for example, metal bars, bird feathers) suggests a population of artisans in the Inka capital that is difficult to identify using the available evidence. At present, we cannot be certain whether craft producers lived in distinct neighborhoods and maintained workshops there, or whether they labored for the Inka elite in palace workshops designated for such purposes. While wealth was an important means for linking Cusco to the provincial regions that it governed, food production in the area surrounding the city was critical for maintaining the city itself. Cusco's municipal boundaries included a number of farming communities, as well as royal estates and country homes of the elite.

There is much that is not known about the layout and socioeconomic organization of the Inka capital, and it may be unrealistic to expect that scholars will discover detailed new ethnohistoric descriptions of Inka Cusco in the coming years. Our reconstructions of the city are more likely to advance through the fieldwork and laboratory analysis of archaeologists. As Peruvian archaeologists and their foreign colleagues excavate in Cusco itself, work in the Cusco Basin and surrounding region will also prove critical for understanding the century or more of urban development that transformed the Inka capital into one of the great native cities of the Americas.

Endnote

1. The population of *yanakuna* in early Colonial Cusco included individuals in the service of the Inka nobility since pre-Conquest times, but it also included individuals attached permanently to the service of Spaniards after the European invasion, making it problematic to consider these figures as an accurate number or proportion of the Inka period urban population.

References

Agurto Calvo, Santiago
1980   *Cuzco—Traza urbana de la ciudad inca.* Proyecto Per 39, UNESCO, INC-Perú. Imprenta Offset Color S.R.L., Cuzco.

Anonymous Conqueror (attributed to Cristóbal de Mena)
1930[1534]   The Anonymous La Conquista del Perú (Seville, April 1534) and the Libro Vltimo del Svmmario delle Indie Occidentali (Venice, October 1534), edited by Alexander Pogo. *Proceedings of the American Academy of Arts and Sciences* 64(8):177–281.

Archivo General de la Nación (AGN), *Títulos de Propiedad*, Legajo 23, Cuaderno 431
1585   Títulos de las tierras denominadas Picoy-pampa, Quillahuasi, Limpihuasi, y otras en el valle de Jaquijahuana, jurisdicción de la ciudad del Cuzco, que pertenecieron a don Alonso Suca, de quien las heredaron don Lucas Sacayco, indios yungas reducidos en la parroquia de Santiago de la ciudad del Cuzco.

Bauer, Brian S.
1998   *The Sacred Landscape of the Inca: The Cuzco Ceque System.* University of Texas Press, Austin.
2004   *Ancient Cuzco: Heartland of the Inca.* University of Texas Press, Austin.

Bauer, Brian S., and R. Alan Covey
2002   Processes of state formation in the Inca heartland (Cuzco, Peru). *American Anthropologist* 104(3):846–64.

Betanzos, Juan de
1999[1551–1557]   *Suma y narración de los incas.* Universidad Nacional de San Antonio Abad del Cusco, Cusco.

Cieza de León, Pedro de
1985[1553]   *La crónica del Perú,* edited by Manuel Ballesteros. Historia 16, Madrid, Spain.
1988[ca. 1550]   *El señorío de los incas,* edited by Manuel Ballesteros. Historia 16, Madrid, Spain.

Cook, Noble David (editor)
1975   *Tasa de la visita general de Francisco de Toledo.* Universidad Nacional de San Marcos, Lima.

Covey, R. Alan
2006   *How the Incas Built Their Heartland: State Formation and the Innovation of Imperial Strategies in the Sacred Valley, Peru.* University of Michigan Press, Ann Arbor.

D'Altroy, Terence N.
2002   *The Incas.* Blackwell, New York.

D'Altroy, Terence N., and Timothy K. Earle
1985   Staple finance, wealth finance, and storage in the Inca political economy. *Current Anthropology* 26(2):187–206.

Diez de San Miguel, Garci
1964[1567]   *Visita hecha a la provincia de Chucuito.* Documentos regionales para la etnohistoria andina, 1. Ediciones de la Casa de la Cultura del Perú, Lima.

Falcón, Francisco
1918[1567]   Representación hecha por el licenciado Francisco Falcón en el concilio provincial, sobre los daños y molestias que se hacen a los Indios. *Colección de Libros y Documentos referentes a la historia del Perú* 9:133–76. Sanmartí, Lima.

Garcilaso de la Vega, "El Inca"
1966[1609]   *Royal Commentaries of the Incas and General History of Peru,* translated by Harold V. Livermore. University of Texas Press, Austin.

González Holguín, Diego
1989[1608]   *Vocabulario de la lengua general de todo el Perú llamada lengua qquichua o del Inca.* Universidad Nacional Mayor de San Marcos, Lima.

Hyslop, John
1990   *Inka Settlement Planning.* University of Texas Press, Austin.

Kendall, Ann
1994   *Proyecto Arqueológico Cusichaca, Cusco: Investigaciones arqueológicas y de rehabilitación agrícola,* Tomo I. Southern Peru Copper Corporation, Lima.

Kroeber, Alfred L., and William Duncan Strong
1924   The Uhle collection from Chincha. *University of California Publications in American Archaeology and Ethnology* 21:1–54.

Levillier, Roberto
1940   *Don Francisco de Toledo, supremo organizador del Perú: Su vida, su obra (1515–1582). Tomo II: Sus informaciones sobre los incas (1570–1572).* Espasa-Calpe, Buenos Aires.

Niles, Susan A.
1987   *Callachaca: Style and Status in an Inca Community.* University of Iowa Press, Iowa City.

Noticia del Perú (attributed to Miguel de Estete)
1968[1535?]   Noticia del Perú. In *Biblioteca Peruana: Primera Serie: Tomo I,* pp. 347–402. Editores Técnicos Asociados S.A., Lima.

Ondegardo, Polo de
1916[1559]   Los errores y svpersticiones de los indios, sacadas del tratado y aueriguación que hizo el licenciado Polo. *Colección de Libros y Documentos referentes a la historia del Perú,* Series I, Vol. 3:3–43. Sanmartí, Lima.

Ortiz de Zúñiga, Iñigo
1967[1562]   *Visita de la Provincia de León de Huánuco,* Vol. I, edited by John V. Murra. Universidad Hermilio Valdizán, Huánuco.
1972[1562]   *Visita de la Provincia de León de Huánuco,* Vol. II, edited by John V. Murra. Universidad Hermilio Valdizán, Huánuco.

Pizarro, Pedro
1986[1571]   *Relación del descubrimiento y conquista de los reinos del Perú,* edited by Guillermo Lohmann Villena. Pontificia Universidad Católica del Perú, Lima.

Rowe, John H.
1967   What kind of a settlement was Inca Cuzco? *Ñawpa Pacha* 5:59–76.

Ruiz de Arce, Juan
1933[ca. 1545]   Relación de servicios en Indias . . . *Boletín de la Real Academia de la Historia* 102:327–84.

Sancho de la Hoz, Pedro
1962[1534]   *Relación de la conquista del Perú.* Ediciones J. Porrúa Turanzas, Madrid.

Santo Tomás, Domingo de
1951[1560]   *Lexicón, o vocabulario de la lengua general del Perú.* Instituto de Historia, Lima.

Sherbondy, Jeanette E.
1987   The Incaic organization of terraced irrigation in Cuzco, Peru. In *Pre-Hispanic Agricultural Fields in the Andean Region,* edited by William M. Denevan, Kent Mathewson, and Gregory Knapp, pp. 365–71. BAR International Series, 359(ii). BAR, Oxford.

Topic, John R.
1990   Craft production in the kingship of Chimor. In *The Northern Dynasties: Kingship and Statecraft in Chimor,* edited by M.E. Moseley and A. Cordy-Collins, pp. 145–76. Dumbarton Oaks, Washington, D.C.

Trujillo, Diego de
1985[1571]   Relación del descubrimiento del reino del Perú que hizo Diego de Trujillo en compañía del gobernador don Francisco Pizarro y otros capitanes, desde que llegaron a Panamá el año de 1530, en que refiere todas derrotas y sucesos, hasta 15 de abril de 1571. In *Francisco de Xérez: Verdadera relación de la conquista del Perú,* edited by Concepción Bravo, pp. 191–206. Historia 16, Madrid, Spain.

Xérez, Francisco de
1985[1534]   Verdadera relación de la conquista del Perú . . . In *Francisco de Xérez: Verdadera relación de la conquista del Perú,* edited by Concepción Bravo, pp. 57–160. Historia 16, Madrid, Spain.

PART III
COMMENTARY

13

Understanding Houses, Compounds, and Neighborhoods

Joyce Marcus

Most ancient capitals offered residents and non-residents a wide range of services and opportunities, some of which occurred there and nowhere else. Capitals could host unique events such as the inauguration of rulers, the dedication of state temples, and special festivities that only took place in royal palaces, plazas, and private courts. Many capitals displayed heterogeneity in architectural styles, residential housing, craft production, occupational specialization, dietary preferences, funerary customs, and ritual practices. Individual households varied in their access to local and imported items, but most items fell along a continuum from relatively scarce to quite abundant rather than present/absent.

One major challenge in studying capitals is obtaining a representative sample of houses that encompass the full range of variability; it is rarely possible to excavate a huge sample of houses from a single capital. Although heterogeneity is precisely what is expected of capitals, it is often difficult to quantify and interpret that diversity, especially when we want to make meaningful ward-to-ward and site-to-site comparisons.

By bringing together scholars with rich and varied excavation data from several ancient capitals, the editors—Linda Manzanilla and Claude Chapdelaine—ensured that this volume would speak to a wide range of issues related to the economic underpinning and sociopolitical web of interactions that integrated these societies. Although other volumes have focused on houses either in Mesoamerica or in South America (e.g., Aldenderfer 1993;

Bermann 1994; Flannery and Marcus 2005; Goldstein 2005; Lohse and Valdez 2004; Manzanilla 1986; Manzanilla and Barba 1990; Ruppert and Smith 1957; Santley and Hirth 1993; Sheets 1992; Stanish 1989; Wauchope 1934, 1938; Wilk and Ashmore 1988), rarely has there been a volume evaluating the data from extensive excavations in the residences in the capital cities of both regions.

In Table 13.1, I note some of the similarities and differences of these two culture areas, some of which will serve as points of departure later in this chapter. Keeping some of these similarities and contrasts in mind, let us see how the contributors to this volume tackled topics such as domestic economy, specialization, heterogeneity, ethnicity, and neighborhoods.

Part I. The Domestic Economy

To understand the domestic economy, most of the volume's contributors rely on a bottom-up strategy—beginning with the household unit; moving to the oft-neglected compound, ward, and neighborhood; and finally moving up to neighborhood-to-neighborhood and sector-to-sector comparisons in order to characterize the socioeconomic organization of an urban center. It is the sum of the analyses of all these constituent components that makes this volume special, thereby counterbalancing books that

Table 13.1. Similarities and differences of the two culture areas, South America and Mesoamerica.

South America	Mesoamerica
emphasis on labor service	emphasis on tribute exaction
no markets	markets
impressive displays of storage	limited display of stored goods
heavy investment in roads, waystations	less investment in imperial roads
resettled whole communities (*mitmaqkuna*)	called in male laborers from nearby hinterland
emphasis on gold, silver, metallurgy	emphasis on jade, serpentinite, *chalchihuites*
camelid caravans	humans with tumplines
yanakuna from nonlocal ethnic groups	local and captured servants
split inheritance	direct inheritance
maize for beer	maize as a staple food
camelid wool, cotton	cotton, maguey fiber, bark paper
chicha, coca leaves	*pulque*, *balché*, *Datura*, *Salvia* seeds
no hieroglyphic writing, but *khipus* (knotted cords for keeping track of items)	hieroglyphic writing
huacas and *apus* as ancestors	sacred mountains as ancestors
ayllu as corporate units	*calpultin* and lineages as corporate units

restrict their focus to the "house" or the "site as a whole" while paying less attention to intermediate units such as the compound and the neighborhood.

A bottom-up strategy is precisely the kind of research design that is needed if we hope to understand urban economics. Such a strategy is rarely implemented at huge urban sites because most funding is directed to the excavation and restoration of monumental public buildings, a strategy often considered more rewarding than investing decades into exposing, in their entirety, the extensive residential zones and walled compounds. Test-pitting and short-term projects, in contrast, rarely expose a sufficient number of square meters to say anything statistically significant about residential diversity, nor do they allow one to demonstrate which customs were actually shared by most or all houses.

Houses

Houses can be associated with many activities, from household rituals to brewing beer to cooking food to the production of multiple crafts and different types of goods. For example, Hendon (see Chapter 6) shows that Maya houses at Copán included a brazier surmounted by a shallow plate that served as a portable stove; manos and metates for grinding maize; jars for storing water; discarded animal bones; and obsidian or chert tools for processing items of wood, leather, shell, and bone, and for cutting up vegetables and meat. Evidence for spinning and for textile production comes from spindle whorls, perforated clay disks, and bone needles, pins, and possible weaving picks. The whorls and perforated disks evidently served as spindle flywheels for spinning thread from different raw materials. Interestingly, Hendon says that weaving elements had their greatest concentration in patios, an open air venue that was also utilized for this activity in the Andes (Marcus 1987, 2008).

Hendon suggests that cooking and food preparation at Copán took place in a location separate from the areas where cloth and shell ornaments were produced. Hendon found that the most elaborate dwelling around a patio was the one where feasting and entertaining were focused, while craft production was practiced elsewhere in the compound.

Unlike some capital cities in this volume, such as Teotihuacan, Copán shows no evidence of a foreign enclave. There is, however, evidence of active exchange with societies to the southeast who were producing Ulúa polychrome. Isotopic analyses of a large number of Copán skeletons helped Hendon rule out the presence of foreign residents as the explanation for the unit containing those imported Ulúa vessels. Isotopic analyses on skeletons at Teotihuacan, in contrast, showed that some walled apartment compounds like Oztoyahualco did house foreigners (see Chapter 2 by Manzanilla).

Walled Compounds

Mesoamerican sites rarely featured huge walled compounds; instead, they usually had clusters of residential units that seem to constitute neighborhoods. As we will see below, walled compounds were much more typical of the Andes.

When walled compounds are found, archaeologists face the challenge of determining whether the wall was built to ensure privacy, to control traffic, to monitor goods arriving and departing, or all of the above.

Another major challenge has been to determine what social units lived and worked in these walled compounds. Were they kin groups, a segment of a corporate unit (for example, a Nahua *calpulli* or Andean *ayllu*), or some combination of permanent kin-related occupants and non-resident unrelated servants and specialists who came to the compound to work during the daytime?

Even though most compounds at Teotihuacan seem to have housed local families, the Oztoyahualco compound (see Chapter 2 by Manzanilla) may have included members from other geographic regions, as indicated from strontium isotope results of their skeletons. In Teotihuacan's apartment compounds, each household had its own kitchen, storeroom, sleeping area, and ritual courtyard where its members venerated a patron deity. One way to explain the presence of local and nonlocal people in the same compound is to suggest that local Teotihuacanos wanted to oversee the activities of nonlocals. A second possibility is that the nonlocal people had a special skill or occupation, for example, the ability to work with valued materials that Teotihuacanos did not want circulating outside the compound until such raw materials could be converted into finished products. A third explanation is that nonlocal groups were not of equal status, for instance, servants or slaves. Indeed, Manzanilla shows that local and nonlocal people lived inside the same compound and were not of the same socioeconomic status. She persuasively argues that a hierarchical organization of residents characterizes each multifamily compound. For example, at Oztoyahualco she shows that only one family worshipped the Thunder Deity as its patron, and that this family had the largest ritual courtyard as well as the greatest access to imported raw materials such as jadeite and slate. In contrast to those worshipping the Thunder Deity, other families worshipped a Fire Deity as their patron. The third socioeconomic group apparently revered a rabbit.

Such hierarchical and socioeconomic organization was even more dramatic in barrio or neighborhood compounds, where people of different statuses lived in contiguous houses arranged around the barrio's ritual sector. The nucleus or focal area of a neighborhood usually featured three temples around a plaza, surrounded by apartment compounds, each of which in turn featured a different craft activity. Manzanilla suggests that this layout of three temples around a plaza was the earliest arrangement at Teotihuacan, and that it was the architectural manifestation of groups who first settled Teotihuacan, including groups fleeing volcanic eruptions in the Tlaxcala and Tetimpa area during the first century AD. Manzanilla emphasizes that such three-temple plaza groups were present in the oldest part of the city (the northwest sector of Teotihuacan), and continued to be constructed in later sectors along the main axis of the city, where these groups were incorporated into still larger compounds (for example, in the Western Plaza and the Street of the Dead Compound).

Manzanilla shows that elite neighborhoods, such as La Ventilla, had compounds for each barrio function—ritual, administrative, craft production, and residential. Excavations in La Ventilla provided detailed data on this neighborhood, with its barrio temple, an administrative building called "The Glyph Courtyard," and the apartment compounds of commoners. Manzanilla suggests that two more sectors, Tepantitla and Teopancazco, may have served as centers for their barrios and included large open areas where gatherings could take place.

Not only has Manzanilla demonstrated intra-compound heterogeneity and compound-to-compound variability, she has isolated two kinds of Teotihuacan artifacts that will probably change our view of that city's administration. These two items are (1) stamp seals that may have been used by different groups to mark products, and (2) round ceramic *tejos* that may have been administrative devices to signal ownership or mark tribute. If the distribution of such stamps, seals, and administrative devices—*or the marks they made*—could be more fully documented, we might know even more about goods entering and leaving Teotihuacan.

Do such walled compounds exist at Xochicalco? In Chapter 3, Hirth says that he was able to recognize households and barrios, but found no evidence for an intermediate unit such as the compound. One of Hirth's goals was to determine if areas of craft production were isomorphic with the limits of the barrio in which they were found. Barrio divisions at Xochicalco were defined by prominent terrace walls, fortifications, walled streets, and visible pathways and corridors. These features helped Hirth divide Xochicalco into fourteen barrios. If Xochicalco's barrios had been organized the same way as Teotihuacan's apartment compounds (or even the Aztec *calpultin*), Hirth suggests that Xochicalco's barrios should show evidence for internal hierarchical organization. He concludes that they do. Thirteen of the fourteen barrios contain either a civic-ceremonial structure or an elite residence, and nine barrios contain both.

Hirth also wonders whether Xochicalco's craftsmen were organized like later Toltec and Aztec craftsmen, who were members of guilds based on a specific craft in addition to their barrio or *calpulli* membership. Aztec artisans "were set apart from the rest of Aztec society by virtue of their separate residence, control over membership, internal control over education and ranking, distinct ethnic origins, commitments to particular patron deities and religious ceremonies, and special relations with the state" (Berdan 1982:26). Although Aztec *calpultin* were the basis of craft guild organization in the sixteenth century AD, we do not know when such guilds first appeared nor do we know how to confirm their presence or absence in the archaeological record.

Hirth estimates that each of Xochicalco's barrios had populations of 100 to 600 persons. In terms of size and social composition, he suggests that these barrios were analogous to *chinámitl* or ward segments. Hirth believes that these ward segments were the level at which craft guilds would have been organized, and he focuses on six obsidian workshops in four residential areas. Since the blades were made on obsidian from three sources (Ucareo, Pachuca, and Zacualtipan) that lie 150 to 200 km away, Xochicalco's craftsmen had two options: either travel to the quarry or rely on trade. If craftsmen procured raw materials directly from quarries, Hirth would expect to see debitage from manufacturing the blades, and no such debitage from modifying cores was recovered from these workshops. Instead, Xochicalco craftsmen only had access to nearly exhausted cores. Thus Hirth convincingly argues that Xochicalco craftsmen got their cores through trade, and that each household obtained its obsidian independently. If centralized procurement or pooling had occurred, each domestic workshop would have had access to obsidian from the same sources in similar proportions; instead, each household evidently developed its own allies and exchange network.

Within the household, Hirth found no evidence of task specialization or division of labor. His analyses indicate that craftsmen carried out all production activities in the same locations, beginning with the rejuvenation of cores and continuing through the manufacture of blades. Although many scholars argue that full-time craft production was restricted to urban settings while part-time production predominated in rural areas, Hirth's research at Xochicalco presents a much more complex picture of artisans engaged in an array of economic activities, many or all of which were conducted on a part-time basis. Examination of craft production elsewhere in Mesoamerica suggests that diversified production and multicrafting were common economic strategies, going back even to the Early Formative (e.g., Flannery and Marcus 2005).

Hirth concludes that each of Teotihuacan's large walled compounds might have been analogous to Xochicalco's *chinámitl* or small barrio, and he suggests that Teotihuacan built enclosed compounds because their downtown area was so crowded.

Although Teotihuacan is unusual for Mesoamerica, walled compounds are much more common in the Andes, occurring at such well-known sites as Wari (see Chapter 10 by Isbell), Viracochapampa, Pikillaqta, Cajamarquilla, and Chan Chan (see Chapter 11 by Topic).

Wari, the capital of an empire, covers 2 km² in the Valley of Ayacucho. Its compounds have stone walls, some still standing 12 m high. As the city of Wari grew, it swallowed up three separate Huarpa communities; thus, much as Monte Albán did in Mexico's Oaxaca Valley, three formerly independent polities were brought together to form a much larger political system. By AD 600–700, Wari's walled compounds typically measured 150 × 300 m, with evidence for ceramic specialists using pottery molds in workshops and ornament makers using massive amounts of turquoise. Hundreds of square kilometers of terraced hillsides were irrigated near Wari, evidently to grow corn for the maize

beer that the elite used to reward workers and entertain guests. Just as Manzanilla has documented the use of possible administrative devices at Teotihuacan, archaeologists indicate that the Wari used the *khipu* (knotted cords) to keep track of goods.

The Wari Empire established colonies and installations from Viracochapampa in the north to Pikillacta in the south. Pikillacta was laid out like giant military barracks, and resembles a huge ice cube tray from the air. Its great enclosure wall is divided into a large number of separate segments, each representing the efforts of a different work gang. From this evidence we might infer that the construction of Pikillacta was the result of *mit'a*, or rotating labor. We suspect that this pattern was similar to that known from Inka times, when each village was required to provide a certain number of workers for state projects for a set period of time. After those laborers finished their turn, they were replaced by laborers from other settlements, while the first group of workers returned to their homes. Some of the buildings at Pikillacta were never finished, and the site was ultimately burned and abandoned, like some other Wari installations.

Mesoamerican and Andean use of labor is worthy of much more attention and could be the subject of another book-length study. Large construction projects in the Andes were often completed by village-level *ayllus* or kin groups. Rather than amassing one huge labor force to work on a project, Andean people generally worked in small groups, with coordination left in the hands of many overseers. Each *ayllu* was assigned a distinct task within a larger project, and that task was to be completed independently of those being carried out by other work groups. Such labor organization can be noted still earlier in the production of adobes in the Huaca del Sol at the Moche capital (Hastings and Moseley 1975).

Walled compounds were also built by the Chimú, who dominated northern Peru from AD 850 to 1450 (see Chapter 11 by Topic). Their capital at Chan Chan, one of the most extraordinary sites in South America, sprawled over 20 km² and had an inner core covering 6 km². Perhaps 6,000 members of the elite lived in thirty adobe-walled compounds, with royalty living in ten particularly huge compounds called *ciudadelas*.

John Topic documents the same kind of hierarchical organization at Chan Chan that we see in Mesoamerica (Chapters 1–7). Some 26,000 craftsmen lived in wattle-and-daub houses, 3,000 of them adjacent to the elite compounds and *ciudadelas*. Various lines of information have been used to show that the ten largest compounds were built in succession, with one clue consisting of the changes in brick size and composition. Geoffrey Conrad (1982) has suggested that the ten *ciudadelas* were the palaces of the legendary Kings of Chimor, with each ruler building one royal enclosure to house himself and his government. In accordance with a law of "split inheritance," in which the ruler's palace passed to multiple heirs after death, his compound and any territory he had captured were retained in his name and administered in perpetuity by a separate bureaucracy. Each new ruler had to build his own compound and conquer new territory, which was then organized and administered in the name of the new king